Hosted Horror on Television

Hosted Horror on Television

The Films and Faces of Shock Theater, Creature Features *and* Chiller Theater

BRUCE MARKUSEN

McFarland & Company, Inc., Publishers
Jefferson, North Carolina

ISBN (print) 978-1-4766-8461-1
ISBN (ebook) 978-1-4766-4328-1

LIBRARY OF CONGRESS AND BRITISH LIBRARY
CATALOGUING DATA ARE AVAILABLE

Library of Congress Control Number 2021030641

© 2021 Bruce Markusen. All rights reserved

No part of this book may be reproduced or transmitted in any form or by any means, electronic or mechanical, including photocopying or recording, or by any information storage and retrieval system, without permission in writing from the publisher.

Front cover: John Zacherle, host of *Shock Theater*, circa 1958 (Photofest)

Printed in the United States of America

*McFarland & Company, Inc., Publishers
Box 611, Jefferson, North Carolina 28640
www.mcfarlandpub.com*

This book is dedicated to the horror historians who have done so much to help us enjoy the genre of horror, while giving us a better understanding and appreciation of the films that have entertained us for so long. These historians, who provided assistance in the writing of this volume, are an integral part of horror culture:

Joe Bob Briggs
Frank Dello Stritto
Greg Mank
Genoveva Rossi
David J. Skal
Harrison Smith.

They are a phenomenal group of writers and speakers. We should value their contributions as much as the films themselves.

Table of Contents

Preface   1

ONE: What Exactly Is Hosted Horror?   5

TWO: The Arrival of "Shock Theater"   8

THREE: The Pioneers: Vampira and Zacherley   16

FOUR: The Movies of "Shock Theater"   21

FIVE: The Movies of "Son of Shock"   56

SIX: Hosts from Coast to Coast   70

SEVEN: *Creature Features, Fright Night* and *Block of Shock* (1931–1969)   88

EIGHT: *Creature Features, Fright Night* and *Block of Shock* (1970–1975)   175

NINE: What Might Happen Next   212

Chapter Notes   215
Bibliography   227
Index   233

Preface

The Books That Hitchcock Didn't Write

Where did my passion, or more accurately my veritable *obsession* with horror movies begin? I have vague recollections from my childhood, back in the early 1970s when I was no more than seven or eight years old, of reading a book that was filled with ghost stories and hauntings. It was the first book that I remember reading cover to cover. I seemed to recall Alfred Hitchcock being involved with the book, either as the author or simply as the editor who had chosen the stories for inclusion. I had a notion of it being a large hardcover book, with lots of great drawings.

For several years, I tried to remember the title of the book. No matter what, I just couldn't bring it back to memory. At one point, I started to doubt that Hitchcock was even involved, or that the book even existed. Perhaps it was something that I had imagined incorrectly, as we sometimes do when trying to recall the fonder times of our youth.

The identity of the book remained a mystery until the summer of 2016. One Saturday in June, I decided to go to the Cooperstown Antiquarian Book Fair. This annual event started back in the 1990s, but I had never attended until now. Walking across the gym floor of the Clark Sports Center where the book fair takes place, I happened to visit the booth of a Syracuse, New York, dealer. I looked up at the top shelf of his booth, and lo and behold, I saw the very book that I had been thinking about so often in recent years.

The book, *Alfred Hitchcock's Haunted Houseful*, was a compilation of the horror master's favorite stories of haunted locations. It wasn't as large as I had remembered, but it was still good-sized and had the same cover as my original copy, a color drawing of an old Victorian house featuring Hitchcock's head on one side! I had forgotten the specific details of that cover and its beautifully creative imagery, but it all came back to me that moment at the book fair.

For much of the 1970s, I simply loved this book, which had been published in 1961 but hadn't made it into our house in Bronxville, New York, until years later. This cherished volume was targeted toward children, or "younger readers" as the front of the book indicated. It had everything, from the entertaining short stories to the wonderful drawings, done in beautiful blue tones by skilled illustrator Fred Banbery. I simply had to buy this book, and more than willingly plunked down $20 for the privilege of having a copy, something to replace the original copy that had been lost in so many house moves years ago.

In talking to one of the owners of the Syracuse bookstore, I learned that *Haunted Houseful* was the first in a series of books that Hitchcock published during the 1960s. He told me that there were at least four or five in the series. The bookseller happened to have another one of them for sale, a volume called *Monster Museum*, which I had never seen before, but just had to have. So I invested another $20 and brought that home as part of my newly rejuvenated Hitchcock collection.

That night, I decided to do further research into the two books I purchased. (In looking up their entries on Amazon, I wanted to kick myself for not going to the Internet sooner. Had I simply entered "Alfred Hitchcock" as the key words to my search, I would have rediscovered *Haunted Houseful* so much sooner. How foolish of me.) As I worked my way through the pages of Amazon, I soon learned the identities of the other books in this series for young readers. They all had alliterative titles, from *Spellbinders in Suspense* to *Daring Detectives* to *Sinister Spies*. From there, I discovered a number of other books that Hitchcock lent his name to, books for adult readers that carried wonderful names like *Alfred Hitchcock Presents: Stories That Scared Even Me*. I never realized that Hitchcock had put his name on so many of these books, numbering dozens in total.

When I first read *Haunted Houseful* back in the 1970s, I thought that Hitchcock had written the stories, or at least selected them for inclusion in his volume. As I thumbed through the book all these years later, I saw that each story had its own author. I soon learned that Hitchcock actually played no part in selecting the stories, or even writing the foreword. He simply lent his name to *Haunted Houseful*, as well as the later books in the series, receiving what I am sure was fairly healthy monetary compensation. That was a little disappointing—I wanted Hitchcock to have some creative involvement—but it didn't dampen my enthusiasm for the book, the quality of the stories, and the beautiful renderings by the artist.

One of the books that came up in my Internet search was called *Ghostly Gallery*. When I saw the cover image, which showed a terrified young boy sitting up in his dark and windowless bedroom, with a human head forming the headboard and a ghostly figure standing in the closet, I realized that I had struck gold for a second time that day. This was the *other* Hitchcock book that I had once possessed, one that I had read over and over as a child, always enjoying the drawings along with that terrific cover image which wrapped around to the back of the book as well.

Haunted Houseful and *Ghostly Gallery* had stirred my interest on a variety of fronts. They motivated me to read more, which was extremely important in retrospect, but they also inspired me to want to experience more ghost stories—not just in written form, but on the television screen. I wanted to see the movies that Hitchcock directed, at least the ones that fell into the realms of the supernatural and the broader world of horror, and I wanted to see other films that dealt with this subject matter. In short, these two books served as the impetus for me becoming a fan of horror films.

As part of this process, I began to search out horror films on television. They were somewhat difficult to find during the daytime hours, but as someone who liked to stay up late, I soon discovered that horror movies could be found more readily after 10 p.m., and sometimes after midnight.

That's what brought me to the discovery of *Chiller Theater*. It was a late-night presentation, shown every Saturday night on WPIX, a local (New York City) station. By the time I started watching, *Chiller Theater* no longer had a horror host; the legendary Zacherley had left the station after appearing on *Chiller Theater* from 1963 to 1965.[1]

Even after Zacherley's departure, *Chiller Theater* continued to use an introduction that featured snippets of black-and-white horror films. This opener began with Vampira emerging from the woods in 1958's *Plan 9 from Outer Space*, followed by a clip from a 1957 film, *The Cyclops*, and then a *Killers from Space* snippet showing a gigantic lizard, followed by *Ape*

Man footage of an ape attacking a man. The montage concluded with a short clip from 1958's *Attack of the 50 Foot Woman*.

By the early 1970s, when I started watching, *Chiller Theater* had made the transition from a filmclip opening to one that relied on animation. Each week, *Chiller Theater* began its presentation with an animated, Claymation opening of a swamp, with a hand emerging from its depths. At first, it appeared to be a normal hand. But within moments, it became apparent that the hand had *six* fingers. As a younger viewer, I was lured by the six-fingered hand. I loved this special effect, even if later viewings would show it to be somewhat hokey. At the time, I thought that the six-fingered hand in the swamp, which *Chiller Theater* also used upon returning from commercial breaks, was just about the coolest thing to appear on my television set. Taken in by the abnormal hand, I was now primed and ready to watch the actual movie itself.

While *Chiller Theater* consumed most of my interest, the New York City market also offered some other avenues for old-time horror films. Another local station, WNEW, or Channel 5 as we always called it, played a daytime movie on Saturdays under the showcase name of *Jeepers Creepers*.[2] The artwork on *Jeepers Creepers* was not as good; the show featured a drawing of an ape-like creature with fangs, not quite at the same creativity level as the six-fingered hand. But it was still decent enough for young fans, like me, who were lacking in discernment but not in passion for horror films.

WNEW's venture into old-fashioned horror did not end with *Jeepers Creepers*. On Saturday nights, the station competed against *Chiller Theater* with *Creature Features*. Host Lou Steele did not wear makeup, but instead wore sunglasses and looked like a hipster.[3] *Creature Features* relied heavily on the classics from Universal, films from American International Pictures, and selections from Hammer Films, making it popular with viewers in the metropolitan area. I didn't watch *Creature Features* as often as *Chiller Theater*, and the show was cancelled by August 1973. I was likely also discouraged by Channel 5's lack of baseball coverage; after all, baseball represented my other area of interest. I tended to watch a lot of WPIX Channel 11 because of its status as the flagship station of the New York Yankees. In watching Yankee games, I often saw the promos for the upcoming *Chiller Theater*. And when the Yankees played on Saturday nights, the broadcast sometimes led directly into the *Chiller Theater* offering. In the age before remote controls, who was I to change the channel as Yankee baseball faded into late-night horror?

There was one other station based out of New York City that showcased late-night horror. Beginning in 1973, WOR (better known as Channel 9 back in the day) ran a program called *Fright Night*, which featured both horror classics from Universal and RKO, and obscure B-movies. *Fright Night* did not have a host, but did give plenty of airtime to films like *King Kong* and *Frankenstein Meets the Wolf Man*.[4] As it turned out, I didn't watch too many of the *Fright Night* flicks, even though Channel 9 was the flagship station of New York Mets baseball. I wasn't much of a Mets fan in the early 1970s, with most of my loyalties given to the other team in the city.

Whether it was *Chiller Theater* or the occasional film from *Creature Features* and *Fright Night*, the late-night showcases provided steady entertainment for a child who had not reached the teenage years but still liked to stay up late on non–school nights. Some of the films were in black-and-white, some were in color, and all of them seemed pretty frightening to me. I can remember watching them from my own bed; the scariest scenes would make me sit up, look behind at the headboard and the wall, and look toward the door to make sure that some unknown, evil presence had not made its way into the room. I found myself most frightened by the stories that involved witchcraft and satanic worship; the villains of those stories always seemed the worst, in part because of their ties to the Devil, but also because they were such duplicitous characters, hiding their sinister traits only to unleash them on unsuspecting victims at the most inconvenient moments.

To a lesser extent, I was also affected by the more visible monsters—the Frankensteins, the vampires, the werewolves, the ghostly apparitions, and the larger-than-life creatures that came from experiments gone wrong. But it was easier to see *them* coming. With those monsters, there was usually a warning of some kind. Still, they too could be intimidating. What I really liked about those monsters was the imagery that they placed on the screen. They created visual portrayals that reminded me of some of the similar images that I saw in the Hitchcock books. In other words, these movies took the flat pages of *Haunted Houseful* and *Ghostly Gallery* and made them into moving images that seemed livelier, almost three-dimensional.

I didn't watch *Chiller Theater* every week, if only because I sometimes had too much homework to do by Monday morning. There were also times that my parents insisted that I go to sleep earlier than the late-night showings would allow. But more often than not, I managed to watch at least part of the film, giving myself enough of a taste of the world of horror to know that this was something I wanted to follow.

By now, I was hooked, the transition from the glorious Hitchcock books to the macabre movies of *Chiller Theater* having completed its course. I was now fully engrossed in the world of what some, including me, would call hosted horror.

Note: Unless otherwise indicated, the film release dates given throughout this book refer to its American premiere, even if it was a limited release. For some of the more prominent films, a larger nationwide release may also be included.

Chapter One

What Exactly Is Hosted Horror?

For some readers, the term "hosted horror" requires no explanation. For other readers, it may cause confusion. So what exactly is hosted horror? Essentially, it refers to the broader era of TV history that began in 1957, when Screen Gems released 58 films, known collectively as the "Shock Theater" package, into the public realm. Not only did Screen Gems allow local television stations to show the pictures, but the company encouraged the stations to create a program complete with a so-called horror host who would introduce each film and interject commentary throughout. These hosted horror showcases became a staple of Saturday afternoon and late-night weekend television, beginning in the fall of 1957 and continuing with a degree of fervor until the mid–1970s, when interest began to fade.

While television stations began airing these horror showcases in the late 1950s, the films that they initially showed—films that had never before aired on television—came mostly from the 1930s and '40s, the time when Universal Studios made a name for itself with its highly successful series of classic horror films. So while horror hosts did not come into being until 1957, the films of the hosted horror actually date as far back as 1931, when iconic films like *Dracula* and *Frankenstein* debuted in theaters.

As TV stations continued to feature these horror showcases, complete with their own local hosts, they added more films to their libraries. In 1958, Screen Gems released a second batch of films, a package known as "Son of Shock." This group of 21 films again represented a concentration from the 1930s and '40s, highlighted by the iconic *Bride of Frankenstein*.

These horror showcases, some of which carried names like *Shock Theater* and *Chiller Theater*, continued into the 1960s. Rather than remain stagnant, they evolved, thanks to a continuing, staggered release of films over the course of many years. These later batch of films made horror and sci-fi from the 1950s available to local TV stations, along with British horror (like Hammer's films), and the Japanese films that delved into the world of giant monsters. Not surprisingly, some of the local TV stations began calling their showcases *Creature Features*, a wonderfully creative and lyrical name for late-night theater.

As the 1960s progressed and gave way to the 1970s, films of more recent vintage continued to be added to TV libraries. By the time that horror hosts started to lose some of their appeal, the first era of hosted horror movies had encompassed parts or all of five decades—spanning from the 1930s to the 1970s.

Given the long span of roughly 45 years, from 1931 to 1975, it would be impractical to detail every horror film. Rather, the mission here is to provide an overall history of the era, while highlighting many of the best horror films, or in some cases, historically important films that made their way into theaters and then onto TV.

Still, that leaves us with a vital question. How do we define the genre of "horror"? Noted historian David J. Skal tries to lend some context to the definition. He points out:

> Horror has rather slippery parameters to begin with: There's supernatural horror, there's suspense horror, there's psychological horror. Horror is like—you know what it is when you see it. It deals with extreme emotions, extreme situations. The supernatural can, or might not, be a part of it, but all the better when it is.[1]

It might be helpful to think of horror as a genre where fear becomes the intended emotion that the director is seeking from the audience. It is "that which is meant to frighten." The director tries to elicit that emotion by putting the viewers in a state in which they feel uneasy, if not completely terrified. That can be done through a monster or a ghost (that is supernatural) or through a killer (that is human) or through both. Additionally, there needs to be a possibility of death, particularly involving the main characters. Without that possibility, the sense of horror is lost.

With an emphasis on horror, I have excluded films that more logically fall into the category of science fiction. Science fiction is a genre that emphasizes setting; it gravitates toward stories that involve creatures from other planets, and toward themes involving futuristic societies. To include all of the classic science fiction offerings, along with all of the wonderful horror films of this time period, would make this book unwieldy. For that reason, I chose not to include most of the films involving aliens, the so-called "flying saucer" films of the 1950s.

The better way for me would be to focus the subject matter, concentrating on the more classic genre of horror, with its man-sized monsters, haunted houses, evil ghosts and supernatural overtones. Horror, in this more traditional sense of the word, is what I know.

I did, however, make a few exceptions for films that emphasize sci-fi over pure horror. One involves the original version of *King Kong*, only the second film in history to present an oversized monster on the big screen.[2] It is such an important film that it needs to be included. I also made an exception for the excellent 1954 film *Them!*, which is perhaps the best of the films involving oversized insects.

In compiling this book, I have placed the emphasis on what I would call straight horror, or at least on films where the traditional horror elements are a considerable part of the presentation. Even after eliminating the pure science fiction genre, there remain hundreds of films to consider. Of course, there is a vast wasteland of bad horror films, making it necessary to eliminate the many films recognized for their poor quality and brutal cheapness: the films of Ed Wood, historically awful offerings like *Manos: The Hands of Fate*, and other films that have been parodied on programs like *Mystery Science Theatre*.

Included in the book are horror films that I would classify as good, at the very least, or at the extreme end, veritable classics of the horror genre. In some cases, I have selected films that are no more than mediocre, but carry some historical significance that make them worthy of selection. In a few instances, I have included films that have been panned by critics, but have become personal favorites.

More specifically, here is what you will find in this book: many of the classics from the Universal heyday of horror, the essential films of horror masters like Boris Karloff and Bela Lugosi, some of the best selections from the careers of Vincent Price, Christopher Lee and Peter Cushing, and iconic films that transcend any era, like *Rosemary's Baby*, *Night of the Living Dead* and *The Exorcist*. And yes, you will also find Alfred Hitchcock, the man who spurred my interest with his self-titled books. While the Master of Suspense was best known for his creation of thrillers and mysteries, his influence on horror cannot be ignored.

As important as the films are, the hosts who enhanced this rich era within the horror genre cannot be ignored. Any compilation of horror hosts must begin with the two pioneers: Vampira, whose first TV appearance predated the arrival of "Shock Theater," and John Zacherle, aka Zacherley. Vampira focused her performance on her appearance and generic sight gags, while Zacherley placed the emphasis on the films themselves, setting a trend for future horror hosts.

The exploits of other hosts, those who became exceedingly popular in local markets along with those who achieved a national presence, will also be covered. Most of these hosts emphasized humor, poking fun at the films in a good-natured way. A few took a more serious approach, stressing the frightening nature of the films, the special effects, and the backstories of the actors. All of the hosts did their best to enhance the films, making the shows less of a conventional late-night program and more of a themed attraction.

Clearly, there is a rich history to be examined when studying the films of this era, along with the hosts who had the most impact. More than 150 horror films will be examined. It is hoped that this core of films will shed some insight into the flavor, the nuances and the evolution of horror during this timeframe. It was a time when the masses were exposed to horror via TV. It represented the start of something that we now take for granted: the opportunity for everyone with a television to have a fair shot at appreciating the world of hosted horror.

I hope the coming chapters will motivate some readers to watch these films—many of which can be found on cable TV stations like Me-TV, and on streaming outlets like Amazon Prime and Roku—from their darkened living rooms during the late hours on a Friday or Saturday night.

Chapter Two

The Arrival of "Shock Theater"

By the mid–1950s, the world of horror in American popular culture had hit one of its low points. The cause of that development could be found in multiple sources. One involved the shift to themes that dealt with science fiction, rather than pure horror. Another factor involved the comic book industry. Horror was becoming persona non grata in mainstream America, in large part because of the controversial content being produced by publications like *The Haunt of Fear*.

The Haunt of Fear was a bi-monthly horror comic put out by EC Comics, the same company that produced similar comic books like *Tales from the Crypt* and *The Vault of Horror*. *The Haunt of Fear*, which ran from 1950 to 1954, featured tales that were influenced by macabre writers like H.P. Lovecraft, Edgar Allan Poe and Bram Stoker, the author of *Dracula*. *The Haunt of Fear* dealt with a variety of horror fare, everything from vampires to witches to just plain old-fashioned murder.

During its short history, *The Haunt of Fear* featured a total of 28 issues. By far the most controversial issue was the one dated May-June 1953. It featured a comic strip called "Foul Play," which was drawn by legendary cartoonist Jack Davis, who would become far better known for his work with *Mad* magazine.

Davis' visual images, in support of the writing of Al Feldstein, brought to life the story of a midnight baseball game being played in a fictional place called Central City. The comic strip started out rather innocently, recalling an earlier playoff game between the Central City team and a team from the nearby town of Bayville. But strange circumstances soon developed. During the game, Bayville star Jerry Deegan was spiked at second base, causing him some pain, but not enough to force his removal from the game. As he came to bat in the ninth, he began acting strangely. Striking out to end the game, he collapsed at home plate. His teammates rushed out, trying to figure out what was wrong. Within moments, they realized that Deegan was dead.

Bayville soon discovered that Deegan had been murdered. He had been intentionally spiked by Central City pitcher Herbie Satten, who had dipped his spikes into a time-release poison. When the spikes penetrated Deegan's uniform and skin, the slow-acting poison entered his bloodstream, killing the young star.

When the Bayville players realized that Deegan was murdered, they concocted an elaborate revenge scheme. Claiming to be a group of Satten fans, they sent the pitcher a letter saying that they wanted to honor him with a plaque at the ballpark. They invited him to meet them at Central City Park at 11 p.m. For some reason, Satten did not become suspicious of the late-night meeting time. Instead, with his ego appropriately tickled, the self-centered Satten made his way to the ballpark.

Fast forward one hour, to the reveal of the comic strip. As the readers learn, a special midnight game is being played. The narrator of the story provides the details:

> So now you know, friends. Now you know why there is a ballgame being played in the moonlight at midnight in the deserted Central City ballpark. Look closely. See this strange baseball game! See the long strings of pulpy intestines that mark the baselines. See the two lungs and the liver that indicate the bases. The heart that is home plate. See Doc White bend and whisk the heart with the mangy scalp, yelling....[1]
>
> "See the batter come to the plate swinging the legs, the arms, then throwing all but one away and standing in the box waiting for the pitcher to hurl the head into him."[2]

The head, along with the other body parts being used in the ghoulish game, all belonged to Satten. The Bayville players, in completing their revenge against the murderous Satten, had committed a murder of their own. They killed Satten during their late night "meeting" and then dismembered him so that his body parts could become a part of the playing field and the equipment used in playing the actual game.

To call this climax gruesome would be a gross understatement. Not surprisingly, this comic created a stir, especially in a relatively conservative 1950s culture. The *Haunt of Fear*'s status as a publication marketed to teenage boys added to the furor. Readers of the comic, particularly adult consumers, were appalled. The following year, noted author and film critic Robert Warshow wrote an essay in which he criticized *The Haunt of Fear* for running the comic strip and described "Foul Play" as "the outer limits … of good taste."[3]

That same year, German-American psychiatrist Fredric Wertham published his book *Seduction of the Innocent*. As part of a scathing critique of the comic book industry, he cited "Foul Play." As pointed out by Wertham, "Foul Play" was not the only comic strip that seemed to exceed the standards of good taste. Wertham cited other examples of what he felt were comic strips that had gone too far, including one in which a young girl was about to have her tongue ripped out.[4] He also described a story in which a ten-year-old murdered her own father.[5] In case after case, Wertham complained of the gruesome comic book imagery that accompanied the written word.

Wertham argued that young readers of such comics were becoming motivated to commit criminal activity themselves, thereby feeding into the continuing problem of juvenile delinquency. Led by the railing of Wertham, other folks joined in the fight against horror comics. The growing list of protesters, all of whom agreed with Wertham's main premise, included parents, schoolteachers, religious men and psychologists. They argued that horror and terror comics were essentially "provoking" young children, particularly teenage boys, causing them to engage in dangerous and even violent behavior.

Congress took note of the growing controversy. In April and June 1954, the Senate Subcommittee on Juvenile Delinquency met, headed up by Senator Estes Kefauver. In April, committee members heard testimony from Wertham. He also presented a blow-up of the "Foul Play" comic strip, complete with the graphically detailed caption that described the various body parts littering the playing field.[6]

Shortly after Wertham addressed Kefauver and the other committee members, EC Comics publisher William Gaines offered a rebuttal. Speaking eloquently, he made a rational and impassioned defense of horror comics, arguing that the behavior of children was not being directly affected by the fiction stories, but rather by the dysfunctional environment in their homes, neighborhoods and schools. That, Gaines argued, is where the blame lay.[7]

Once Kefauver and the other committee members heard from both sides, they came to a conclusion. They did not come out and place outright blame on the comics industry for juvenile delinquency, but they did suggest that publishers tone down the content of their product. They hinted that the comic book industry could face censorship if it did not clean up its act.[8]

In the fall of '54, the comic industry formally reacted to the hearings. They avoided outside censorship by creating the self-regulatory Comics Magazine Association of America (CMAA) and a Comics Code Authority (CCA); the industry placed severe restrictions on violent comic book genres. According to the Code, publishers could no longer use basic words like "terror" and "horror" in their titles. Furthermore, they could no longer depict zombies, werewolves, vampires, ghouls and other sinister characters of supernatural origin. Subjects like cannibalism and torture could not be broached. To put out their magazines, publishers now needed a visible seal of approval which would appear on the cover of their comic books.

Gaines rightly believed that his titles were being targeted by the Code and realized they were doomed to future failure. Rather than compromise and water down his product, he announced the cancellation of *The Haunt of Fear* in September 1954; the last issue was dated November-December 1954. Eventually Gaines also cancelled *Tales from the Crypt* and *The Vault of Terror*. By the end of 1955, all three of the magazines were gone from shelves. *Haunt* and *Vault* would never return; *Tales from the Crypt* made only a brief comeback in 2007, long after Gaines' passing.

For the next decade and a half, the Comics Code Authority had a profound effect on the industry. During that time, a few underground comic books sprang up, but mainstream horror comics were essentially sidelined, or if they persisted, their content was emasculated. It was not until 1971 that the Code restrictions were significantly lessened, allowing for the depiction of "vampires, ghouls and werewolves," particularly when they were faithful to such classic stories as Dracula and Frankenstein.

Without true horror comics to stir the passions of younger fans, the overall genre of horror stagnated in the mid– to late 1950s. Logically, it would have seemed that teenage and young adult fans could turn to horror on film, but even that option was becoming limited. In the 1950s, movie studios had transferred their emphasis from horror stories to science fiction themes, replacing the concept of the classic supernatural monsters like Dracula and the Mummy with alien invaders, enormous insects and other creatures that seemed to come from outer space, or were rooted in the side effects of nuclear and atomic accidents. Yes, there were still a few true horror films of quality being produced; viewers could see the films during their theatrical releases, but once they had their initial runs, in the era long before home video or the onset of the Internet, they essentially disappeared from view.

What of the horror films from the 1930s and '40s? They would have made logical fodder for the new generation growing up in the late '50s, but circumstances did not cooperate. Television stations might have seemed like a logical destination for those classics, but they did not show these films, simply because they could not. TV stations did not have the rights to show many horror films.

That all began to change in June 1957. That's when Screen Gems, a film distribution company that served as a television subsidiary to Columbia Pictures, leased the television rights to a whopping 550 films from Universal. The deal gave Screen Gems the TV rights to the films for the next ten years.

That October, Screen Gems announced the official release of 52 of the Universal films into TV syndication. That meant that, in exchange for a fee, local TV stations around the country could air the films. Screen Gems referred to the group of films as the "Shock Theater" package.

All 52 films had come out prior to 1947. None came out before 1931, so silent classics like *The Phantom of the Opera* and *The Hunchback of Notre Dame* (also products of

2. The Arrival of "Shock Theater"

Universal) did not make the cut. A little more than half of the films germinated from the genre of horror, or a blend of horror and mystery, with the other half representing a mix of crime dramas, straight mysteries, thrillers and films noir. The horror films provided a wonderful cross-section of Universal's horror classics from the 1930s, everything from *Dracula* to *Frankenstein* to *The Mummy* and *The Wolf Man*. The "Shock" package also included second-tier classics like *The Invisible Man*, *The Black Cat* and *Murders in the Rue Morgue*. Several other campy favorites, including *Frankenstein Meets the Wolf Man*, *Son of Dracula*, *Son of Frankenstein* and *Night Monster* helped round out the better half of the package.

Here is a complete list of the films in the "Shock" package. The films that are underlined are featured in this book:

Title	Date	Genre
Dracula	1931	Horror
Frankenstein	1931	Horror
Murders in the Rue Morgue	1932	Horror
The Mummy	1932	Horror
Secret of the Blue Room	1933	Horror-Mystery
The Invisible Man	1933	Horror
Secret of the Chateau	1934	Crime-Mystery
The Black Cat	1934	Horror
Chinatown Squad	1935	Crime-Drama
Mystery of Edwin Drood	1935	Horror-Mystery
The Great Impersonation	1935	Drama
The Raven	1935	Horror
Werewolf of London	1935	Horror
Dracula's Daughter	1936	Horror
The Invisible Ray	1936	Horror
Night Key	1937	Crime-Thriller
Reported Missing	1937	Thriller
The Man Who Cried Wolf	1937	Crime-Drama
The Last Warning	1938	Mystery
The Spy Ring	1938	Adventure-Crime
Mystery of the White Room	1939	Mystery-Crime
Son of Frankenstein	1939	Horror
The Witness Vanishes	1939	Adventure-Mystery
Enemy Agent	1940	Adventure-Mystery
The Invisible Man Returns	1940	Horror
The Mummy's Hand	1940	Horror
A Dangerous Game	1941	Adventure-Crime
Horror Island	1941	Horror
Man Made Monster	1941	Horror
The Wolf Man	1941	Horror
Destination Unknown	1942	Drama
Mystery of Marie Roget	1942	Horror
Nightmare	1942	Crime-Mystery
Night Monster	1942	Horror
Sealed Lips	1942	Crime-Drama
The Mad Doctor of Market Street	1942	Comedy-Horror

Title	Date	Genre
The Mummy's Tomb	1942	Horror
The Strange Case of Doctor Rx	1942	Horror-Mystery
Calling Dr. Death	1943	Horror-Mystery
Frankenstein Meets the Wolf Man	1943	Horror
Son of Dracula	1943	Horror
The Mad Ghoul	1943	Horror
Dead Man's Eyes	1944	Horror-Crime
Weird Woman	1944	Mystery
The Mummy's Ghost	1944	Horror
Pillow of Death	1945	Horror-Mystery
The Frozen Ghost	1945	Horror-Mystery
Danger Woman	1946	Drama
House of Horrors	1946	Horror
She-Wolf of London	1946	Horror-Mystery
The Cat Creeps	1946	Mystery
The Spider Woman Strikes Back	1946	Horror-Thriller

Based on a reasonable calculation, no fewer than 34 horror titles found homes in the "Shock Theater" package. The films featured a strong sampling of titles starring the early legends of the horror genre: Boris Karloff, Bela Lugosi, and Lon Chaney, Jr. For fans of horror, the announcement of the "Shock" package created a wave of excitement in the later months of 1957. Theatergoers who were old enough to see the movies during their initial releases could now enjoy them again in their living rooms, and at no charge. Even more importantly, young horror fans, born after the glory days of 1930s horror, would now receive their first crack at watching the films that had made Universal the king of horror.

Screen Gems did have one recommendation for local television stations that aired the "Shock Theater" movies. It was not a firm condition, nothing that would make or break the deal, but simply something that Screen Gems encouraged. The company felt that TV stations would be wise to show the films as part of a format accompanied by a host, someone who would introduce the films and then make comments during the commercial breaks.

TV stations might have lazily bypassed the suggestion for a horror host, which would have required the hiring of another announcer, or given added responsibilities to someone already employed by the station. Remarkably, most of the local stations reacted favorably to Screen Gems' suggestion, bringing in actors who would serve as hosts. With that, local TV stations initiated the era of "hosted horror."

It did not take long for WCAU, a Philadelphia station, to hire its first horror host. On October 7, WCAU debuted its "Shock Theater," hosted by a young radio personality named John Zacherle. A broadcaster with a passion for the theater, Zacherle had shown little to no prior interest in horror. But he turned out to be the right choice for the new position that had been stimulated by the "Shock Theater" release.

Rather than play the role straight, Zacherle adopted the persona of Roland (pronounced Ro-*land*, emphasis on the second syllable), a lanky man who wore a long black coat that one would associate with an undertaker. Zacherle's routine as Roland, which emphasized his ghoulish, costumed appearance, along with sight gags and wisecracks, became a hit with viewers, boosting the ratings for WCAU.

The character of Roland became a template for other horror hosts around the country.

In New York City, WABC hired a faceless host who could only be heard from an off-camera location; he was called "The Voice." In Chicago, Terry Bennett played Marvin, a character with thick glasses who played up the humor but occasionally tried to scare audiences, too. In San Francisco, a local television station featured a host named Terrence.

In smaller but still substantial markets, other hosts took hold. In Fort Worth, Texas, Gorgon took to the airwaves, the name stirring up memories of the mythical creature Medusa. By 1958, a man named Ray Sparenberg was playing Selwin in Indianapolis, Indiana. Selwin's catchphrase was "Friday night is Fright Night on Channel 8." Beginning in 1959, New Orleans became the home of a character named Morgus, a play on the word "morgue."

Equipped with their new horror hosts, these stations, and many others, aired the showcases on weekends. Generally speaking, the horror hosts and their films took center stage during the late hours of Friday or Saturday nights, or during the early afternoon on Saturdays. In many cases, the stations referred to their programs as *Shock Theater*, as WCAU did, borrowing the name used by Screen Gems.

Despite the lack of prime ratings slots, "Shock Theater" was a great success across the country. In five key markets, including New York, Philadelphia, Los Angeles and San Francisco, the airings of the horror films lifted local TV ratings by significant margins. In some cases, the ratings increase measured 38 percent. In others, the ratings went through the roof, improving by over 1000 percent the ratings of programs previously seen in those same time slots.[9]

Thanks to the boost prompted by the airing of the "Shock Theater" selections, Screen Gems decided to do a follow-up just one year later. In 1958, they announced the release of 20 additional films in a package called "Son of Shock." This time, horror films comprised the vast majority of the selections. No fewer than 17 of the 20 films came from the horror genre; the other three could be classified as crime dramas or mysteries with some horror elements.

The "Son of Shock" package featured the following films. The films that are underlined are featured in this book:

Title	Date	Genre
Behind the Mask	1932	Horror-Crime
Night of Terror	1933	Horror-Mystery
Bride of Frankenstein	1935	Horror
The Black Room	1935	Horror-Crime
The Man Who Lived Twice	1936	Crime-Drama
The Man They Could Not Hang	1939	Horror-Crime
Before I Hang	1940	Horror-Crime
Black Friday	1940	Horror-Drama
Isle of Doomed Men	1940	Crime-Drama
The Man with Nine Lives	1940	Mystery–Science Fiction
The Devil Commands	1941	Horror–Science Fiction
The Face Behind the Mask	1941	Crime Drama–Horror
The Boogie Man Will Get You	1942	Comedy-Horror
The Ghost of Frankenstein	1942	Horror
Captive Wild Woman	1943	Horror–Science Fiction
House of Frankenstein	1944	Horror
The Invisible Man's Revenge	1944	Horror–Science Fiction
The Mummy's Curse	1944	Horror-Fantasy
House of Dracula	1945	Horror
The Jungle Captive	1945	Horror–Science Fiction

Of the 20 "Son of Shock" films, the prize release was *Bride of Frankenstein*, the hugely successful and critically acclaimed 1935 sequel to *Frankenstein*. The film, like the original, starred Boris Karloff, whose film credits highlighted the "Son of Shock" package. Karloff appeared in no fewer than 10 of the "Son of Shock" films. The Frankenstein theme also dominated this grouping, with the Monster appearing in four of the movies: *Bride of Frankenstein*, *The Ghost of Frankenstein*, *House of Frankenstein* and *House of Dracula*.

While "Son of Shock" lacked the sheer volume of the initial "Shock" package, it had a positive impact on the local TV ratings. With its emphasis on more recent (1940s) releases (14 in total), "Son of Shock" felt newer and hipper, making it even more attractive to younger viewers.

Not only did the "Shock" and "Son of Shock" packages succeed with local TV stations, they created an influence in other avenues. Most prominently, the popularity of the films (particularly the initial "Shock" package) contributed to the creation of a new magazine, an iconic piece of horror literature called *Famous Monsters of Filmland*.

The magazine was the brainchild of two men: East Coast publisher James Warren and a Californian named Forrest J Ackerman, the country's No. 1 collector of science fiction and horror memorabilia. Ackerman loved science fiction with the passion of a child, while his interest in horror ran second.

With Ackerman providing the creative genius and Warren laying the publishing groundwork, they collaborated on the idea of a one-shot publication focusing on film monsters from the 1930s and '40s. Warren initially called the magazine *Wonderama*, but the title gave him pause.[10] On second thought, he renamed the magazine *Famous Monsters of Filmland* (a far better and more accurate title). Ackerman, with his knowledge of the industry and his creative, innovative way of thinking, agreed to be the primary writer and editor.

The magazine hit newsstands on February 27, 1958, and fans snapped it up as if it were paper money. The one-shot publication sold out of its initial print run.[11] Within a few days, letters started to pour into Warren's office, expressing their gratitude for the magazine and its unprecedented subject matter. The wave of fan letters continued day after day.

Famous Monsters of Filmland became such a hit that Warren realized he could not let it pass with just one issue. He quickly formulated plans to make the magazine a regular production; by 1960, he was publishing the magazine four times a year, and by 1962, he was up to six issues. Warren relied on Ackerman as the driving force behind both the written content and the imagery. The so-called "monster magazine" paid homage to the old horror films through wonderful black-and-white photographs—many culled from Ackerman's personal collection.

In writing up stories and photo captions, Ackerman emphasized his love of puns, word play and cute nicknames. He printed fan letters under the name of "Fang Mail." Another regular feature of the magazine became known as "You Axed for It!" To top it off, Ackerman referred to himself as the Ackermonster and Dr. Acula. His house, full of movie memorabilia, became known as the Ackermansion.

Ackerman estimated that at one point, he received hundreds of letters a month, ranging from letters of appreciation to story submissions for future issues. The wave of letters became so overpowering that Ackerman enlisted his mother's help in sorting out legitimate inquiries from frivolous ones.

One fan of Ackerman and the magazine was a young David J. Skal, who was just becoming interested in monsters and horror films. With limited access to the films themselves, Skal enjoyed them courtesy of the editor of *Famous Monsters of Filmland*. "Forrest J Ackerman was a personal hero of mine when I was 14,"[12] says Skal, now a leading horror historian and the author of numerous books about horror films and supernatural subject matter. "Thank God for those magazines because there was no other way to experience these films. When you're that young, the idea of waiting six years for something, when you're six years old, is like half a lifetime,"[13] says Skal. "Forry Ackerman did cast a spell on me with his magazine. It did what it intended to do. It created a special aura around monsters. And they were very important. They were my first real passion in life."[14]

Inspired by Ackerman's fun literary style, not to mention all of the terrific black-and-white photographs and the colorful cover art (some supplied by the brilliant artist Basil Gogos), fans like Skal devoured copies of *Famous Monsters of Filmland*. Having found its audience, the magazine continued the success of its surprising debut. With the new magazine making regular appearances on newsstands and through subscriptions, horror fans now had more than just the movies themselves at their disposal. They now had the opportunity to read and learn about the films and the actors, along with a collectible keepsake that reflected their love of the genre.

While *Famous Monsters of Filmland* established a strong niche of its own, it eventually spawned a number of similar publications. The list of monster magazines included *Castle of Frankenstein* and *Monster Mag*, each of which developed a following, though not at the same level as *Famous Monsters*. Unlike the comic books, the monster magazines were not subject to the Comics Code Authority, allowing them to delve freely into the world of vampires, werewolves and witches.

From the nadir of the Wertham witch hunt to the excitement of "Shock Theater" to the euphoria created by *Famous Monsters of Filmland*, the world of horror had undergone a remarkable transformation in the late 1950s. Within a span of only five years, horror had gone from being an unwanted stepchild to re-taking its hold on at least part of mainstream popular culture.

While *Famous Monsters of Filmland* contributed to the bounce-back, the reemergence of horror manifested itself most popularly through film and television. It was buttressed by the strong followings of established shows like *Alfred Hitchcock Presents* (which had started in 1955 and remained on TV for years) and newer programs like Rod Serling's *The Twilight Zone* (1959–1964) and Boris Karloff's *Thriller* (1960–1962). Along with the surprising emergence of hit films like *Psycho*, horror on both the small and large screens had gotten a hold on the American populace. The public had a taste for horror, particularly when it came to visual imagery and presentation. Feeding that hunger was the weekend ritual on local television, aided by costumed characters and other kinds of persona, all of which gave horror fans a chance to watch and re-watch both the old classics and the new wave of film gems.

The era of hosted horror, spawned in the latter days of 1957, was now more fully formed and ready to take its place in American culture for the next decade and a half.

Chapter Three

The Pioneers
Vampira and Zacherley

The first horror host predated Screen Gems' 1957 release of the "Shock Theater" package. A full three years before "Shock Theater" made its way into syndication, KABC-TV (Channel 7) in Los Angeles debuted 31-year-old Finnish actress Maila Nurmi as the hostess who would introduce a late-night horror film each week. And thus, Vampira was born.

In creating a costume for a local masquerade party, the rail-thin Nurmi borrowed a look from Charles Addams' cartoons, specifically the "Addams Family" character that would later come to be known as Morticia. Dressed in a long, skin-tight black dress featuring tattered sleeves, Nurmi had a 17-inch waist that was so thin it seemed to defy the laws of physics. Sporting fingernails the length of Nosferatu's and arched eyebrows that created a look of impending doom, Vampira (pronounced vamp-*eye*-ruh) looked something like Dracula's daughter, funereal but also alluring.

In winning the masquerade contest, Nurmi drew the attention of an ABC executive who offered her a job hosting a different horror film each week. The introduction of Vampira's show became iconic, displaying a fog-filled back alley, empty at first, but then revealing a figure at the far end of the street. At first, the figure approaching the camera appears to be some sort of creature, but within seconds, it is evident that it is a strangely dressed woman. She lets out a blood-curdling scream, followed by a pleasant and seductive "Good evening." And with that, the notion of a horror host was off and running.

Beginning with the early episodes in April 1954, Nurmi appeared in taped segments that aired before, during and after the movie. Her short sketches emphasized morbid comedy. One week, she would take a bubble bath in what appeared to be a boiling cauldron of water. In another, she might discuss the bizarre ingredients of one of her vampiric recipes.

Like any good vampire, Nurmi delivered her lines deliberately, her voice breathy, seductive and deep, but with an American accent. As Vampira, her form of humor was corny to the extreme, particularly by 21st century standards, but 1950s audiences loved it. Nurmi's Vampira possessed an excellent sense of timing and an ability to turn a humorous pun. Thanks to her presence, the ratings for the horror films skyrocketed, with fans tuning in to see Vampira as much as they wanted to see the featured film. In fact, fans seemed more interested in what Vampira would say and do next than anything having to do with the film itself.

Even though Vampira appeared on a local affiliate in Los Angeles, she almost immediately became a national sensation. Shortly after debuting on KABC, Nurmi's character was featured within the pages of *Life* magazine.[1]

As the first horror host, Vampira turned out a performance that was very different from the mostly male hosts that succeeded her with the advent of the "Shock" packages.

3. The Pioneers: Vampira and Zacherley

Vampira (circa 1955): Played so hauntingly and provocatively by Maila Nurmi, Vampira gazes into the camera, accompanied by a skull, a creepy doll and spider webs. She looked like no TV character who had come before her, complete with diagonal eyebrows, dagger-like fingernails and a tiny waist that could have fit in a ship's porthole (Photofest).

In contrast to the later hosts, Vampira did not focus her sketches on the film being shown. She did not talk about the films, or offer insight into them. Instead, the sketches centered on Vampira's fictional persona and lifestyle, with an emphasis on ghoulish behavior that often drifted into comedy. The audience didn't seem to mind the disconnect between Vampira and the movies. They were fully entertained, as evidenced by the soaring ratings.

Given the ratings success, it might have seemed probable that Nurmi would remain with KABC for years. It didn't happen. After roughly a year and a total of 50 episodes, the station canceled the show and released Nurmi. The reasons for the fast exit remain somewhat in dispute; Nurmi always contended that KABC wanted her to relinquish all rights to the Vampira character,[2] and that when she refused, the station fired her, causing her to be blackballed by the rest of the TV world.[3] By April 1955, Vampira's show had come to an end.

With Vampira ousted, the horror host remained in limbo for three years, finally resurrected with the advent of the "Shock Theater" package. The first of the new wave of horror hosts was 38-year-old John Zacherle, a man who loved the theater and had experience creating characters for the live Western TV series *Action in the Afternoon*. Zacherle had never watched horror films prior to signing a contract to serve as horror host for WCAU in Philadelphia. (His father did not approve of horror films, even the classics like *Dracula* and *Frankenstein*, and would not allow his son to watch them.[4]) Like Nurmi, Zacherle adopted a fictional personality, becoming a cadaverous character known as Roland.

The character wore a long frock coat and took on the appearance of an undertaker who seemed to be near death, almost ghoulish in appearance. To enhance Roland's tall and skeletal look, the TV station supplied him with makeup that turned his eye sockets into dark circles and gave his lips a series of stitches, making them look like they had been sewn onto his face.

The WCAU stage purported to show Roland's home, a crypt where he lived with his unseen wife, whom he always referred to as My Dear, and laboratory assistant Igor. Realizing that the some of the horror films that Roland would introduce were of poor quality, WCAU's station manager encouraged Zacherle to play up his role fully, almost as if he were providing a distraction from the film. With his theatrical nature and sense of comedy, Zacherle was more than happy to oblige through his characterization of Roland.

Unlike Vampira, Roland's sketches did not take place in isolation from the film being shown. Rather, Roland's skits provided a commentary about the film, essentially forming a parody of the movie being shown that night. Ad libbing much of his dialogue, he poked lighthearted fun at everything from the characters to the plot to the horror genre in general. WCAU executives didn't seem to mind; they understood that many of the horror films were of B-quality, or lesser stature. In fact, the lesser the quality of the film, the more that Roland brought out the needle during his skits, which occasionally ran simultaneously over the movie's soundtrack. Once the brief skit ended, the visual feed of the film was restored.

Much like Vampira, Roland became an immediate hit with late-night television viewers. "They were both deadpan comedians," says horror historian David J. Skal. "There was a kind of a Charles Addams quality about the early horror hosts."[5]

WCAU decided to hold an open house in Philadelphia, giving fans a chance to meet the new horror host. The TV station expected only a small turnout of diehard fans, perhaps a few hundred, to attend the event. The executives were taken aback when a crowd of approximately 13,000 rabid fans showed up at the open house, overwhelming the horror host and his co-workers.[6] Roland was a certified hit.

Zacherle also enjoyed simultaneous success in recording an album. His friendship with Dick Clark, the popular host of *American Bandstand,* gave him the opportunity to cut a single called "Dinner with Drac," which featured a mix of music and horror sound effects. At first, Zacherle's recording was too gory for Clark's taste, so he recorded a second, toned-down version. The two versions occupied both sides of a bestselling 45 which brought him to a wider audience.

Not only did Clark help Zacherle's musical career, he also advanced his reputation as a horror host. It was Clark who dubbed Zacherle "The Cool Ghoul,"[7] a nickname that would stick for the rest of his life.

In 1958, WCAU was purchased by CBS, a move that prompted Zacherle to pull up stakes and move to New York City, where he was hired by WABC. His new employer wanted Zacherle to continue hosting a late-night horror film, but they decided to abandon the Roland persona, instead opting to use a variation of his real last name. Adding a "y" to Zacherle, he

Zacherley (circa 1958): The ghoul-faced John Zacherley poses in a coffin while sifting through a mountain of fan letters. Although his tenure as a TV host ended by the mid–1960s, he would remain a popular cultural force up until his death in 2016 (Photofest).

became known as Zacherley, which would remain his stage name for the rest of his career. His new WABC show was called *Zacherley at Large*.

As he did at WCAU, Zacherley thrust himself into the horror films. At times, he would pretend to have conversations with the various monsters being shown on screen. At other times, the focus became the sight gags supplied by his imaginary on-stage home, where he carried on conversations with his wife, who was lying in a coffin with a stake driven through her heart, or with his son Gasport, who was supposedly encased in a burlap sack hanging from a rope.

Not surprisingly, Zacherley provided the same kind of ratings boost to WABC that he had already provided for WCAU. In his first year with the station, WABC's ratings tripled. For those who thought that Zacherle was a fluke in Philadelphia, his New York success proved otherwise.

Zacherley remained with WABC through 1960. Then he took his talents to WOR Channel 9, another New York City station. After a brief stint there, he moved on to WPIX Channel 11 where he served as host of several shows, including the iconic *Chiller Theater*.

By the mid–1960s, Zacherle had ended his tenure as a regular late-night host, but he would continue to foster his persona in other avenues. He made appearances in numerous documentaries and also had cameos in two horror films, *Brain Damage* and *Frankenhooker*. He recorded a wide variety of singles and full-length albums in which he told stories and even sang while using the same vocal style of his on-air persona. Right into his late 80s, Zacherle continued to make TV appearances, often during the Halloween season. His last

TV appearance was in 2008 when WPIX brought him and *Chiller Theater* back for a special presentation of the 1955 film *Tarantula*. Zacherle regularly attended horror and sci-fi conventions, a practice that he maintained through 2015.

Maintaining an active schedule nearly to the end, Zacherle passed away in 2016 at the age of 98, leaving behind a legacy as the most famous horror host in history.

Much like Zacherley, Maila Nurmi continued to perpetuate her image as Vampira well beyond her one-year horror hostess heyday. As she wrapped up her stint on late-night TV, she made a celebrated appearance on *The George Gobel Show* and acted in a number of films, most notably Ed Wood's *Plan 9 from Outer Space* (1958). Generally regarded as one of the worst science fiction films of any era, the movie briefly featured Vampira in a non-speaking role.

In the early 1960s, Nurmi opened Vampira's Attic, a Hollywood boutique specializing in antiques and featuring some of her own handmade clothing and jewelry.[8] In the early 1980s, she reached an informal agreement to resurrect her Vampira persona for KHJ-TV, but the proposed show never made the airwaves due to creative differences. Shortly thereafter, Nurmi made news when she sued Cassandra Peterson for her portrayal of Elvira, a horror hostess that bore a close resemblance to Vampira. The courts ruled against Nurmi, allowing Peterson to continue her career as a leading horror host of the 1980s and '90s.

In her later years, Nurmi authorized the creation of both a plastic model based on Vampira (much like the Aurora models of the 1960s and '70s) and a pre-painted figurine made by Bowen designs. It was all part of her effort to make ends meet, as she lived a modest but acceptable life in Southern California.

In 2008, Nurmi, 85, died of natural causes. Though not as popular or enduring as Zacherley, Nurmi left a sturdy and unquestionable legacy as the pioneer of televised horror hosts.

Chapter Four

The Movies of "Shock Theater"

There is little doubt that John Zacherle played an enormous role in the success of "Shock Theater." Without his on-air presence, "Shock Theater" might have faltered. But like most horror hosts who followed, Zacherle relied heavily on the films he presented as his source of inspiration. While horror hosts such as Zacherle completed the package through their insights, bits of trivia and comedic touch, it was the content of the films that maintained the lifeblood of late-night horror.

Much of the appeal of the original "Shock Theater" package stemmed from the inclusion of two iconic films that were well known by the late 1950s. Without these two landmark productions, "Shock Theater" would not have been picked up by so many local television markets in 1957. Without such films, television viewership would have suffered dramatically, perhaps bringing an early end to the era of hosted horror.

Of the 52 films in the package, *Dracula* was the earliest on the list. It premiered in Asheville, North Carolina, on February 9, 1931, before premiering in New York City on February 12 and then "going wide" on February 14. Beyond the chronology, the impact and legacy of *Dracula* also place it first on the "Shock Theater" list.

That is not to say that the original *Dracula* is a great film, or even a very good one; it has an array of shortcomings. It is slow-moving, with stiff dialogue, poor special effects, glaring continuity errors and overacting from many of its performers. At times, it is hard to follow the storyline presented by director Tod Browning. Compared to other Universal Horror classics from the 1930s and '40s (*Frankenstein*, *Bride of Frankenstein*, *The Wolf Man*), it does not hold up well.

Yet, as flawed as *Dracula* might be, it remains a critically important film, one that adapted the successful Hamilton Deane stage play, which in turn was based on Bram Stoker's brilliant Gothic novel. Universal originally intended a more direct and more expensive adaptation of the famed Stoker novel, but the onset of the Great Depression made the studio reluctant to spend such a sum of money.[1]

The film begins with real estate agent Renfield visiting Count Dracula's Transylvanian castle to complete a deal, unaware that his host is a vampire. Bitten by Dracula, he falls under the count's influence and becomes his servant. Renfield assists the vampire in making the trek by sea to England, where he can feast on a larger population of victims. Upon arrival at Carfax Abbey, Dracula embarks on a series of attacks, including a young victim named Lucy. He then turns his attention to Lucy's friend Mina. Dracula's obsession with Mina leads to confrontation with the astute vampire hunter, Prof. Van Helsing.

Dracula was a huge box office success, creating the impetus for other Universal Horrors.

The sixth-highest grossing American film of 1931,[2] *Dracula* showed Hollywood that horror could be highly profitable. The film also made a star of Bela Lugosi as the title character. He had already performed the role on the stage, which led to Universal's decision to give him the film role. But Lugosi was far from the first choice. The studio preferred the legendary and well-established Lon Chaney of *Hunchback of Notre Dame* and *Phantom of the Opera* fame, but he was ill with cancer at the time and passed away shortly before filming began. The studio looked at other actors, like Ian Keith,[3] before settling on Lugosi, who was not considered bankable by some within Hollywood. It turned out that he most certainly was.

Horror historian David J. Skal, the leading authority on Stoker and arguably the highest-ranking expert on the 1931 film, says that *Dracula* represented a groundbreaking change for the moviemaking industry: "It was the first time that a studio took a chance on a supernatural topic. Hollywood didn't believe the public would buy the supernatural. It was considered inappropriate for the screen. Universal took that chance. It was a freak success.... *Dracula* and *Frankenstein* probably saved Universal from bankruptcy."[4]

Although *Dracula* became available to TV viewers in the late 1950s, Skal did not see it until the late '60s, when he saw it on a large screen:

> It was not until I was in high school, it was 1968, when Universal made new theatrical prints of *Dracula* and *Frankenstein*, and they went out on the road with some of their W.C. Fields movies. There was this kind of nostalgia craze brewing, and we had a theater locally; they showed these films. I went back several times to watch. In those days, you could just sit in the movie theater and watch things over and over and over.[5]
>
> *Dracula* kind of *underwhelmed* me. I had expected so much. Lugosi was there, and his presence is the most impressive thing about the film. But I almost thought if I kept watching it, I might catch other things. Maybe there were Munchkins committing suicide back in the shadows! [*Laughs*] I don't know. I became obsessed with the film. I could probably recite every line of dialogue in it. I've probably seen it hundreds of times over the years. I've introduced many, many screenings of it during my late-life career as a horror historian.[6]

For Skal and many others, the stirring performance of Lugosi makes the film a landmark, even though the actor had limited command of the English language at the time he worked on *Dracula*. As Skal points out, Lugosi's then-rudimentary knowledge of English forced him to memorize the words without always knowing what each word meant. As a result, Lugosi spoke slowly—mouthing each word forcefully. "It was certainly his voice that was the voice of Count Dracula," Skal says. "It's a voice that you never forget. It's one of the most imitated voices in theatrical history. It's not precisely a Hungarian accent. It's the voice of a Hungarian actor who is learning his English-language roles phonetically. One … deliberate … syllable … at a time."[7]

In addition to the language barrier, Lugosi faced the problem of transitioning his portrayal of Dracula from the theatrical stage to the medium of film. "For the screen," said Lugosi, "in which the actor's distance from every member of the audience is equal only to his distance from the lens of the camera, I have found a great deal of repression was an absolute necessity. Tod Browning has continually had to 'hold me down.'"[8]

Beyond the proper level of restraint, Lugosi's intimidating presence, achieved through his penetrating stare, helps make his portrayal of Dracula iconic. For example, we never see Dracula blink in any of his close-up scenes. Lugosi also delivers one of the best-remembered lines in horror history when he reacts to the baying of the wolves by declaring, "Listen to them. Children of the night. What music they make."[9] The line induces chills to this day.

Beyond Lugosi, the film has a good supporting cast, headlined by Edward Van Sloan

4. The Movies of "Shock Theater" 23

Dracula (1931): Fully draped in his trademark black cape, Bela Lugosi's Dracula looks over the three coffins of Transylvanian soil that have been transported to the cavernous Carfax Abbey in England. According to vampire lore, the creature must sleep in a coffin filled with dirt from his native land during the daylight hours (courtesy of Frank Dello Stritto).

and David Manners. One of the best performances is delivered by the tragic Dwight Frye, who portrays the psychotic Renfield in the same year that he played Fritz, the deformed assistant to the doctor in *Frankenstein*. Frye was 31 when he appeared in *Dracula*; he would die only 12 years later from a heart attack. An extremely versatile character actor, Frye could portray the role of a wild-eyed, fly-eating lunatic (like Renfield) better than anyone of his era.

Unfortunately, he became typecast in that kind of role, preventing him from fully displaying his talents in other characterizations.

While *Dracula* succeeds in cultivating much of the vampire myth and creating a template for future portrayals of the undead, there are also some misconceptions about the film and its correspondence to the vampire legend. For example, Lugosi never displays fangs in the film; that would be left for future interpretations of Dracula and other vampires, particularly those portrayed by Christopher Lee and Jonathan Frid. Also, we never see any actual bite marks on Dracula's victims; they are only referenced verbally by some of the characters.

Dracula's initial theater release also produced an interesting footnote that is not well known. "*Dracula* was actually released with theater titles because not all theaters were wired for sound in those days," says Skal. "Hollywood was just getting its legs."[10] Clearly, *Dracula* is a flawed film that accurately represents the early era of talking movies, a time when films were still trying to find their way with the new technology of sound. *Dracula* features almost no music, leaving numerous dead spots when the actors are not speaking.

In what is believed to be a publicity still for *Dracula*, Dwight Frye takes on the freakish look that made him famous. In *Dracula*, Frye plays Renfield, the real estate lawyer that the vampire turns into a madman. A gifted actor, Frye performed so well that Universal brought him back as the hunchbacked Fritz in *Frankenstein* and as the unhinged Karl in *The Bride of Frankenstein*. Universal used him often in similar roles, even though he was capable of much more (courtesy of Frank Dello Stritto).

Horror fans expecting a great film will be disappointed by *Dracula*. The lack of attention given to the film by director Browning, who was afflicted with alcoholism, is quite evident in the final print. At times, Browning left cinematographer Karl Freund with the duty of directing entire scenes. Due to the lack of oversight, *Dracula* simply does not hold up, unlike many of the other horror Universal releases. But when enjoyed for some of its basic components, particularly its dark Gothic sets and shadowy, mood-filled atmosphere, and when appreciated for the breathtaking presence of the legendary Lugosi, it has special value.

Dracula is also a historically vital film, one that broke ground by developing much of the current mythology of vampires. For that reason alone, it is a substantial part of horror's legacy. "Shock Theater" simply would not have been as successful, commercially or artistically, without it.

Without question, *Dracula* is the film that launched the popularity of horror films for Universal, but in many ways, the second film on the "Shock Theater" list deserves to be known as the king of the Universal monsters—and perhaps all monsters. No horror movie has ever established a more iconic monster than the other powerhouse release from 1931: *Frankenstein*, which debuted in Detroit on November 19 before receiving a nationwide release two days later.

Without its vampiric predecessor, *Frankenstein* might not have been made. "*Frankenstein* soon followed because of *Dracula*'s success," maintains Skal.[11] Based on the novel by Mary Shelley, *Frankenstein* recounts the pioneering efforts of Henry Frankenstein. With the help of his demented hunchback assistant Fritz, Frankenstein obtains body parts of corpses and then creates a new "man" out of the remains.

The doctor has noble intentions of advancing science, but his plan soon descends into madness and tragedy. The Monster first murders Fritz as payback for the way that the hunchback repeatedly tormented him. He is later subdued by Frankenstein and his mentor, the wise old Dr. Waldman. As Dr. Waldman prepares to dissect and destroy him, the Monster regains consciousness and murders the doctor, before escaping the laboratory and terrorizing the countryside.

The movie takes the monster saga to new levels, creating the lasting imagery that has set the standard to this day. When we think of *Frankenstein*, we think of the movie first—and the book second. That is no insult to Shelley; it is a tribute to the work of legendary director James Whale, the quality of the sets and scenery, and the lasting portrayal of the Monster by Boris Karloff.

Makeup man Jack P. Pierce departed from the Monster's appearance contained in Shelley's vision. Studying human anatomy and medical surgery, he equipped the Monster with a flattened head and two bolts protruding from the neck, the latter serving as electrodes through which the life-giving electrical current flows. Pierce gave the Monster sunken cheeks and heavily shaded eyelids, so as to portray a kind of sleepy lifelessness for the resuscitated creature. In a brilliant use of costuming, Pierce decided to fit the Monster with boots which weighed close to 15 pounds each and accentuated Karloff's height. As a final touch, Pierce gave Karloff a poorly tailored suit jacket that made his arms seem longer than they actually were, while also exposing suture marks at the wrists.[12]

It is this image of the Monster that stands to this day. Any other portrayal, even in good productions from Hammer Films in later years, feels as if it is a misfit. That sense has come about, at least in part, because of Universal's decision to copyright the costume and look of the Monster, preventing other studios from replicating it.

Of course, none of that physical imagery would have mattered if not for Karloff's surprising performance. Despite his experience as an actor, he was still a relative unknown at the time, obscure enough that the movie's producers chose not to invite him to the film's premiere. He was also the clear-cut second choice, after the role had been offered to and rejected by Bela Lugosi, who didn't like the wild-haired look originally conceived for the Monster. "Lugosi was originally announced," says Skal. "He looked like the Golem. He was also offended that he had no dialogue [as the Monster]."[13]

It was a decision that Lugosi came to regret, but he wanted no part of a non-speaking role that made him look like "a scarecrow"—far different from the appearance that Karloff would attain through the work of Pierce. Lugosi's decision led to the casting of Karloff, whose identity was kept secret during the opening credits. Rather than listing his name, a large question mark appears next to "The Monster" in those credits, part of the film's promotional effort to keep the identity of the actor shrouded in mystery.

While Karloff was unknown to most moviegoers, he did not lack for service time in the

Frankenstein (1931): Frankenstein's Monster, played so forcefully and at times sympathetically by Boris Karloff, stands in his prison chamber. The Monster would escape, only to meet a more violent fate at the film's conclusion (Photofest).

film industry. As Skal points out, "Karloff was a seasoned actor at that time."[14] A veteran of films since 1919, the 44-year-old Karloff did an impressive screen test for Whale, convincing the director that he was the right choice. Karloff's Monster does not appear until after nearly 32 minutes of the film have elapsed, but when he does, he dominates the screen with an imposing, towering presence. Karloff also gives the Monster a sense of humanity, even sadness. He is not merely an evil beast raging at every turn; he is far more nuanced and complicated, someone that we sympathize with at times, and do not merely loathe. Karloff makes sure to deliver both the Monster's sensitivity and his own fears, particularly an extreme phobia of fire, along with a temper and a tendency toward destruction. Simply put, Karloff gives the Monster a soul.

Later comments by Karloff clearly indicate that he understood the importance of showing the Monster's vulnerable side. "This was a pathetic creature," said Karloff, "who like us all, had neither wish nor say in his creation and certainly did not wish upon itself the hideous image which automatically terrified human beings whom it tried to befriend."[15]

Karloff's layered and complex performance makes him the star of *Frankenstein*, but he is ably supported by two veteran actors who were more well-known at the time, but have now receded behind the legacy of Karloff. Edward Van Sloan introduces the film out of character, warning viewers of its disturbing theme, and then delivers one of his typically fine "good guy" performances as the kindly Dr. Waldman. And Colin Clive is a perfect fit as the obsessed Frankenstein, frantic in his desire to create a new "man" out of the parts of others. Clive's wonderful delivery of the repeated line, "It's alive! It's alive!" has become the subject of both imitation and parody, a sure sign of its iconic nature.

Clive also delivers the equally memorable and far more controversial line: "Now I know what it's like to be God." Whale's original film featured that critical line of dialogue, but the re-release of the film in the late 1930s deleted it because of objections from the censors, who considered it blasphemous.[16] In the edited version, the line was replaced by a loud clap of thunder, but it was eventually restored to the print and remains part of the film today.

Another controversial piece of editing involved the famous scene involving Maria, the young girl at the lake. She shows him flowers and then tosses them one by one into the water, where they float. She gives the Monster a handful of flowers, and he imitates her by throwing them into the water. But when he runs out of flowers, he picks up the small child and tosses *her* into the water, where she drowns. The censors demanded that Whale cut the scene short, preventing us from seeing what the Monster did with Maria, and how he was simply trying to imitate what the girl had done with the flowers. Based on the follow-up scene, where we see the father carrying the young girl's body through a street celebration, we can only imagine that the Monster has murdered her intentionally and willfully. (It was a case of unintended consequences for the censors, whose decision actually made the Monster even more sinister.) The original scene would not be restored to the film until the 1980s. It was only then that viewers knew with certainty that the Monster, innocently believing that the young girl could float, accidentally drowned her.

Frankenstein is a film that deserves to be seen in its original, uncut form. Fortunately, that is the case today. It is a film with only one flaw: a relatively short running time of approximately 70 minutes, a common trait (and problem) of films from the 1930s. When the film ends, we want to see more. Other than its length, *Frankenstein* is nearly the perfect horror film—a masterpiece. From its distinctive imagery to its creative storyline to the performances of Karloff and Clive, it is a monumental horror classic that delivers in every way.

Thanks in large part to *Frankenstein* and *Dracula*, and with an assist from *Dr. Jekyll and Mr. Hyde* (a Paramount release), the year 1931 became a landmark in horror history. As Skal puts it succinctly, "Nineteen thirty-one was the greatest year for monsters."[17]

After the dual moneymaking successes of *Dracula* and *Frankenstein*, Universal continued its journey into the world of horror with the February 21, 1932, release of *Murders in the Rue Morgue*, another key part of the "Shock Theater" package. While it has never achieved the iconic status of its two Universal predecessors, the film has won acclaim as a minor classic, one that utilizes the sinister talents of Bela Lugosi, who manages to steal scene after scene with his wonderfully creepy portrayal of a deranged doctor.

Ostensibly based upon the work of Edgar Allan Poe, *Murders in the Rue Morgue* brings the world of Lugosi's Dr. Mirakle to the screen. Living in 19th century Paris as the operator of a carnival, the mad Dr. Mirakle is determined to prove a connection between ape and man by abducting innocent women and injecting them with the blood of a gorilla. He ultimately hopes to find a girlfriend for his main sideshow attraction, an ape named Erik (played by an uncredited actor in a convincing gorilla suit). Unfortunately, Mirakle's experiments involving the mixing of blood kills each of the women, including a prostitute, whose body is found in a river and taken to the local police. When a young medical student, Pierre Dupin, learns that his girlfriend Camille has also been taken by Dr. Mirakle, he asks the police for help in saving her and bringing the murdering scientist to justice.

Lugosi carries the film, portraying Dr. Mirakle with the proper mix of fiendishness and oddity. With his mesmerizing eyes and theatrical movements, Lugosi commands each scene. Compared to many of his earlier film roles, Lugosi is almost unrecognizable, with thick, curly hair and overgrown eyebrows, but his performance is classic Lugosi. He might be second-billed in the credits, after the beautiful and innocent Sidney Fox (Camille), but he is clearly the star of this movie.

While *Murders in the Rue Morgue* would not have succeeded nearly as well without Lugosi, who was given the role as somewhat of a make-good deal for dropping out of the cast of *Frankenstein*,[18] director Robert Florey also deserves credit. Florey was originally supposed to direct *Frankenstein*, before being pulled at the last minute, so *Murders in the Rue Morgue* was essentially a gift for him, too. Florey ran with the project, overseeing the production of vivid sets with appropriate lighting and the layout of a nightmarish atmosphere that helped make the movie a favorite among horror fans. Clearly, Florey was a talented director, one who might have done justice to *Frankenstein*.

As effective as Lugosi and Florey proved in advancing *Murders in the Rue Morgue*, one wonders how much more powerful the film would have been if not for the censors. Originally scheduled to run 80 minutes, *Murders in the Rue Morgue* was cut down to just over an hour. Among the footage that was eliminated was part of a prostitute's death scene; she was originally shown being stabbed and then being tied to crossbeams.[19] The censors of the early 1930s would not allow such imagery, forcing Florey to make unwanted cuts.

Even with the elimination of some of the more graphic scenes, *Murders in the Rue Morgue* managed to touch a nerve with audiences. The film appeared to violate some of the unwritten rules of the early 1930s, such as the open portrayal of a prostitute and the suggestion of a relationship between an ape and a woman. Such taboo subjects might explain why *Murders in the Rue Morgue* did not achieve more box office success in 1932.

The film really has only one major flaw; the imposition of forced and generally unfunny comedy, which was meant to relieve tension for the audience, but which only serves to undermine the general terror of the film. Other than that, *Rue Morgue* is a fine film with good makeup and special effects, a worthy follow-up to Universal's first forays into the world of monsters.

As effective as *Murders in the Rue Morgue* was, it did not emerge as the most famous horror film of 1932. That honor belongs to another movie within the Universal Horror and "Shock Theater" galaxies: *The Mummy*, which made its first theatrical appearance on December 22.

The Mummy has never been as widely popular as *Dracula* or *Frankenstein*. Based on its own merits, *The Mummy* is a good film, not a great one, deserving a ranking as one of the studio's second-tier classics. The presence of Boris Karloff and the guidance of director Karl Freund, who was helming his first American film, make the movie work on many levels, even if it does fall short of some of the other 1930s monster movies.

Freund's effectiveness can be found in his ability to create a distinct atmosphere and deliver a moody rendering of the occult. His sets are also top-notch, from scenes taking place in Egyptian excavation sites to the museum and hotel imagery employed in the film.

In forging a dual portrayal of Imhotep and his reincarnated being, Karloff plays a mummified figure from ancient Egypt who is unwittingly revived by a foolish archeologist during a 1921 expedition. Ignoring a written curse inscribed on a small casket containing a scroll with supernatural powers, the archeologist opens the casket and unfurls the document, reviving Imhotep and causing himself to fall into madness.

Ten years after his return, Imhotep is shown as a modern-day man, a mysterious Egyptian scholar who goes by the name of Ardath Bey. He begins to stalk a beautiful woman (Zita Johann) whom he believes to be the reincarnation of his long-deceased lover. His goal is to use mind control to hypnotize the woman, kill her, blend her into his lover's mummified corpse, and then revive her completely in her new hybrid form. As he did so skillfully with the Frankenstein Monster, Karloff gives Bey a sliver of humanity and a strong sense of intelligence, along with a streak of sinister creepiness. The complexity of the character makes him more than a one-dimensional creature. It is yet another testament to Karloff's gravitas as an actor.

As the antagonist, Karloff squares off against another actor of considerable talent: Edward Van Sloan. Just as he did with his portrayal of Van Helsing in *Dracula*, Van Sloan poses a formidable challenge to the evils of Karloff's Bey-Imhotep, despite the latter's advantage in his possession of supernatural powers.

There was a tense relationship between Freund and leading lady Zita Johann. Freund initially told Johann that she would have to portray her character topless[20] (a threat he never enforced), filmed one scene with dangerous lions while offering no protection to the actress, and even refused to provide her with an off-screen chair featuring her name.[21] Johann withstood the shabby treatment and managed to endure throughout the difficult filming process.

While Freund's behavior was inexcusable, his talents as a director were considerable. In *The Mummy*, he uses lighting to enhance the atmosphere and pacing to create suspense. His direction of Karloff also helped bring out the best in an actor who was fast becoming a Hollywood legend.

Makeup man extraordinaire Jack P. Pierce also deserves a mention, even if his efforts were left somewhat unrewarded. Pierce spent eight hours a day applying the cotton-based makeup to Karloff's Mummy. He applied so many layers of makeup, so as to create Imhotep's wrinkled appearance, that Karloff could barely move his mouth in an effort to speak.[22] It is somewhat of a mystery as to why Karloff and Pierce went through such a process. As detailed as Pierce's makeup was, we are only given momentary glances of it: Early in the film, we see brief glimpses of the creature's head and hands, and the rotting nature of the bandages stemming from his feet, but that is the extent of our exposure to Karloff as the actual Mummy. At no point does Freund give us the chance to see Karloff's Mummy in a full-length shot, or while he is walking. Instead, we see Karloff almost exclusively as Ardath Bey, with a face full of creases (beautifully done by Pierce), but no bandages or wrappings covering his body.

Given the quality of Pierce's makeup and the skill of Karloff, it's a shame that the mummified figure of Imhotep is given so little screen time. Perhaps this is why the film pales in comparison to some of the other Universal classics. The absence of the iconic imagery that we see in the other Universal films hurts *The Mummy*. Others have suggested that *The Mummy* has been betrayed by its misleading title. One of the film's working titles was *King of the Dead*, which might have been a more powerful and accurate name for the movie that Freund directed.

In spite of these flaws, *The Mummy* is an entertaining film. Its story, acting, atmosphere and mood are all quite good. More importantly, Karloff is excellent as Ardath Bey, in what was his only venture into the world of mummified corpses. As such, *The Mummy* is still a must-see event for horror fans with an appreciation of the classics.

After the high impact of the first four "Shock Theater" films, a letdown arrives in the form of the fifth: *Secret of the Blue Room*. This July 20, 1933, release from Universal is far from a heavy-hitting classic, and involves only tangential elements of horror rather than fully encompassing the genre. But it does offer enough entertainment to be worthy of viewing and discussion.

The story centers on the titular blue room located within a dark castle. It is a room in which three murders took place 20 years earlier, and it is now locked; no one has entered since the deaths occurred. Now in the present day, three men have become suitors to a beautiful young woman, who has just turned 21, and they pledge to take turns spending the night in the deadly and haunted room so as to prove their courage to their prospective bride. Will they each survive the night, or will they be doomed to repeat the tragedy of two decades earlier?

While the cast lacks the presence of a horror legend, the film does feature a solid cast, headlined by the capable Lionel Atwill, who plays the young lady's father. Atwill's top billing is deceiving, however, as his role is relatively small. A young Gloria Stuart, whose career would enjoy a rebirth many decades later with the 1997 epic *Titanic*, is the more substantial player here. She portrays Irene von Helldorf, while Paul Lukas, Onslow Stevens and Edward Arnold lend capable support as two of her suitors and a homicide detective, respectively. They all handle the material well, especially given the whirlwind six-day shooting schedule imposed on director Kurt Neumann.

The opening of *Secret of the Blue Room* is reminiscent of the start of *Dracula*. That's because the film employs the same music that *Dracula* used in its opening, a decision that has drawn some criticism. Other than that, there is one small similarity between the two films: Lukas' heroic character speaks with a Hungarian accent that is similar to Lugosi's delivery as the famed vampire. *Secret of the Blue Room* also reuses some sets from earlier Universal ventures, including *The Old Dark House*, another film that featured Stuart in a prominent role.

The film is held back by two weaknesses. One is the lack of an obvious monster, which we come to expect in so many of Universal's films. The other is the inability to provide an explanation or resolution to some of the film's secondary mysteries. Given the latter shortcoming, the ending to *Secret of the Blue Room* will leave some viewers dissatisfied.

Universal likely billed *Secret of the Blue Room* as a horror film because it is set in a dark, foreboding castle. In truth, the film is much more of a whodunit or a thriller, one that is contained within a setting that only hints at the horror genre. It will never be confused with the legendary horror pictures of the 1930s, but it does provide enough atmosphere and sustain enough mystery to hold our attention for its 66-minute running time.[23]

A later 1933 release continued Universal's run as a producer of horror classics. This film would also supply a creative twist in the way that horror was presented. In contrast to the other Universal horror classics, *The Invisible Man* succeeds in striking fear by presenting what we *cannot* see. Premiering in Boston on November 3, 1933, the film has become iconic for the creative way in which it uses sound and the spoken word over visual imagery.

The Invisible Man begins with the arrival of the mysterious Dr. Jack Griffin, cloaked strangely in clothing from head to toe, at a local English establishment called the Lion's Head Inn. We soon learn that Dr. Griffin has come up with a formula for human invisibility by experimenting with a rare and dangerous drug, monocane. After throwing the innkeeper, Mr. Hall, down a flight of stairs in a fit of anger, and then revealing himself to be completely invisible to villagers and the local police, Griffin makes his way to the home of one of his colleagues, Dr. Kemp. He forces Kemp to become his accomplice, starting with a visit to the inn and the retrieval of his notebooks on his invisibility experiments. The police become involved, determined to arrest Griffin, who kills one of the officers. This murder, the first in a long series of killings by Griffin, intensifies the search for the man who is becoming increasingly mad because of the effects of monocane.

For most of the film, we only hear the voice of Claude Rains, who portrays the brilliant but violent Dr. Griffin. At times, we see him clothed, his head wrapped in bandages, sporting large sunglasses and white gloves, thereby creating an iconic image in early horror history. Griffin's face is hidden from us for the majority of the film, but the character frightens us through his powerful voice, his threatening manner of speaking, and the sense of the unexpected. After all, if we can't see him, how will we know when he will strike?

In fact, we don't see Rains' face until the very end of the film. Yet Rains is so skilled as an actor that he manages to create a persona without the benefit of facial expression or physical movement. Rains is brilliant in portraying the transformation of a doctor who begins his experiments with noble intentions, only to have his personality (and sanity) altered by moncane's effects. At times, Griffin plays only harmless pranks on his victims, but all too often his actions regress into outright murder.

The Griffin character ranks as one of the most brutal of the Universal villains. In a series of memorable scenes, he murders at least four people directly on screen and also derails a train full of more than a hundred innocent passengers, resulting in their deaths as well. By the end of the movie, Rains' Griffin is a veritable monster, still human in his physical qualities, but as vicious and unyielding as Dracula, Frankenstein's Monster and The Mummy—perhaps even more so.

It was a role that almost didn't come to Rains. Universal originally wanted Boris Karloff for the lead, but he turned it down because of a dispute that developed between him and director James Whale.[24] Rains turned out to be brilliant. The clarity of his voice makes the character what it is. He delivers his lines with such piercing force that they underscore the ruthlessness of his character. As great as Karloff was, it's hard to imagine him turning in a performance any better than the accomplished Rains.

Rains is ably assisted by Gloria Stuart, who remained busy in 1933 after her starring role in *Secret of the Blue Room*. Stuart plays Griffin's fiancée, the innocent Flora Cranley. Another significant player is Henry Travers, best known for his later portrayal of Clarence the Angel in *It's a Wonderful Life*. Travers plays Flora's father, Dr. Cranley, who is also Griffin's employer. Perhaps the only real flaw to the movie is its brevity. As with many of the horror films of the 1930s, the running time is a hindrance. The film lasts for only 71 minutes, leaving viewers wanting more.

Though not as beloved as *Frankenstein* and *Dracula*, *The Invisible Man* is an excellent film and an integral part of the Universal library. Carried by Rains, it deserves its place as one of the studio's most significant films among its early efforts in horror.

Universal continued its run of success in 1934 with the May 3rd premiere of *The Black Cat*. Not only an entertaining film, it is also an important piece of film history. For the first time ever, Boris Karloff and Bela Lugosi are paired on screen. Of the eight films they did together, some have called this their greatest collaboration, though that contention remains open to debate.

The Black Cat pits Lugosi directly against Karloff. Lugosi is the more sympathetic of the two characters, playing a Hungarian psychiatrist named Dr. Vitus Werdegast, who has been a prisoner of war for 15 years before returning to his hometown to learn the fate of his wife and daughter. While on the train, Lugosi's Werdegast meets young newlyweds, Peter and Joan (David Manners and Julie Bishop). The three later decide to share a bus, but it crashes, leaving Joan injured. Werdegast and Peter assist her in walking to the home of Hjalmar Poelzig (Karloff), the man who had abandoned Lugosi during the war and allowed him to be imprisoned. The visit will allow Werdegast to exact his revenge against Poelzig, but will also put the young couple in danger.

Lugosi acts strangely throughout, an indication of the after-effects he feels from his long tenure as a prisoner of war. His character represents one of Hollywood's first depictions of PTSD, a term that had not yet been invented at the time, but an effect of war that was no less real. While Lugosi's character is one with which we can sympathize, at least partially, Karloff's is pure evil, a cowardly man who betrayed his own soldiers and is now a Satan worshipper with no redeeming qualities.

At one point, we see Karloff conducting a black mass in the bowels of his strange art deco mansion; it's one of the film's most memorable sequences and one that somehow made it past the the Motion Picture Production Code (better known as the Hays Code). The Code, which was actually adopted in 1930 but not enforced until 1934, set strict guidelines as to film content that was considered taboo. One of the Code's guidelines included limits placed on "brutality and possible gruesomeness."[25]

According to rumors of the day, production of *The Black Cat* also had to deal with the issue of supposed tension between Karloff and Lugosi, who were highly competitive on the set. That contention may have some merit, but is probably exaggerated. It seems true that Lugosi resented Karloff because of the latter's success and higher billing, and worried that Karloff might steal the scenes when they both appeared on camera; that, along with Karloff's natural tendency for reclusion, prevented them from doing much off-camera socializing during the film.[26] Over time, however, Karloff and Lugosi would come to enjoy a better relationship. Although they never became close friends, certainly not in the way of a Peter Cushing and Christopher Lee, they got along fairly amicably for most of their subsequent films together.

The Black Cat is not only iconic for the presence of the two horror greats but it is particularly gruesome, especially for the 1930s. The movie depicts the practice of black magic and devil worship. It also includes a scene in which Karloff's character is skinned alive. Censors in at least three countries—Austria, Finland and Italy—banned the film.[27] In the United States, it received "outraged reviews" from a number of media outlets, including *The New York Times* and *Variety*.[28]

Prior to *The Black Cat*'s release, editors at Universal expressed their concerns about the film's extreme content. After the initial cut was viewed, director Edgar G. Ulmer was ordered to make some edits and reduce the level of violence. Unbeknownst to them, Ulmer did the exact opposite, intensifying the horror and adding a scene that underscored the evil tendencies of Karloff's character.[29]

Based on the promotion of the film, *The Black Cat* was supposed to be based on the Edgar Allan Poe masterpiece of the same name, but the film bears no resemblance to its source. In fact, the only mention of cats comes with Lugosi's character, who has an extreme phobia of feline creatures. After the film's release, Ulmer admitted that the supposed connection to the Poe short story was announced simply for promotional purposes.

The Black Cat became a commercial hit. Artistically, it ranks as a minor classic. If there is a criticism of the film, it is its length. The running time is only 65 minutes, limiting the development of the antagonism between the characters played by Karloff and Lugosi. For those who wanted more of the two film legends on screen simultaneously, that is simply not enough time. But those viewers only had to wait one year for their next collaboration.

Not every horror film can be a financial success. In 1935, Universal experienced its share of box office failures, beginning with a film that completely flopped in theaters: *Mystery of Edwin Drood*. The relatively little-known film debuted on February 4 and did so poorly that it has become underrated; it's a quiet gem that skillfully re-appropriated some of the same sets used in *Bride of Frankenstein*. It also gave us a look at such Universal Horror favorites as Claude Rains, David Manners and Valerie Hobson.

Boris Karloff was considered for the lead role,[30] but it went to Claude Rains. He plays John Jasper, a Church of England choirmaster in 1864. Addicted to opium, he becomes obsessed with one of his female students. Unfortunately for Jasper, she is already engaged to the title character, who happens to be Jasper's nephew. Manners, best known for his supporting appearances in *Dracula* and *The Mummy*, plays the innocent character of Drood, who is caught between his fiancé and the troubled Jasper. Drood then goes missing, with the suspicion falling on a rival student—and Jasper.

The film is based on a Charles Dickens novel that went unfinished at the time of his death. With no conclusion to the book, director Stuart Walker had full freedom to devise his own climax. Walker and his team of writers deliver nicely, putting forth a compelling finish that was filmed on the same crypt set used in *Bride of Frankenstein*.

Universal gave Walker plenty of financial support, allowing the director the use of lavish sets and extensive furnishings. At the time, the studio was already floundering, but executive Carl Laemmle, Jr., foolishly allowed the oversized budget.[31] The film would then fail badly at the box office, putting Universal into further economic chaos.

It's hard to fault Walker for the film's financial failing. His direction is very good, particularly the opening scene, which is actually an extended hallucination caused by Jasper's heavy use of opium. *Edwin Drood* has no actual monsters—no vampires or creatures made in a laboratory—but it does reproduce the feel and atmosphere of many of the Universal classics while giving us a solid mystery. Those qualities make it worthwhile viewing on a weekend night.

Another 1935 Walker film also disappointed during its theatrical run, but it did reattach Universal to the concept of monsters. There exists a common misconception that *The Wolf Man* represented Universal's first venture into the werewolf industry, but that's not the case. Universal's treatment of man-turned-wolf actually began with the May 13, 1935, release of *Werewolf of London*, which became the first mainstream film to deal with the subject of lycanthropy. Though not nearly as good as the Lon Chaney Jr. classic of 1941, *Werewolf of London* is a decent handling of the werewolf legend and a reasonable effort by director Walker.

The film stars Henry Hull, whom some regarded as a quasi–Boris Karloff lookalike, in the title role. When Hull is not a werewolf, he is Dr. Wilfred Glendon, who travels to Tibet in search of a rare flower. While on the botanical expedition, he is attacked by a man-like animal. Upon his return home, he begins to turn into a werewolf on a nightly basis, with each foray resulting in a murder. He is advised by another scientist, Dr. Yogami, to use an extract from that rare Tibetan flower as an antidote to his werewolf condition.

Makeup man Jack P. Pierce applied the wolf-like regalia to Hull—and wanted to plaster him in heavy facial hair and extreme levels of paint that would have made him look particularly beastly. Hull supposedly objected to the exaggerated application, insisting on more subtle makeup that made him more human and less monstrous; but that contention was refuted by Hull himself many years later.[32] In actuality, the producers made the demand because they were concerned that if Pierce went too far with his makeup, censors might not approve the film.[33] The end result: Hull looks more like a cousin to Eddie Munster (as played by Butch Patrick in the 1960s TV series *The Munsters*) than the later Wolf Man. But the makeup is still well-done, even if less frightening.

Hull is capable in the role, but he is also cold and aloof, lacking Chaney's ability to elicit sympathy and compassion from the viewer. His werewolf character also lacks the viciousness and rage of Chaney's Wolf Man. Perhaps the most powerful actor in the film is Warner Oland, who would become most famous for his work in the Charlie Chan films. Oland portrays the mysterious Dr. Yogami, who knows all about werewolves and also possesses his own set of secrets. Bela Lugosi was originally considered for the part, but turned down the offer because of his involvement in *Mark of the Vampire* at the same time.[34]

Though forgotten today as a director, perhaps because of his early death in 1941, the underrated Walker does well in overseeing the creation of sets that actually look like London. He also creates an intriguing love triangle within the horror motif and stages a climactic fight scene featuring the film's two headline characters.

On its own merits, *Werewolf of London* is perfectly acceptable as 1930s horror fare. It's only when mentioned in the same breath as the 1941 Universal classic that it inevitably suffers by comparison, leaving it well short of classic status.

Premiering on July 8, 1935, *The Raven* also struggled during its initial run, despite the presence of its two headline performers. It is not as good as *The Black Cat*, the first Bela Lugosi-Boris Karloff collaboration, but for fans of disturbing horror, it is well worth the investment of 61 minutes.

The Raven showcases both Karloff and Lugosi in the roles of villains, though Lugosi is the more detestable. He portrays Richard Vollin, a brilliant neurological surgeon with an enormous ego. After much persuasion, he is convinced to come out of retirement to save the life of a judge's daughter, Jean Thatcher, who has been seriously injured in a car accident. But Dr. Vollin has a dark side. He becomes infatuated with the daughter, even though she is much younger and engaged to be married to another doctor. When the judge begs Vollin to end his infatuation, he angrily refuses while reiterating his love for her.

Even more disturbing is Dr. Vollin's willingness to blackmail and torment, which is evident in his relationship with Karloff's character, Edmond Bateman. A career criminal, Bateman approaches Vollin to seek a new identity after his escape from prison, but also to improve his facial features, which have resulted in him being called ugly and grotesque since childhood. Bateman believes that he will be able to change his criminal ways—if only he has a new face. Initially, Dr. Vollin says that he will perform the surgery only if Bateman commits a murder for him. Vollin then relents, putting Bateman under the scalpel immediately. When Bateman wakes up from the operation, he finds himself in a room of mirrors, forced to gaze upon his hideous new look: The right side of his face has been completely disfigured.

The demented operation represents only the surface of the doctor's sins. Vollin tells Bateman that he will fix his facial features if he commits the murders that he originally desired. Vollin forces Bateman to become his servant for a weekend house party, so that he can torture and murder Jean's fiancé and her father.

Shot in only 15 days,[35] *The Raven* does not adhere to the Edgar Allan Poe poem of the same name, but it does pay homage to the author of the macabre. Lugosi's Vollin is obsessed with Poe, to the degree that he has collected a variety of torture devices modeled on weapons from the writer's books. Lugosi keeps the instruments of pain and death in his basement, which might accurately be called a dungeon, where they are eventually shown to Bateman.

Some film critics have called this Lugosi's wildest and most maniacal role. Director Lew Landers (who made the film under his real name of Louis Friedlander) gave Lugosi wide latitude in fleshing out the character, an opportunity that the actor could not pass up. As Lugosi's Vollin grows increasingly insane, Karloff gives his character a two-tiered performance. He is not the embodiment of evil, in the way that Vollin has become, but repeatedly shows reluctance to carry out the murders, leaving hope that he may provide help to Jean, her father and her fiancé.

Given the deranged qualities of the two lead characters, it's not surprising that *The Raven* reaches a particularly gruesome level. As pointed out by horror historian Gregory Mank, critics around the country railed at the film's "sadism, torture and ugliness."[36] Censors in New York, Ohio and Pennsylvania demanded the elimination of scenes they considered most offensive, with much of the consternation stemming from a scene in which a victim is held below a swinging pendulum.[37]

The film did not receive such treatment in the U.S., to the delight of American horror fans who wanted to soak up *The Raven*'s violence and torture. Those fans were not disappointed. Modern-day fans wishing to see Lugosi at his evil best and Karloff willing to take him on should also be fully satisfied.

In 1936, Lugosi would become involved in another release from Universal. *The Invisible Ray* is not part of Universal's series of *Invisible Man* films, but a stand-alone feature that showcases Lugosi and Boris Karloff for a third time. It's an underrated film that capably combines horror with science fiction in creating another entertaining blueprint for the two screen legends.

Karloff takes the lead in this 1936 gem, which premiered on January 20. He plays Dr. Janos Rukh, a loner scientist who has devised a telescope that can photograph light rays, thereby providing a look at events from the past. Rukh shows two skeptical scientists, including Felix Benet (Lugosi), an event from over a billion years ago: a meteorite crashing on Earth. Duly impressed, the two scientists convince Rukh to make an expedition to the crash site, located in Africa. There Rukh becomes exposed to Radium X. The radiation makes him deadly to others—simply by touch—and also affects his mind. Dr. Benet tries to help Rukh, but in coming up with an antidote, he only complicates the situation. To make matters even worse, Rukh's wife has become involved with another man, motivating the scientist to seek revenge.

A dynamic pairing, Lugosi and Karloff deliver their typically fine performances. Karloff's character elicits both our sympathy (for his unfortunate diagnosis) and contempt (for his ill-advised revenge), while Lugosi performs a rare role for him: a good man who tries to help his fellow doctor without a hidden agenda. For those critics who claimed that Lugosi could handle only villain and monster roles, *The Invisible Ray* clearly proves otherwise.

Additionally, the supporting cast behind Karloff and Lugosi is very good. Three excellent actresses—Frances Drake, Violet Kemble Cooper, and Beulah Bondi—enhance the film with their brief but distinctive performances.

Raising the level of the movie even further are the special effects, which were created by the masterful John P. Fulton on a paltry budget of $4500.[38] Fulton's effects were considered brilliant for the mid–30s. Ever the perfectionist, Fulton did his work so meticulously that it delayed the completion of the film.[39]

Considering all of its strengths, it's puzzling why *The Invisible Ray* remains such an underrated film. Perhaps it's because there is no actual monster—simply a damaged scientist—or maybe it's because of the lack of supernatural overtones. Yet all of the elements of good horror are here, from an entertaining storyline to laudable special effects and some creative science, all capped off by the inevitable conflict between two film giants. *The Invisible Ray* is a quiet classic of the 1930s.

By the time 1936 arrived, a full five years had elapsed since Universal's groundbreaking release of *Dracula*. The lack of a sequel surprised some within the film industry, but Universal finally delivered an indirect follow-up in 1936 with the intriguingly named *Dracula's Daughter*. Debuting on May 11, the sequel turned out far differently than originally intended. *Frankenstein* director James Whale was scheduled to head up *Dracula's Daughter*, but he submitted such an outrageous and risqué script that the producers turned in a different direction.[40] At various times, Bela Lugosi, Boris Karloff, Colin Clive and Jane Wyatt were each linked to the project, but none ended up in the film.[41]

Lugosi, star of the original *Dracula*, would have made perfect sense for *Dracula's Daughter*. Lugosi had asked for more money after the success of the original movie. While Lugosi and the producers couldn't come to an agreement on salary, the film's promoters did use his image on *Dracula's Daughter* posters. Lugosi allowed his photo likeness to be used in exchange for a $4,000 payday.[42]

The 1936 film is intriguing, but most critics agree that it would have been far better with Lugosi. As such, it is a pale effort compared to many of the Universal classics. There are also a few too many strained attempts at silly comedy, which detract from the atmosphere of the film.

If not viewed in the context of other superior Universal efforts, *Dracula's Daughter* can be described as decent fare. When the film is serious, it is quite good. British actress Gloria Holden does commendably in trying to carry the picture as the title character, whose actual name is Contessa Marya Zaleska. Though her delivery of dialogue is somewhat stiff, she has an exotic appearance, which is supplemented by the hypnotizing gaze of her searing eyes (which never seem to blink and are reminiscent of Lugosi). She also creates a sympathetic portrayal of the female vampire, one who is trying to separate herself from her evil heritage.

Curiously, none of the actors in the sequel appeared in the original *Dracula* with the exception of Edward Van Sloan. He reprises his role as Prof. Von Helsing, who immediately faces charges for the murder of Dracula, at least until the countess steals the body and eliminates the necessary evidence. Soon after her arrival in London, citizens turn up dead. Unlike her father, the countess is not satisfied with a murderous life as a vampire; by chance she meets a psychiatrist, Jeffrey Garth, who may hold the key to ridding her of the evil duality. American actor and onetime matinee idol Otto Kruger is capable in portraying Dr. Garth, and brings a sense of logic and calm reason to the wild supernatural surroundings. The movie draws some of its plot from the Bram Stoker short story "Dracula's Guest,"[43] which was supposed to be published as part of his original classic novel, but was removed in order to shorten the book. The short story was finally published in 1914, shortly after the death of the author.

The film also suffers from the strict guidelines that governed movies in the 1930s. "The censors played havoc with *Dracula's Daughter*," says Skal.[44] As a result of the Hays Code, which was strictly enforced at the time, some of the sexual tension contained in the original print was removed, ultimately harming the film. Even with such censoring, there are still lesbian overtones to the film. They are simply not as overt, but clearly hold their place. *Dracula's Daughter* is satisfactory in some ways, and is certainly worth seeing, but it is far from being one of the top-tier Universal classics.

As fate would have it, *Dracula's Daughter* turned out to be the final Universal horror film assembled under the leadership of Carl Laemmle, Jr. Four days after production ended, Universal's creditors took control of the company and forced the entire Laemmle family to the sidelines.

The "Shock Theater" package contained no horror films from 1937 or '38, instead drawing from the combined genres of thriller, crime drama and mystery. Chronologically, the next horror film emanated from 1939, a significant year in Hollywood history, but less so on the horror front. One of the better films of 1939 came out on January 13; it represented an extension of a familiar franchise that had begun with *Frankenstein* and *Bride of Frankenstein*.

If for no other reason, the simultaneous presence of Boris Karloff, Bela Lugosi and Basil Rathbone makes *Son of Frankenstein* a must-see on the list of horror classics. Yet there is far more to this film than these three giants of horror. It is not just a worthy sequel to *Frankenstein* and *Bride of Frankenstein*, but an underrated film that is heavy on atmosphere, passion and old-fashioned 1930s horror.

The story introduces us to Baron Wolf von Frankenstein, son of the deceased Henry Frankenstein, who created the Monster. Wolf returns to the Frankenstein home after living in America, only to find that the local villagers resent him because of the sins of his father, who had unleashed such terror upon them. Ygor, a blacksmith and grave robber, lives in exile in the old Frankenstein laboratory. He shows Wolf that the long-lost Monster is still alive, but in a coma. After reviving the creature, the baron comes into conflict with Ygor, who maintains his own bizarre and obsessive hold over the Monster, and with Police Inspector Krogh.

Rathbone plays Wolf, assuming the lead role ahead of Boris Karloff, who returns as the Monster, and Bela Lugosi, who takes on the role of Ygor. Rathbone was not the first choice for the role; Peter Lorre had agreed to play the baron, but he fell ill and had to bow out.[45] Rathbone did not like horror films, even though he appeared in many during his prolific career. His dislike of the genre certainly does not show in the film. He attacks this role in an over-the-top fashion, seizing the viewer and making himself mostly a sympathetic figure, at least at first, in his grapple with Lugosi's Ygor. As the film progresses, Wolf becomes less rational and more frenzied, increasingly susceptible to fits of anger as his nerves continue to fray. He also becomes fearful that Inspector Krogh (Lionel Atwill) will discover that he has revived the Monster. At times, Rathbone becomes carried away in his performance, but he certainly commands attention, a difficult achievement in a film featuring Lugosi and Karloff.

Lugosi, given third billing, supplies a brilliant portrayal of the deformed Ygor, a convicted body snatcher who somehow survived his own hanging, but at the price of a broken neck. Lugosi's Ygor protectively keeps watch over the Monster, whom he treats like both an adopted son and a cherished pet. But he also uses the Monster for his own gain, instructing him to murder the jury members who had found him guilty and sent him to the gallows. Lugosi does his best to make Ygor seem superficially ignorant and unaware to the other characters, but he is far more intelligent than he lets on, and highly devious, allowing him to give the role a truly fiendish flair. In executing the supporting role, Lugosi steals practically every scene in which he appears. Critics have called this one of Lugosi's best performances, and it is quite possibly his greatest, even more impressive than Dracula.

Caught in the power struggle of Ygor and the baron is the Monster. Strangely, the Monster is again mute, despite having gained the ability to speak in *Bride of Frankenstein*. Karloff is still effective in the role, but his character is clearly different. Not only is he silent, but he seems less human, with little of the soul that he showed in the first two films. The Monster shows little compassion for others, with the exception of one or two moments. He is also more obedient, taking instructions from the evil Ygor, the only human for which he truly seems to care.

Physically, Karloff's Monster also assumes a different look. In *Son of Frankenstein*, he sports a vest of fur, something not seen in the first two *Frankenstein* films. The vest, apparently given to him by Ygor, gives the Monster something of a pathetic quality, making him seem even more primitive than usual.

Son of Frankenstein represented Karloff's final feature film appearance as the Monster. The actor believed that the character was becoming the brunt of jokes and parody, and he felt it better to back off from a role that had become so repetitive. It seems that viewers didn't necessarily agree with that assessment. *Son of Frankenstein* emerged as a box office sensation, a major boon for Universal, which had been struggling financially.

In retrospect, it's surprising that *Son of Frankenstein* turned out so well. The script was written at the last minute, giving the actors little time to prepare before facing the camera. But their performances remained stellar, as did the makeup of the brilliant Jack Pierce. The film also featured more depth than many of the other Universal classics, in part because of the 99-minute running time, the longest for any of the studio's horror ventures. In properly showcasing the talents of three of horror's legendary figures, *Son of Frankenstein* attained excellence.

The theme of horror sequels continued in 1940. On January 12, Universal released *The Invisible Man Returns*, an able successor to the 1933 film. Even without Claude Rains, the sequel sustains quality while introducing us to a new acting legend of the genre.

The movie tells the story of Geoffrey Radcliffe, who has been framed for the murder of his brother. Facing the death sentence in the form of a public hanging, the desperate Radcliffe receives a visit from Dr. Frank Griffin, brother of the original Invisible Man. Frank supplies Geoffrey with the formula of invisibility, allowing him to escape from prison. Capably filling the role of Geoffrey, Vincent Price makes his horror film debut at the age of 30. Eight years later, he would memorably supply the voice of the Invisible Man at the conclusion of *Abbott and Costello Meet Frankenstein*.

Price is far more sympathetic than the original Invisible Man, portrayed so skillfully by Rains seven years earlier. (Technically, Rains does make an appearance in the sequel, but only in the form of a photograph.) With help from his sympathetic fiancée (Nan Grey), Price's character fights back against the dangerous effects of the invisibility formula (now known as duocane, a name made up for the film) and tries to retain his sanity while attempting to find the true murderer. He does show a few moments of madness, such as when he kidnaps his brother's actual killer, played devilishly by Cedric Hardwicke, and angrily attempts to coerce a confession out of him. Noted actor Alan Napier also makes a memorable appearance as a villainous and drunken superintendent of the Radcliffe family's mining operation. Many years later, Napier achieved fame portraying Alfred Pennyworth, the butler on the 1960s TV series *Batman*.

There is a scene in which only the outline of Price's figure can be seen against the

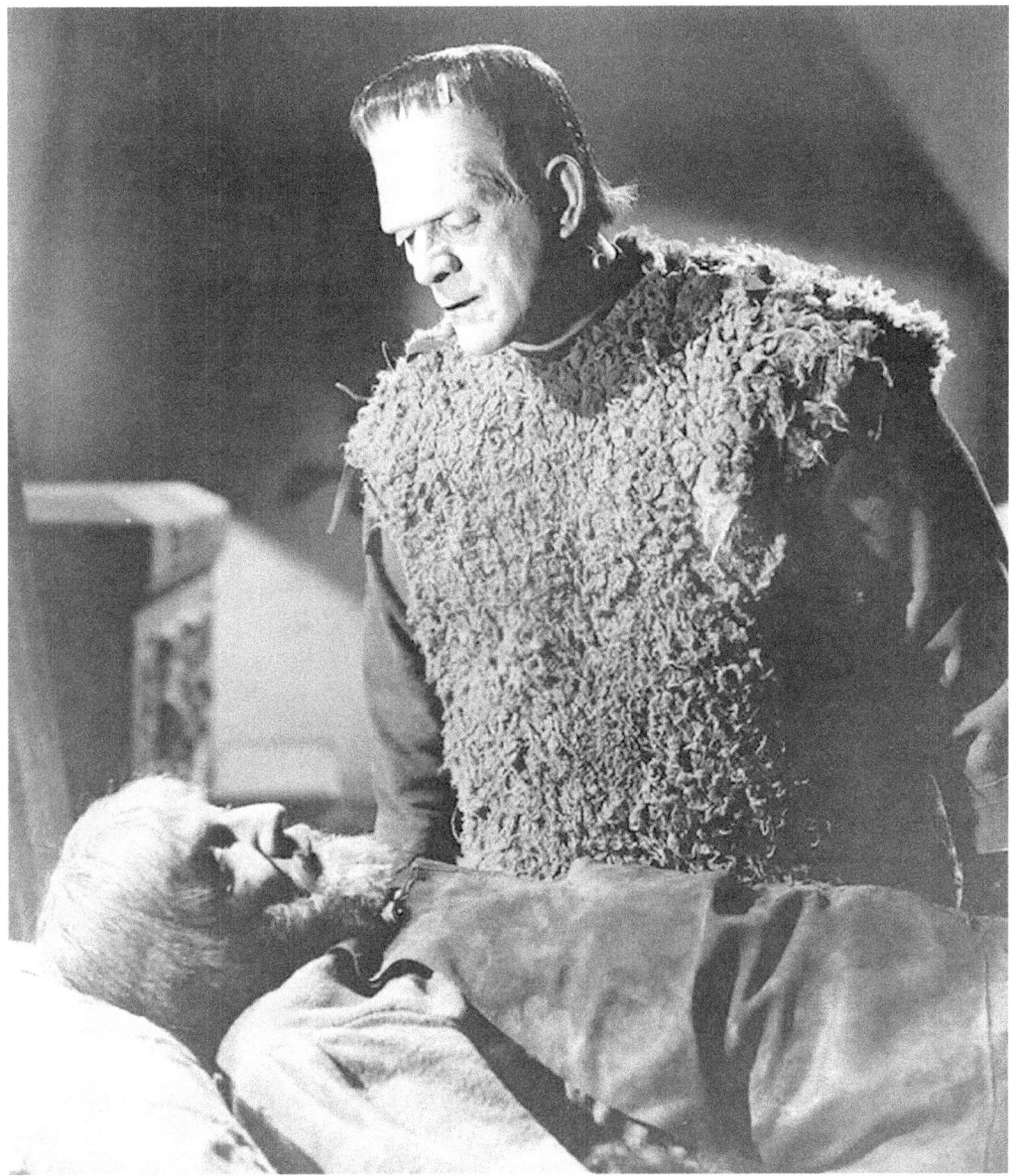

Son of Frankenstein (1939): Frankenstein's Monster (Boris Karloff) looks with concern at the seemingly lifeless body of his only friend, Ygor (Bela Lugosi). For the third of Universal's *Frankenstein* films, famed makeup artist Jack P. Pierce fitted Karloff's Monster with a strange fur vest that he wore. The reason for the vest is never explained (courtesy of Frank Dello Stritto).

backdrop of falling rain, a testament to the special effects team headed up by John P. Fulton. Otherwise, Price is completely wrapped in clothes and bandages, or unseen. At the end of the film, the transformation from invisibility to visibility is skillfully done through a series of dissolves.

Price's voice, much like Rains, is strong and distinctive, which helps him fulfill the role quite skillfully, despite his previous lack of experience in horror. Price's ability to speak another language also aided the production. The director, a German film pioneer named Joe May (*née*

Joseph Mandel), spoke very little English. May co-wrote the story and was given a chance to direct the film, despite his obvious lack of familiarity with the language. Price spoke some German, allowing him to better communicate with May and sometimes informally act as a translator. At times, Price exhorted May to speak to him in German, because his English was so jumbled that he was unintelligible.[46] But the other actors struggled mightily in taking direction from May, particularly Hardwicke, who developed a strong dislike for the director.[47]

Like most sequels, *The Invisible Man Returns* is not as good as the original, but it is certainly entertaining fare. Thanks to the horror debut of Price, and solid contributions from Hardwicke, Napier and Cecil Kellaway as a suspicious Scotland Yard detective, the film takes solid footing among Universal's second tier of classic horror films.

On September 20, 1940, Universal dipped its toes into the sequel waters once again, this time presenting a not-so-typical follow-up. Rather than pick up the story directly from where *The Mummy* left off, *The Mummy's Hand* represents a reimagining of the story about a mummified creature that has somehow come back to life. In this film, a living mummy and a mystic guard a 3000-year-old tomb while doing battle with archaeologists determined to find the remains of an Egyptian princess.

An Egyptian (George Zucco) is given orders by a high priest to guard the mummy of Kharis. The Mummy is currently in a passive state, but can be revived through the burning of tana leaves. Archeologist Dick Foran and his sidekick Wallace Ford, spurred on by the financing of a stage magician, embark on an expedition to find the sarcophagus of the princess Ananka. The expedition members will encounter a problem, since Kharis remains in love with Ananka.

Tom Tyler, a former amateur weightlifter better known for his roles in cowboy movies, assumed the mummified role of Kharis. In choosing a replacement for Boris Karloff (who had played Imhotep in the original film), the moviemakers selected Tyler because of his height and physical similarities to screen legend Karloff, making it easier to match newly filmed scenes of Tyler to stock footage from the 1932 film. That was deemed necessary because of the frequent use of flashback scenes. While Tyler was no Karloff, he does bring a solid physical presence to the role, in spite of the many physical problems, including rheumatoid arthritis, which caused his early death in 1954.

Makeup creator Jack Pierce applied his complicated, layered, cotton-based makeup to the Mummy—at least for the close-up scenes. But in order to save time and money, Pierce also created a mummy mask that Tyler used for scenes in which he was filmed from a distance.[48]

Given the absence of Karloff, *The Mummy's Hand* lacks the star power of the original film. The sequel also fails to match the dark, shadowy atmosphere of *The Mummy*. In fact, it has a more comical feel, thanks in part to the two unemployed, bumbling archaeologists who open the film by discovering evidence of the burial place of Princess Ananka. Cecil Kellaway, portraying the eccentric magician known as The Great Solvani, also brings a humorous touch to his role.

One of the film's strengths is the elaborate tomb set that was originally created for another film, *Green Hell*.[49] The large, lavish interior, adorned with Incan iconography, provides a terrific setting for some of the film's most important scenes.

The Mummy's Hand is nowhere near as powerful as the original film, but it is probably the second-best of the three Mummy follow-ups that Universal produced in the 1940s. While it fails to frighten, it does provide some enjoyment at a lower level. It's certainly not a classic, but the quality sets and an acceptable performance from Tyler make it adequately entertaining fare.

Even with its growing reliance on sequels, Universal still found some time for completely original material in the early 1940s. In particular, 1941 stood out as a year for releases that did not stem from earlier projects.

On March 28, Universal simultaneously released *Horror Island* and *Man Made Monster*. With its lack of big-name stars, *Horror Island* is clearly a B-movie, the product of a very small budget. Despite the financial impediment, this 1941 film works as basic entertainment because of its second-half fast pacing and its rather surprising ending.

Desperate for money, hard-luck businessman Bill Martin, owner of Morgan's Island, decides to turn the remote location into a treasure hunt tourist expedition. As part of the scheme, Martin falsely promotes Morgan's Island as haunted. On his first visit to the island, Martin and his passengers stumble upon a series of strange accidents, along with the possibility that a phantom might exist. They will also encounter a killer, whose identity remains a mystery to Martin.

Parts of *Horror Island* were filmed on previously used Universal sets, including the Carfax Abbey stone staircase from *Dracula* and several sets from the 1939 film *Tower of London*.[50] If one is willing to forgive their recycled nature, the old sets do create a proper atmosphere for the film.

Remarkably, the film was shot and produced so quickly that it debuted in theaters only 25 days after production began,[51] a particularly notable achievement given the horrendous weather that plagued the filming. In order to meet the imposed deadline, director George Waggner ordered the crew to work until midnight on several occasions. One of the film's stars, Dick Foran, came down with a severe cold due to the long nights and wet weather, forcing him to miss a day of work and resulting in the cutting of his final scene.[52] The extended work schedule represented a clear violation of union rules, which were supposed to limit actors to only eight hours per day.

Somehow, the cast and crew of *Horror Island* completed the picture within two weeks. The end result is an uneven film, one that is overly silly in some places (with the comedy working only occasionally) and at times a serious mystery. The pacing is too slow at the beginning and then lightning-quick toward the end. Clearly, the film has many flaws, but the acting is surprisingly effective and the story is good enough to hold our attention. *Horror Island* entertains the audience with a befuddling mystery before giving us a surprise ending that leaves us with a satisfied feeling.

Man Made Monster also comes from the category of B-movies. When compared to Universal's classics, *Man Made Monster* pales badly in finding a meaningful niche in the genres of horror and sci-fi. But on the scale of B-list films, it stacks up very well against the competition of its era. Some observers have called it one of the studio's best efforts in the realm of B-movies, perhaps only a notch below *The Raven*.

Man Made Monster stars Lon Chaney, Jr., who was relatively little known at the time but would begin to develop a niche for himself at Universal because of his memorable performance as the title character. He plays Dan McCormick, a sideshow performer who is the miraculous sole survivor of a bus crash into an electrical tower. A well-intentioned scientist wants to study Dan to learn more about his electrical immunity, but his colleague, Dr. Rigas, has far more nefarious intentions. Played in an over-the-top fashion by Lionel Atwill, Rigas makes Dan the subject of experimentation that is designed to create an army of electrical creatures. The evil doctor gives him increasing doses of electricity that make him deadly to the touch, while also altering his mental state.

The movie was based on a story called "The Electric Man." Universal had purchased the rights to the story years earlier, with the intention of featuring both Bela Lugosi and Boris Karloff. In 1940, looking for a new leading man to head up its horror genre offerings, Universal turned to Chaney.[53]

Man Made Monster turned out to be one of Universal's least expensive productions. It was filmed at a cost of $86,000,[54] a remarkably low price for the era. That might explain why the running time of *Man Made Monster* is only 59 minutes. With some additional creative editing, the short film could have fit into a one-hour television time slot.

Its biggest weakness is the relative lack of action and violence over the first three-quarters of the movie's duration. The last act is terrific, full of twists and unexpected developments, as Chaney's character, who is both sympathetic and frightening, becomes the subject of a police investigation. One of the film's strengths is the makeup applications made to Chaney, whose physical condition deteriorates from start to finish. The special effects are also top-notch, thanks to the work of John P. Fulton, who creates a glowing perimeter around Chaney's body.

Chaney and Atwill carry the film, making it something of a cult classic. It was also the first recognizable film in Chaney's horror career, indicating the future success that he would have as the Wolf Man, the Mummy and others. Bolstered by Chaney and Atwill, the movie provides basic fun for horror and sci-fi enthusiasts.

While *Man Made Monster* and *Horror Island* made their marks in smaller ways, Universal managed to forge one of its truly classic films later in 1941. It would elevate Lon Chaney to superstar status, putting him just a rung below Karloff and Lugosi. On December 9, just in time for the Christmas season, Chaney's *The Wolf Man* premiered in Los Angeles theaters.

The release of *Dracula* in 1931 had kickstarted the Universal Horror franchise. Ten years later, the *Wolf Man* debut launched the second phase of Universal's glorious reign of horror classics. *The Wolf Man* is in many ways a superior film to *Dracula*, especially in terms of dialogue, special effects and continuity, even if *Dracula* remains more famous and groundbreaking. The story of werewolves is well told by screenwriter Curt Siodmak and director George Waggner. They lay out the tragic tale of Larry Talbot (Chaney), who comes back to his ancestral home in Wales after 18 years in America.

Returning because of the sudden death of his older brother, Larry reunites with his titled father (Claude Rains), who wants him to take over the reins of the family estate. Larry soon meets young Gwen (Evelyn Ankers), who draws his romantic interest but also happens to be engaged. That night, he accompanies her and a friend to a local fair so that they can have their fortunes told by gypsies. Gypsy fortune teller Bela (Bela Lugosi) turns into a werewolf and attacks Gwen's friend. Larry comes to her assistance and kills the creature, but not without paying a large price for his heroism.

Siodmak's scenery, particularly the atmospheric, fog-ridden Welsh forest, has become iconic. The special effects and the makeup are also excellent. Jack Pierce, given more freedom in applying makeup to Chaney than he had been in *Werewolf of London*, took full advantage, creating the Wolf Man out of a mix of yak hair, dark greasepaint and a rubber snout. (The process took three to four hours for the application and another three hours for removal.[55]). For the transformation scene, Pierce applied the makeup in stages; after each stage, additional film of Chaney would be shot. By using time lapse dissolves, the filmmakers created the masterful effect of Larry transforming gradually into the werewolf.

Of all the processes applied by Pierce, Chaney felt that the removal of the makeup at the end of the day was the most exhausting. "What gets me is after work when I'm all hot and itchy and tired," said Chaney, "and … I've got to sit in the chair for 45 minutes while

Pierce just about kills me, ripping off the stuff he put on me in the morning."[56]

Chaney does a lot more than merely display Pierce's heavy makeup. As the Wolf Man, he is ferocious and unyielding. As Larry, he is at first charming and amiable, but after his encounter with Bela, he turns forlorn, a man doomed to become a monster. In retrospect, it's fascinating to consider that the studio originally wanted Boris Karloff to take the role before accepting Chaney. As horror historian David J. Skal points out, "Siodmak thought the casting of Chaney was ridiculous."[57] It turned out that Siodmak, who had little regard for Chaney as an actor, was wrong. Of all the film roles that Chaney assumed, the roles of Talbot and the Wolf Man became his own; he handled the dual roles in five Universal films, and no other actors would portray the characters during Universal's long run of horror films in the 1930s and '40s.

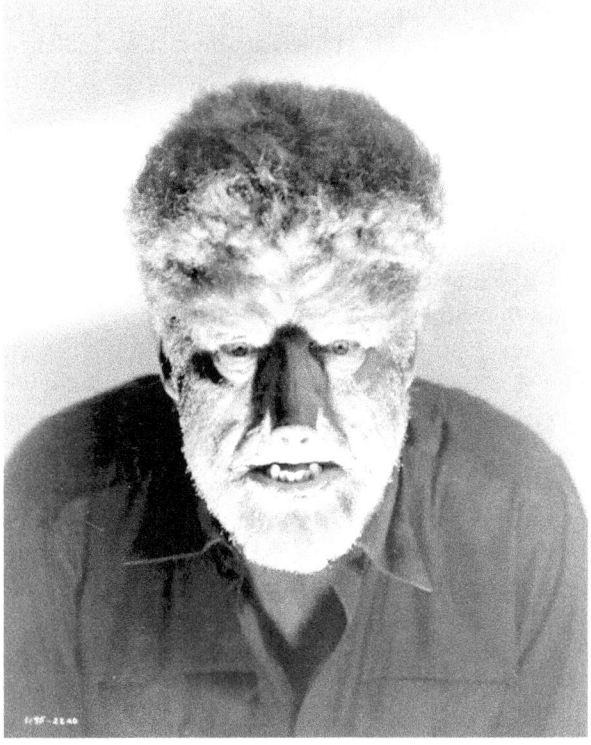

The Wolf Man (1941): A close-up publicity still gives us a detailed view of the makeup donned for Lon Chaney for his signature role. Makeup artist Jack Pierce used a strange combination of ingredients, including yak hair, in creating the iconic look. Chaney reprised the werewolf role four times, culminating in 1948's *Abbott and Costello Meet Frankenstein*.

Chaney also achieves on-screen chemistry with co-star Ankers. This was no small trick, given that the two actors disliked each other intensely. Chaney called her "Shankers," a mocking play on her last name, and delighted in scaring her by sneaking up on her in his full Wolf Man regalia.[58] The actress did not appreciate such hijinks. But there is no evidence of that antagonism in the film; the two actors succeed in portraying a budding love affair that is doomed by his monstrous transformations.

The other *Wolf Man* actors support Chaney and Ankers beautifully. In fact, the film's cast was one of the strongest ever put forth by Universal. Rains is very good as Talbot's proper and highly respected British father; Lugosi (who had actually campaigned for the lead role) does well in the small role of the gypsy; Ralph Bellamy is solid as Col. Montford, and the legendary Maria Ouspenskaya steals a number of scenes as Maleva, a wise fortune-telling gypsy (and mother to Bela). There is nothing B-list about this group. The acting, the atmosphere, and the mood come together beautifully in *The Wolf Man*. "It's a very nice and moody film," says Skal. "It clicked."[59]

In addition to being a strong film on its own merits, *The Wolf Man* also changed popular culture. A number of popular werewolf myths (which remain to this day) gained acceptance via the movie, including the belief that the moon would initiate the transformation and the stipulation that one could become a werewolf if bitten by a werewolf. The film also promoted the notion that werewolves and their victims had pentagrams appear on their bodies, along with the idea that only a silver bullet could destroy one of the beasts.[60]

The Wolf Man succeeds on every level: culturally, cinematically and as pure entertainment. It remains an absolute classic from the Universal library.

Of all the films released as part of the initial "Shock Theater" package, *Mystery of Marie Roget* is one of the least known. Debuting on April 23, 1942, it lacks monsters and Hollywood superstars, but it has enough horror and a sufficiently entertaining mystery to make it necessary viewing in the hosted horror era.

The premise is quite simple: A young actress dies under a set of strange circumstances, and a detective digs deeper into her demise. The story is based loosely on the Edgar Allan Poe story of the same name, published in 1842 as a follow-up to his famed "Murders in the Rue Morgue." Screenwriter Michel Jacoby did away with many of the characteristics of Poe's original work (and also moved up the time period of the story by some 50 years), but did keep the setting in France.[61]

Patric Knowles, an accomplished British actor, takes the lead as amateur detective Paul Dupin, who assumes the challenge of solving the mystery despite his lack of professional credentials. He is very good as this Sherlock Holmes clone. Also effective is *Wolf Man* veteran Maria Ouspenskaya, who plays the grandmother of the victim.

There is a tendency to categorize *Mystery of Marie Roget* outside of the horror genre, but its status as a work of Poe carries several Gothic elements, including the presence of a predatory animal, a frightful murder weapon and a dramatic horse-and-carriage chase.

Thanks to these features, along with solid acting from all of the main players, *Mystery of Marie Roget* emerges as an above-average feature from the 1940s. In retrospect, director Philip Rosen could have been more faithful to Poe's work and placed more of an effort in emphasizing the horror that Poe created, but he does adequate work in making the film a compelling and worthwhile mystery.

An October 1942 release from Universal falls more comfortably into the genre of straight horror. But it is a deceiving film in another sense. For fans of Bela Lugosi, *Night Monster* might turn out disappointing; Lugosi is top-billed (for the final time in his Universal career),[62] but he is really no more than a supporting actor making intermittent appearances. Despite this bit of false advertising, *Night Monster* is a solid horror film, one that mixes in some mystery with an inherent creepiness and a good use of black-and-white film techniques.

Veteran actor Ralph Morgan places fifth on the billing list, but he plays a starring role as Kurt Ingston, a paralyzed recluse who lives in a large, dark mansion near a slough. He summons the three doctors who failed to cure his paralysis. A psychiatrist, Dr. Lynn Harper, also makes her way to the mansion. Accompanied by a mystery writer who helped her when her car broke down in the swamp, she has been summoned by Ingston's mentally disturbed sister Margaret. Margaret hopes that Dr. Harper will declare her sane and allow her to escape the control of her brother.

Suspicion soon arises that Ingston may have laid out a trap for the doctors, holding them responsible for his invalid condition. After an Egyptian skeleton materializes out of thin air and is seen by the guests, the doctors are done in one by one, leading to the inevitable question about the killer's true identity. The killer menaces Dr. Harper before the mystery writer comes to her aid.

Morgan does well in the role of the wheelchair-bound Ingston, a strange man who is nonetheless respected within the community. Other good performances are turned in by the accomplished Lionel Atwill as one of the doctors, Leif Erickson as the beefy and crude chauffeur, and Robert Homans as a humorless police captain with a level of irritation that becomes endearing.

Lugosi is relegated to the role of Rolf, the Ingston family's autocratic butler, who has enough sinister qualities to make him a suspect in the murders taking place in and around the mansion. Typically, Lugosi performs well in his role as a servant, which he plays in a far more understated way than his monster roles. Critics have questioned why he was not given a larger role as either Ingston himself or as one of the attending doctors, especially in a film that promoted him as the star. Sad to say, the reduced role seems to have been a form of continuing mistreatment from studio executives, who had come to overlook the talents of Lugosi.

Those willing to accept the undercard role for Lugosi will appreciate the film for its spooky atmosphere, its ability to cast mystery over the main characters, and its wonderful use of shadows. Both the fog-ridden swamps and the immense mansion provide excellent backdrops for the key parts of the film, creating an appropriate atmosphere of spookiness and tension for a plot filled with mystery and murder.

One of *Night Monster*'s biggest fans was none other than Alfred Hitchcock. Attending a screening so that he could observe supporting actress Janet Shaw, whom he was considering for one of his own films, Hitchcock came away highly impressed with the work of fellow director Ford Beebe. Hitchcock particularly marveled at Beebe's ability to complete the production within only two weeks' time.[63]

Like many of Universal's 1940s efforts, *Night Monster* was a B-film shot on a limited budget. While the lack of money (resulting in relatively hokey special effects) and the diminished role of Lugosi detract from the film, it is good for what it is: a movie that skillfully combines the genres of horror, mystery and thriller while giving us a series of surprising twists. It's no surprise that the film became a staple of the hosted horror era, making it a favorite among the films released as part of the original "Shock Theater" package.

In terms of sheer volume, 1943 was a prominent year for horror films, and in turn, for the "Shock Theater" package. No fewer than four horror movies from that year were included in "Shock," including two sequels and two new ventures.

One of the sequels involved *two* monsters, giving the creatures the chance to battle head to head. Though not a great film technically, *Frankenstein Meets the Wolf Man* is a fun venture and provides several worthwhile moments for vintage horror fans. It also marks a milestone for one of the most recognizable actors of the genre.

Released on March 5, 1943, the film begins with the return of the Wolf Man, played by Lon Chaney. The opening features an excellent and highly atmospheric graveyard scene, where the Wolf Man is accidently unleashed by two bumbling grave robbers. When they remove the wolfbane from the coffin, Talbot's body is revived. He soon turns into a werewolf and kills one of the grave robbers before eventually returning to his human state. Brought to a hospital, he tells his doctor and the police who he is but they don't believe him, given that Talbot died four years earlier.

Once again turning into the Wolf Man, he escapes from the hospital and eventually finds the gypsy Maleva, hoping that she can help him find a way to die, as opposed to living eternally as a werewolf. She brings him to the home of Dr. Frankenstein, only to discover that the doctor has already passed away. Talbot eventually stumbles upon Frankenstein's Monster, encased in a block of ice. Hoping that the Monster can lead him to Dr. Frankenstein's papers, Talbot chips away at the ice until the Monster is freed.

The film marks Bela Lugosi's only film appearance as the Frankenstein Monster. It was a role that Lugosi turned down for the original *Frankenstein* film in 1931. The choice of Lugosi as the Monster in *Frankenstein Meets the Wolf Man* made sense in at least one tangible way; in an earlier film, *The Ghost of Frankenstein*, Lugosi's Ygor had his brain transplanted into the creature as a central part of the plot.

Originally, Lugosi's role in the 1943 release was much larger and had him delivering dialogue, but that plan was scuttled. Director Roy William Neill decided to cut out Lugosi's speaking parts, erasing all of his voice tracks from the final print, even though there are clearly scenes that show Lugosi moving his lips but with no words coming out. The reason for the cuts remains a mystery; there doesn't seem to be a consensus among participants or observers. Some have speculated that Lugosi did a poor job handling his lines, causing the producers to panic and order the elimination of his voice work, while others contend that Lugosi's doomsday "conquer the world" dialogue was deemed inappropriate during a time of Adolf Hitler's rise.[64] Screenwriter Curt Siodmak claimed Lugosi's dialogue came across as comical, mostly because of his heavy Hungarian accent, and prompted laughter from test audiences.[65] Whatever the actual reason, Lugosi is reduced to roughly five minutes of screen time—and no spoken lines.

Lugosi was a questionable choice to begin with; he was already 60 and incapable of handling most of the physical demands of the Monster. That's why several additional minutes of the Monster's time are handled by skilled stunt men Gil Perkins and Eddie Parker, who split time as the doubles for Lugosi. Both Perkins and Parker play the Monster during the climactic fight scene with the Wolf Man.

In another curiosity, Lugosi played the part as if the Monster were blind; that's why he walks with his arms extended throughout the film, establishing a stereotype of behavior for future portrayals of Frankenstein. (That stereotype also became fodder for parodies of the Monster, in which actors would exaggerate its lumbering gait and awkward arm extensions.) In actuality, Lugosi was simply following the orders of the script, but the words of Siodmak's screenplay, which had explained the creature's blindness, were cut from the film when Lugosi's words were removed.[66] This left viewers a bit puzzled as to the Monster's strange manner of walking. Critics initially mocked the Monster's movements, only to realize later the pattern of behavior that Lugosi was trying to establish.

Frankenstein Meets the Wolf Man marks another milestone: two Universal monsters on screen at the same time, making it the first of the studio's so-called "monster rallies." Pitted against Lugosi's Monster is the reluctant Wolf Man, who really deserves top billing over Frankenstein in the film's title. Chaney is typically outstanding in his performance, creating the necessary level of sympathy for the werewolf. Unfortunately, Chaney's scenes as the Wolf Man are too few and far between. Most of the time we see Chaney as a sad and angry Larry Talbot, not in his ferocious werewolf role.

In contrast, one of the film's most entertaining scenes involves the Festival of the New Wine, a nighttime street celebration that culminates in a memorable loss of temper by Talbot. The final scene of the film also involves a compelling fight sequence between the two monsters, but the climactic brawl should have been allowed to play out longer. It's possible that some of the fight scene ended up on the cutting room floor, too.

Unfortunately, too much of this film ended up being removed and essentially lost forever, despite efforts to retrieve the abandoned footage. Otherwise, we might have been talking about another Universal classic. Instead, we are left with something less substantial. Still, *Frankenstein Meets the Wolf Man* is an entertaining and essential part of 1940s fright

Frankenstein Meets the Wolf Man (1943): A worried look on his face, Lon Chaney's Lawrence Talbot discovers Frankenstein's Monster (Bela Lugosi) encased in ice. Chaney and Lugosi had previously worked together in both *The Wolf Man* and *The Ghost of Frankenstein*; in the latter film, Chaney played the Monster and Lugosi the evil Ygor (courtesy of Frank Dello Stritto).

film history. It gave Chaney an additional turn as his iconic character and placed the great Lugosi in an out-of-the-box role that he could have had a dozen years earlier. For those reasons, horror fans should be grateful.

The other sequel from 1943, which also involved Chaney, first hit theaters that fall. The release of *Dracula's Daughter*, back in 1936, made it inevitable that there would be a *Son of Dracula*. The latter film became a reality on November 5, 1943.

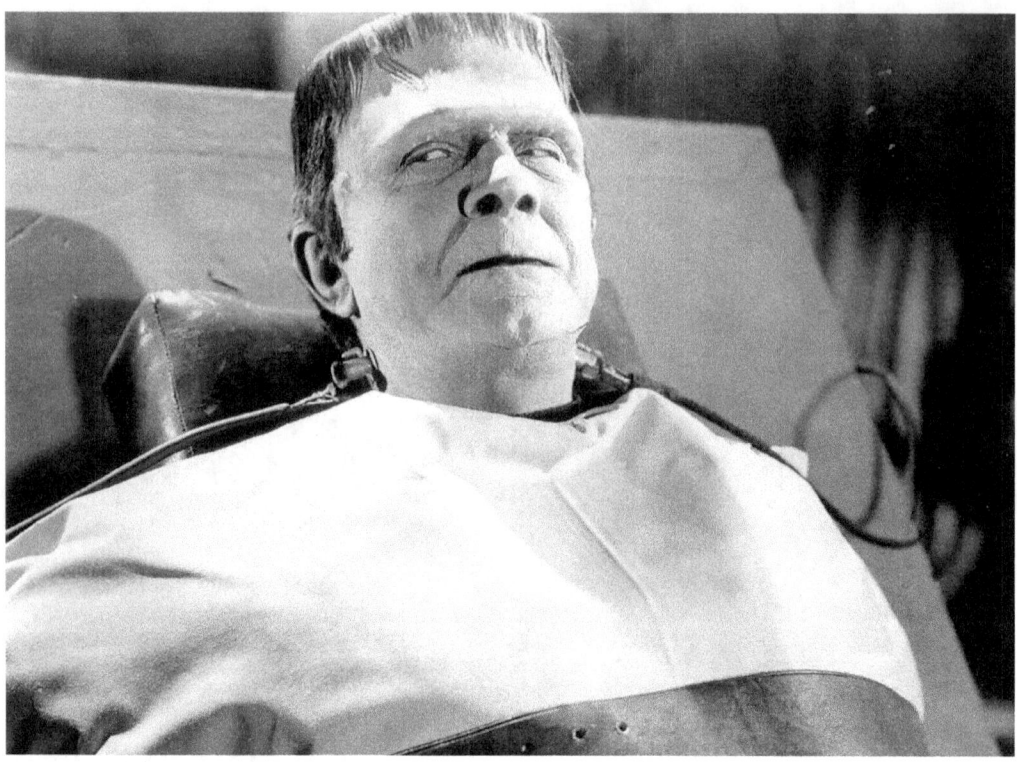

Frankenstein Meets the Wolf Man (1943): Strapped to a surgical table, Bela Lugosi purses his lips, in what turned out to be his lone portrayal of the Monster. Although it is never explained in the film, Lugosi's Monster is blind, which clarifies why he walks stiffly with outstretched arms (courtesy of Frank Dello Stritto).

Set on a Southern American plantation rather than in England, *Son of Dracula* never acknowledges *Dracula's Daughter*, but does serve as a delayed sequel to the original classic. Right from the beginning, *Son of Dracula* creates a paradox for the viewer. The title and the opening credits initiate the confusion: is the film really centered on Dracula, or is it instead focused on his son? The opening credits introduce Chaney as Dracula, but throughout the film he is referred to as Count Alucard, who is presumably Dracula's son. So is this Dracula, or is he disguising himself as his own offspring? In actuality, Dracula's son is never mentioned in the script, so we must assume that this is the original count. What we also know is this: In taking the name Dracula and spelling it backward as Alucard, the film introduces a gimmick that would be used in future films, including some parodies of the legendary vampire.

Once again, Lugosi was passed over as part of the sequel. Lugosi was deemed too old to capture the romantic angle of the lead role,[67] so the part went to Chaney. The selection of Chaney was considered controversial at the time. In fact, the debate has raged ever since. Some critics felt that the oversized Chaney lacked the grace and gravitas of the Carpathian vampire; others felt that he was the logical choice, given the aging of Lugosi. What really matters is Chaney's ability to pull off the character. With his icy, reserved personality, Chaney makes the character work. He features slicked-back hair and a larger frame than Lugosi, but Chaney looks slimmer and more refined than in most of his other films, which helps in his characterization of the vampire. He also

Son of Dracula (1943): Lon Chaney in one of his most underrated performances, as Count Alucard, an alias for Count Dracula. In this scene, a sleek-looking Chaney moves in for the kill on Colonel Caldwell, played by prolific actor George Irving (Photofest).

moves smoothly and slickly, in contrast to his more hulking movements in other monster roles. Chaney might not be Lugosi, but he is capable enough in his only film portrayal of Dracula.

The film begins with Dracula-Alucard's arrival at a Louisiana plantation owned by Col. Caldwell, prompted by an invitation from the colonel's daughter Katherine. Soon after Dracula's arrival at Dark Oaks, the colonel dies, ostensibly because of a heart attack. The Dark Oaks plantation is left to Katherine, who has secretly become romantically involved with Dracula even though she has a longtime boyfriend, Frank Stanley. When Frank learns of the affair, he confronts Dracula, which leads to unwanted tragedy.

The female lead of Katherine is played by Louise Allbritton, another interesting casting choice given her extensive background working in comedies, not horror. Still, Allbritton is cold and calculating as Katherine, a young and wealthy woman who has become obsessed with Dracula—and the supernatural in general.

Son of Dracula is one of the more innovative of the Universal films. For the first time ever, we see the on-screen transformation of Dracula into a flying bat. Additionally, Chaney's character is given remarkable physical strength, something that was not featured by Lugosi's Dracula. And for the first time in a theatrical film, Dracula departs the old world of Europe and comes to America, thanks to the plan hatched by Katherine.

The film has its share of memorable imagery, including a scene where we see a casket rising out of swamp water. Emerging initially as mist from the casket, Chaney's Dracula then materializes and appears to glide along the top of the water as he approaches the expectant Katherine. It is a beautifully executed scene, particularly for the time period.

In another iconic scene, Dracula appears as mist as he makes his way under a locked door and into an office where Dr. Brewster and Prof. Lazlo are plotting to bring him down. The mist soon solidifies into the form of Dracula. Now standing only a few feet from them, Dracula's presence stuns the two men, who realize that the vampire has heard every word of their plan.

Although conceived as a B-movie, *Son of Dracula* succeeds at a higher level because of the quality of the script and its dark, shadowy atmosphere. Some have called it *horror noir*, and that's probably an apt description for a film that is singularly creative and quite different from its many counterparts.

Just one week after the release of *Son of Dracula*, Universal unleashed a different kind of film on the American cinema. Debuting on November 12, *The Mad Ghoul* is a wonderfully titled film that fails to live up to its name—or the studio's high standards. It has some appeal for fans of the horror genre, but its lack of marquee actors, eye-catching special effects and genuine chills make it mediocre in the realm of Universal horror. What makes it worthy of at least one viewing is the excellent performance of George Zucco as Dr. Alfred Morris, along with Universal's usual collection of wonderful set designs.

The movie tells the story of Dr. Morris, a university professor who performs chemical experiments on animals using an ancient Mayan nerve gas. Dr. Morris then decides to use the gas on a human, the brilliant medical student Ted Allison. When Dr. Morris becomes infatuated with Ted's girlfriend Isabel, he decides to apply the gas to Ted as a means of killing him. The results are predictably disastrous, with Ted repeatedly becoming a ghoul who must consume the fluid from human hearts in order to survive. Deciding to unleash the ghoul on society, Dr. Morris directs Ted to rob graves as a way of obtaining hearts. Dr. Morris also instructs Ted to murder a man who has become the object of Isabel's desire.

While the premise has potential, the execution is disappointing. We never see the student, played by David Bruce, make the transformation from human being to ghoulish figure. Instead, he suddenly appears in his monstrous state, with makeup that is lacking the convincing depth of Universal's best efforts. The script by Brenda Weisberg and Paul Gangelin is also lacking. Director James Hogan, who died from a heart attack shortly after the completion of filming but before the film's release, was unable to overcome the weaknesses of the screenplay, making this a less-than-triumphant swan song for the filmmaker.

Cast members Bruce, Zucco and Evelyn Ankers (as Isabel)—all mainstays of Universal's horror run—do solid work, but the lack of a Karloff or a Lugosi makes it difficult to lift the script or the direction above the level of mediocrity. Ankers was supposed to do her own singing in the film, but the tight production schedule forced the producers to use old recordings of another singer-actress, Lillian Cornell.[68]

Zucco's performance as the mad scientist, along with a creative storyline, make *The Mad Ghoul* appealing to horror diehards and ardent followers of Universal films. But the film has little else of value to help it connect with a mainstream audience. It lacks the bite of truly outstanding hosted horror. It does provide decent and entertaining filler for a Friday or a Saturday night, as long as one's expectations remain reasonable.

On December 17, 1943, Universal debuted the first in a new series of films. The studio borrowed from a popular radio show of the era, "Inner Sanctum." and devised a series of films that starred Lon Chaney, Jr. Each film featured an introduction by a floating head that could be seen within a crystal ball. The film then laid out a basic murder-mystery, with

Chaney at the center of the storyline while simultaneously providing narration via a stream-of-consciousness delivery.

The first of the Inner Sanctums featured the eye-catching title of *Calling Dr. Death*. In the first scene, a close-up of a crystal ball reveals the twisted face of actor David Hoffman, who welcomes viewers with the following proclamation: "This is the Inner Sanctum. A strange, fantastic world, controlled by a mass of living, pulsating flesh—the mind. It destroys, distorts, creates monsters ... commits murder. Yes, even you, without knowing, can commit murder!"[69]

As part of the Inner Sanctum inaugural, Chaney plays Mark Steele, a highly successful neurosurgeon but also a man whose wife is obviously cheating on him with several other men. When Maria leaves for the weekend, Dr. Steele blacks out and does not regain consciousness until Monday. When he awakes, he learns that his wife has been murdered and her face disfigured. Steele suspects that he himself may be the killer. To find out for sure, he instructs his nurse to hypnotize him, with the hope that he will be able to recall his activities from his lost weekend.

Calling Dr. Death is not a great film, and is actually more of a mystery–film noir than pure horror, but it is an above-average effort for a B-movie created on a scant budget and completed within a 20-day time frame.[70] Chaney plays his part with palpable vulnerability and is ably assisted by Universal veteran J. Carrol Naish, who hounds Dr. Steele as the doggedly tough Police Inspector Gregg. Naish plays his character with obsessive determination, convinced that Chaney is responsible for the murder.

The Chaney-Naish exchanges highlight the film, creating an interesting byplay as both men attempt to solve the crime and find the killer. The musical score is also quite good, adding to the atmosphere of *Calling Dr. Death*, which takes on a film noir quality. Rather than outright horror, the film places an emphasis on the terror of the mind, a psychological exploration of Chaney's tormented character.

At 63 minutes[71]—all of the Inner Sanctum offerings had a running time in the vicinity of an hour—*Calling Dr. Death* is a modest film that doesn't pretend to be high art. With its low budget and lack of supernatural monsters, it will never be confused with one of the Universal classics, but it is good for what it is: an effective thriller and an above-average vehicle for Chaney's talents.

The second film in the Inner Sanctum series debuted on March 1, 1944. *Weird Woman* is an oddly titled but decent thriller–horror film. While not horror *per se*—it's more of a mystery with threatening tones—the movie does skillfully mix in elements of the supernatural, giving viewers an intriguing premise and some real doubts about the true nature of the title character.

Like all of the films in the series, *Weird Woman* stars Chaney—but not in the title role, obviously. This time he plays Prof. Reed, who vacations in the South Seas and meets an exotic woman named Paula. The two marry, but when Reed brings his new wife back to his hometown, the reception is rather cold. Reed's colleague Ilona resents Paula because she believed that her own meaningful relationship with Reed would have resulted in marriage. Other members of the community come to dislike Paula because of her adherence to voodoo and a general belief in the supernatural. After the death of one of Reed's colleagues, the finger of suspicion points toward the new wife.

Weird Woman treats its subject matter with a high level of campiness, making it a fun rather than frightening film. The pace moves quickly, making up for the lack of deep-seated horror within the running time of 63 minutes.[72]

Chaney delivers a mediocre performance as the professor, but Anne Gwynne is especially good as his wife. The real standout of the movie, however, is horror veteran Evelyn Ankers, who plays Chaney's spurned girlfriend and casts her objections in the direction of Gwynne's Paula. Ankers normally played innocent and wholesome characters, but *Weird Woman* gave her a chance to showcase her more sinister side of acting—which she does with special relish. Additionally, there are several other female characters given screen time, all with quirky personalities, calling into question exactly who the title character might be.

The byplay between Ankers and Gwynne is particularly enjoyable. Ankers' character shows real animosity toward Gwynne, despite their real-life relationship: The two actresses were the best of friends, and they often broke into laughter during the filming of their scenes together.[73] But there is little evidence of that friendship in the film, as both succeed in creating an on-camera appearance of a heated rivalry.

Of the six Inner Sanctum films, *Weird Woman* is one of the better offerings, just a little lacking in comparison to *Calling Dr. Death*. Much of that is due to the efforts of Ankers and Gwynne, as both took advantage of the rare 1940s script that allowed the female characters to outshine their male counterparts.

Chaney continued to play a major role in Universal's horror world in 1944. On July 7, his latest film, *The Mummy's Ghost*, premiered. It was a sequel that improved on the mediocre quality of *The Mummy's Tomb*, which was an earlier follow-up to the original version of *The Mummy*. Although there is no actual ghost, the 1944 film adds the considerable talents of John Carradine to the cast, while also featuring the return of Chaney, who adds a little more depth and versatility to his portrayal of the monster.

The storyline is familiar to the *Mummy* series: High priest Yousef Bey (Carradine) makes a journey to America in search of the remains of the Egyptian princess, Ananka, and her guardian, who is none other than the mummified Kharis. Bey's mission is to bring both back to Egypt. The Mummy runs loose, resulting in a series of murders. Carradine gives his role his usual doses of gusto and campiness. He is a capable complement to Chaney, who shows far more emotional range in this portrayal of the Mummy than in his first performance. Chaney hated playing the role, but once the camera started to roll, he delivered, exhibiting anger, sadness and exasperation at the appropriate times. In fact, Chaney's emotion may have been overcharged. In one scene, he strangles a college professor, played by veteran actor Frank Reicher. Chaney applied such force to his fellow actor's throat that Reicher exclaimed, "He nearly killed me!" The next day, director Reginald LeBorg noticed marks on Reicher's neck.[74]

While Chaney went overboard in filming that scene, this is clearly his best effort in the role of the Mummy. Unfortunately, the supporting cast behind Chaney and Carradine is not as good. A stunning actress named Ramsay Ames replaced an injured Acquanetta as Amina, a beautiful young Egyptian woman, and while Ames' physical charms make a strong presence, her acting fell short of the standards of Chaney and Carradine. Similarly, Robert Lowery is mediocre as college student Tom Hervey, Amina's love interest.

Some critics point to *The Mummy's Ghost* as the best of the lot of *Mummy* sequels. The reasons are many: a wonderful musical score, atmospheric sets, legendary actors Chaney and Carradine near the top of their game, and an offbeat ending that will leave viewers surprised. All of these elements make *The Mummy's Ghost* a nice follow-up to the original classic.

Chaney's impact continued to be felt on June 1, 1945, with the release of the oddly titled but entertaining film, *The Frozen Ghost*. The fourth film in the Inner Sanctum series, it was released on a double feature with *The Jungle Captive*.[75]

Regarded as one of the more effective of the Inner Sanctum films, *The Frozen Ghost* stars Chaney as Gregor the Great, a mentalist-hypnotist who is embarrassed by a drunken fan while on stage. Gregor becomes enraged when the heckler calls him a fake, and makes him part of the act in an effort to prove his abilities. When the heckler dies suddenly under his hypnosis, Gregor feels responsible, even though the medical examiner rules that the drunken man died from a heart attack. Overcome by guilt, an emotion always well portrayed by Chaney, Gregor breaks his engagement to his girlfriend, gives up his stage career and begins working as a lecturer at a wax museum, where strange events are beginning. It's an intriguing premise (part of a fairly complicated plot that moves in several different directions) and one that is carried out well amidst the creepy atmosphere of the wax museum.

The film co-stars Evelyn Ankers, the Universal favorite who had developed a reputation as a leading scream queen from the era. Ankers portrays Gregor's girlfriend, one of the three women who is pursuing him. Ankers is more than capable in the role, which she performs with a degree of sympathy, in contrast to her other appearances in the Inner Sanctum series. Milburn Stone is effective as Gregor's business manager, a figure who is not to be trusted. Finally, Martin Kosleck is very good as Rudi, a plastic surgeon-turned-sculptor who enjoys throwing knives and also has a habit of talking to lifeless wax figures. Playing the role with gusto, Kosleck received stronger reviews for his performance than Chaney did in the lead role. Those opinions apparently did not sit well with Chaney, who felt he deserved more credit for his role as the film's star.

There is one caveat to *The Frozen Ghost*: the title is deceiving. There is no ghost in this film, not a frozen one or even an unfrozen one. The producers simply liked the title and felt that it would attract viewers. This kind of strange titling happened frequently with Universal, which never placed title accuracy high on its priority list. As with many films, the title was designed to attract viewers, rather than accurately inform them.

While the movie has its merits, including the above-average level of acting and the effective backdrop, it lacks much of a supernatural element and fails to rise above the usual standard of Inner Sanctum movies, which were generally fair to acceptable but never outstanding. Still, viewers who are willing to accept a premise that has nothing to do with the title will find some enjoyment here.

The tail-end of the "Shock Theater" package gave us two memorable films, both released in 1946, one of which showcased the commanding screen presence of Rondo Hatton. Released on March 29 as a follow-up to the 1944 Sherlock Holmes hit *The Pearl of Death*, *House of Horrors* is one of the films in Hatton's famed Creeper series. This B-movie tells the story of unsuccessful sculptor Marcel De Lange. As he prepares to commit suicide, he notices a drowning man who happens to be a serial killer known as the Creeper. De Lange revives him and becomes his friend. He decides to make the Creeper the subject of one of his sculptures *and* he begins to use the Creeper to wreak revenge against the art critics who ruined his career.

Hatton plays the monstrous Creeper, and it's easy to see why: His massive frame and his unusual facial features give him the look of a menacing figure bent on destruction. Hatton suffered from a disease called acromegaly,[76] which usually originates with a tumor in the pituitary gland. The disease gradually results in deformation of the head, hands and feet.[77] The revelation of Hatton's disease led some to criticize Universal for exploiting Hatton's physical appearance, though it's debatable whether studio executives fully understood the actor's deteriorating physical condition.

Sadly, Hatton never lived to see the release of *House of Horrors* or his final Creeper film,

The Brute Man. He died from a heart attack on February 2, 1946, before the two films made their ways into theaters. Universal had planned to make more Creeper films, but the exact number remains unknown. While Hatton's career lasted only a few years and consisted of many uncredited appearances, his impact on the genre would become considerable. He is still remembered today, in part through the annual Rondo Awards, a popular fan-based set of awards that honors standouts in horror films and literature each year.

Given his relatively brief career, it's fair to ask why Hatton's name has lived on. While he was not a formally trained actor, and he delivered his lines in a sluggish manner, he played the role of the Creeper with a degree of soul that made the character sympathetic, in much the same way that Boris Karloff portrayed Frankenstein's Monster. *House of Horrors* viewers tend to feel for the Creeper and the misfortune of his physical deformity. Hatton's ability to elicit favor and sympathy, in spite of his deformity, stand as a testament to the heart of the actor.

In contrast to the Creeper, we feel no sympathy for De Lange, the vengeful sculptor who is played skillfully by German actor Martin Kosleck. Nor do we have much compassion for the art critics depicted in the film; they seem to delight in ruining the careers of others, even if their subsequent "punishments" are far too extreme. Some reviewers have credited *House of Horrors* for its success in delivering a biting commentary on the elitism of the art world and its critics.

House of Horrors has been described as a bizarre film; given the storyline and the physical presence of Hatton, this is certainly accurate. It is also a film heavy in atmosphere, deep in chills, and surprising in its ending. Of the Creeper films that Hatton appeared in, it probably runs second to *The Pearl of Death* in terms of quality, but it is the one that truly helped make Rondo Hatton an iconic figure in horror history.

Shortly after *House of Horrors*, Universal came out with a werewolf-themed film, *She-Wolf of London*. While it's certainly not one of the strongest horror films of the 1940s, it does lay out a good mystery, with excellent photography and palpable atmosphere.

Debuting in theaters on May 17, *She-Wolf of London* stars June Lockhart as young heiress Phyllis Allenby, who lives in a mansion near a park where a series of murders is taking place. The murders, all involving young women with their throats torn, point to a werewolf. Some witnesses claim to have seen a "wolf woman." Lockhart suspects that she has fallen victim to the curse of the Allenbys, which has placed her under the spell of lycanthropy and put her into the role of murderer.

Far better known for her work in two TV shows, *Lassie* and *Lost in Space*, during the 1950s and '60s, Lockhart was an interesting choice to star alongside Don Porter, a veteran B-movie actor of the 1940s. Porter was given top billing in *She-Wolf of London*, but Lockhart is clearly the star. She was still very young (only 20) when production took place, but delivers a solid performance, as do most of the main players.

Clearly a Universal B-film, *She-Wolf* was partly shot at what was known as the Hacienda set, where many of the studio's westerns were produced.[78] Filming took place over the course of two weeks in December 1945, but several of the cast's key performers had to return later in the month to complete retakes. As a result, filming did not wrap up until Christmas Eve.[79]

Despite the low budget, the sets are quite good. So is the atmosphere created by director Jean Yarbrough and cinematographer Maury Gertsman, who create nighttime scenes full of fog and mist. The photography is top-notch, emblematic of many of the Universal offerings of the era.

Perhaps its largest flaw is the relative lack of horror. Universal billed *She-Wolf of London* as a film of the horror genre, but that was a deceiving label. It contains a few elements of horror, but fits more comfortably into the genres of mystery and thriller. Fans expecting pure horror will be disappointed, but those who are willing to forgive the shortcomings and concentrate on solving the mystery will find themselves engaged for the duration of the movie. All in all, *She-Wolf of London* is an above-average film that represents competent fare from the 1940s. No one will confuse it with the classic monster movies of the 1930s and '40s, but on its own merits, it provides an adequate degree of entertainment.

From *She-Wolf of London* to *Dracula*, "Shock Theater" made its presence felt, while encompassing every aspect of horror, from werewolves to vampires to monsters to human killers. Of the 34 horror films released as part of "Shock Theater," the 29 films featured in this chapter laid a strong base for horror fans of the late 1950s to enjoy watching, or rewatching, a number of classic and cult films.

The skyrocketing TV ratings that "Shock Theater" produced in late 1957 and early 1958 not only confirmed the success of the Screen Gems concept, but offered proof that horror was worthy of a higher place than the ugly stepchild in the family hierarchy of film. Horror films, if packaged and promoted properly, could sell.

In fact, those films sold so well that Screen Gems decided to duplicate its efforts in 1958. It would do so with a reprisal of the brand names of Frankenstein, Dracula and the Wolf Man, and a heavy dose of acting from the king of horror, Boris Karloff.

Chapter Five

The Movies of "Son of Shock"

With "Shock Theater" an unquestioned success, it only made sense for Screen Gems to put together its own sequel to the initial batch of horror and thriller films. So the company negotiated a second deal with Universal, this time adding a selection of Columbia films to the mix. The combination of Universal and Columbia releases, made available to TV stations in 1958, formed what Screen Gems billed as "Son of Shock."

In contrast to the earlier "Shock" release, Screen Gems placed almost all of its emphasis on one genre. Playing down the genres of crime drama and mystery, Screen Gems released 20 films—almost all coming from the world of horror. Some involved monsters of a supernatural kind, while other villains came strictly from the human ranks.

Much like the first "Shock" package, "Son of Shock" needed a headliner. It had just that in *Bride of Frankenstein*, the highly successful sequel to the original *Frankenstein*. The film once again starred Boris Karloff as the Monster while adding Elsa Lanchester to the franchise as the Bride. Not surprisingly, Karloff emerged as the featured player throughout the "Son of Shock" package. Of the 20 films that Screen Gems made available, exactly half featured Karloff in a starring role.

The Frankenstein Monster appeared in four of the "Son of Shock" movies. In addition to *Bride of Frankenstein*, he reared his hideous head in *House of Frankenstein* (with Karloff taking on a different but no less villainous role), *The Ghost of Frankenstein* with Lon Chaney as the Monster and *House of Dracula* with Glenn Strange assuming the role. Sequels to *The Mummy* and *The Invisible Man* added to the brand name value and appeal of "Son of Shock."

"Son of Shock" also introduced younger horror fans to the talents of actors Peter Lorre and John Carradine, each of whom appeared in three of the movies. The work of underrated director Nick Grinde also gained some exposure, as Grinde collaborated with Karloff in three of the films. While *Bride of Frankenstein* topped the "Son of Shock" list in terms of impact, it did not lead off the release from a chronological standpoint. That honor went to *Behind the Mask*, a 1932 crime drama–mystery with Karloff in a supporting role as a gangster.

The first actual horror film on the "Son of Shock" list came out on April 24, 1933, and reintroduced "Shock" viewers to an old friend who had headlined the first TV package. A Columbia picture, *Night of Terror* has all of the elements of classic horror and mystery. First, there's the setting of a spooky old mansion. Second, a séance takes place at night. And then there's the presence of Bela Lugosi, who brings his usual dose of chilling stares and sinister creepiness to the production.

As with many of his films, Lugosi's star power was used to promote the film, even though he had relatively few lines to speak. The promotional poster showed Lugosi's head, topped by a turban, with his face colored in an odd greenish hue. Curiously, Columbia also put out publicity stills that showed Lugosi wearing a full mustache, giving us a different look at the horror legend. But he sports no mustache throughout the movie, perhaps indicating a last-second change of mind by the director.

Some critics have contended that Lugosi was wasted by director Ben Stoloff in his role as Degar, a household servant who is a peripheral character. The improper use of Lugosi is a legitimate complaint, but Lugosi physically appears in most of the scenes, often silently, and his presence is vital to creating the proper mood of the film. Wallace Ford takes on a greater speaking role; he plays fast-talking reporter Tom Hartley, who covers the murder of businessman Richard Rinehart. The murder appears to be the latest in a series of slayings by a killer known as The Maniac, who takes down his victims with a large knife.

After the death of Rinehart, the heirs to the family fortune attend a nighttime séance at the Rinehart estate. If they do not attend, they will be cut out of the inheritance. But they will first have to survive the arrival of the mad killer. Suspicion centers on Lugosi's Degar, a man who appears to have mystic abilities.

In many ways, the old Rinehart mansion is the true star of *Night of Terror*. The house has a full complement of secret passages, narrow tunnels and sliding wall panels, creating a perfect backdrop for the story. The characters themselves add to the atmosphere with their offbeat personalities and weird tendencies. In many ways, it's a menagerie of madness—and it all contributes to the fun of the film. The ending adds to the enjoyment. It is bizarre and unexpected, a fitting conclusion to a film filled with so many macabre elements and unforeseen twists.

A few critics have derided *Night of Terror* for being too clichéd, too over-the-top in its presentation. That is all true, but it's also part of what makes this a thrill ride for horror fans. Sadly, it is also a film that has been rarely shown on television in recent years, and has yet to receive a home video release.

Bride of Frankenstein deserves recognition at the highest level of horror films. The consensus of genre film critics places it at the top of the list of the Universal horror classics. I suppose that contention is debatable—this author sees the original *Frankenstein* as the slightly superior film—but ultimately the comparison matters little. Like the original film, *Bride of Frankenstein* remains somewhere near the summit of all-time horror, successfully continuing the story from the first film while adding two key characters and new elements that involve the Monster's ability to speak and find friendship.

Premiering in selected theaters on April 19, 1935, *Bride of Frankenstein* came from the directing genius James Whale, who had delivered the first *Frankenstein*, along with *The Old Dark House* and *The Invisible Man*. But Whale took on the new project reluctantly, only willing to embrace the making of the film when the studio promised him full artistic authority. Whale certainly took advantage of the opportunity.

Whale opens the film by introducing us to Mary Shelley, the author of the famed *Frankenstein* novel, while giving us a summary of the developments in the first film. He then unleashes a surprise: establishing that the Monster is still alive. He survived the catastrophic fire at the mill by falling into an underground pool of water below the structure. As for Henry Frankenstein (again played keenly by the tragic Colin Clive), his presumably lifeless body is brought back to his mansion, but he suddenly regains consciousness in front of his wife Elizabeth (Valerie Hobson).

Henry is forced by a scientist of questionable sanity, Dr. Pretorius (Ernest Thesiger), to create a Mate for the original Monster. Pretorius has devised his own way of creating life, by growing miniature humans from seeds, and hopes to merge his methods with those of Henry. In the meantime, local authorities attempt rather futilely to incarcerate the Monster, who eventually encounters Pretorius in an underground tomb before reuniting with his reluctant creator, Henry Frankenstein.

Dr. Pretorius is played brilliantly by Thesiger, an actor somewhat forgotten by time, but one of the driving forces behind the success of *Bride of Frankenstein*. His distinctively odd appearance, complete with bony facial features and wild hair, and his unusually pronounced way of speaking make him one of the stars of the film. He is someone to be feared almost as much as the Monster. It is clear from the beginning that Pretorius has sinister intentions, and as the plot unfolds, Thesiger's portrayal only grows more evil.

The film also showcases a young Elsa Lanchester in a dual role, playing both Mary Shelley at the beginning of the film and the Monster's Mate at the end. As the Bride, Lanchester's screen time amounts to fewer than four minutes, but that's more than enough time for her characterization to become iconic. Right after being born, she twitches, jerks her head and hisses loudly. Her reaction to the sight of the Monster is also classically memorable, and not what Dr. Pretorius, Henry Frankenstein or the Monster himself had in mind. Interestingly, the opening credits to the film do not list Lanchester as the female monster; instead, there is a question mark next to her name, just as was done with Karloff in the first Frankenstein movie.

Karloff again plays the Monster—and does it brilliantly. Since he was so well-known by the time that *Bride of Frankenstein* came out, he is simply listed as KARLOFF in the credits. As effective as Karloff is, he protested the director's decision to have the Monster learn how to speak, as laid out in the classic scene in the Hermit's hut.[1] Reluctantly, Karloff went along with this plotline, which helps to explain why he did not remove his partial bridgework from his mouth. Karloff had removed the bridgework for the first film, to give the Monster more of a sunken cheek look. But in order to speak relatively clearly in *Bride of Frankenstein*, he needed the bridgework in place.[2] Without it, he would have had great difficulty mouthing the words.

In retrospect, Karloff regretted the film. He remained steadfast in his belief that the Monster should not speak, and felt that *Bride of Frankenstein* made him too human, less of a destructive creature. Karloff's thoughts turned out to be the minority opinion, as most critics applauded Whale's decision to make the Monster evolve.

Karloff's feelings toward the film may have been colored by his experiences on the set. According to accounts of the filmmaking, Karloff lost about 20 pounds on set because he sported hot, heavy makeup and a cumbersome costume.[3] He also suffered a dislocated hip early in the production, so it's understandable why he needed to take frequent rests during filming.[4] Clearly, *Bride of Frankenstein* was a physically exhausting film for the actor, made even more difficult by the fact that he was now four years older than he was during the production of *Frankenstein*.

Karloff was not the only critic of the film. Censors in several foreign countries expressed their displeasure with the scene at the climax, as the Monster gazes longingly at his new bride. The censors felt that the scene suggested necrophilia, but the footage was allowed to remain.[5]

While *Bride of Frankenstein* received its share of criticism at the time, it has now become a full-fledged horror classic. David J. Skal considers it the best of all the Universal releases from the 1930s, '40s and '50s. "*Bride* is the gem in the Universal crown," contends Skal. "It's that rare sequel that is better than the original."[6]

Bride of Frankenstein (1935): The four key players in the highly successful sequel to 1931's *Frankenstein* make their presence felt. Mesmerized by his new bride (Elsa Lanchester), Frankenstein's Monster (Boris Karloff) is held back by the evil Dr. Pretorius (Ernest Thesiger). On the left is creator Henry Frankenstein, played so maniacally by Colin Clive (Photofest).

Skal finds agreement from current-day director Harrison Smith, a horror historian and longtime fan of the Universal classics:

> *Bride of Frankenstein* really stands out to me. It's one of the greatest sequels ever made. It's just as good now, if not better, than when it was made. It's because stylistically James Whale took chances; he didn't just give us the same story again. *Bride* did what a good sequel should do. He took the story and took us off in a whole different direction while bringing along many of the same characters. Stylistically, it's beautiful. Thematically, it's beautiful. It was elevated. It was above the material of the original *Frankenstein*. James Whale was a pioneer with visual style and surreal sets, and he was a big influence on me.[7]

The work of heavy-hitting legends like Karloff, Lanchester, the underrated Thesiger and the energetic Clive only adds to the appeal of *Bride of Frankenstein*. Other than some over-the-top attempts at humor within the first few minutes, the film has relatively few weaknesses. With its caliber of acting, wonderful sets and iconic scenes, *Bride* advances Mary Shelley's classic story in a way that horror fans still find engrossing to this day.

Two months after giving us his reprisal as the Monster, Karloff once again entered theaters with the release of *The Black Room*. This time, he did not appear on behalf of Universal, but instead for Columbia. The film represented one of the studio's most successful ventures into the world of 1930s horror.

Aside from *Bride of Frankenstein*, *The Black Room* may have been the best of the 20

"Son of Shock" films. Debuting on July 15, 1935, *The Black Room* finds Karloff in a dual role; he plays twin brothers born to an aristocratic family. One of the brothers has a physical deformity that prevents him from using his right arm; he is the good brother, while the other is decidedly not. The malicious brother, Baron Gregor, becomes a ruler who relies on murder. The good brother, Anton, visits Gregor at his castle, shocked to hear of the baron's evil ways. Given his general kindness, Anton wins favor with the local citizens, who storm the castle and force Gregor to abdicate the throne to his brother. This leads to a confrontation in what is known as the Black Room, where a violent family prophecy will be fulfilled.

Critics of Karloff who claimed that he could only portray men of an evil nature are quickly disproven upon a single viewing of *The Black Room*. He is superb in both roles, playing each man with subtlety and nuance, giving us a fine portrayal of both characters. *The Black Room* was one of a handful of films that allowed Karloff to display his full range and expressiveness as an actor, and he does not fall short of fulfilling the mission. Karloff's distinctive speaking voice, always one of the strengths of his acting, is showcased in all of its glory, allowing him to command each scene.

The rest of the cast, which lacks the presence of a strong character actor like a Lionel Atwill or a Dwight Frye, is not up to the standard of those two legends. But the other actors don't need to be, given the standout nature of Karloff's performance. While the casting call could have been more effective, director Roy William Neill ably supports Karloff by laying out excellent sets, dressing his characters in authentic outfits, and brilliantly using the effects of lighting to create an appropriately Gothic atmosphere. In a relatively low-budget scenario, Neill maximized his resources beautifully.

The Black Room deserves to be considered a minor classic, even though it has become something of a forgotten film. Its relative obscurity might stem from its lack of connection to Universal, which has promoted its horror movies so well over the years, in contrast to Columbia. Or it could have something to do with a lack of physical monsters. We're so used to seeing Karloff in monstrous roles, like Frankenstein's Monster and the Mummy, or as an evil scientist creating something otherworldly, that it becomes more difficult to grasp the legendary actor as someone with more mundane human qualities.

Whatever the reason, *The Black Room* deserves a more substantial legacy. It is essential viewing for fans of the hosted horror era, and doubly so for those who regard themselves as fans and followers of the great Karloff.

Of the other Columbia films released as part of the "Son of Shock" package, *The Man They Could Not Hang* is another strong offering. The film, first seen in theaters on August 17, 1939, also foreshadows an important advancement in medical science: the ability to transplant a human heart from one person to another.

Boris Karloff plays the title role: mad scientist Dr. Henryk Savaard, who becomes obsessed with the notion of bringing the dead to life. Made aware of Savaard's bizarre and illegal experiments by his nurse, the police arrest him. He is tried, found guilty of all charges, and sentenced to death by hanging. Savaard swears revenge against all who have sealed his fate, from the district attorney to the judge and jury. Savaard will have that chance when his corpse is resuscitated by his assistant, using the very technique that the doctor had developed. That technique involves the transplant of a mechanical heart, something that was unheard of in 1939. Writers Karl Brown and George W. Sayre deserve credit for their foresight in developing this concept.

Some critics have relegated *The Man They Could Not Hang* to B-movie fare because of its low budget, but Karloff elevates it with an excellent performance as the crazed scientist.

The above-average script features several twists, and the cameraman's use of light and dark are also quite effective.

Perhaps the most legitimate criticism of the film is its length. At 64 minutes,[8] it goes by too quickly. A longer film would have done justice to a good story and given us more of Karloff, who is simply superb in the use of his voice and his facial expressions. Other than the weakness of brevity, this film is highly enjoyable, particularly in the way that director Nick Grinde uses a secluded and deserted house as a supposed refuge for the potential victims of the resuscitated doctor. With its atmosphere and commanding lead performance, *The Man They Could Not Hang* is a must-see event for Karloff fans.

Karloff also takes center stage in *Black Friday*, which premiered on February 29, 1940. In addition to Karloff, it also stars Bela Lugosi, but it is a third actor who steals the show. That is relatively little-known character actor Stanley Ridges, who puts forth arguably the best performance of his career in playing two different characters. Thanks to Ridges, and with some help from the two horror legends, *Black Friday* becomes a more than serviceable example of 1940s horror.

Karloff plays Dr. Ernest Sovac, a man who is desperately trying to save the life of his good friend, college professor George Kingsley. In order to do so, Sovac transplants the brain of gangster Red Cannon into the professor, indeed saving his life but creating a Jekyll-and-Hyde side effect that splits his personality into two separate entities. Ridges skillfully plays both the gangster and professor, setting the two characters distinctly apart while still maintaining their believability.

Though he was second-billed, Lugosi takes on the relatively minor role of a second gangster who becomes involved when he learns that Cannon had hidden away a small fortune. Under the original film plan, Lugosi was scheduled to play Dr. Sovac, while Karloff was given the dual roles of the gangster and Prof. Kingsley. But Karloff did not want to play the professor-gangster role (for reasons that are not clear and have been disputed),[9] so director Arthur Lubin recast Karloff and Lugosi in different parts, lessening the work of Lugosi, and creating the dual opening for Ridges. In what is sure to disappoint fans of horror, Lugosi and Karloff share no scenes together. Ordinarily, the lack of a connection might have ruined a film in which both appeared, but Ridges' performance saves *Black Friday* from mediocrity.

How good was Ridges' portrayal? Some film historians believe that the British-born actor was so convincing as both characters, especially the brutal gangster, that he deserved an Academy Award.

At the time, the film created a stir because of reports that Lugosi had actually been placed under hypnosis for a crucial scene by the film's technical advisor, Manly P. Hall. Universal propagated that myth, as did both Lugosi and Karloff, who played along for the sake of the film. It was not until years later, after Lugosi's death, that the myth was debunked by director Lubin.[10] Lugosi's survivors maintained that the hypnosis claim had been a ploy by the studio to generate publicity. The ploy didn't work, as *Black Friday* turned into a box office disappointment, one that led studios to believe (falsely) that Karloff and Lugosi were no longer bankable in tandem.

Black Friday is an unusual film, in that it mixes the gangster theme with elements of science fiction and horror. It is also a film that is bound to disappoint viewers who want to see Karloff and Lugosi together. But on the merits of the storyline, the efforts of the two legends, and the rousing performance of the unheralded Ridges, it is worthy of a viewing by horror fans of the era.

Karloff's busy 1940 continued with a film that was released on April 18. For Karloff, *The*

Man with Nine Lives continued his association with director Nick Grinde. After the success of *The Man They Could Not Hang*, Grinde and Karloff again teamed up for Columbia. Their new collaboration on *The Man with Nine Lives* gives us another strong look at Karloff as an obsessed scientist, but this time with a different twist: Dr. Leon Kravaal has been missing for a number of years. One day, a medical researcher and his nurse break into the doctor's abandoned home, where they find his body, which has been frozen in a state of suspended animation. Through a series of flashbacks, the revived Kravaal tells his story. At first, he appears to be a morally grounded man of medicine who is nobly determined to develop a cure for cancer, but the progression of the story reveals a more sinister side.

Kravaal tells of his experiments, which involve freezing a patient, a method that is reminiscent of the controversial belief in cryogenics. When it appears that Dr. Kravaal has frozen one of his patients to death, the man's family comes to the doctor's home, setting the stage for a climactic confrontation.

Once again, director Grinde succeeds on a small budget, making up for a lack of elaborate props and special effects with very good use of lighting and shadow. Grinde's set designs are also outstanding. In particular, the director devised a wonderful backdrop of an underground laboratory, the perfect setting for Karloff and his experiments. The actors do their part, especially Karloff, who always seemed to deliver in his role as a mad scientist, even when the good side of his character does battle with the bad. That moral conundrum serves as fuel for the audience members, forcing them to consider the ethics of creating life out of death, and whether human beings should be made unconscious for long periods of time before being brought back to vitality.

The Man with Nine Lives does have its down points. At times, the pace is plodding and lacking the breakneck speed of *The Man They Could Not Hang*. In contrast to its predecessor, it seems too long at 74 minutes.[11] It also has its share of plot holes and continuity errors. Still, it's an entertaining film and another in a long line of productions that showcase the ample talents of the great Karloff.

The third collaborative effort between Karloff and Grinde debuted on September 17, 1940. *Before I Hang*, while not a standout film, is notable for the work of its featured actor. As with his other performances for Grinde, Karloff is stellar in playing a doctor who has become motivated to conduct bizarre experiments, as always with unwanted consequences.

Without Karloff, *Before I Hang* would have become a forgotten film, but once again, the actor elevates the material in his role as a scientist gone mad. Karloff plays John Garth, who has been imprisoned and unjustly sentenced to death for committing the equivalent of a mercy killing on an elderly, dying friend. While awaiting the penalty of death, Garth is allowed to continue his research, thanks to the prison warden and a scientist, Dr. Ralph Howard. In tandem with Dr. Howard, Garth develops a serum that will reverse the effects of aging. Garth is injected with the serum by Dr. Howard, just before he is scheduled to be executed.

At the last minute, Garth's death sentence is commuted, and he is given a life sentence instead. The serum also begins to take effect, making him look and feel younger, but there's a side effect: the urge to kill. When Garth is later given a full pardon for his original crime, he is free to commit murders.

In contrast to the other Grinde-Karloff films, *Before I Hang* has a stronger supporting cast, thanks mostly to the presence of Edward Van Sloan. In what was one of his final credited roles, Van Sloan is very good as Dr. Howard, and B-movie staple Evelyn Keyes capably handles the role of Garth's daughter.

Before I Hang has its flaws. The science portrayed in the film stretches credibility (even beyond the usual standards of horror), the plot is too predictable, and the story falls apart somewhat as it nears its conclusion. Clearly, it's not as strong as the other tandem efforts of Karloff and Grinde. Karloff does makes it worthwhile, even if it is the weakest of the three "Son of Shock" films directed by Grinde.

While Karloff was reaching prolific levels in the early 1940s, he was not the only man making a name for himself in the era's horror genre. Peter Lorre's ample talents came to the forefront in the January 16, 1941, release, *The Face Behind the Mask*. While Lorre did not like this movie, and hated the experience of making it, those sentiments should not detract from an objective assessment of this gem. Not only was Lorre excellent in his performance, but the other characters and the general storyline all provide intrigue that is beautifully handled by accomplished director Robert Florey.

Lorre plays Janos Szabo, a friendly and hopeful Hungarian watchmaker who comes to America, only to be badly disfigured in a fire on his first day in New York City. With his facial features so badly damaged, he is unable to find work. Desperate to support himself, he turns to a life of crime, specifically the disabling of alarms. He later becomes the leader of a gang of robbers, earning enough money to purchase a lifelike mask that successfully covers his scarred face. After falling in love with a blind woman, he decides to change his ways and stop committing robberies, but the other members of his gang will have none of it.

In portraying a kind man turned criminal, Lorre gives us an in-depth look at his remarkable acting range. He displays all of his character's traits in believable fashion, from good to bad to those in the middle. Even in committing crime, Lorre gives us the sense of Janos as the reluctant villain, a man who regrets his actions almost at the very moment that he commits them.

Lorre's work was notable to begin with, but it becomes more laudatory in light of his ability to simulate the wearing of a mask. In actuality, Lorre wore no mask, but instead sported prosthetics and tape, and had to constrict his facial muscles so as to create the illusion of a mask.[12] This level of self-discipline led to great discomfort for Lorre, explaining why he hated making the film, but also underscores his extraordinary skill as an actor.

The Face Behind the Mask, while a finely made film, has drawn some criticism for not being pure horror. There is truth in that assessment, which could be applied to many of the "Son of Shock" films. But there is at least some horror, in the form of Lorre's disfigurement and the use of the surreal mask, and it is mixed beautifully with elements of drama, crime, thriller and even film noir. *The Face Behind the Mask* does not fit neatly into any one genre, but to exclude it completely from the field of horror would be somewhat inaccurate and unfair.

As the director, Robert Florey showed a willingness to experiment. He introduced some unusual techniques which add to the stark imagery and the overall visual experience. He accomplished this while working on a minuscule budget, which makes *The Face Behind the Mask* even more impressive.

As 1941 progressed, Karloff continued to hone his performance as the obsessed scientist, one who often began with noble intentions before descending into evil. *The Devil Commands*, a February 3rd Columbia release, is another of those films. While not quite as good as some of the other examples of Karloff's work in this area (like *The Man They Could Not Hang*), it skillfully mixes horror with science fiction while creatively adding elements of the occult to the scheme.

Karloff plays Julian Blair, a scientist who has been engrossed in experiments involving human brain waves. When his wife dies in a car accident, Dr. Blair alters the focus of his work so that he can attempt to communicate with the dead—specifically his wife. Although discouraged from pursuing this connection with the occult by his daughter and his colleagues, he persists, moving his laboratory to a secluded location in New England and bringing with him some questionable characters to serve as his new assistants. While Karloff is clearly the star, one of his assistants is worth more than a mention. Dr. Blair's hulking manservant Karl, played by Ralph Penney, is a memorable part of the film, if only because of his oversized presence on the screen.

Another key player in the film is veteran character actress Anne Revere, who portrays Mrs. Walters, a purported psychic who is nothing more than a phony medium. Revere is excellent in the ominous role as an advisor to Dr. Blair, just as effective as Karloff is in his portrayal.

The Devil Commands is clearly a B-picture made on a limited budget. It's a thin film, only 65 minutes in length,[13] and lacks the depth of some of Karloff's other mad scientist efforts. But the performances of Karloff and Revere, some very good direction from Edward Dmytryk, and an excellent séance sequence make this a very serviceable movie. *The Devil Commands* has developed something of a cult following and become part of the essential Karloff library.

As much of a role as Karloff continued to play in 1940s horror, he chose not to sustain his active connection to the Frankenstein Monster. On March 13, 1942 (Friday the 13th), *The Ghost of Frankenstein* made its way into theaters without Karloff. It became the first of Universal's Frankenstein films that did not feature the talents of the legendary actor, who turned down the role as the Monster, setting the stage for the reins to be handed over to Lon Chaney, Jr., who had established his stardom in *The Wolf Man*. As such, the film represented a changing of the guard for the Frankenstein franchise.

While there is no Karloff, there is plenty of Bela Lugosi, who returns as the evil and demented Ygor. When the local mayor gives the villagers permission to blow up the castle laboratory where the Monster had allegedly died and thereby rid themselves of all remnants of his legacy, they discover that Ygor is determined to protect it. (It's impressive to learn that Ygor survived two bullets to the stomach in *Son of Frankenstein*.) Although the Monster had also appeared to die in a burning sulfur pit at the end of the previous film, Ygor finds the Monster alive, his body preserved in layers of hardened sulfur. Ygor extricates the creature and brings it to a neighboring village, where the Monster seizes a little girl (played beautifully by Janet Ann Gallow), but intends her no harm; he only wants to help her retrieve a ball that she had been playing with. Noticing the Monster carrying the girl, the villagers seize him and bring him to the local court, where he is chained to the witness stand.

Among those in the court room is Ludwig Frankenstein, the brother of Wolf von Frankenstein, who had been featured in *Son of Frankenstein*. Played by the capable Cedric Hardwicke, Ludwig becomes consumed with the idea of replacing the Monster's current brain, which is criminal in nature, with one that comes from a more law-abiding member of the community.

The Ghost of Frankenstein succeeds in providing entertainment, but it doesn't meet the high standards of the first three films in the series. Chaney's size and stature add to the brutality of the Monster—and the makeup that was applied make him look like a larger version of Karloff, complete with the flattened head and the protruding bolts. But he lacks the emotional range and facial expressions that Karloff used so well in creating a character that was simultaneously vicious and sympathetic. With Chaney's Monster, there is little in the way of humanity; he is generally expressionless, at least before those moments that he becomes a raging creature. It also didn't help that Chaney drank heavily during production. At one point, he allegedly became so drunk while playing the Monster that he actually lost his way walking through a maze of corridors that had been created as part of the set.[14]

Chaney was also short-tempered during the filming. Fitted with a rubber headpiece that was attached to his forehead, Chaney complained repeatedly about how uncomfortable the attachment felt:

> I must have been allergic to the headpiece or the glue, because I broke out in a rash under that gray-green greasepaint and I started to itch—all down my back and around my forehead and scalp. The makeup men refused to take off the headpiece without [Jack] Pierce's permission and no one else would help, so I tried to take it off myself, and part of my forehead came off with it.[15]

Chaney had to take a week off to recover.

While Chaney's behavior affected production, Lugosi was also rumored to be enduring personal problems that diminished his performance, which fell short of the level that he had achieved in *Son of Frankenstein*. Still, Lugosi's portrayal of the sinister Ygor remains a memorable part of the film. (It is also quite the sight later in the film, when we hear Lugosi's voice coming from Chaney's Monster.) Beyond Lugosi and Chaney, the supporting cast helped matters and made the storyline a bit more credible and believable; Hardwicke, Ralph Bellamy, Lionel Atwill and Evelyn Ankers, all familiar and reliable members of the Universal stable, deliver solid performances. Atwill is particularly good as a duplicitous doctor who creates all manner of trouble for the protagonists.

The Ghost of Frankenstein suffers by comparison to its predecessors, all of which have achieved classic status. The movie's outdoor scenes and indoor sets are very good and atmospheric, but the acting from the two main stars does not quite meet the standard set in earlier releases, and the running time of 67 minutes[16] is not long enough to allow for character development amidst all of the chaotic action. But if the viewer is willing to overlook such comparisons and judge the film on its own merits, *The Ghost of Frankenstein* is still a very solid film, more than acceptable for fans of the Universal monsters.

Two years later, Universal tinkered further with its Frankenstein franchise, releasing *House of Frankenstein*. Some filmgoers refer to it as Universal's first official "monster rally," though that honor could also go to 1943's *Frankenstein Meets the Wolf Man*. Debuting on December 1, 1944, *House of Frankenstein* brings three major monsters together for the first time, throws in a hunchback for good measure, and stirs the pot of murder and revenge for an hour and 10 minutes.

The film, which had the working title of *The Devil's Brood*, showcases Dracula, the Wolf Man and the Frankenstein Monster. Interestingly, the three are never seen at once, as Dracula is kept separate from the other two. At one point, the plan also included the presence of the Mummy, but it was ultimately decided that *four* monsters were too much of a good thing. Budget restrictions also played a role in the decision to keep Kharis out of the proceedings.

House of Frankenstein represents the return of Karloff to Universal, but not in the role of the Monster. Instead, Karloff plays Gustav Niemann, a decidedly evil scientist who has been imprisoned for his deranged experiments, along with his loyal hunchbacked servant. The two escape when a lightning bolt strikes the prison, collapsing the walls and leaving an enormous hole in the prison floor. The two miscreants soon encounter the trio of monsters. While Karloff plays the doctor, Glenn Strange makes his initial appearance as the Monster. When not engrossed in his own role, Karloff provided tutelage to Strange on playing the creature in an appropriate way. Strange took the counsel to heart, often crediting Karloff for his wisdom and generosity.

The Ghost of Frankenstein (1942): In his sole appearance as Frankenstein's Monster, Lon Chaney towers over child actress Janet Ann Gallow. Of all the actors who played the Monster for Universal, Chaney was the bulkiest, carrying 230 pounds on his 6'2" frame. He brought brute power to the role, but lacked the soul of Karloff's Monster (Photofest).

Karloff gave the film his full effort and performs well as Dr. Niemann, but didn't think much of the finished product. In a later interview, Karloff described the movie as "a monster clambake."[17] With so many monsters running amok, Karloff felt the film had become ridiculous.

In addition to Frankenstein's Monster, a vampire and a werewolf, *House of Frankenstein* also features a hunchback. Karloff's assistant Daniel is played exceedingly well by J. Carrol

Naish. While the title of the film implies that the monsters are the focus of the plot, the human characters played by Karloff and Naish are actually the central figures, with Naish's hunchback the far more sympathetic of the two. Naish gives Daniel a more nuanced portrayal, kind and caring at times, especially in becoming attracted to a gypsy dancer, but also quick to lose his temper and turn to violence. As the true villain, Karloff's Niemann coldly seeks revenge against those who imprisoned him, and continues his murderous ways by ordering Daniel to kill the owner of a traveling chamber of horrors which features the skeletal remains of Dracula.

Pretending to be Prof. Lampini, proprietor of the horror show, Niemann unintentionally revives Dracula by removing a stake from his rib cage. On a trip to the Frankenstein ruins, Niemann finds the Wolf Man and the Monster, both encased in ice, and revives them. In the meantime, Naish's Daniel pines for the gypsy girl he saved from a cruel beating, making us root for him in the process. Daniel also establishes the common template for the hunchbacked assistant, complete with the delivery of the trademark line, "Yes, master!"

Naish and Karloff are supported well by Lon Chaney, who returns in his iconic Wolf Man role amidst hopes that Niemann can find a way to destroy him and end his werewolf curse. John Carradine steps in to play Dracula (who now goes by the alias of Baron Latos), giving the role a new look and feel, capped off by a top hat and an elegant manner

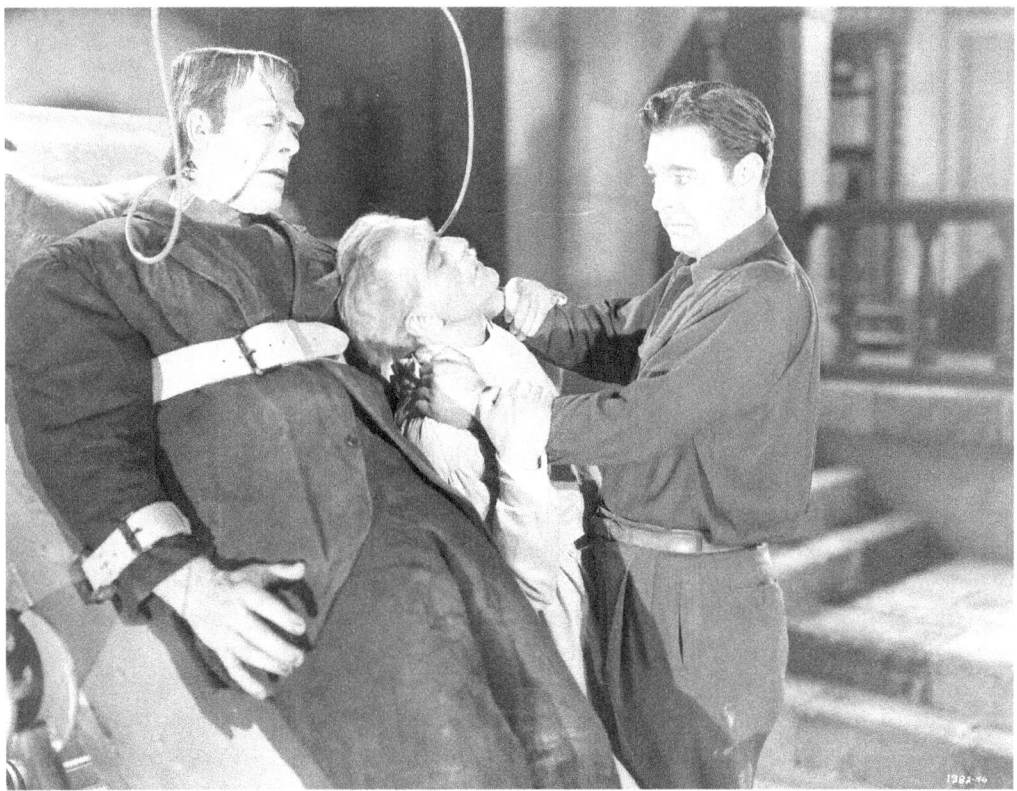

House of Frankenstein (1944): Lon Chaney's Larry Talbot (right) chokes the sinister Dr. Niemann (Boris Karloff). Observing the madness is a grimacing Monster, played by the underrated Glenn Strange. Strange was given bottom billing in the screen credits, but he handled the role well and twice returned to play the Monster (Photofest).

of speaking. Carradine's presentation is especially interesting, but his Dracula is killed off far too quickly. The Monster is also given too little in the way of screen time, even though Strange displays a nice combination of strength and emotion in his brief role.

Despite its flaws, *House of Frankenstein* has a big-budget feel. Universal allotted over $350,000 for the making of the film and also provided a 30-day window, instead of the usual 15 to 20 days. Filming actually spanned more than 30 days, giving director Erle C. Kenton extra time to finish the film as desired.[18]

The end result is a fun film. As Karloff said, it is a movie that is silly at times, one that is lacking in sophistication and character development. No one will ever confuse it with the early triumvirate of classic Frankenstein films. Still, *House of Frankenstein* is full of adventure, action and a trio of our favorite monsters, a combination that will appeal to most classic horror fans.

Universal liked what it saw in *House of Frankenstein*, so the studio returned to the well one year later with another monster rally. Just like *House of Frankenstein*, the December 7, 1945, release *House of Dracula* gave us three marquee monsters in the same film. While it's not nearly as good as the first monster collaboration, *House of Dracula* does provide another confluence of activity for Dracula, the Frankenstein Monster and the Wolf Man.

Dracula, the Wolf Man and the Monster were all presumed dead at the end of *House of Frankenstein*, but the new film opens with the revelation that the Monster is still alive, covered in quicksand while holding onto the skeleton of Dr. Niemann. In contrast, the survivals of Dracula and the Wolf Man are never explained; as with many of the Universal follow-ups, the monsters have miraculously lived to see another day.

The plot of *House of Dracula* involves desperate efforts by Dracula and the Wolf Man to find remedies for their monstrous afflictions. In their quest for help, they both—in a coincidence of ridiculous proportions—approach Dr. Franz Edlemann, a brilliant man of science who is played effectively by the underrated Onslow Stevens. Dr. Edlemann agrees to make the effort to help both of them. Simultaneously, we learn about the fate of the Monster.

The film features many of the Universal regulars, including Chaney, Carradine, Strange and the venerable Lionel Atwill. (There is even a brief appearance by Karloff, though it happens only in a dream sequence and consists of no more than archival footage from the Universal vault.) Although Chaney is given top billing as the Wolf Man—while curiously sporting a mustache as the continually troubled Lawrence Talbot—Carradine is quite good in the secondary lead role of Baron Latos (his alias for Dracula). A mysterious figure purportedly seeking the elusive cure for vampirism, Carradine's character is given much more screen time in this film than in *House of Frankenstein*, allowing for a more substantive interpretation of Dracula.

Sporting a top hat and featuring a much taller and thinner frame than previous Draculas like Chaney and Lugosi, Carradine creates a strange, cadaverous quality for the famed vampire. His seemingly noble intentions of ending his vampire curse also come into question when he attempts to impose his hypnotic powers on one of Dr. Edlemann's nurses.

The filming was especially difficult for Atwill, who was in the late stages of a battle with cancer and passed away four months after the film's premiere.[19] Strange, while much younger and healthier than Atwill, had to endure the unpleasant duty of filming the scene in which Frankenstein's Monster emerges from the quicksand-filled caves where it was presumed that he had died. After spending hours in the chair having his extensive makeup applied, Strange then had to spend most of the day practically buried in cold, liquefied mud that doubled for the quicksand.[20]

The presence of so many cinematic legends, particularly Carradine and Chaney, carries the film to an extent, but doesn't completely make up for the many plot holes and some of the inevitable silliness of having three monsters in one movie. There is also insufficient screen time given to Strange's Monster, who seems deserving of a larger presence. Certainly, *House of Dracula* lacks the gravitas and character development of many of the Universal releases. It's hardly a legitimate classic, but it is still an enjoyable romp for the old monsters and their loyal fans who want to see them together one more time.

Culminating with a film like *House of Dracula*, the "Son of Shock" package did well in continuing the new tradition that had been launched by the first "Shock" package. "Son of Shock" also widened the genre's focus, which initially had been restricted to Universal selections but now expanded to include pertinent films from Columbia's vault. The new package succeeded in cementing Karloff's reputation as the king of horror, while reintroducing viewers to some of the best work of less famous but substantial actors like Peter Lorre and John Carradine.

Essentially, "Son of Shock" proved that the initial "Shock" package was no fluke, and that interest in vintage horror could be sustained. Yet, many horror fans did not want to be pigeonholed into nostalgia exclusively. They had a desire for newer films which could be placed into the late-night and Saturday afternoon slots that made weekend TV viewing so much more captivating.

Those films would come to TV, but under a different name. "Shock" would give way to a new era of packaged movies that could be called anything from "Creature Features" to "Block of Shock."

Chapter Six

Hosts from Coast to Coast

Shortly after John Zacherley debuted in Philadelphia in the fall of 1957, other horror hosts began to carve out their own legacies—smaller than Zacherley's, but still significant and vital to the success of "Shock Theater" and "Son of Shock."

One of the earliest was Terry Bennett, who was beginning to display his talents in another major market, Chicago. On December 7, 1957, he debuted as Marvin, hosting WBKB-TV's version of "Shock Theater."[1] Also known as Marvin the Nearsighted Madman, Bennett took a different approach to his alter ego. Instead of becoming a vampire or a ghoulish undertaker, his character could best be described as a demented beatnik. Looking a bit like a young Dustin Hoffman, he wore ridiculously thick glasses and a dark turtleneck sweater, giving him the appearance of someone who would frequent night clubs at all hours of the night. As with Zacherley, Marvin appeared with his wife, whom he only referred to as Dear. The camera never showed her face.[2]

Marvin's offbeat appearance worked. Like Zacherley, he emphasized humor, poking fun at the films that he hosted. At other times, he played the role straight, attempting to scare the audience with dramatic and serious readings. The mix of fear and comedy worked beautifully. The show became a ratings hit, so successful that the station created a half-hour show that aired after the movie: *The Shocktale Party* featured a number of characters created by Bennett, including a hunchback named Orville and a giant who wore a Frankenstein mask and bore the nickname of "Shorty."[3] Bennett also employed a band called The Deadbeats, whose members all wore white face paint with black circles around their eyes.

The Shocktale Party became such a hit that it actually spawned a Marvin Fan Club. Some fans became so rabid that they called the Bennetts' home number, sometimes as early as four a.m. Unfortunately, Bennett's popularity did not maintain his presence at the TV station. In 1959, WBKB cancelled "Shock Theater," replacing it with the ABC Network's *Fight of the Week*. Bennett fans were so angered that they drew up a petition and acquired thousands of signatures.[4] Stubbornly, the station refused to admit its mistake, leaving Bennett and Marvin out in the cold. The station did, however, retain Bennett as the host of its Saturday morning show *The Jobblewocky Place*."[5] That show, targeted at young children, allowed Bennett to showcase his talents as a ventriloquist and remained his first love.

Like his characterization of Marvin, Bennett's life turned out to be all too short. He continued to have success in broadcasting, and was nominated for Emmys on three occasions, then died in 1977 after a two-year illness. He was only 47.

In San Francisco, Russ Coglin took on the persona of Terrence, with an emphasis on the first four letters of his name matching the letters in the word "terror." Terrence hosted the horror showcase *Nightmare* for KRON-TV. A journeyman broadcaster who had once done cartoon voice work, Coglin was a tall, angular man, but he didn't always appear onscreen for

KRON. Instead, only his voice could be heard, and in some ways that enhanced the creepiness of the character. When he did appear on screen, he did not wear a costume, but sported a formal dress suit, complete with jacket and tie.

Coglin unwittingly became involved in controversy on the night of November 17, 1957.[6] As he hosted a showing of the original *Dracula*, he jokingly announced that "Berkeley believers will meet at the Big C at midnight tonight." The "Big C" was a reference to the University of California campus. Sure enough, thousands of Terrence's devoted watchers showed up the campus at midnight, many of them dressed as vampires or as vampire victims. Many of his fans chanted "Dracula" while others decided to howl like werewolves. The gathering became so loud and boisterous that campus security called the police to the scene. A total of 32 policemen made their way to the University of California, creating a bit of a fracas before order was restored.[7] Coglin did remain on the job for a few years, then gave way to fellow broadcaster John Barclay, who continued the persona of Terrence.[8]

With Terrence in the Bay Area, Marvin in Chicago and Zacherley in Philadelphia and then New York, horror hosts had most of the largest markets covered. But even medium-sized markets created and developed their own hosts of late night horror. One of those markets was located in the Midwest, where Selwin took Indianapolis, Indiana, by storm.

In 1958, TV station WISH Channel 8 introduced its first venture into horror films with the catchphrase, "Friday night is fright night on Channel 8."[9] Ray Sparenberg became the embodiment of that catchphrase through his portrayal of Selwin. WISH actually held auditions for its initial venture of horror hosting, choosing Sparenberg from a short list of candidates. "I heard that Ray Sparenberg, a producer-director for Channel 8, had a theater background and he auditioned," WISH program manager Dave Smith told the *Indianapolis Star*. "He gave an evil laugh in the audition, and that sealed it."[10]

Sparenberg did face one problem. While he had the right look and voice for the role, not to mention the appropriately maniacal laugh, he had no experience either writing or ad-libbing his lines. All of his lines had to be prepared by Smith, who helped Sparenberg map out each show.[11]

The odd name Selwin came from Smith, at least indirectly. One day, he was meeting with a representative from an Indianapolis TV magazine. The man suggested Selwin, a distinguished British-sounding name. Smith liked it, and felt it would be a good match for Sparenberg.[12]

Sparenberg himself selected the costume and makeup that he wanted for the role. Influenced by Zacherley, he donned white makeup that made his face look pale. He added another kind of makeup so that his cheeks would appear sunken, swept his eyebrows up to create a menacing appearance, and grew out his sideburns long and large. Instead of a frock coat, he adopted a cape and a bolero hat, which created some separation between his character and that of Zacherley. He also tried using a pair of rubber gloves that looked like gnarled claws, but the gloves made it difficult for him to handle props and were soon discarded.

At the beginning of each show, Selwin emerged from a revolving bookcase and delivered his opening monologue. The set also featured what appeared to be an ancient Egyptian sarcophagus. The sarcophagus became a key prop, often used in Selwin's sight gags. At the end of his closing skit, Selwin signed off by declaring, "Good night ... whatever you are," repeating the line that Zacherley used to finish his programs.

Selwin's character emphasized humor rather than terror. He typically poked fun at the film being shown, but also mocked the sponsors and even the local culture. The humor worked; Selwyn became a hit in the Indianapolis market. A fan club emerged, complete with the wonderful name of Selwin's Society of the Shroud.[13]

The following Halloween, the station decided to bring Selwin out of the studio and have him tape a show at the Riddick Building, while inviting the public to come out and watch the taping for free. Station executives were shocked when hundreds of people lined up outside of the Riddick Building, all hoping to squeeze into a 150-seat theater area. To accommodate everyone, the station rotated visitors by groups through the building, allowing them to watch one skit before leaving and making room for another group to watch the next skit. Selwin repeated each of the skits several times, so that all fans had the chance to see each skit in its entirety.[14]

Selwin and his Friday night fright night took such a foothold that the station managed to bring in Vampira, played as always by Maila Nurmi, as a guest. Vampira and Selwyn taped a memorable sketch in which Selwin offered her a drink, but she continued to talk. Finally, Selwin strayed from his script, delivering an ad-lib of classic proportions. "Better drink it, darling," Selwin implored, "before it clots!"[15]

Sparenberg's stint as Selwin came to an end in 1963. He later became a host for other genres of movies, taking on costumed roles as an astronaut and safari hunter. Sparenberg died in 2001 at the age of 72.

Selwin was not the only host to make an impact in the Indianapolis market. In the early 1960s, another interesting character took a foothold at a rival station.

At first glance, the name Sammy Terry might seem like an odd choice for a horror host. But if you place the emphasis on the first syllable in Sammy and place less stress on the second syllable, then the play on words becomes more apparent: It sounds a bit like "cemetery." That explains the reasoning behind the name of this other horror host based in Indianapolis, one who remained there for much of the 1960s, '70s and '80s.

The character of Sammy Terry was the brainchild of Bob Carter, who worked for WTTV in Indianapolis. Carter was offered the chance to host the station's version of *Chiller Theater* in 1962. At first, his interludes during the late-night Friday night horror film consisted merely of still photographs, seen during Carter's voiceovers. Despite its rather dull format, the show became popular, spurring Carter to change the name to *Nightmare Theater*, ditch the photographs and develop an on-screen character.[16] Donning a red cloak and skull cap, and some white makeup that made his face appear ghoulish, Sammy Terry arose from a coffin with a foreboding laugh, introduced the film, and then proceeded to offer commentary. He also added a floating rubber spider, which he called George.

Carter ad-libbed much of his dialogue, at times talking to the spider and at other times, speaking directly to his unseen audience. Like many other horror hosts, Carter relied on camp humor and sight gags to fill in the gaps in and around his Friday night double features.

Even though Indianapolis was a relatively small TV market, Sammy Terry's popularity approached that of horror hosts in larger metropolitan markets. Enjoying long-term success, Carter remained on the air until 1989. Even after leaving his regular role, he returned on occasion to make special appearances while wearing his full regalia. In 2010, his son Mark continued the on-air tradition of Sammy Terry. Three years later, the elder Carter died at the age of 83.

To the south of Indianapolis, another medium-sized market became involved in horror hosting, starting in 1959. This host was based in New Orleans. Played by actor Sid Noel Rideau, Morgus the Magnificent debuted on January 3, 1959, as part of a showcase called *House of Shock*.[17]

Morgus was not a supernatural character, merely a mad scientist, helped by an executioner named Chopley (played by actor Thomas George), an unsuccessful face transplant recipient who had to wear a full head mask, with a zippered mouth, to cover his disfigurement. Morgus also relied on his assistant Eric, who appeared as a talking skull in the early years of the program. (In the 1980s, Eric took the form of a talking computer, a reflection of advancements in technology.) The three men (or creatures) resided in an upstairs room that was said to occupy the top floor of the Old City Icehouse, located in New Orleans' French quarter.[18]

With his wild hair, heavy eyebrows and dark circles under his eyes, Morgus took on the look of a madman, almost a mix of Dr. Jekyll and Mr. Hyde. Morgus enjoyed conducting strange experiments in sketches that took place during the showing of the horror film. Typically, Morgus' experiments failed badly, creating the comic aspect to his mad scientist routine.

Morgus gained such a following in New Orleans that he actually became the star of a feature film, *The Wacky World of Dr. Morgus*. The film, which co-starred George as Chopley and featured a blend of comedy, horror and science fiction, received regional distribution in 1962.[19]

In 1964, Morgus left New Orleans to ply his trade in Detroit, where he replaced a relatively forgettable host named Mr. X. Morgus hosted a show with the simple name of *Morgus Presents!* It gained a hold in popularity, but then interest faded. By the latter part of 1965, Morgus was ready to return to his true home in New Orleans.

As a horror host, Morgus remained on New Orleans TV through the mid–1980s, when the show was cancelled. To the delight of many horror fans in the South, Morgus returned to New Orleans TV in 2005, still played by Sid Noel Rideau. Off the air, Rideau became known for his community work, including his efforts to encourage children to read through programs offered by the New Orleans Public Library. In October 2019, Rideau made a celebrated appearance at the city's Orpheum Theater, regaling many of his longtime fans with stories of his career as an actor and host.[20] Rideau died in 2020 at age 90.

Another Southeast city also initiated a strong tradition of horror hosting. During the summer of 1958, a character named Dr. Lucifur made his debut on WSIX (Channel 8) in Nashville. Played by local announcer Ken Bramming, Dr. Lucifur wore a black tuxedo with a white tie and sported a black eyepatch. Carrying himself with a slick and smooth demeanor, he came across as a mix of Bela Lugosi, Vincent Price and John Carradine.[21]

Unlike many of the horror hosts of the era, Dr. Lucifur rarely commented directly on the film being presented that night. Instead, he and his supporting cast of strange characters, including one named Granny Gruesome, performed rehearsed skits in which they parodied current events and popular TV shows of the day.[22] With Dr. Lucifur at the helm, WSIX garnered excellent ratings through the mid–1960s. Even with the ratings maintaining a high level, Bramming and WSIX executives decided that the show had run its full course.[23] In 1967, they agreed to end the show, with Bramming leaving TV to pursue a career in radio. Bramming made periodic returns as Dr. Lucifur before passing away in 1995.

Four years after Bramming left WSIX, another Nashville station decided to continue the tradition of hosted horror. In 1971, WSM (Channel 4) premiered *Creature Feature*, a show hosted by a character known as Sir Cecil Creape. Rather than call on an announcing talent, WSM chose a behind-the-scenes player, a film editor named Russ McCown.[24] With McCown serving as the driving force, Sir Cecil had a presence like no other host. He was not a vampire, or a mad scientist, or a ghoulish figure; no, he was actually a hunchback. With his balding head, unsightly teeth and heavyset frame, Sir Cecil was quite the sight during late-night B-movie presentations.

Sir Cecil Creape became a Nashville sensation, even more popular than his predecessor Dr. Lucifur. WSM helped fuel that popularity by making the identity of Sir Cecil a mystery. The station created a Cecil Creape Fan Club and showcased the heavily made-up hunchback at public events.[25]

With Sir Cecil established as a cult favorite, WSM then made a strange decision. In the fall of 1973, the station moved Sir Cecil from a late-night slot to Saturday afternoons. Young viewers became interested in the character and the show, but the foolish and unnecessary move to daytime froze out many of the show's teenage and adult viewers.[26] By December 1973, Sir Cecil had lost enough of his audience that the show was cancelled.

But Sir Cecil's career in Nashville did not come to an end. By the early 1980s, cable TV had established a niche in Nashville. McCown was working for a new cable station, the Nashville Network, which desperately needed local programming. So the network's executives tapped McCown to reincarnate his Sir Cecil act.[27] From 1983 to '85, Sir Cecil hosted "The Phantom of the Opry" and once again attracted a strong following, though not quite as fervent as his first go-round. Even after the show's cancellation, McCown made guest appearances as Sir Cecil through the early 1990s, before passing away in January 1994.

One other host would have a major impact on Nashville. In 1999, writer-artist Larry Underwood debuted Dr. Gangrene, the host of *Chiller Cinema*, on one of the city's public access channels. The show was originally created as a stand-alone half-hour program before becoming part of a horror film presentation. In creating his persona, Underwood paid tribute to Sir Cecil Creape, whom he had watched in the 1970s and '80s.[28] Dr. Gangrene, who sports a white lab coat that features a patch with the words Sir Cecil's Ghoul Patrol, continues to serve as a Nashville-based host through the spring of 2020. His show is now known as *Dr. Gangrene's Cinetarium*.

With horror hosts having established early momentum in the late 1950s and early '60s, the phenomenon began to gain numbers and popularity during the latter decade. One of the most successful of the hosts was found in the Midwest, where he mesmerized young horror fans, including budding historian David J. Skal:

> My [horror host] in Cleveland was an announcer named Ernie Anderson, who presented himself as Ghoulardi. He had quite a long run, and his successors did too. There was The Ghoul, who wore the same kind of get-up, and the Son of Ghoul.
> Ghoulardi is a beloved memory in Cleveland. He was my first reason to stay up late on a Friday night. I watched mostly these dreadful AIP [American International Pictures] movies—I guess they were being shown for the first time on television—but the very first thing I saw with a horror host was *Queen of Outer Space* with Zsa Zsa Gabor and Eric Fleming and all these people. And the Bert I. Gordon films. And the Roger Corman films, not the Poe films, but the black-and-white cheapies, back in 1957 and '58.
> Ghoulardi started out [in January 1963] with a rather macabre aura that he kind of got rid of; he was a beatnik-like character with a mustache and a beard and a wig that he put on. He became more and more anarchic and transgressive in ways that had nothing to do with sick humor and horror. It had more to do with other local television personalities and the large Polish community, and polkas and kielbasa. It was completely crazy; it was kind of a cult segment of the community. But everybody loved Ghoulardi in Cleveland.[29]

Skal had the chance to meet Ghoulardi during one of his public appearances in Cleveland:

He made an appearance at a local movie theater. I can't remember what they were showing, but Ghoulardi was there, and they had a camera crew. I raised my hand, and he called me up on stage for some reason. I presented him with a profile portrait that I had drawn. I was thinking that I was going to be an art student, though I never did. I liked to draw too many monsters, I think that was the problem! My art teachers weren't giving me a lot of encouragement in that way. He signed the copy to me. He asked me, "Could you make one of these for me, too?" I said, "Yes." I made a copy and sent it off to Ernie Anderson. And so that was a thrill. That was my first television appearance ever.[30]

In 1966, Anderson left Cleveland for Los Angeles, ending the successful run of Ghoulardi. He turned to acting and voiceover assignments, continuing to work up until his death in 1997. Anderson was 73.

By the mid–1960s, horror hosts had become so entrenched in popular culture that mainstream TV series incorporated them into their scripts. The most celebrated example of this occurred in 1966 during the run of CBS's *The Munsters*. In the second season episode "Zombo," the plot pivoted on a local horror host named Zombo who becomes the object of affection of the Munsters' son Eddie. Young Eddie begins to revere Zombo, as his hero, causing his father Herman to become jealous.

Eddie wins a contest that allows him to visit Zombo at the local TV station. When Eddie meets Zombo minutes prior to his makeup transformation, he realizes that his hero is nothing more than a character in costume. At first disillusioned by what he now considers a fraud, Eddie becomes angered, damages the studio and removes part of Zombo's makeup, forcing the host to cut short his show.

In a strange way, the actor playing Zombo is relieved that he has been exposed, mostly because he had grown tired of playing the role. He then takes a moment to sit down with Eddie, explaining that Zombo is nothing more than a character on TV, and that the boy should regard his father, a real man, as his hero and idol.

"Zombo" became one of the most popular of the *71 Munsters* episodes that aired over two seasons. The portrayal of Zombo was so realistic that a number of fans, both children and adults, came to believe that the character was an actual horror host of the era. With his shocking white hair, darkened eye patches and large fangs, Zombo had a frightening appearance that made him convincing.

In addition to the wonderful makeup, the performance of Louis Nye helped make Zombo a hit, even if only in the imagination of *Munsters* viewers. A longtime comedian who specialized in playing arrogant characters, Nye's mannerisms and voice work helped him capture Zombo's identity spectacularly. Many years later, a similarly named horror host, Zomboo, took on an appearance nearly identical to Nye's.

While most of the horror hosts who came directly after Vampira were men, at least one female horror host made an impact on 1960s television. Lisa Clark, a newscaster for KOGO (Channel 10) in San Diego, debuted as a hostess called Cosmomina, but that character lasted only a few weeks.[31] Ditching the persona of Cosmomina, Clark transformed herself into the character's cousin, known by the catchier name Moona Lisa. Clark wore a black, low-cut cat suit with stiletto heels, complementing her long, straight black hair.[32] She played the role for sex appeal, making her popular with young teenage boys who claimed to be interested in the horror and science fiction movies, and not the beautiful girl on parade.[33]

In contrast to most horror hosts, Clark used live props, in the form of a variety of snakes. At times, she wrapped a large python around her body, creating an image like no other seen on late night horror television. Moona Lisa spoke softly and seductively, only adding to her alluring act. She developed several catchphrases, including her standard greeting of "Hello, earthlings." At the end of each show, she signed off by saying, "Happy hallucinations, honeys."

Moona Lisa remained on the air in San Diego until 1972 when she moved to Los Angeles, replacing Seymour as the host of *Fright Night*. But the show did not catch on in the larger market, prompting Clark to return to San Diego, this time working for KFMB. The return to San Diego didn't take, so Clark took Moona Lisa to KMOX in St. Louis. That gig lasted only a year, marking the end of Moona Lisa's tenure as a horror hostess.[34]

Another Los Angeles–area host also enjoyed success before his program, and eventually his life, ended far too abruptly. In 1969, actor Larry Vincent became the host of two separate shows in the Southern California market. On KHJ-TV, he hosted *Fright Night*, and on KTLA, he hosted a Saturday night show called *Seymour's Monster Rally*. In both cases, he portrayed a comical character known as Sinister Seymour (or Seymour for short).

Vincent brought with him plenty of acting experience, having previously appeared on such popular TV shows as *The Flying Nun*, *Get Smart*, *Mannix* and *Mission: Impossible*. As Seymour, he often criticized the film he was hosting, using a style of commentary that could best be described as heckling. He typically appeared wearing a dark cape and a black hat, making himself look like some sort of vampire hunter. Some in Hollywood have speculated that the character of Peter Vincent, portrayed by Roddy McDowall in *Fright Night* (1985), was based in part on the Larry Vincent character.

In contrast to most of the horror hosts, Vincent's Seymour shared much of his screen time with the actual movie that he was presenting. As the film ran, Vincent's character would pop up in a window in the corner of the screen, make a quick comment or two poking fun at the featured film, and then disappear.[35] At other times, he would superimpose himself into the actual film through blue screen effects, making it appear that he was interacting with the characters in the movie.[36]

Vincent's success turned out to be short-lived. The *Fright Night* program ended in 1974. Vincent, who often looked gaunt in appearance, died in March 1975, a victim of stomach cancer. He was only 50.

In 1981, KTLA producers decided they wanted a female host for the show. At first they settled on Vampira, but a dispute soon developed with Maila Nurmi and resulted in the termination of the relationship. The station then held an open audition, which was won by young actress Cassandra Peterson, who had previously played small roles in a number of B-type films.[37] Peterson's character was Elvira, Mistress of the Dark. When Nurmi heard about the hiring of Peterson, she sent a cease-and-desist letter to the station, but the courts eventually ruled in Peterson's favor.[38] The station proceeded with the show, known as *Elvira's Movie Macabre*.

For her role as Elvira, Peterson donned an outfit similar to what Vampira wore: a tight-fitting black gown that was low-cut and highly revealing. But Peterson's vocal delivery was much different than Vampira. It was less Bela Lugosi and far more like a "Valley Girl." As Elvira, Peterson specialized in double entendres, risqué material that often referenced her figure and other themes of a sexual nature.

Much like Vampira, Elvira's fame skyrocketed, but with much more lasting effect. Throughout the 1980s, Peterson signed endorsement deals with numerous companies to create Elvira products, everything from action figures and plastic models to comic books and Halloween costumes.[39] Elvira appeared on a number of magazine covers, with her fame far outreaching the range of the local TV market in Los Angeles.

Elvira's initial KTLA run ended in 1986, but her career received a major boost two years later when Peterson appeared as her alter-ego in a film, *Elvira: Mistress of the Dark*. A horror-comedy written by Peterson, it emphasized humor over scares. It received decent reviews, in spite of its cornball humor, and made Elvira even more popular, fully establishing her as a national presence in American pop culture.

Continuing to make her presence known through public appearances and endorsements, Elvira returned to the TV airwaves in 2010, when *Elvira's Movie Macabre* debuted in syndication. The new horror venture remained on the air through 2014. Elvira then debuted a new show on Hulu. As of 2020, she continues to build on her Elvira brand and still makes frequent appearances at horror and sci-fi conventions.

While most horror hosts of the 1960s, '70s and '80s wore a distinctive costume and relied on goofy humor, mixed in with some slapstick comedy, another West Coast host succeeded with a different approach. Bob Wilkins instead dressed in a suit and tie. With his eyeglasses and neatly combed hair, he looked nothing like the prototypical horror host. He still relied on humor, but it was dry, more subtle, and rarely over the top.

Wilkins' on-screen career began at KCRA in Sacramento, where he was given the opportunity to host horror films on a program called *Seven Arts Theater*. The show developed such a strong following that it led to another opportunity: Former KCRA station manager Tom Breen, who had moved on to the Bay Area, encouraged Wilkins to make the move to KTVU, Channel 40, in San Francisco. With demand for his talents high, Wilkins also did on-air work for KTXL, Channel 40 in the Oakland market.[40]

Of his two Bay Area gigs, the work that he did for KTVU dominated his resumé. For weeks the station hyped his debut via a series of promotional spots. Finally, on January 9, 1971, Wilkins debuted as the host of *Creature Features*. The first film he hosted was hardly a landmark, the campy *The Horror of Party Beach*, but it proved an immediate ratings hit with viewers.[41] Not long after, KTVU became the first TV station in the country to air *Night of the Living Dead*,[42] a far more significant horror film. The airing cemented Wilkins' popularity in the Bay Area.

On some Saturdays, Wilkins' show scored a higher local rating than some of the network offerings, including *Saturday Night Live*.[43] His following became so strong that KTVU made *Creature Features* a twin bill of horror movies each Saturday night. At one point, the station added a Friday night feature, giving Wilkins even more exposure.

Wilkins hosted the films in his unique style, delivering commentary in a soft, low-key voice, but providing lots of subtle, sarcastic humor. He brought a level of sophistication to the industry of horror hosting. While some hosts appealed to the lowest common denominator with silliness and slapstick, Wilkins tried to bring a more adult level of humor to his show, while also adding insight to the films he showcased.

KTVU executives became so enthralled with Wilkins that they allowed him to host a number of TV specials, including *The Bob Wilkins Super Horror Show* and *The Star Trek Dream*.[44] They also encouraged him to make frequent public appearances, allowing his fans to meet him in person.

Wilkins remained a KTVU fixture until 1979, when he decided to leave television and start his own advertising agency. But *Creature Features* persisted, thanks to the groundwork that he had laid. The show remained on KTVU until 1984, completing a nearly 15-year run and enduring far past the expiration date of many similar horror programs. Remaining a beloved figure in the Bay Area, Wilkins was stricken with Alzheimer's disease in his later years. In 2009, he passed away at the age of 76.

While Wilkins had a huge impact on the West Coast, another horror host matched his magnitude on the East Coast. In 1963, Pittsburgh's WIIC (Channel 11) debuted its own version of *Chiller Theater*, hosted by veteran broadcaster Bill Cardille. Cardille had worked as a commercial pitch man and host of numerous other shows on WIIC—in fact, he was the first voice heard on the station when it debuted in 1957—so he seemed like a natural fit for Pittsburgh's version of horror hosting.

Station management made a wise choice is Cardille. Becoming known as "Chilly Billy," he had an approach that was similar to Wilkins. Rather than sport a garish costume and makeup, he essentially played himself. His conversational style, mixed with humor that came from a supporting cast of characters, became a hit in Pittsburgh, where his remarkable run as a horror host lasted nearly 20 years.

As part of his role as a horror host, Cardille lent his support to the production of the 1968 film *Night of the Living Dead*, which was filmed in the Pittsburgh area. For several weeks on his show, Cardille talked about the production of the film and the need for funding. He invited director George Romero, writer John Russo and actor Russell Streiner to appear on his show to promote the film. A number of Cardille's viewers came through with monetary donations, helping Romero complete the project.[45] Cardille appeared briefly in the film, appropriately enough as a television newscaster. It was one of eight acting credits on his film resumé.

On the *Night of the Living Dead* set, Cardille became friends with Streiner, who plays Johnny in the film's memorable opening graveyard sequence. Streiner believes that Cardille's long-term success as a host stemmed from his charismatic nature. "I think the popularity of Bill Cardille in the Pittsburgh area started with his own personality," Streiner explains. "He was naturally outgoing, naturally engaging. And when the opportunity presented itself through the television station—the NBC outlet in Pittsburgh—when that opportunity was presented to do late-night horror, Bill fit the bill quite well."[46] With his wisecracking personality and natural gift for humor, Cardille succeeded in laying down a comic touch for his audience, in a way that was lighter than the over-the-top comedy of hosts like Selwin and Morgus. Streiner recalled Cardille's vast experience:

> Cardille had been in broadcasting since he was a very, very young man. He did some of his early radio work in Erie. Then he moved to the big market of Pittsburgh. The television station would purchase or license certain packages of films. Bill didn't have much to do with the quality of the films; it was whatever was in the package, he would do a double-billed Saturday night screening that would come on right after the prime time news. I think it started at 11:30 Saturday night—he did the show live—and it would run for the full length of two feature films. So he ended up hosting until the early hours of Sunday morning. He did it live.
>
> Not only did he host late-night horror on his *Chiller Theater*, he also during the afternoons would host wrestling, which was very, very popular back in the early days of television. [It aired] Saturday afternoons, and even sometimes during prime time. *Studio Wrestling* was the name of his show in Pittsburgh.
>
> [As a horror host,] he was kind of the commander of the ship. But he had a zany cast of characters around him that created various humorous scenarios. And this all allegedly took place in a castle!
>
> He was surrounded by characters that you could hardly tell what was going to come out of their mouths. And Bill would roll with the punches. He would marshal all of these zany characters together and bring some reason to what was taking place in the castle. He never got too far overboard with silliness on *his* part. He let the zaniness and the humor come from the characters around him. He was always the voice of reason.[47]

The format of Cardille's show scored with the Pittsburgh audience, which grew into a rabid following. "It was probably some of the very early days, in Pittsburgh, of 'destination television,' for people who would tune in faithfully every Saturday night just to see Bill Cardille," says Streiner. "And more to see *him*, in many cases, than the films themselves. The films themselves became kind of second banana to Bill and to the antics of he and his cast of characters."[48]

Chilly Billy became influential in other ways, too. His on-air persona became so popular that it motivated comic actor Joe Flaherty to develop a routine for Second City Television, better known as SCTV.[49] In the 1980s, Flaherty introduced Count Floyd, the host of the imaginary *Monster Chiller Horror Theater* sketches that appeared regularly on *SCTV*. Flaherty, a native of Pittsburgh, had watched Cardille for years and said that Cardille's work motivated him to create the sketches. With Cardille having planted the seed, Flaherty based Count Floyd on Bela Lugosi's portrayal of Dracula, adding an appropriate level of parody to the role.[50]

When *Chiller Theater* came to an end in 1984, Cardille turned to radio broadcasting. He worked as a host for WJAS in Pittsburgh until 2014, when he retired. Two years later, his family revealed that Cardille was suffering from cancer. He died in 2016 at the age of 87, leaving behind a legacy as the king of Pittsburgh's late-night horror.

Of all the trailblazing horror hosts, perhaps none had a better name than Sir Graves Ghastly, who dominated the Saturday afternoon airwaves in Detroit from 1967 to 1982.[51] After the departure of Morgus the Magnificent, the management of WJBK-TV (Channel 2) approached veteran radio and TV broadcaster Lawson J. Deming, who had previously worked on a children's program, about hosting a horror show on Saturday afternoons. Deming was particularly skilled at mimicking a variety of dialects, allowing him to give unique voices to imaginary characters.[52]

The Cleveland-born actor agreed to take the job as a horror host at WJBK. Station management wanted him to create a character similar to that of Ghoulardi, the iconic host in Cleveland. But Deming preferred a fresh approach. He devised a character that took on the persona of a vampire, complete with an exaggerated laugh, light-hearted humor, and a general over-the-top demeanor. With help from his wife, Deming brainstormed a number of ideas for his new challenge.

With his prominent dark mustache, goatee and slicked-back hair, Sir Graves Ghastly served as a parody of some of the vampires portrayed in films during the years of classic horror; in a sense, he took some of the portrayals of Bela Lugosi and John Carradine and ramped up the level of camp for comedic effect. Thus, *Sir Graves Big Show* was born.

The show began with the camera panning over a set made to look like a cemetery, accompanied by a howling wind and the sounds of creaking doors. Eventually becoming known as *Sir Graves Ghastly*, the sketch show featured a steady stable of peripheral characters, including Sir Graves' main sidekick Baruba, who dressed in monk's clothing and wore a hood that covered his face. There was also an apparition named the Glob, whose face was featured in the moon that hung above the main set. Typically, the Glob lip-synched silly song parodies of horror themes. The cast also included a castle maid named Tilly Trollhouse who spoke with a Lugosi-like Hungarian accent. Each show regularly featured an appearance of another character, a smallish caretaker named Reel McCoy, who kicked off the show by removing a movie reel from what appeared to be a grave and presenting it as that afternoon's film discovery.[53]

During commercial breaks, and in between films, Sir Graves and his cast of characters performed sketch comedy pieces that were heavy on slapstick and double entendre. While WJBK-TV (Channel 2 in Detroit) promoted Sir Graves Ghastly as a show for children, a good portion of the humor was aimed at older viewers. Adults comprised roughly one-third of Sir Graves' audience,[54] so it made sense for Deming to appeal to that demographic.

The show's popularity reached a new level in 1969, when WJBK acquired the rights to the classic Universal horror films. Now able to show such classics as *Bride of Frankenstein* and *Dracula*, among others, Sir Graves saw his viewership climb higher.

For a span of 15 years, Sir Graves hosted a Saturday afternoons double feature of horror. On occasion, he hosted a Friday night special that showcased especially popular movies like *Frankenstein* and *King Kong*. Sir Graves developed such a following that Deming marketed his show to his native Cleveland and to Washington, D.C., and it developed a similarly strong appreciation in both locales.

The growing popularity of televised sports in the early 1980s led to the demise of Sir Graves. Opting for live sports coverage on Saturday afternoons, the station started to feature Sir Graves on occasional Sundays, often with little to no promotion. By November 1982, WJBK put Sir Graves on hiatus, but without explanation. A few months later, a change in station management resulted in the cancellation of the program.[55] With Graves approaching his 70th birthday, some TV observers speculated that advancing age had played a part in that decision. But age mattered little to Deming, who soldiered on with his creation. Even after the show fell by the wayside at WJBK, he remained popular in Detroit, speaking at various venues. He continued to make public appearances into the mid–1990s, when he was well into his eighties, before finally retiring his act.[56]

In his later years, Deming suffered from congestive heart failure. He died in 2007 at the age of 94.

While we might not think of chilly Syracuse, New York, as a hotbed of horror, the city produced several popular, if not widely famous, hosts of the genre. The first was Baron Daemon, who debuted for WNYS-TV (Channel 9) in 1962.[57] Played by 23-year-old station news reporter Mike Price, the Baron looked like a parody of a vampire, with a long black cape featuring a high collar and a ridiculously oversized set of eyebrows that made him look far more comical than frightening.

Pretending to hail from Transylvania, Baron Daemon spoke in an exaggerated Bela Lugosi–Dracula accent. But he relied more on energetic slapstick comedy rather than verbal humor. The baron resided in a castle dungeon in which he shared time with two sidekicks: Very Hairy, a silent character who looked like a derelict, and Boris, a diminutive creature who resembled a downsized Frankenstein's Monster.[58]

Although Baron Daemon lacked any kind of sophistication in his approach, he developed such a strong following with his late-night show that the station added a daily afternoon children's show called *The Baron and His Buddies*. In the guise of the baron, Price recorded a song called "The Transylvania Twist." The 45 sold over 10,000 copies, a remarkable number for a local performer. His performance, backed up by two bands, became particularly popular in Syracuse around Halloween.[59]

Despite his popularity in Central New York, Baron Daemon's five-year run ended in 1967. Price remained at NewsChannel 9 for a total of 46 years before finally retiring in 2008. As of 2020, he continues to live in the Syracuse area.

Even before Baron Daemon left the air in the late 1960s, another Syracuse station had already stepped into the business of hosting horror films, this time with a different approach. In 1968, WSYR (Channel 3) brought viewers *Monster Movie Matinee,* which remained a staple of its Saturday afternoon lineup until 1980.[60] The primary host of the show, Dr. E. Nick Witty (a play on the word "inequity"), was portrayed by station weatherman Alan Milair.

Although he didn't attain national fame, he became one of the country's most highly praised horror hosts. In an interesting twist, only Nick Witty's hands could be seen on camera. Viewers were never permitted to see his face, allegedly because he was so gruesome that his mere visage would cause the camera to explode and fans to faint in horror. Originally, Milair intended this only as a promotional gimmick, and planned to show himself eventually. But the gimmick worked so well, leaving something to the imagination of the viewers, that he remained off camera throughout his long run.

Milair's sidekick, a character known as Epal, provided the fodder for many of his routines. A one-eyed werewolf played by announcer Willard Lape (which is Epal spelled backwards), he typically became the subject of Dr. Witty's experiments. Epal underwent a neverending series of operations at the hands of the doctor, who at various times boiled, baked and even beheaded his sidekick.[61]

One of the strongest points of the show was its introduction. With music from *This Island Earth* on the soundtrack, *Monster Movie Matinee* began with a moving camera shot that seemed to move through a scale model graveyard and over a bridge that led to a creepy mansion surrounded by thick fog. The camera would then move inside of the house, proceed up a twisting staircase and close in on a darkened room where a man sat in a chair, only his arm visible to the viewer. From there, Nick Witty began speaking with his distinctly baritone voice. Given the limited budget of WSTM, this creative opening proved highly effective, with special effects far better than the typical fare offered by most local TV stations of the era.

After a change in station management brought the show to an end in 1980, Milair and Lape soon found another forum for their characters: They moved their act to Channel 13 in Syracuse, renamed the show *Tales of Horror* and continued to entertain viewers until 1985.[62] Lape, who was also known by the name Bill Everett, died in 2004. Milair died in 2012, at the age of 81.

The tidal wave of horror-hosting, which reached a peak in the 1960s, showed few signs of abating in the early 1970s. One of the most popular hosts was the Cool Ghoul (not to be confused with Zacherley), a character played by Dick Von Hoene. The veteran reporter and news anchor originated the character on radio in 1961, and had transitioned the act to television by 1969. That's when he joined fledgling TV station WXIX, Channel 19 in Cincinnati.[63] Continuing the persona of the Cool Ghoul, Von Hoene added a creepy costume to complete the move to TV. At first, the costume was deemed too frightening for children, so Von Hoene toned down the look, placing an emphasis on silliness more than fright.

The highlight of the costume was a bright orange-red wig, which became the Cool Ghoul's trademark. The wig, with its long, stringy hair, had an interesting back story. According to Von Hoene, it came from a local morgue; it had belonged to a woman who had died in a car accident. The wig had supposedly been cut in half, the front piece remaining with the woman in her coffin, and the back piece joining Von Hoene and his act![64]

With Von Hoene's long-haired wig, accompanied by a funky, multi-colored hat and a bright red vest, the Cool Ghoul looked a bit like a hippie. Now equipped with a distinctive look to go with his tongue-fluttering, high-pitched verbal style, including his trademark shouts of "Bleeeh!," Von Hoene began hosting a Saturday night show in the early 1970s. He dubbed the show *Scream-In*,[65] a play on the popular comedy sketch series *Rowan and Martin's Laugh-In*.

Von Hoene played the character for laughs, emphasizing a campy sense of humor that became popular with both younger viewers and adults. He played his humor off of his frequent guests, including the puppet character Hattie the Witch. Perhaps the most impressive part of his act was his ability to deliver voice impressions, particularly his memorable rendering of the great Boris Karloff. Von Hoene's Karloff imitation was said to be so good that it once fooled Karloff's secretary, who had worked for him for 30 years.[66]

Scream-In lasted three and a half seasons on WXIX. Von Hoene did not allow the cancellation of the show to end the character. Given the popularity of the Cool Ghoul, he continued to make public appearances in character. As the Cool Ghoul, he also filmed commercials and made local TV appearances during the Halloween season. With the Cool Ghoul still having an impact, Von Hoene eventually came back with his own regular show: Von Hoene moved from Cincinnati to New Bern, North Carolina, where the show found another niche with late-night horror fans into the 1980s.[67]

Von Hoene continued to periodically host TV specials, his last appearance occurring in 2003. The following year, he suffered a fatal heart attack. Von Hoene was 63.

When WKEF in Dayton, Ohio, began looking for ways to beef up its Saturday night offering and improve ratings, one station employee, Barry Hobart, suggested the addition of a late-night horror show. The station liked the idea, and some of Hobart's colleagues recommended that he himself audition for the part as the horror host. Hobart obliged, coming up with a costume that included a monk's robe, makeup that made his face look like a skull, and a set of fangs. Calling himself Dr. Death, Hobart secured the role.[68]

Station management liked Hobart's performance, but some of the powers-that-be felt that his act needed to be toned down. Believing that the character was a bit too frightening, even in a late-night time slot, they told Hobart to rid himself of the skull makeup and fangs and change his character's name. Hobart devised a new name, Dr. Creep, and debuted his alter ego on WKEF in 1972.[69]

As the host of *Shock Theater* (or *Shock Theatre*, as it was later spelled), Dr. Creep introduced a B-movie each Saturday night, playing his part for laughs rather than scares. The show did well, but station management eventually moved its time spot, believing that *Shock Theater* would play better on Saturday afternoons while targeting a younger audience.[70] In 1977, WKEF moved the show back to Saturday nights with the new title *Saturday Night Dead*, a perfect follow-up to NBC's hit comedy sketch show *Saturday Night Live*.[71] In the 1980s, Hobart decided to change the tenor of the humor, making it more risqué and adult-oriented. Some higher-ups at the station did not like the change. By 1985, after a series of battles between Hobart and these executives, WKEF cancelled the show but kept Hobart on staff as a master control operator for six more years. The character again appeared on public access television in the late 1990s: *The New Shock Theater* ran off and on until 2005.[72]

In his later years, Hobart's health declined, primarily due to leg and respiratory problems. Even though he was using a wheelchair, he continued to make public appearances as Dr. Creep until a series of major strokes in December 2010. He passed away in January 2011 at the age of 69.

Yet another Ohio host made his mark at virtually the same time as Dr. Creep and the Cool Ghoul. This character, known simply as The Ghoul, represented a resurrection of an earlier character. Young broadcaster Ron Sweed had previously worked as a production assistant for Ernie Anderson, the creator of Ghoulardi. In 1970, Sweed approached Anderson about the possibility of the veteran broadcaster reviving Ghoulardi, but Anderson was not interested. He did, however, give Sweed permission to revive Ghoulardi on his own.[73]

Renaming the character The Ghoul, Sweed approached Cleveland station WKBF in 1971. Station management liked the idea, giving Sweed the go-ahead to host a new show. At first, Sweed treated the endeavor as a tribute to Ghoulardi, but fans did not take well to what they considered a copycat. So Sweed began to develop his own persona for the Ghoul. Relying heavily on sight gags, the Ghoul performed a number of regular routines, including the setting-off of firecrackers, beating up a rubber frog named Froggy, and blowing up model aircraft and ships.[74] In the Ghoul's mind, the wackier the behavior, the better. And while most of his behavior seemed targeted for a children's audience, the skits also found favor with older viewers.

The Ghoul also made his mark on the films themselves. Sweed liked to create amusing sound clips from novelty records and albums, and then insert them at appropriate times during the films, especially the bad ones. As part of his regular routine, whenever a film character took a drink on screen, Sweed played a recording of a loud belch.[75]

By the early 1970s, the Ghoul had achieved such popularity that Kaiser Broadcasting, the parent company of WKBF, decided to syndicate the show. The Ghoul played in a variety of markets, including Boston, Chicago, Detroit, Philadelphia and San Francisco.[76] The show did not do well in Boston and Chicago, but prospered in Detroit. Despite its success, Kaiser Broadcasting cancelled the show in 1975, largely because of complaints from parents who objected to what they considered its low-grade content.[77] In 1976, the Ghoul returned to independent television in Detroit. In 1998, he made a comeback in Cleveland, this time on WBNX Channel 55. Sweed also dabbled in radio and the Internet and wrote a book titled *The Ghoul*, about his experiences in TV. Sweed remained active until November 2018, when he suffered a heart attack. Never quite recovering from the episode, Sweed died in April 2019 at the age of 70.

The East Coast also had its share of performers. In St. Petersburg, Florida, the character Dr. Paul Bearer developed a following that would last for years. The character, whose name was an obvious play on the word "pallbearer," was the brainchild of Dick Bennick, Sr., whose earlier attempt at horror-hosting had failed. Bennick's Count Shockula did not find favor, so he turned to his Paul Bearer persona at a small North Carolina station in the mid–1960s. The character did not take hold until Bennick joined WTOG in St. Petersburg beginning in 1973.[78]

With his hair parted in the middle and slicked straight down on the sides, and loads of mascara under his eyes, the tuxedo-wearing Dr. Paul Bearer took on the look of an insane mortician. Bennick had an artificial eye, which he sometimes turned to the outside so as to create a twisted look as he peered into the camera. During public appearances, particularly in his later years, Bennick was accompanied by a hearse, his name emblazoned on the side of the vehicle.

Speaking with a gravelly voice, Paul Bearer often referred to the WTOG studios as being located in "St. Creaturesburg."[79] He emphasized silly puns and jokes as part of his act, often delivering them from the confines of a coffin. At times, he lip-synched songs while pretending to play a baby grand piano. And at the end of each show, Paul Bearer declared, "I'll be lurking for you."[80]

Despite his mocking of the films, Paul Bearer remained on the St. Petersburg airwaves until the mid–1990s, making him one of history's longest-running horror hosts. Bennick's tenure ended in 1995 when he died after undergoing open heart surgery. He was 66.

WTOG brought back Dr. Paul Bearer (now played by Richard Koon) in 2009 to serve as the host of *Creature Feature*. In 2015, WTOG renamed its late-night show *Tombstone Tales*[81] and put an emphasis on newer films, including some with no connection to the genre of horror. The show, which remains on the air in 2020, has drawn come criticism because of its relative lack of horror-themed films.

Another long-lasting host made an impact on the nation's capital. Known as Count Gore De Vol, the vampire-like figure debuted on WDCA in Washington, D.C., in 1973. Count Gore is played by announcer Dick Dyszel, who at one time had portrayed Bozo the Clown on local TV.[82] Dyszel has said that the name is a play on the name of author Gore Vidal – but also that it refers to a prominent funeral home, bearing the name of De Vol, that he drove by each day.[83]

Whatever the thinking in creating the name, Dyszel has taken a more sophisticated approach as the host of the show he called *Creature Feature*. Rather than focus his humor on childish sight gags and campiness, Dyszel has appealed to adults through his willingness to offer political satire. As the Count, Dyszel takes shots at Washington politicians, ad libbing his comments as he satirizes the current state of political affairs. The humor might mean little to younger viewers, but has registered with adults in tune to the latest political news from the Beltway.

Dyszel delivers all of his commentary as the Count, a vampire with jet black hair, a widow's peak, dark eyebrows and mustache, and a full black cape straight out of Central Casting. Gore De Vol has no official sidekick, but once shared the stage with the character of Countess Von Stauffenberger, played by actress Eleanor Herman.[84]

The Gore De Vol–Von Stauffenberger exchanges typified the more adult nature of *Creature Feature*. Their conversations included plenty of sexual innuendo and double entendres. The count also showed his proclivity for sexual themes by bringing in a number of Penthouse Pets as in-studio guests.

Ever the daring pioneer, Count Gore De Vol has taken chances in other ways. He became the first horror host to air a completely unedited version of *Night of the Living Dead*,[85] which other stations and hosts considered too graphic for over-the-air TV.

De Vol's *Creature Feature* remained a WDCA staple until 1987, when the station cancelled all of its local programming as a cost-cutting measure. Even without a regular venue, Dyszel continued to make public appearances as Count Gore. In 1998, he took his character to the Internet, becoming the first horror host to present a weekly show online.[86] Dyszel now hosts a show on his own Roku Channel, and regularly appears at monster and horror-themed conventions.

While the one and only Zacherley will always be remembered as Philadelphia's premier horror host, the city received a boost in the 1970s when Dr. Shock took to the airwaves. Based on Zacherley's character of Roland, and with full permission from the legendary host, the character of Dr. Shock was created by amateur magician Joseph Zawislak, who also worked as an insurance salesman, a truck driver and a pinball arcade manager.[87]

Zawislak made Dr. Shock look eerily similar to Roland, a zombielike figure with slicked-back hair and a black frock coat. At the beginning of each show, he emerged from a coffin, later to be joined by his hunchbacked assistant, the one-eyed Boris. Dr. Shock typically ended each show by declaring, "Let there be fright." Those words became an unofficial mantra for Philadelphia schoolchildren, a key segment of Dr. Shock's audience.

Dr. Shock debuted on WPHL in March 1970. He hosted *White Zombie* for his debut show and quickly developed a cult following. But the station cancelled the show after only 13 weeks, spurring over 10,000 angry letters from faithful viewers and an actual protest march.[88] Feeling the pressure, WPHL management brought back Dr. Shock, but only after significant changes. The station demanded that Zawislak tone down the act and make it less frightening, a common reaction from conservative station management in the 1960s and '70s. In response to the demands, Zawislak brought his nine-month-old daughter Doreen onto the show as a kind of unofficial sidekick. Her presence made Dr. Shock less ghoulish and more familial and sympathetic. The show also went through a number of name changes over the years, including *Scream-In, Mad Theater* and *Horror Theater*.[89] No matter the name of the show, Dr. Shock remained popular throughout the 1970s, establishing a late-night niche in Philly. While still serving as host of the show in 1979, the hard-working Zawislak, 42, suffered a massive and fatal heart attack.

Played by broadcaster Jerry Harrell, Doctor Madblood was first seen as part of a Halloween special in early November 1975.[90] Airing on WAVY-TV in Tidewater, Virginia, his show was created as a one-time event, with a number of vignettes that aired during a presentation of the classic *House of Frankenstein*.[91]

Harrell resisted making his character a vampire, believing that too many horror hosts had chosen such a role. He wanted a more creative touch and opted for the less conventional mad doctor. Harrell's doctor was not frightening in appearance, but goofy and comical. He wore a white lab coat and sported a wig of wild and curly silver-colored hair, while specializing in quirky bits of humor. The comic element of the show proved such a hit that WAVY quickly decided to make Doctor Madblood a weekly program, calling it *Doctor Madblood's Movie*. Each week, Harrell made appearances during commercial breaks of films drawn from a package known as "Universal 77 Horror Hits."[92]

The show remained a WAVY staple until 1982, when it was cancelled. Harrell took his act to another Tidewater outlet, public TV station WHRO. Airing in syndication on a half-dozen affiliates, *Doctor Madblood's Nightvisions* provided late-night entertainment for much of the 1980s.[93]

After a successful run in syndication, Harrell moved on in 1989, signing on with WTVZ, an affiliate of FOX, and bringing back the title *Doctor Madblood's Movie*. Harrell incorporated several characters into his vignettes, including a wisecracking sponge-like entity called Brain, a vampire named Count Lucudra and a boxer known as Kid Exorcist.[94] This incarnation of the doctor proved especially popular and remained on the air until 2002.

Doctor Madblood then moved to cable in the Hampton Roads market, joining WSKY-TV as the host of *Doctor Madblood Presents*. For this weekly show, he provided wrap-around material for showings of two vintage TV programs, Boris Karloff's *Thriller* and *Alfred Hitchcock Presents*, before switching to *Rod Serling's Night Gallery*. The Madblood show came to an end in 2007, capping a run of over 30 years,[95] but the character continues to make public appearances in the Hampton Roads market.

While many of the horror hosts of the 1960s and '70s have faded away, either because of changing tastes or the deaths of the actors, a few new hosting talents have managed to carry on into the 21st century. One of the more prominent is a man who does not wear a formal costume, but has succeeded in taking on the persona of an alter-ego, a comical and insightful character named Joe Bob Briggs.

Briggs was born John Bloom in Dallas, Texas, where he would eventually establish himself as an award-wining investigative reporter for local newspapers. Given his love of drive-in and B-movies, Bloom began writing satirical reviews of such films under the pseudonym Joe Bob Briggs. In one of his articles, he penned a parody of the song "We Are the World," calling it "We Are the Weird." That created enough controversy that the *Dallas Times-Herald* decided to fire him.[96]

Undeterred, Bloom developed a one-man comedic stage show that led to his being hired as a horror host for The Movie Channel. From 1987 to 1996, he hosted *Joe Bob's Drive-In Theater*. Rather than wear a full costume like other hosts, Bloom took on the persona of Briggs by sporting casual, western-style clothing and promoting himself as a Texas redneck who specialized in sarcastic humor.[97] Like most hosts, Briggs would poke fun at the late-night film, but would also provide insights into the making of the movies, along with information on the whereabouts of the actors involved.

When the Movie Channel changed its format in the early 1990s, Briggs took his talents to TNT, where he became even more popular as the host of *Monster Vision*. During the last half of the 1990s, Briggs and *Monster Vision* provided late-night entertainment on Friday nights. With his passion for films of the genre, and his likable and amusing on-air manner, Briggs became a huge hit with audiences.

In spite of the success, TNT cancelled *Monster Vision* in 2000, forcing Briggs to reemphasize his writing career, which he had never fully abandoned even during his television stints. Writing under the name of Briggs, Bloom penned freelance articles for a number of national outlets, including *Rolling Stone* and *Playboy*,[98] and authored several books, some of which included his humorous reviews of a variety of B-movies, chillers and various other exploitation films.

In 2018, Briggs made a celebrated return to broadcasting by signing on with the streaming service Shudder, where he hosted special marathons of movies on three occasions. The marathons drew so many subscribers that Shudder made his show a weekly Friday night event. *The Last Drive-In with Joe Bob Briggs* scored well with audiences, prompting Shudder to renew the program for a second season in 2020. With his cutting humor and encyclopedic knowledge of horror films, Briggs remains a major force in the field of horror hosting.

Along with Briggs, another prominent host to emerge in contemporary culture is Svengoolie, who lives on as a Saturday night staple of Me-TV. But the actor who currently plays Svengoolie is not the same man who created the role in 1970; that was the late Jerry Bishop, who debuted Svengoolie for WFLD in Chicago.[99]

Bishop's show aired originally under the name of *Screaming Yellow Theater with Host Svengoolie*, a strange title that stemmed from a yellow popcorn snack known as Screaming Yellow Zonkers.[100] Residing in a brightly colored coffin, Svengoolie looked like a cross between a hippie and a ghoul. (That makes sense since "Svengoolie" is a combination of "Svengali" and "ghoul.") Bishop sported long hair wrapped with a headband, along with an elongated mustache and a beard, all set against a face whitened with makeup and topped off by a pair of dark sunglasses. In completing the picture, Svengoolie typically wore garish multi-colored striped pants that could only have been worn during Woodstock.

In offering comments about the films he presented, Svengoolie emphasized silly, cornball comedy that was typical for hosts of the era. As the original purveyor of Svengoolie, Bishop presided over the show until the late summer of 1973, when Kaiser Broadcasting took over WFLD and cancelled the weekly offering.[101]

Then came the second incarnation of Svengoolie, which resulted shortly after Field Communications reassumed the leadership of WFLD. Bishop and one of his loyal fans, a young man named Rich Koz, began to discuss the possibility of a comeback for the character. In June 1979, *Son of Svengoolie* came to WFLD, this time with Koz in the role and Bishop serving as an advisor. With Bishop's permission and endorsement, Koz carried on the legacy of hosted horror.[102] Having shed the hippie appearance, the now top-hatted Son of Svengoolie looked much different than his predecessor, but retained the tradition of corny, vaudeville-type humor.

Bishop eventually left his advisory role and returned to his roots in radio, working in that field until his death from a heart attack in 2013. In the meantime, Son of Svengoolie remained a Chicago TV staple, and also aired in other markets like Boston, Detroit and San Francisco, until Field Communications sold the station to Rupert Murdoch in 1986. Once again cancelled, *Son of Svengoolie* remained in mothballs until 1995, when Koz joined independent station WCIU and resurrected the character for a second time, but with an alteration. Now claiming that Son of Svengoolie had "grown up," Koz dropped "Son of" from the name, simply calling himself Svengoolie.[103] Koz's character, along with sidekicks like Kerwyn (a rubber chicken) and Doug Graves (a musician who plays the keyboard), has become a staple of television ever since.

Beginning in 2011, Koz and Svengoolie transitioned from local television to a national presence when he joined the cable network Me-TV, where has continually hosted a Saturday evening presentation of classic horror films, usually ranging from the 1930s to the 1980s. He also retains a strong presence in the Chicago area, where he makes frequent public appearances in costume.

While the sheer volume of hosts is not now what it once was, the horror personalities of today have succeeded in reviving the concept of a late-night host, and some with the benefit of a national forum. If anything, there seems to be a growing interest in the concept of horror-hosting, as fans of the genre clamor to be a part of a community. In an age when Facebook and Twitter have brought the average citizen into the public spotlight, allowing them to interact (and often clash) with others, it only makes sense that like-minded horror fans would seek out ways to come together while watching their favorite films, especially those of a vintage nature. The horror hosts of the 21st century have been charged with the responsibility of galvanizing that community—and that can only be a good development for those who share a passion for ghosts, monsters and creations of the imagination.

Chapter Seven

Creature Features, Fright Night and *Block of Shock* (1931–1969)

There is no question that the 1957–'58 "Shock" packages gave the horror genre a dynamic and energetic boost at an important time in cinema history. Without those films coming into syndication, a previous era of horror might have been ignored and eventually forgotten, and a new generation of horror fans might have been stunted.

As well-executed as the packages were, they represented a relatively small sampling of horror. Fewer than 50 horror films were released in the two packages, and of those, only about 40 could be considered good or even above-average movies. Based on sheer volume, that small vault of films figured to satiate horror appetites for a few years, but would likely become tired and overdone if aired over and over again, particularly within the same repeated format of hosted horror.

In order to continue generating interest in the genre, new films needed to be added to the cauldron of syndication. Those additions would come throughout the 1960s, not necessarily in the form of a large, formalized package of films, but rather through a constant trickling of smaller film packages, variously referred to as "Creature Features," "Fright Night," "Block of Shock" and other names.

While there is no single package of films that had quite the impact of the two "Shock Theater" deliveries, these packages of films encompass everything from that first glorious era of horror in the 1930s to the more graphic films of the 1960s and '70s. (In some cases, the films from the later years were cheesy and inexpensive, and not exactly classics of the genre.) Many of the films could be categorized as straight and conventional horror, but many could also be classified more accurately as science fiction, particularly those with a futuristic bent. Some easily cross both genres.

In finding films that truly represent the horror genre, there is no shortage of viable *Creatures Features* or *Fright Night* offerings. In terms of a chronological order, we'll date them back to the remarkable year of 1931, when horror made a huge step in its transition from silent films to the talking picture era.

Arguably the most influential year in horror film history, 1931 certainly received its due in the initial "Shock Theater" package, thanks to the release of *Dracula* and *Frankenstein* to local TV stations. But the "Shock Theater" package did not include another important horror film which originally debuted in New York City on New Year's Eve 1931. That's because *Dr. Jekyll and Mr. Hyde* was not a product of Universal, but came from another formidable studio, Paramount, which hoped to cash in on the recent box office success of the horror genre.

Dr. Jekyll and Mr. Hyde has been adapted onto film numerous times, both before and since the Paramount version, but never better than when Fredric March passionately took on the two title roles. March's performance as both characters turned out so brilliantly that he earned an Academy Award for Best Actor and carried the film to legendary status among early horror films. March became the first actor to claim an Oscar for his or her performance in a horror movie.

Based on Robert Louis Stevenson's famous novella, "The Strange Case of Dr. Jekyll and Mr. Hyde," the film places the focus on the work of Dr. Henry Jekyll (pronounced as JEE-kul in this film version). Dr. Jekyll believes that man's evil side can be separated from the good and ultimately dispatched. Using himself as his own experimental body, Dr. Jekyll concocts a chemical potion that helps transform him from a kind, rational, even-keeled physician into a raving madman that he calls Edward Hyde.

As the beastly Hyde, his manner is coarse and vulgar; he treats others abominably and commits horrific crimes, giving Jekyll feelings of guilt. His actions as Hyde include cheating on Jekyll's fiancée Muriel by his involvement with a prostitute, Ivy Pearson, whom he abuses sexually and psychologically. Jekyll eventually responds to the guilt by no longer ingesting the chemical formula, but he finds that the corrective measure is too late: He now cannot control the transformations, and continues to become Mr. Hyde against his will.

March is brilliant in both roles, showing his full range as an actor. At one moment, March is charming and amicable as Dr. Jekyll; the next, he is the raving lunatic Hyde. It's almost as if two different actors took on the two characters, but it is indeed March all along, displaying a wide range of acting emotions and making us believe every moment of it. March is ably supported by the excellent direction of Rouben Mamoulian, who oversees seamless camera work and a fine use of light and shadow. Showing a creative touch, Mamoulian begins the film by giving us the point of view of Dr. Jekyll, before switching the camera smoothly to a third-person perspective. Unlike many films of the early 1930s, *Dr. Jekyll and Mr. Hyde* does not suffer from the awkward and clunky movements of camerawork typical of the early days of the sound era.

Even the special effects, depicting the gradual transition of Jekyll into the beastly, werewolf-like Hyde, are well ahead of their time, accomplished through the use of color filters that are removed one by one.[1] The treatment applied to March's face by makeup man Wally Westmore was very effective, but was also accentuated by the actor's extraordinary skill in conveying the facial expressions of a madman.

In directing *Dr. Jekyll and Mr. Hyde*, Mamoulian succeeds in creating a dark and violent film, one that concerned the censors, even in the days before the enforcement of the Motion Picture Production Code (also known as the Hays Code). The film delves into controversial and provocative themes, including the prominent role for prostitute Ivy Pearson, played by Miriam Hopkins. There is more than a hint of sexuality in both the skimpy clothing worn by Pearson and the suggestive dialogue between her and Hyde. The censors demanded a number of cuts, but Mamoulian found his way around most of those demands, at least for the initial theatrical release of the film. In 1936, Paramount re-released the film, this time with roughly eight minutes of footage eliminated.[2]

One of the few weaknesses of *Dr. Jekyll and Mr. Hyde* is the sometimes melodramatic dialogue assigned to the female characters, a common problem with films during the early years of sound. The by-play between Jekyll and his fiancée, who is discouraged from marrying him by her overbearing father, can be cringe-inducing, but those exchanges don't last long enough to detract from the rest of the film.

March's acting overshadows this small pitfall. Another strength involves the spectacular sets and scenery, which are photographed beautifully. A total of 35 studio sets, all regarded as historically accurate,[3] were created for *Dr. Jekyll and Mr. Hyde*. The end result is a film that looks far different than *Dracula* and *Frankenstein*, two films that featured far more primitive film techniques. *Dr. Jekyll and Mr. Hyde* looks more like a movie from the 1940s or '50s, simply based on its level of sophistication.

The film proved a huge success for Paramount, which was hoping to match the popularity of Universal's *Dracula* and *Frankenstein*. Unfortunately, the flow of income did not prevent the studio from declaring bankruptcy in 1933.[4] But those financial concerns matter little in the context of the quality of the film, the first from the genre of horror to earn an Academy Award of any kind. Of all of the adaptations of the Stevenson story, this one is likely the best. *Dr. Jekyll and Mr. Hyde* is a veritable classic, bolstered by its lead actor, its elaborate backdrops, and a well-told story of good doing battle with evil.

Shortly after *Dr. Jekyll and Mr. Hyde*, another classic from the era became a late entrant into the hosted horror sweepstakes, but did not gain traction on American television until the 1960s. MGM's *Freaks*, directed by Tod Browning, debuted in Los Angeles theaters on February 12, 1932, and then disappeared for decades. Why did it take so long for *Freaks* to make its way into living rooms? The reason is rather simple: There was no more controversial film of the hosted horror era than *Freaks*. The film used deformed circus and carnival performers as actors, creating such a stir among critics and fans that it was banned in parts of the United States. But it is a film that is effective in large part because it is so realistic, not to mention how diabolical it is in content and tone.

In *Freaks*, beautiful trapeze artist Cleopatra (Olga Baclanova) shows interest in Hans (Harry Earles), a sideshow dwarf. (Earles appeared in *The Wizard of Oz* seven years later.) Cleopatra is already romantically tied to another performer, Hercules the strongman, and is only interested in Hans because he is about to inherit money. She convinces him to leave his fiancée for her, and Hans foolishly agrees. At their wedding party, a drunken Cleopatra poisons Hans while also letting slip her true feelings about him and the other freaks. This leads the deformed carnival performers to exact revenge on her.

Browning, best known for his direction of *Dracula* one year earlier, succeeds in creating a realistic backdrop for *Freaks*, one that is tinged with an atmosphere of dread and unhappiness. Browning knew well about this kind of venue, having left his family as a teenager to work for a traveling circus. That knowledge helped him create especially authentic sets for the film. Browning also advanced the film through his ability to build suspense, which explodes into a crescendo of violence at the end.

The realism of the film is aided by Browning's employment of genuine circus performers who suffered from a variety of physical deformities. Browning's cast included conjoined twins, a bearded woman and so-called "pinheads," who featured misshapen skulls. Browning took heavy criticism for his casting decisions, which many considered exploitative.

Prior to its official release, the studio ran test screenings of *Freaks*. Browning's original print included an extended scene showing the freaks attacking Cleopatra, along with a brutal scene where Hercules is castrated. Test audiences responded with such revulsion that MGM made a number of cuts to the film, hoping to lessen its graphic nature.[5]

Even with the offending scenes gone, the February theatrical release still horrified viewers and film critics alike. *Freaks* upset most established critics, who wondered how Browning could create such a distasteful story. "*Freaks* was disowned by the studio," says horror historian David J. Skal.[6] That is no exaggeration. In response to the outcry, MGM decided to pull

Freaks from theaters, cutting short its scheduled release in the U.S. In the meantime, Browning's career was essentially ruined; he would make only four more films, two of which were uncredited.

The long-term reaction was no better. For nearly 30 years, most American television stations refused to show *Freaks*. The United Kingdom, because of complaints from British censors, banned the movie outright for three decades.[7] It was not until the early 1960s that a renewed interest in *Freaks* led to it being shown more regularly in the U.S. By then, some movie theaters presented Browning's film in special midnight screenings. By the 1970s, *Freaks* had become a staple of late-night television horror.

Although the film technically remains banned in some states, much of the controversy surrounding *Freaks* has died down. Still, the film is debated for other reasons. The dialogue is subpar at times, and the acting from the real-life circus performers leaves something to be desired. There are also those critics who contend that *Freaks* is really not a horror film, but actually a drama that is almost documentarian in style. There may be some merit to all of these criticisms, but the atmosphere, the characters and the story of revenge all reek of legitimate horror, making it an uncomfortable but essential part of the genre.

While *Freaks* disappeared for decades because of controversy, another 1932 film also became lost for different reasons. At one point, it was believed that *White Zombie* was gone forever, all prints having disappeared from circulation. But the film was retrieved in the 1960s, albeit in relatively poor quality. Restoration efforts have made the film's condition better over time, though not up to par with other films from the 1930s.

Many critics have called *White Zombie* overrated, citing the over-the-top performances by the supporting cast members and its slow pace. Upon its New York City release on July 28, 1932, it received poor reviews but drew good crowds. The film is historically significant for its groundbreaking treatment of the theme of zombies and for the visual character created by its star, Bela Lugosi.

Coming just one year after the release of Lugosi's *Dracula*, *White Zombie* features Lugosi as Murder Legendre, an unscrupulous voodoo witch doctor and owner of a sugar cane mill. Murder is asked for help by a wealthy plantation owner, Charles Beaumont, who hopes to romantically entice a young woman, even though she is committed to another man. Beaumont gives her a strange potion provided by Murder, which makes her fall for him, but also turns her into an emotionless, zombie-like creature. Beaumont pleads with Murder to reverse the effects of the potion, but he refuses. Beaumont himself begins to slip into a zombie-like state.

Lugosi reportedly received a meager salary for his participation, and this became a sore point with the horror legend.[8] Based on the stunning visual and audible presence that he created with his character, Lugosi was severely underpaid. He takes on a menacing, almost satanic appearance, fully equipped with a bizarre goatee, while voicing his lines with his trademark slow-paced, eerie delivery that underscores every evil word he utters. The stare of his piercing eyes, reminiscent of his appearance in *Dracula*, adds to his wonderfully sinister character. Lugosi's effort stands out in the film.

The makeup effects of the zombies are quite good; they are made to look utterly lifeless, as they follow the commands of the despicable Murder. Director Victor Halperin (assisted by his brother, producer Edward Halperin) succeeds in creating a creepy tone which is enhanced by an excellent musical score and intriguing voodoo sound effects. *White Zombie* presents some of the most memorable film images from the 1930s, including the infamous sugar mill staffed by a team of zombies, along with the silhouetted appearance of the creatures as they walk lifelessly along a hillside, set against the backdrop of the moon.

The ending of the film, dramatically shot at the seaside residence of Murder, is also quite good. All in all, the Halperins present a disturbing film, one that was particularly shocking to audiences of the early 1930s.

Where *White Zombie* fails is in its snail-like pacing, a lack of physical action, and the exaggerated acting efforts of some of the supporting cast, some of whom seem stuck in the performing style of the silent era. The film, shot on a shoestring budget, features poor sound recording, making it difficult to hear some of the dialogue. With filming completed in only 11 days,[9] the final product clearly shows symptoms of being rushed. As a result of all of these flaws, *White Zombie* does not hold up as well as many of the classic horror films of the 1930s.

While the film is not particularly entertaining or engrossing, it has become a worthwhile movie for historical reasons. Perhaps its one-time status as a lost film has increased appreciation for its value. To lose the movie would have been particularly galling since it is the first full-length feature film to deal with zombies. As such, it has become a model for future filmmakers and TV directors, some of whom have borrowed from the makeup and acting techniques seen in *White Zombie*. Without *White Zombie*, we might not have received the benefits of later films like *The Plague of the Zombies*, *Night of the Living Dead*, *Sugar Hill* and the original *Dawn of the Dead*, or in a more modern context, a TV show like *The Walking Dead*. While *White Zombie* has its share of shortcomings, its pioneering effort makes it an important film—and a significant showcase for the unique talents of Lugosi.

The theme of lost films continued with another 1932 release, *The Old Dark House*. The Boris Karloff venture is as much comedy as it is pure horror and received more criticism than praise at the time of its initial limited release on October 19, followed by a full release on the 20th. Yet, in retrospect it has gained favor as a cult classic, in part because of a stand-out cast boasting the talents of not only Karloff, but Ernest Thesiger, Charles Laughton, Eva Moore, Raymond Massey, Melvyn Douglas and a very young Gloria Stuart. All of them performed well under the direction of the brilliant James Whale. Along with *Frankenstein*, *Bride of Frankenstein* and *The Invisible Man*, *The Old Dark House* is considered one of Whale's classic horror films, making him one of the most successful directors in genre history.

The Old Dark House tells the story of several travelers, trapped in a driving rainstorm that is creating floods and landslides, who find refuge in a secluded mansion in a remote part of Wales. The travelers soon discover that the residents, the Femm family, consist of a collection of certified weirdos—highly unpredictable characters who are headlined by an intoxicated and violent butler, played by Karloff. In addition to the butler and the Femm family residents who are allowed to roam free throughout the large house, there is also a mysterious family member who is kept locked in one of the rooms because of his violent and unpredictable nature.

For many years, *The Old Dark House* was believed to be a lost film. It remained so until 1968, when Curtis Harrington, a friend of Whale, found a print in a Universal vault and convinced the George Eastman House to restore it.[10] After initial efforts, the film's appearance remained somewhat murky and dingy, but it has since been digitally remastered and now looks superb.

In this case, as with *White Zombie*, perhaps absence led to greater appreciation. Upon its restoration, *The Old Dark House* became the recipient of much praise—and with good reason. Karloff is wonderful as the drunken and mute butler, a frightening man and a brutish force who seems capable of doing just about anything. Laughton plays his role as one of the stranded strangers with offbeat but charming bluster. Then there is Ernest Thesiger as homeowner Horace Femm, foreshadowing his memorable *Bride of Frankenstein* role,

7. Creature Features, Fright Night *and* Block of Shock (1931–1969) 93

The Old Dark House (1932): With an overgrowth of beard, a crooked nose and tussled hair, Boris Karloff takes on the role of the film's crazed, alcoholic butler, Morgan. In his clutches is Margaret, one of five stranded guests at the house. She is played by a young Gloria Stuart, who was all of 22 during filming (Photofest).

while stealing scenes with his odd appearance, his distinctive speaking style and his general strangeness. Just as effective is Eva Moore, who portrays Femm's malevolent and deranged sister with gusto. Moore, Thesiger and Laughton deliver their lines in an over-the-top style, but it all seems right in creating a wonderful blend of comedy and sinister tension.

Perhaps Whale's most intriguing casting decision involved the role of Sir Roderick Femm, the ancient family patriarch who lives in a secluded room on the house's top floor. The credits list John Dudgeon as the actor playing Roderick, but in reality, the role was handled by an actress named Elspeth Dudgeon.[11] In viewing the film, it is quite obvious that Dudgeon is female portraying a male. Whale never explained the strange casting choice, but ultimately, it doesn't detract from the overall effectiveness of *The Old Dark House*.

Whale also manages to create another character through the house itself, which consists of a combination of finely detailed Gothic sets. Some have called *The Old Dark House* the first haunted house movie, though there are no ghosts present in the building. It is a highly atmospheric film that establishes an excellent prototype for future films set in large, dark houses. The atmosphere is also aided by the soundtrack, which is full of booming thunderclaps timed to coincide with critical moments throughout the story.

Some of the original criticism of *The Old Dark House* still carries through today. Some viewers have claimed that the comedy sometimes overwhelms the horror, demeaning it in the process. Clearly, Whale wanted to create a parody of horror films of that time period. He may have gone too far, at least in the eyes of some. It is a point that will continue to be debated.

The Old Dark House was not included in the original "Shock Theater" package,[12] despite being a Universal release from the same time period as the other films. The absence from the "Shock" package makes it one of those old-time horror films that has been seen by relatively few fans of vintage horror. That is a shame, but the situation will likely be corrected as the film continues to receive air time on networks like Turner Classic Movies. With its blend of comedy and horror and its eclectic collection of great acting talents, *The Old Dark House* is a film that deserves to be seen by any fan of the genre.

Of all the 1932 horror releases, one of the best came out in December. *Island of Lost Souls* is a classic that boasts the talents of Charles Laughton and Bela Lugosi. Based on the H.G. Wells novel, the film caused major controversy upon its release.

Laughton takes center stage as Dr. Moreau, an intelligent but completely obsessed and deranged scientist who has been conducting experiments in evolution. Moreau's end result is the creation of a race of half-human, half-creature abominations that reside on his remote island, where Moreau has apparently been banished. The island residents included pig-men, dog-men, wolf-like beings and other mixed breeds of beastlike creatures that represent samples of Moreau's horrific experiments.

Shipwreck survivor Edward Parker comes into conflict with the detestable captain of the vessel that rescued him. As a consequence, the captain throws him off the ship and into a boat belonging to Dr. Moreau, who has no choice but to take Parker to his island. At first, Moreau is charming and welcoming, but Parker eventually learns about the doctor's secret experiments and their grotesque results. Parker's arrival spurs Moreau to a new goal: the mating of Parker with a panther woman named Lota, his most perfect human-animal to date.

The idea of creating half-human, half-animal mutants was dangerous material, regarded by some as taboo in the early 1930s and controversial to the point of spurring censorship, even in the days before the enforcement of the Hays Code. Objecting to the radical themes and the suggested violence, some Midwestern theaters chose not to play *Island of Lost Souls*. Additionally, British censors refused to put their stamp of approval on it. The film remained banned in England until 1958.[13]

While Laughton received top billing, Lugosi had to settle for something less. No higher than fourth-billed, he was paid roughly $800,[14] largely because he had declared bankruptcy in mid–October and badly needed employment.[15] While it is a relatively small role, Lugosi is effective and impactful as the Sayer of the Law, who shouts out and repeats the rules to the other island creatures. The Sayer roughly resembles a werewolf but seems to have more articulation and intelligence than the island's other abominations.

As with all films from the early 1930s, *Island of Last Souls* bridges the transition gap from the silent era to the era of sound. At times, the placement of sound seems like an afterthought, creating some awkwardness within the film. The pace is also too slow for more modern tastes, but it is not so lagging that it destroys the picture's effectiveness. Laughton is excellent in his portrayal of Moreau; he is charismatic on the outside, but truly menacing and malicious in character. Laughton claimed that he based his appearance on that of his dentist. Whatever the inspiration, the characterization worked for him.

Island of Lost Souls did not come without difficulty—and near-tragedy. One of the film's

7. Creature Features, Fright Night *and* Block of Shock (1931–1969) 95

uncredited actors, Joe Bonomo, nearly drowned when he fell into a large tank of water. The foam rubber in his costume began to absorb water and became heavy. Bonomo began to sink, but was rescued from drowning.[16]

Director Erle C. Kenton completed the picture, only to be greeted with largely negative reaction due to its content. That criticism abated over time, and the film is no longer banned. The performances of Laughton and Lugosi, the willingness to tackle a controversial theme, and a strong, pulsating, fast-paced climax make *Island of Lost Souls* a must-see film that stands out for its shock value in the early years of the sound era.

In terms of volume, 1933 turned out to be a relatively thin year for horror films. One 1933 film, *The Invisible Man*, helped fill out the roster of the initial "Shock Theater" package. The other would have to wait until later to make its mark on late-night TV.

There's little doubt that the original *King Kong*, which premiered in New York City on March 2, 1933, is a full-fledged classic and an important film, but there are a few who debate whether it's truly horror or merely science fiction. Given the amount of death and destruction that the giant beast inflicts on the landscape and his captors, I think it's safe to say that the film fully encompasses the genre of horror. And without question, it's an essential film from the early history of 1930s talking pictures.

In presenting what has become a well-known story, *King Kong* unveils the plan of director Carl Denham, who wants to travel to an exotic and mysterious location, Skull Island, so that he can film his next wildlife picture. Needing a leading lady, Denham becomes so desperate that he literally searches the streets for an actress, before stumbling upon an unemployed performer named Ann Darrow. He convinces her to travel with him by ship to the island, based largely on the promise of adventure and excitement. Traveling with Darrow and his crew to the remote Skull Island, Denham soon discovers why it has been regarded as such a mysterious destination; it is inhabited by prehistoric creatures, including a gigantic gorilla.

As Darrow and his crew secretly observe a native ceremony in which a young woman is about to be sacrificed to the beast, they are spotted. The native chief expresses a desire to trade six of his women for Ann, so that she can be sacrificed, but the offer is rejected. Later that night, the natives sneak aboard the ship, kidnap Ann and offer her to the beast, who becomes smitten with the actress. Ann's new love interest, Jack Driscoll, begins pursuing the monster through the treacherous jungle in an effort to rescue her. Driscoll extracts Ann from Kong, and then Denham and his crew capture the gorilla. Denham makes the ill-fated decision to transport him to New York, setting the stage for tragic mayhem in a crowded city ill-equipped to handle a large prehistoric beast.

King Kong's stop-motion animation effects, which were devised by Willis O'Brien, are now outdated, but for the early 1930s, they were considered groundbreaking. The rest of the film, from the visual presentation to the performances of the lead actors, raises it to a level of high cinematic achievement. Fay Wray brings beauty and grace to the character of Ann, while Robert Armstrong and Bruce Cabot are more than capable as Denham and Driscoll, respectively. Yet, they are all overshadowed by the 50-foot ape known as Kong.

The imagery and camerawork push *King Kong* into the territory of a remarkable film. At one point, there is a ten-minute gap in dialogue, with the story told only through visual images. Uncredited directors Ernest B. Schoedsack and Merian B. Cooper lay out the outdoor scenery in incredible detail, presenting both Skull Island and New York City in a dynamic and revolutionary way. The use of music is also critical; *King Kong* was one of the first films to feature a full-length, symphonic musical score,[17] which enhances the

King Kong (1933): Now captive in New York City and shackled at the wrists, waist and ankles, the gargantuan Kong is showcased like a grand zoo attraction. At the bottom left, Jack Driscoll (Bruce Cabot), Ann Darrow (Fay Wray) and Carl Denham (Robert Armstrong) greet the audience, unaware that chaos that is about to ensue (courtesy of Frank Dello Stritto).

drama of the story and the fear that the monstrous gorilla imposes on the human characters.

Not only does *King Kong* succeed artistically, but it proved to be a savior for RKO, which had lost significant money in 1932. During its opening weekend of theatrical release in 1933, *King Kong* brought in a gross sum of $90,000, a record-setting total for the time.[18] The film debuted at New York City's two largest theaters, the Roxy and Radio City Music Hall. Shown in each theater ten times a day during the opening weekend, the *King Kong* screenings sold out each time.[19]

As a film that involves horror, fantasy and adventure, *King Kong* continues to have an impact. One of the most innovative films in history, it was only the second movie to showcase a monster of oversized proportions; *The Lost World*, a silent film, was the first to do so in 1925.[20] Additionally, *King Kong* employed special effects and visual techniques that had never before been attempted. The editing style was also unique, emphasizing sudden and surprising action over the usual emphasis on unnecessary scene-setting. And then there is the epic ending, the memorable sequence featuring the monster atop the Empire State Building, some 102 stories above the ground.

For all of these reasons, *King Kong* has influenced a number of film directors – not just those who have attempted remakes of the original, but other filmmakers within the larger scope of the horror and science fiction genres. All these years later, *King Kong* remains as powerful as the beast who became its star.

A smaller, but still significant monster also made its debut in 1933. Boris Karloff's talents were put to use in the English-made *The Ghoul*, a Gaumont British production. Debuting in

7. Creature Features, Fright Night *and* Block of Shock (1931–1969)

King Kong (1933): Perched atop the Empire State Building (which in real life features 102 stories), and with a broken shackle attached to his left wrist, an angry Kong swats at one of the Curtiss Helldiver military planes attacking him with gunfire (courtesy of Frank Dello Stritto).

America on November 25, *The Ghoul*'s longtime status as a lost film has contributed to its less-than-stellar reputation. Now that an original, uncut version has been found, and the film can finally be seen in all of its intended glory, it has taken its place as part of the Karloff essential library.

The first British horror film of the sound era, *The Ghoul* stars Karloff as the title character, an Egyptologist named Morlant who is bedridden and dying from some unknown, disfiguring disease. Morlant has acquired a precious jewel, known as the Eternal Light, which he believes will allow him to be rejuvenated. Prior to his death, Morlant instructs his manservant Laing to prepare his body for burial by placing the jewel in his hand and wrapping it in bandages. Instead of doing as told, Laing steals the gem, inspiring the arrival of several intruders who want the gem for themselves. At the next full moon, Morlant rises from the dead, seeking revenge against those who dared to betray him.

Some critics claim that Karloff's Ghoul looks like a cross between Frankenstein and the Mummy. In one of Karloff's most impressive scenes, he commits an act of self-mutilation, permissible in the years before the enforcement of the Hays Code. Karloff is capably supported by an excellent cast that includes the inimitable Ernest Thesiger, who plays the manservant in a deadpan way that carries a comedic quality, and Cedric Hardwicke, who plays a scheming solicitor. The film also marks the debut of young Ralph Richardson, who would later reinforce his horror reputation in such films as *Tales from the Crypt*.

After its initial run in theaters, *The Ghoul* was not seen for decades. With no prints believed to remain in existence, it was considered a lost film, at least until a poor nitrate copy was finally discovered in the Czech National Archives in Prague. It contained several bad splices, which affected the continuity and flow of the film.[21] *The Ghoul*'s public domain status also contributed to the problem. When the original copyright holder failed to renew, bootleg filmmakers made numerous copies, which often appeared blurry and featured numerous sloppy edits.[22] The film was seen in this subpar condition for years, leading to its reputation as a below-average film.

Then workers at Shepperton Studios in England found the film's nitrate negative—and in nearly perfect condition. The British Film Institute ordered new prints of the film to be made, clearing the way for the English network, Channel 4, to air the complete original version. Seen in this incarnation, the way it was intended to be, *The Ghoul* gained a new appreciation among fans who had only been treated to the heavily edited and blurred versions.

In its true form, *The Ghoul* is a much better film, buttressed by creepy individual performances, surprisingly humorous dialogue, shadowy photography (including some atmospherically lit street scenes) and excellent sets, including an eroding old mansion that is musty, moldy and mysterious. The film has its drawbacks, too. Karloff is given scant screen time, less than some of the supporting players,[23] and that's simply not enough for a film in which he is top-billed. The plot is also difficult to understand at times; *The Ghoul* tries to be more complicated than it should be, and that only leads to confusion.

The Ghoul is a worthwhile experience. It's not a classic, and there is certainly not enough of Karloff on display, but fans of the legend will want to see the movie for his monstrous presence alone.

After a lean year in 1934, in part due to the restrictions placed on Hollywood by the newly adopted Hays Code, horror made a comeback with a strong showing in the spring of 1935. On April 26, Tod Browning executed his own comeback in his effort to recover from the financial disaster of *Freaks*, returning to the forefront with the release of *Mark of the Vampire*, his third venture into the world of blood-seeking creatures. Essentially a remake of the silent film *London After Midnight*, it was also Browning's follow-up to his 1931 classic *Dracula*. While not as well-known as the original *Dracula*, in some ways it exceeds its predecessor, particularly with better and more creative camerawork, improved effects, and the superior development of an atmosphere that is eerie and ghoulish.

In *Mark of the Vampire*, a nobleman is murdered in his mansion, left with two wounds on his neck and drained of all his blood. The attending doctor and one of the nobleman's friends believe that he has been killed by a vampire, but the police refuse to believe such a wild tale. Prof. Zelen, an expert in the occult, also suspects that a vampire is at large, a belief that is only underscored when it appears that vampires are menacing the nobleman's daughter in the family mansion. Suspicion will soon fall on a count and his daughter. To determine the identity of the murderer, the professor devises a plan that involves hypnosis, which will produce a remarkably surprising answer to the mystery.

The film stars Bela Lugosi as Count Mora, who is much like Count Dracula in appearance and manner but carries a different identity and now has Czechoslovakian (instead of Transylvanian) ancestry. Lugosi is believable in the role, even if many of his lines were stripped from the final cut. (He does not actually speak until the end of the film.) His co-star, the youthful Carroll Borland, is also quite capable as the Count's daughter Luna. At the time, Borland was a drama student at Berkeley and had virtually no experience as a working actress. Borland is convincing and creepy in the role.

The one down note among the cast members is the performance of Lionel Barrymore in the top-billed role of Prof. Zelen. Barrymore overacts so blatantly that he becomes overly comical, reducing the film to a level of parody. While humor can have a place in horror films, Barrymore's exaggerated efforts at comedy detract from this movie's effectiveness.

Mark of the Vampire also created controversy because its original script featured a theme of incest, in the form of a sexual relationship between Count Mora and his daughter. The censors would have none of that, not in 1935 with the Hays Code in effect. MGM agreed to eliminate any on-screen romance between the father and daughter.[24] The removal of this storyline helps explain the bullet wound that can be seen on Count Mora's temple. In delving into the inappropriate relationship between Mora and his daughter, the original script depicted the Count becoming so overwrought with guilt that he shot himself.

Coming off the box office failure of *Freaks*, Browning had no power to fend off the demands of the censors. He cut out all specific references to incest, resulting in the elimination of 20 minutes of footage and leaving the film at a relatively scant 60 minutes. But there was no chance to remove the bullet wound from Count Mora's makeup, so that last piece of evidence remained.[25]

For some censors, Browning's cuts fell short of the mark in making the film acceptable. Even with the deletion of the incest theme, the film was still banned in Poland, and shown in Lugosi's native Hungary only after additional censorship.

While it lacks the fame of the 1930s classics, *Mark of the Vampire* stands on its own as a worthy piece of horror. MGM mading the film look like an A-list production, full of all the trappings (including bats, cobwebs and spiders) of a vampire movie. The ample budget allowed Browning to import large South American bats, create visually stunning sets, and procure some of the best available acting talent. And Browning supplied determined direction, particularly in creating a complicated scene in which Borland appears to fly like a bat; that scene reportedly took three weeks to film. In another scene, Borland and Lugosi appear to walk through a monstrous cobweb, yet the cobweb remains undisturbed. The film's greatest flaw is likely its ending, one that remains a source of controversy. Many critics feel that it the film and left many viewers feeling cheated.

While the ending was ill-conceived, the rest of the film is a testament to Browning's creative touch. *Mark of the Vampire* succeeds in overcoming some of the flaws that come with a screenplay that was revised so many times that it did not always make sense. The end result is an atmospheric, sensual and unnerving film.

By 1935, vampire themes had become mainstream in Hollywood. So too had human monsters. On July 12, 1935, a horror film with an unlikely title made an impact, while continuing to reveal the talents of a foreign-born actor. On the surface, *Mad Love* sounds like some kind of a dramatic romance, or even a romantic comedy. But do not let the title deceive; even with a few romantic elements, this MGM release is a true horror film, and a brilliant vehicle for the talents of Peter Lorre, who remains underappreciated in horror history.

Making his MGM debut, some four years after showing his penchant for villainous roles in the German production *M*, Lorre stars as Dr. Gogol, a Paris surgeon who agrees to perform life-saving operations. But Dr. Gogol has a dark side; he enjoys attending public executions and regularly patronizes the Grand Guignol Theater, where he delights in the often horrifically themed stage productions.

Gogol becomes dangerously obsessed with actress Yvonne Orlac (Frances Drake), who rejects his unwanted advances. Yvonne is married to an acclaimed concert pianist, Stephen (Colin Clive), whose hands become mangled in a train wreck. The actress begs Dr. Gogol to help her husband, which he agrees to do. He believes that the best solution is to graft the hands of an executed murderer, one who specialized in throwing knives, onto her husband. Not so shockingly, this turns out to be a bad idea, leading to a series of undesirable side effects.

In his American film debut, the Hungarian-born Lorre turns in a phenomenal performance. With his baldheaded appearance (reminiscent of an evil Daddy Warbucks) and his large bug eyes, he puts forth an off-kilter portrayal of the crazed surgeon. Director Karl Freund often shows Lorre in extreme close-ups, putting his star in a spotlight that might have been uncomfortable for lesser actors. Lorre does not disappoint, with an elasticity in his face that allows him to unleash his full range of acting emotions. After watching *Mad Love*, the legendary Charlie Chaplin called Lorre the best actor he had ever seen on screen.[26]

Another fine actor provides good support behind Lorre. Colin Clive, far better known for his work in the Frankenstein films, performs capably as the ill-fated pianist, but his screen time is limited. In retrospect, Freund should have relied more heavily on the veteran actor. Otherwise, Freund capably delivered the goods with his direction. His experience as a cinematographer helped him use light and shadow; the end result is a beautifully filmed movie in glorious black-and-white.

Mad Love created some controversy. During its initial run, a warning aired prior to the credits, letting viewers know of the violent and explicit nature of the film. Given the inclusion of scenes that showcased torture and the use of a guillotine, *Mad Love* traumatized a few viewers while skirting the new regulations of the Hays Code. As a result of the graphic imagery, some countries banned the film.[27] After its initial release, the studio ordered the cutting of roughly 15 minutes of footage, including the scene in which new hands were grafted onto the hands of the pianist.[28]

In its full form, *Mad Love* is a wonderful example of early horror. Allowed to roam free, Lorre showed himself capable of carrying a film and establishing a reputation as one of the finest actors of the horror genre—or any other, for that matter.

In recent years, *The Walking Dead* has become a phenomenon among TV series. But on March 1, 1936, in New York City, Warner Brothers gave us the first taste of something called *The Walking Dead*—a feature film starring Boris Karloff. It has nothing to do with zombies and a post-apocalyptic world, instead telling the story of a luckless man named John Ellman (Karloff), framed for first-degree murder by a gang of racketeers. Ellman is found guilty and sentenced to death. New evidence then comes forth that proves Ellman's innocence, but it arrives too late to save him from the electric chair. A doctor, aware of the case, decides to try an experimental procedure on Ellman, one that will bring him back to life. The resurrected Ellman takes a most unusual kind of revenge against those who framed him.

The Walking Dead was made at lightning speed over the course of only 18 days. Director Michael Curtiz supposedly approached the film as if it were a throwaway project; he wanted to make it as quickly as possible and move on to productions he considered more important.[29] So it probably surprised him when the film received mostly critical praise, with reviewers lauding it for its creepy atmosphere, beautiful camerawork and effective lighting. Karloff is excellent in the lead, carrying the story as an innocent man who is given a chance to render justice. Even in delivering payback, Karloff manages to give Ellman a sympathetic tone throughout the film.

For much of the film, *The Walking Dead* comes across as a gangster picture, a kind of movie that was popular during the 1930s. But the resurrection of Karloff's character, coupled with his urge for vengeance, give it a supernatural tinge with significant elements of horror. It's a film that tends to become forgotten amidst the classics that Karloff made in the 1930s and '40s, but it's an above-average effort that showcases his ability to portray a nuanced character. For classic horror fans, and certainly for Karloff fans, *The Walking Dead* ranks as necessary viewing.

"Shock Theater" had plucked most of the top horror films from 1937, '38 and '39, but at least one crucial film remained untouched from the latter year. It is a film that some critics might categorize outside of the horror genre, perhaps putting it more safely in the category of drama, but it contains so many elements of classic horror that it should be included.

The Hunchback of Notre Dame, released on December 29, 1939, ranks as one of the decade's finest films. In 1923, the silent version of the Victor Hugo tale debuted. Fully determined to make the new talking version of *Hunchback* the definitive adaptation, RKO poured $1.8 million into the production and included a significant budget for promotional purposes. The production costs also included a $250,000 replica of the famed Cathedral of Notre Dame.[30] The investment turned out to be worthwhile; the film looks every bit as good on the screen as its nearly $2 million price tag would indicate.

It also turned out to be a profitable film, covering all of its vast expenses and making a modest profit. Although some moviegoers expressed reservations about viewing a horror film during the December holidays, *Hunchback* counteracted the unusual timing by drawing huge crowds.

Charles Laughton stars as Quasimodo, a deformed man forced to perform menial tasks for France's chief justice during the late Middle Ages. The chief justice, a horrible man named Frollo, is smitten with a gypsy girl named Esmeralda (played by the beautiful Maureen O'Hara) and orders Quasimodo to capture her and bring her to his quarters. The twisted Frollo eventually frames Esmeralda for murder. After she confesses under torture, the authorities sentence her to death by hanging, an injustice that Quasimodo becomes determined to prevent.

The end result did not disappoint. Laughton and O'Hara are both magnificent in their performances. So is Cedric Hardwicke, who gives the evil Frollo a particularly despicable streak. The choice of Laughton to play the title role came only after RKO considered a long list of heavy-hitting performers. Lon Chaney, Jr., Bela Lugosi, Claude Rains and Orson Welles all received substantial looks before RKO settled on Laughton.[31] The British actor turned out to be a wonderful choice. It's hard to believe that any of the other actors, as accomplished as they might have been, could have surpassed Laughton; he runs the full gamut of emotions in portraying a beast-like figure who is horrible to look at but is also full of humanity and heroism. Laughton succeeds in becoming the definitive film version of *Hunchback*, no easy task given that Lon Chaney had played the role so skillfully in the 1923 film adaptation.

The makeup applied to Laughton only enhanced his characterization. It took roughly two and a half hours each day to make Laughton look the part of Quasimodo, with his offset eyes, hunched back and an unusually muscled torso.[32] Given the heat wave raging through Los Angeles at the time, which raised temperatures into the 100s, Laughton suffered through a remarkably uncomfortable experience. The lengthy and pains-taking application, which involved layers of foam rubber and an aluminum framework for the Hunchback's hump,[33] ultimately paid off, resulting in one of the most memorable appearances for a character in a horror film.

Adding to the realism, Laughton suffered actual pain during the filming. For the scene in which Quasimodo received a whipping, Laughton felt the sting of the lashes, which seeped through his bodysuit and costume, leaving him with a series of bruises. Laughton also instructed one of the assistant directors to twist his ankle off-camera so as to create a greater sense of pain and advance his performance even further.[34]

It's difficult to believe, but at the time of the film's release, a reviewer for the *New York Times* derided the picture, calling it "a freak show."[35] That criticism simply does not hold up. It isn't often that horror films are nominated for Academy Awards, as *The Hunchback* was, which becomes even more impressive given the volume of great films released in 1939. With its elaborate sets and cathedral replica, detailed costumes and makeup, a riveting musical score and iconic performances, *The Hunchback of Notre Dame* deserves recognition as a standout film and legitimate horror classic.

As horror moved into the 1940s, a shift from straight horror to more futuristic themes involving science fiction and weird inventions began to take place. One of the earliest films of the new decade to cross this barrier was *Dr. Cyclops*, an entertaining release that debuted in New York City on April 10, 1940. Not only did the new film blend horror with science fiction, it also made history in its use of color, at a time when most horror films were still being produced in black-and-white.

The film stars Albert Dekker as Dr. Thorkel, an ingenious physicist who invites four scientists to his jungle home in Peru. After he asks them to identify a specimen under his microscope, they are dismissed. Upset that they have been asked to travel a long way to make a single identification, they decide to remain on the premises and later inspect the doctor's laboratory. Catching them in his lab, Dr. Thorkel admits that he has been working on experiments in which he uses a unique source of radium to physically shrink living creatures, including a horse. Shortly thereafter, Dr. Thorkel makes a transition to human subjects by capturing his visitors and shrinking them to approximately one-fifth of their original size.

While the plot is preposterous and the beginning of the film is slow-paced, Dekker is fun in his over-the-top performance as the evil Dr. Thorkel. Full of camp, he plays the part with relish. This might not have worked in another genre, but it meshes perfectly with a 1940s film blending horror and science fiction. *Dr. Cyclops* became Dekker's signature film role. When he died in 1968 at the age of 62, almost every one of his obituaries led with a mention of his starring role in *Dr. Cyclops*.

Directed by Ernest Schoedsack (one of *King Kong*'s directors), *Dr. Cyclops* broke from the conventions of the day; it became the first science fiction film to be shown in three-color Technicolor,[36] giving it a far different look from most of its contemporaries. The color imagery is quite memorable, as are the special effects and sound effects, which are both above-average for the era.

In some ways, the special effects overwhelm the film, which has drawn criticism for its lack of character development and the absence of any major stars. Clearly, this is not a deep film; it lacks the gravitas of many of the Universal classics from the 1930s. But the special effects are so eye-catching and the color so bright and graphic that it commands and keeps the viewers' attention throughout its duration. It is a fun film, if not one that is to be taken very seriously.

Another amusing film debuted during the summer of 1941. When we think of the great comedians Bud Abbott and Lou Costello and their association with horror, we tend to gravitate toward the comedy classic *Abbott and Costello Meet Frankenstein*. Before the comedic duo produced that successful venture into horror-comedy, they tackled the theme of the supernatural in *Hold That Ghost*, which premiered in New York City theaters on August 7.

The film is very much a vintage example of Bud and Lou's ability to mix slapstick comedy with a tinge of horror. They play inept gas station attendants who become the beneficiaries of a gangster whose will stipulates that whoever was with him at the time of his death will receive his inheritance. They inherit a hotel-tavern purportedly containing the gangster's hidden fortune, prompting them to wade their way through a series of clues in search of the money, all the while having to deal with the ghosts that may or may not dwell there.

The movie was inspired by Abbott and Costello's famed "moving candle" routine, which is featured in *Hold That Ghost*. But the candle bit is just a small part of what makes the movie successful. Abbott and Costello are at their comedic best throughout, and are ably supported by a cast that includes Richard Carlson (later the star of *Creature from the Black Lagoon*), horror stalwart Evelyn Ankers, and even a brief appearance by Shemp Howard of Three Stooges fame. But none of the supporting cast tops the performance of Joan Davis, who proves to be just as funny as Abbott and Costello and provides an ideal foil for the lead comedians.

Hold That Ghost features a series of musical numbers in a nightclub, but they do not detract from the main theme of the film: that of a haunted house. The end result is a lighter touch than the comedians' later monster movies, but there is still just enough of a supernatural tone, thanks to the wonderfully creepy house setting and its ability to induce a few scares, along with sufficient doses of murder and mystery to keep the interest of horror aficionados. For fans of Abbott and Costello, and for fans of 1940s horror, *Hold That Ghost* is a necessary part of the film library.

During the 1940s, it would be difficult to find a writer-producer more influential in the horror genre than a visionary named Val Lewton. *Cat People* remains his signature piece. Premiering in New York City on December 5, 1942, it is a movie that lacks outright terror or violence of any kind, but is a perfect example of psychological horror. Some critics have called it the finest horror film of the 1940s.

As the head of the horror division at RKO Pictures, Lewton produced and sometimes co-wrote a whirlwind of 11 films during a three-year span.[37] Those films saved RKO, which had fallen into terrible economic straits. Lewton made the films cheaply, but with a high degree of skill and ingenuity. While it's arguable whether *Cat People* is Lewton's best—cases could be made for *The Body Snatcher* and *I Walked with a Zombie*—it is almost certainly his most famous film.

The plot of *Cat People* is intriguing and offbeat. The theme comes from one of Lewton's own phobias: a fear of cats. French actress Simone Simon excels in her role as Irena, a Serbian immigrant who has moved to New York City and become a fashion designer. Irena meets an American, but retains a strange phobia, a belief that she is descended from actual "cat people" in her native Serbian village and will turn into a panther if she becomes intimate with anyone. In spite of this oddness, the man asks Irena to marry him. When she persists with her beliefs, he persuades her to see a psychiatrist, but that does little to solve Irena's bizarre problem.

Director Jacques Tourneur builds on Lewton's story by using lighting creatively in *Cat People*. Many of the scenes are filmed in dark shadow, creating a sense of mystery and a feeling of the macabre. Tourneur also relies heavily on sound, with no better example than the scene where footsteps can be heard pursuing one of the main characters. Tourneur builds tension and suspense throughout the story, before finally revealing a monstrous presence at the end of the film.

Tourneur's methods, along with the influence of Lewton, become even more impressive given the lack of a budget. RKO put forth only $150,000, forcing the filmmakers to improvise. To save money, Lewton re-used sets from an earlier Orson Welles film, *The Magnificent Ambersons*.[38] Tourneur also managed to complete filming within 18 days, satisfying RKO's demands for a fast and inexpensive production.[39]

When Lewton showed the final print to studio executives, they were hesitant. The film seemed too subtle in its horror presentation; they wanted something more direct and overt in its approach to horror, something filled with obvious monsters, like one of the 1930s films that Universal had produced. As it turned out, the executives were wrong. *Cat People* became a huge success, remaining in theaters for months and turning an enormous profit. In fact, the film did so well that RKO actually delayed the release of two other Lewton features, not wanting them to come into direct competition with *Cat People*.

While *Cat People*'s absence of outright horror, along with a lack of brand-name actors, might make it less appealing to some genre fans, it remains a powerful piece and a terrific example of the horror of the mind. Simon's performance, one of the first and most effective examples of a female monster unleashing terror on the screen, carries the film to high cinematic status. It is an example of Lewton—and Tourneur—at or near their best.

Lewton's influence may have reached even greater heights with *I Walked with a Zombie*, which premiered in Cleveland on April 8, 1943. The strange title makes the film sound like a combination of comedy and horror, but it is not. Despite the offbeat moniker, this is horror through and through, and a legitimate classic of the 1940s.

Young Canadian nurse Betsy Connell (Frances Dee) has been summoned to a Caribbean island to care for the wife of sugar plantation owner Paul Holland (Tom Conway). The wife has been acting strangely, seemingly the result of a fever that has caused mental paralysis. Or has she simply lost all of her willpower because of the way that Paul has treated her? While tending to the wife, Betsy falls in love with Paul, but she remains committed to finding a cure for the wife, even if it means resorting to voodoo.

A veteran of horror, Conway also co-starred in *Cat People*. Not so coincidentally, that film was directed by Jacques Tourneur, who also oversaw *I Walked with a Zombie*. With an excellent screenplay co-written by Curt Siodmak, Tourneur succeeds in creating an atmospheric gem, full of creepy imagery, creative sets and vibrant locations which add to the feelings of mystery and suspense. The film reaches a crescendo with a hypnotic scene that captures a voodoo ceremony, which is beautifully shot by Tourneur and his crew. Unlike most of the other Lewton–RKO efforts, the horror of the film is not merely suggested, but is actually shown—and done so effectively—in the form of the walking dead.

Although *I Walked with a Zombie* is now considered one of the best 1940s horror films, critics did not take kindly to it upon its initial release. A *New York Times* reviewer referred to it as "a dull, disgusting exaggeration of an unhealthy, abnormal concept of life."[40] Such criticism has not held up well over time, at least based on the consensus of most historians.

With his innovative use of light and shadows, and his ability to build tension and atmosphere from start to finish, Tourneur completed one of the best horror films to come out of RKO. Tourneur's horror career continued to burgeon in later years with his 1957 film *Curse of the Demon* and 1963's *The Comedy of Terrors*. At a time when horror was beginning to lose steam after its 1930s peak, *I Walked with a Zombie* gave the genre some new life.

So too did a film that debuted on November 11, 1943. *The Return of the Vampire* is one of only three films in which Bela Lugosi played a genuine vampire. Long underrated, it is not as well-known as the original *Dracula*, or as entertaining as *Abbott and Costello Meet Frankenstein*, but it showcases Lugosi in the vampire role that he mastered in film and on stage. And while the title vampire is not called Dracula, the character shares many features with the iconic figure from the 1931 classic.

Opening in the World War I era, *The Return of the Vampire* tells the story of a British family being plagued by vampire Armand Tesla, who is assisted by a werewolf, Andreas. A friend of the family, a medical doctor named Lady Jane Ainsley, stakes the creature, which not only destroys the vampire but allows the werewolf to resume human form.

Roughly 25 years later, Tesla's body is unearthed when a cemetery is hit by German bombs during the Second World War. Workers remove the metal stake from the body, not realizing that this will rejuvenate the vampire. Now revived, Tesla seeks revenge on the family and Lady Jane, but first enlists the help of his onetime servant, Andreas, forcing him to once again deal with the curse of lycanthropy. The pairing of the two supernatural creatures represents the first time in cinematic history that a vampire and a werewolf appear in the same movie, predating several monster rally movies from Universal.

When Universal learned that this Columbia film was being made, studio executives refused to give the rival studio permission to use the name Dracula.[41] Columbia reacted, not by changing the content of the film, but by removing the name of Dracula and altering the names of other characters. In essence, Columbia produced a Dracula film but without the names or references to the Dracula story, in order to avoid legal troubles. As he did in *Dracula,* Lugosi nails the role, performing it with his usual passion and gusto.

Although director Lew Landers relied heavily on the Dracula story, he also showed creativity in filming *Return of the Vampire.* Not only does he introduce us to the groundbreaking vampire-werewolf combination, but he does something highly unusual: making the werewolf speak in full sentences, a first in film history. As played by character actor Matt Willis, the werewolf acts more human than monstrous; he wears a suit and performs the duties of a vampire's servant. Landers, who had previously directed Lugosi in *The Raven,* also succeeds in presenting an on-screen destruction of a vampire, executed in the form of a visible disintegration. This was something done in the 1922 silent film *Nosferatu,*[42] but not delivered on screen in the original *Dracula.* In general, the special effects of the film are far superior to the 1931 classic, an indication of improved filmmaking techniques that occurred over the 12-year gap.

With engaging effects, a creative storyline, and Lugosi at his vampiric best, *The Return of the Vampire* is, in some ways, a better film than *Dracula,* and certainly a worthy venture in 1940s horror. It is

The Return of the Vampire (1943): Sporting makeup that was far less fearsome than what was given Lon Chaney in *The Wolf Man,* little-known actor Matt Willis takes on the persona of the werewolf, assistant to the vampire. Willis' werewolf was given the ability to speak, a decision that was panned as comical by some, but creative and effective by others (courtesy of Frank Dello Stritto).

a must-see for fans of classic horror—and for anyone regarding themselves as a devoted follower of Lugosi.

By the mid–1940s, horror films were beginning to take a step up. One of the decade's best came out on January 19, 1944, a product of 20th Century–Fox. The premiere of *The Lodger* helped make Laird Cregar a star, even if only for a brief time.

The film is set in Victorian London, in the midst of Jack the Ripper's spree of murdering actresses and prostitutes. At the same time, an aging London couple named the Burtons decides to take on a lodger as a way of alleviating recent financial troubles. The lodger is played brilliantly by Cregar (pronounced cray-GAR), who is at first charming and gentle before revealing another side to his personality. Eventually, the Burtons begin to suspect that he is indeed the Ripper. By the end of the film, Cregar's character has become a "rampaging monster," in the words of historian and Cregar biographer Gregory Mank.[43]

The Lodger caused controversy for its strong sexual content, which broached areas out of the 1940s mainstream. Cregar's character, known as Mr. Slade, hints at having an incestuous and homosexual relationship with his brother. The suggestion of incest somehow passed muster with the censors, but did cause a stir with some critics and fans.

Mank points to *The Lodger* as memorable for two other features: the inability of the female actresses to scream, simply because they are vocally paralyzed by the horror of what they see; and the magnificent presence of Cregar, who is "breathtaking."[44]

Cregar's performance is so overpowering that it resulted in him being typecast. Given his convincing effort, Hollywood would only cast him in the role of homicidal maniacs. Wanting to transform himself into a leading man, Cregar became obsessed with losing weight and went on a starvation diet, which resulted in a rapid weight loss of over 100 pounds.[45] But the sudden and radical changes to his body also led to two heart attacks and then his sudden death in December of 1944. Cregar was only 30 years old.

While Cregar has been forgotten by Hollywood, *The Lodger* remains a masterpiece, a reminder of Cregar's talent. Mank regards *The Lodger* as one of the three best horror films of the 1940s, along with *Hangover Square* (another Cregar film) and *The Body Snatcher*. As Mank puts it, *The Lodger* is "a fantastic horror movie."[46] There is no disagreement here.

In terms of an old-fashioned story of a ghost haunting a house, it's difficult to find much better than *The Uninvited*. Premiering in Washington, D.C., on February 10, 1944, this film features high-end acting, a good story and wonderful atmosphere, providing an excellent example of horror in the black-and-white era.

Adapted from a 1941 novel by Irish author Dorothy Macardle, *The Uninvited* stars Ray Milland and Ruth Hussey as siblings who purchase a Gothic mansion on the British coast. Originally excited (they bought the house at a bargain price), they become disenchanted when they learn about the house's strange history from the previous owner's daughter, played by tragic actress Gail Russell. (Russell would die from alcohol abuse at the age of 36.) Becoming a romantic interest of Milland's character, she informs them of some of the tragic events that have taken place, stories that disturb the new residents. The Milland and Hussey characters also begin hearing unexplained sounds within the mansion at night, leading them to the conclusion that the house is haunted.

There is no violence or gore in *The Uninvited*, but there is plenty of atmosphere and a sense of foreboding that instills chills in the viewer. The house is beautifully and eerily photographed, creating a nearly perfect backdrop for a seaside ghost story. Directed by first-time film director Lewis Allen, the film represented Hollywood's initial attempt at a completely serious haunted house venture, without the camp or the comedy of earlier productions such as *The Old Dark House*.⁴⁷ In contrast to earlier films, there is no real-world resolution behind the happenings of the house; the root causes are all supernatural.

Allen succeeds in creating a legitimate and sophisticated ghost story; he gives us a good, well-developed plot, one that is enhanced by the mature presence of Milland, Hussey and supporting players Donald Crisp and Alan Napier. The film also sustains a sense of mystery; exactly who is this ghost and what is its motivation? We won't find the answers until the very end.

The Uninvited is one of the few horror films that has ever been nominated for an Academy Award. Cinematographer Charles Lang received a nod in the category for best black-and-white cinematography, but did not win. Still, the nomination alone speaks to the quality.

The Uninvited has become an influential film. Modern-day director Guillermo del Toro has called it one of his favorite horror films. Martin Scorsese listed the film as one of his 11 favorite "scary" films of all time.⁴⁸ *The Uninvited* has also been referenced in subsequent movies, including the 1982 ghost story classic *Poltergeist*.

It would be difficult to find much fault with *The Uninvited*. Yes, it is slowly paced at times, but the cinematography, the musical score, the sound effects and even the visual ghost effects are all well done. Simply put, it is one of the better supernatural thrillers, an essential part of cinematic horror history.

Another excellent (and underrated) film kicked off the year of horror in 1945. On February 7, *Hangover Square* premiered in New York City, ahead of a nationwide release. *Hangover Square* has often been described as a crime drama, but contains just enough of a horror element that it served as the inspiration for the musical *Sweeney Todd*.

Hangover Square also represents the final film in the all-too-short life of Laird Cregar, who had passed away in December 1944. It's set in London during the Victorian Era and the tormented actor plays composer George Harvey Bone. While working furiously on a piano concerto, Bone blacks out from time to time due to stress. Waking up, he finds himself in a remote part of the city, unaware of how he arrived there. After each incident, Bone reads a local newspaper account describing another London murder. Bone wonders whether he himself is committing the murders.

As he did in *The Lodger*, Cregar delivers a *tour de force* performance, even though he appears frail as the result of the aforementioned rapid 100-pound weight loss. As explained by historian Gregory Mank, Cregar had wanted no part of making *Hangover Square* because of his dissatisfaction with being typecast as maniacal and demented killers. Cregar wanted to become a leading man, motivating his efforts to undergo radical weight loss and plastic surgery.⁴⁹ When he learned that *Hangover Square* would be similar in tone to *The Lodger*, he initially refused to participate and was suspended by 20th Century–Fox. Two weeks later, he gave in to the studio's executives and agreed to make the film.⁵⁰

During the shooting, the ailing Cregar had difficulty remembering his lines. He also became temperamental, quarreling with director John Brahm.⁵¹ In spite of his fits of temper, and his rapidly deteriorating health, Cregar succeeded in putting forth a masterful portrayal of the troubled composer who wonders whether he is responsible for a series of heinous crimes.

Cregar is ably supported by co-star Linda Darnell, who plays a dancer and a love interest of the composer. (Darnell was a stunning actress who would also die young, perishing in a house fire.) George Sanders, a close friend of Cregar who made efforts to defend the actor against the studio,⁵² is also effective as a friendly doctor who tries to help Bone deal with his blackouts.

With strong performances all around, and wonderful atmosphere and suspense created by director Brahm, *Hangover Square* becomes one of the more effective horror-thrillers of the 1940s. Along with *The Lodger*, the film stands as a testament to the enormous talents of Cregar, one of Hollywood's most tragic figures.

February 1945 would see the release of another historic film. First shown in St. Louis theaters on February 16, *The Body Snatcher* is one of those understated horror gems that showcases Boris Karloff at his finest. While this production from RKO and the genius of writer-producer Val Lewton has never received its due, it stands as one of the best horror films of all time.

Based on the short story by Robert Louis Stevenson, the film centers on the plight of Dr. MacFarlane (portrayed by veteran English actor Henry Daniell), who is being harassed by a cab driver. Played brilliantly by Karloff, the ruthless cabbie, John Gray, regularly provides MacFarlane with cadavers for his medical practice, but also pesters and harasses him, constantly reminding him of the "dark secret" that would ruin his career and reputation. Mac-Farland's assistant, a top-tier medical student named Fettes, eventually comes to realize that the cab driver is obtaining the bodies through murderous means. Fettes shows the corpse of a murdered man to MacFarlane, but the doctor advises him to keep quiet and refrain from telling the police.

A medical school janitor (Bela Lugosi) visits Gray and attempts to blackmail him about the body snatching operation, leading to a dramatic skirmish between the two men, and setting the stage for a violent climax involving the evil cabman and the tormented Dr. MacFarlane.

The film opens with footage that is purported to represent Edinburgh, Scotland, but was actually shot on the studio ranch in California, using an exterior set from the 1939 film *The Hunchback of Notre Dame*.[53] From there, the story and the characterization pick up enormously, with Karloff laying out one of the greatest performances of his career. He gives a full and nuanced portrayal, showing not only Gray's wicked side, but also a friendly demeanor that helps him gain the trust of the local citizens, including children. Often flashing a wry smile in his interactions with others, Karloff plays the role with both humor and ruthlessness, alternating those two character traits according to his particular needs of the moment.

Some critics have called this Karloff's best performance. One of those critics is historian David J. Skal, who believes that Karloff's effort reflects his skills as an actor. "My favorite [of all the Karloff roles] is his portrayal of John Gray, the grave robber in *The Body Snatcher*," says Skal. "I think indisputably [Karloff] is the most polished actor ever to become a famous monster.... He was a very subtle actor.... He could be terrifying, he could be charming, but [he gave] very, very nuanced performances."[54]

While the role of Gray is not as famous as Karloff's appearances in the Frankenstein movies, *The Body Snatcher* demanded that the actor do more than create a memorable pantomime or mouth a few syllables; it asked him to cover his full range as an actor. Karloff, who felt the Frankenstein franchise had run its course, gave Val Lewton much of the credit for challenging him and resurrecting his career via *The Body Snatcher*. In a *Los Angeles Times* article from 1946, writer Louis Berg described Lewton "as the man who rescued [Karloff] from the living dead and restored, so to speak, his soul."[55]

In addition to Karloff's career-peaking performance, *The Body Snatcher* also gives us the added bonus of Lugosi, who plays the small but important role of Joseph, the blackmailing janitor. The character was not part of the original story, but was added to "accommodate the casting of Lugosi," as explained by director Robert Wise.[56] Lugosi was added to the cast

7. Creature Features, Fright Night *and* Block of Shock (1931–1969) 109

The Body Snatcher (1945): Played to perfection by Boris Karloff, evil cabman John Gray hauls away his latest victim, to be used in medical school classes. The Frankenstein Monster will always be Karloff's signature role, but some critics have called his portrayal of the cabman his finest acting effort ever.

at the last minute, forcing Wise and Lewton to create a role for him. When Lugosi officially signed his contract with the studio, filming on *The Body Snatcher* began.[57]

In the film, Lugosi and Karloff share relatively little time on the screen, but their last scene culminates in a frightening physical confrontation. For the viewer, the opportunity to see Karloff and Lugosi grappling with each other presents a rare and thrilling treat. The scene is also historic: This was the eighth and final film in which the horror legends appeared together. Appropriately, their final film as a duo is one of their best.

Karloff is outstanding, Lugosi is good, and the rest of the cast (particularly the classically trained Daniell as the brilliant doctor who lacks a bedside manner) holds its own in lifting *The Body Snatcher* to classic status. Lewton's influences of subtlety and suggestion are on full display, and well executed by Wise. Their work is perhaps best exemplified in the riveting climax scene, which involves Karloff and Daniell and a harrowing horse-and-carriage ride through a driving rainstorm. The filmmakers added to the scene's effectiveness by applying a spray to Karloff's body, making his skin glisten in the rain. A number of years later, a writer asked Karloff if he remembered the substance that was used to illuminate him. "I really can't recall," Karloff said, "but you can be sure that it was something *foul*."[58]

Having watched that climactic scene, viewers can be satisfied in having seen not only one of the best horror films of the 1940s, but a veritable classic that deserves more recognition than it has received.

Premiering in New York City on March 1 and set in Victorian London, *The Picture of Dorian Gray* is an excellent adaptation of the Oscar Wilde novel. It has a terrific cast delivering at a high level, along with award-winning cinematography, making it one of the stronger horror films of the 1940s. It's also an unusual film, in that it was shot mostly in black-and-white but also contains a few moments in color.

Relatively little-known Hurd Hatfield plays the title character, a wealthy young man who poses for a portrait and then receives it as a gift. When Dorian sees the portrait, he wishes out loud that only the portrait would age, and that he himself would remain unchanged. By making the wish in the presence of an Egyptian statue of a cat, Dorian has actually given himself more than he can handle.

Shortly after the portrait's acquisition, Dorian meets a woman and decides to become engaged. Unfortunately, he continues to be influenced by the corrupt Lord Henry Wotton. On the advice of Lord Wotton, Dorian breaks off the engagement and begins to live a life of debauchery and immorality. And Dorian does not age at all. Instead, the portrait grows uglier through supernatural means, reflecting the life of corruption that Dorian has chosen.

Hatfield, an American actor affecting a British accent, is good in his role as Gray, playing it in a reserved and understated way, so as to mask the emotions of his duplicitous character. George Sanders is even better in portraying the evil Lord Wotton, giving him a humorous side with his flair for fast-paced wit. And a young actress named Angela Lansbury received an Academy Award nomination for her performance as Sibyl Vane, a singer and Gray's initial love interest. Lansbury, who was not even 20 at the time of filming, lost the Oscar to Anne Revere for her work in *National Velvet*, but won praise for her demure characterization of the innocent Sibyl. It is here that director Albert Lewin broke from Wilde's original work; Wilde had portrayed Sibyl as a sophisticated woman, in contrast to the more naïve interpretation in the film.

Other key players include Donna Reed (who was originally promised the part of Sibyl but settled for a lesser role)[59] and English actor Peter Lawford, making this one of the strongest casts ever assembled for a horror picture in that era. Lewin capably oversees the performances, allowing each to showcase their talents. The director also displays a sense of innovation. While most of the film is shot in black-and-white, Lewin presents the painting of Dorian Gray in color on four different occasions (all from the perspective of Gray himself), creating a stark visual contrast that gives the portrait a life of its own.

Lewin's film is beautiful and atmospheric, the perfect backdrop for an elegant horror

7. Creature Features, Fright Night *and* Block of Shock (1931–1969)　　111

story. It is the rare horror film that won an Oscar (for Best Cinematography), and that alone makes it essential viewing. The performances of Lansbury, Sanders and Hatfield only add to a strong argument in favor of *The Picture of Dorian Gray*.

In the same year that Karloff wowed in *The Body Snatcher*, he also found success with *Isle of the Dead*, another Lewton RKO. In this case, Lewton found inspiration in a painting called "Isle of the Dead" which at least partly became the basis for his written script.[60]

The film is set on a Greek island in 1912, in the midst of the Balkan Wars. A Greek general (Karloff) becomes upset when he visits the island and discovers that his wife's body has vanished from its crypt. The next day, the general and all other visitors to the island become trapped there because of an apparent plague; no one is allowed to leave. The general begins to wonder if something more sinister than the plague is at work here. To add to the mix, a local peasant woman suspects that a young Greek girl named Thea is actually a kind of vampire, known as a vorvolaka.[61] This leads to speculation that the vampire is actually responsible for the spread of disease.

Director Mark Robson presents a good story, which he supplements with some beautiful and atmospheric black-and-white photography. Robson creates a strange moodiness that governs the plot, hovering over the characters throughout each scene. Each of Robson's key actors delivers a solid performance, including Karloff, who is typically good as the general. Lewton originally had reservations about Karloff, whom he felt was limited to playing monsters and other ghoulish figures. Lewton so came to appreciate Karloff's ability to handle a "thriller" type role that he collaborated with him on two other RKO movies.

The production of *Isle of the Dead* did not come without some difficulty. Filming began in July 1944, but had to be temporarily suspended because Karloff came down with severe back problems. Karloff's condition required surgery, forcing a delay in the proceedings. While waiting for the rest of the cast to become available again, Lewton took time to make *The Body Snatcher*, also with Karloff.[62] As a result of the unexpected delay, *Isle of the Dead* lost one of its key actresses, Rose Hobart, who was forced to move on to her next scheduled film.[63]

While the absence of Hobart hurt, the delay could not have been avoided; *Isle of the Dead* needed Karloff, and Karloff at his physical best. The end result was a solid film. Although not as powerful as *The Body Snatcher*, *Isle of the Dead* is an effective film, full of claustrophobic atmosphere, an appealing mystery and plenty of surprising scares.

In many ways, the span of the 1940s represented the decade of Val Lewton. After the dual successes of *The Body Snatcher* and *Isle of the Dead*, it made perfect sense for Lewton and Karloff to venture into the studio a third time. The pair collaborated on *Bedlam*, the last of the horror films that Lewton produced for RKO. Lewton never worked with Karloff again.

The 1946 death of RKO chief Charles Hoerner would lead to massive changes at the studio, including the dismissal of Lewton. Hoerner had been a huge supporter of Lewton, but his successor felt no such loyalty.[64] Now out of work, Lewton fell into bad health and suffered a heart attack. His career badly affected, Lewton succumbed to a second heart attack at the age of 46.

A few years before his death, Lewton succeeded in putting the finishing touches on *Bedlam*, which premiered in New York City on April 16, 1946. The story of *Bedlam* puts the spotlight on the notorious St. Mary's of Bethlehem Asylum, a fictionalized version of an actual mental institution. Nell Bowen, played heroically by Anna Lee, has been assigned to observe the asylum. Horrified by the corrupt institution known as Bedlam, she wants to initiate a series of reforms. But her plans are interrupted by the evil head of the institution, Master

George Sims. Played by Karloff, Sims falsely accuses Nell of being mentally unsound, has her committed to the asylum, and makes sure that she is treated poorly. At first it appears that Sims will get away with his nefarious maneuver, at least until the other inmates decide to take matters into their own hands.

Karloff takes on his role with gusto, playing Sims as a man who sees the asylum as a means of enjoyment, a way to entertain his VIP guests. There is nothing redeemable about Karloff's character, an evil man who places a higher priority on providing ghoulish entertainment for his friends than he does the well-being of his inmates.

Some critics of *Bedlam* have taken shots at the film for its supposed lack of horror, but there are enough chilling moments to place it safely within the genre. Lewton and director Mark Robson do well in creating sophisticated dialogue that gives the film an elevated air. Robson also gives Karloff and co-star Lee plenty of room in which to roam. When the two are on screen together, the film really shines.

Despite its lack of outright horror, *Bedlam* succeeds by creating tension. While not quite as good as the two earlier Karloff-Lewton efforts, it is a worthy film. It's also a sad reminder that we could have had more of Karloff and Lewton together, if not for the unfortunate politics of the movie studio—and ultimately, the premature death of a creative genius.

By the mid–1940s, several studios had established reputations for their general excellence in handling the horror genre. In addition to RKO and Universal, rivals like Columbia and Paramount made their marks. Another studio, a much smaller one, decided to venture into the territory of horror as well.

In the 1940s, very few British studios were making horror films, which had essentially been banned throughout England during World War II. Ealing Studios broke that trend, making its first and only attempt at a horror film.[65] It turned out to be a good one. *Dead of Night*, which had been first released in the United Kingdom in the fall of 1945, made its way into American theaters on June 28, 1946. An example of an early horror anthology, the film presents five different but interlinked stories, all delivered in flashback form. Well executed and acted, *Dead of Night* became a template for future horror anthologies, particularly those of the 1960s and '70s.

The film centers on architect Walter Craig, who is played by accomplished British actor Mervyn Johns. In search of legitimate work, Craig receives an invitation to visit a country home and serve as a consultant on some renovations. When he arrives, he feels as though he has already met all of the home's residents in a recurring nightmare. The sight of these familiar residents convinces Craig that he is mired in the nightmare, but before he can emerge and wake himself, he must listen to a series of supernatural tales that are spun by the inhabitants of the house.

Of the five tales, which are directed by four different directors, the most memorable is "The Ventriloquist's Dummy," which stars Michael Redgrave. After the dummy acquires the power of actual speech from Redgrave's character, Redgrave becomes overly possessive, to the point that he shoots down a rival ventriloquist who has become too "close" to the dummy. Another scary sequence is "Hearse Driver," the story of a man who dreams of repeatedly seeing another man behind the wheel of a hearse.

The "Haunted Mirror" segment is also chilling; it's one that featured the smashing of an actual mirror. As explained by actress Googie Withers, that needed to be done in one take because the studio, with a limited budget, had only one large mirror on hand.[66] The other two *Dead of Night* segments, "Christmas Story" and "Golfing Party," were not as strong, but are still well above average. Upon the film's release, the U.S. distributor cut those two segments, because they felt the movie was too long. This ill-advised decision created continuity problems for viewers, who became confused by the sudden appearance of actor Michael Allan during a nightmare sequence.[67]

Those segments have been restored to *Dead of Night*, which is now shown in its full rendition. It is a film that deserves recognition for its good storytelling, its disturbing sense of doom, and a twist ending that most could not have seen coming. *Dead of Night* continues to earn praise from modern-day directors as one of the best horror films of all time.

At least one more film from the 1940s deserves mention in recalling the history of hosted horror. Even though some critics have tended to treat the film as a comedy classic, *Abbott and Costello Meet Frankenstein* remains a favorite of horror buffs. Shown in Great Britain under the title of *Meet the Ghosts*, it blends the two genres nicely, while providing a frenzied and entertaining forum for three of our favorite Universal monsters.

Released in the U.S. on June 15, 1948, *Abbott and Costello Meet Frankenstein* has always been billed as a comedy first and foremost—and it *is* legitimately funny—but it is still, at its core, a horror film that creates a sense of tension and terror in a number of key scenes. There is not only screen time given to the title character of Frankenstein's Monster, who is played capably by Glenn Strange, but also to his villainous cohort Dracula (Bela Lugosi) and a well-intentioned Wolf Man (Lon Chaney), who intends to take down the other two monsters. (At one point, the Mummy was scheduled to be included as part of the ensemble classic, but that idea was scrapped before filming.[68])

Abbott and Costello Meet Frankenstein gives us that rare opportunity to see a comic genius like Lou Costello share screen time with Strange, Lugosi and Chaney Jr. Costello and Bud Abbott portray Wilbur Gray and Chick Young, respectively, a pair of Florida freight handlers overseeing a shipment of large crates that have been sent from Europe to McDougal's House of Horrors. One crate contains the body of Dracula, who has somehow been restored to life and has conceived of the idea to revive the Frankenstein Monster through a series of electrical charges.

Larry Talbot, aka the Wolf Man, will soon join the proceedings, but not as an ally to the other monsters. Instead, he join forces with Wilbur and Chick, attempting to convince them that both Dracula and the Monster are real and must be stopped. To complicate matters, Wilbur has become romantically involved with an attractive woman, Dr. Sandra Mornay (Lenore Aubert); little does he know that Mornay is conspiring with Dracula to capture Wilbur and have his simple brain transplanted into the Monster's body. Wilbur accompanies Sandra on a date to a costume party, along with Chick and a female insurance investigator (Jane Randolph), eventually setting the stage for an action-packed showdown at Dracula's island castle.

Lugosi will forever be associated with Dracula, but he played the role on film only twice, with the Abbott and Costello film marking his final film appearance as the famed count. It also represented his final film role with a major Hollywood studio. In some ways, Lugosi is better here than he was in the original *Dracula*. While he does look considerably older than his 1931 appearance (who wouldn't, given the passing of 17 years?), he delivers his lines more naturally and comfortably, and not as deliberately as he did in the original. Despite his advancing age, Lugosi is just as intimidating, particularly through the intensity of his stare.

Thanks to its late 1940s release, the music and the special effects in *Abbott and Costello Meet Frankenstein* are superior to some of the Universal efforts of the early 1930s. The animation effects, which involve Dracula's transformation from man to bat, and vice versa, have

Abbott and Costello Meet Frankenstein (1948): Having just been freed from his coffin, Dracula (Bela Lugosi) examines the Frankenstein Monster (Glenn Strange), who has yet to be revived (courtesy of Frank Dello Stritto).

drawn some criticism, but they tend to work within the lighter, more comic atmosphere felt throughout the film.

Lou Costello initially wanted nothing to do with the script, which he referred to as "crap" and something that his daughter could have done a better job of writing; he changed his mind when the studio promised a $50,000 advance,[69] along with the involvement of director Charles Barton. Costello regarded Barton as a friend and one of his favorite directors.[70]

The dichotomy between comedy and horror, often a tricky balance, could have failed in this picture, but thanks to Barton's direction, the decision to have the various monsters play their roles in a serious manner, and the genuine efforts of Costello and partner Abbott, the film works beautifully.

A degree of controversy hovered over the film upon its release. Some horror purists felt that a film with such comic overtones was an affront to the Universal monsters. Chaney himself felt as if the seriousness of the monster movies had been undercut. That opinion was not

7. Creature Features, Fright Night *and* Block of Shock (1931–1969) 115

Abbott and Costello Meet Frankenstein (1948): Dracula (Bela Lugosi) makes a move on Joan (Jane Randolph), even though she is accompanied by Wilbur and Chick. The film marked Lugosi's second and last film performance as Dracula. For Randolph, it was her only role in a Universal horror picture, though she did appear in RKO's two *Cat People* films (courtesy of Frank Dello Stritto).

shared by Lugosi, who felt that the dignity of Dracula remained. "All I had to do was frighten the boys [Abbott and Costello], a perfectly appropriate activity," said Lugosi. "My trademark stands unblemished."[71]

In later years, a lesser controversy developed regarding *Abbott and Costello Meet Frankenstein*. Should it be regarded as part of the long-running series of Universal monster movies, or as a stand-alone film? The answer to that question is really a matter of bookkeeping, and should matter little in the grander scheme: the viewers' enjoyment of a wonderful mixture of horror and comedy, graced by the presence of so many legends from the two genres. With its fast pace, well-choreographed fight scenes, and the atmospheric backdrop of a Gothic castle, it is a film that entertains to no end.

As horror moved into the 1950s, it began to take on more of a science fiction feel, especially in terms of oversized monsters that came from alien civilizations. While some of these films wandered into silliness, and did little in terms of producing fright, a few exceptions managed to provide legitimate and well-executed scares. There is perhaps no better example of this than the 1951 release *The Thing from Another World*. It became such an influential film that it would be remade several decades later, under an altered and simplified title.

In some cases, both the original and the remake can prove to be classics of horror filmmaking. Such is the case with *The Thing from Another World* and John Carpenter's 1982 remake, *The Thing*. Even though the films come from completely different eras, they are both effective in creating a sense of isolation and dread. The original film stands as one of the best horror–sci-fi films of the '50s, with its stark black-and-white presentation adding to the overriding feelings of terror.

The film is supported by excellent storytelling, eerily set in a remote Arctic research station. Responding to reports of an unknown aircraft having crashed in the vicinity of the station, a team of scientists and airmen uncovers the spacecraft buried in ice. They attempt to thaw out the spacecraft, but that only results in its destruction. The men then discover a strange body, buried in ice, seemingly dead. They excavate the large block of ice containing the body and take it back to their outpost, where a storm is brewing. That's when the scientists and airmen begin to debate whether to thaw out the corpse or leave it intact. Thanks to an electric blanket that has been accidently tossed onto the ice block, the body thaws out, releasing the alien. The creature loses its arm while being attacked by sled dogs, but it will eventually return to the outpost and seek out victims among the airmen and scientists.

Debuting on April 5, 1951, in Cincinnati and Dayton, Ohio, *The Thing from Another World* begins with an unusual series of credits, which don't feature the names of any of the actors. Although we eventually learn their identities, there has always been some mystery as to the involvement of the two reported directors of the film. Christian Nyby received on-screen credit as the director, but producer Howard Hawks reportedly became heavily involved after filming started. Some of the cast and crew who participated in the film claim that Hawks became the true driving force of the picture, while others claim that it was Nyby's film, first and foremost. Nyby himself gave credit to Hawks in a 1982 interview, saying that the film reflected Hawks' style.[72]

Whoever deserves the most credit certainly did excellent work in creating some of the more memorable scenes in horror history, including the early visual of the scientists forming a ring around the alien aircraft. The scientists are also presented as fully developed characters who are generally sympathetic figures worthy of our attention. This is another characteristic that separates *The Thing from Another World* from much of the ordinary sci-fi fare of the 1950s. We find ourselves rooting for at least some of these characters, who are more likable than their counterparts from the 1982 film, in their quest to fend off the mysterious monster of unknown origins.

The director(s) also made an excellent choice in removing several close-up shots of the Thing, which is played by legendary actor James Arness. In so doing, the monster becomes more mysterious and nebulous, and there is no disappointment when it finally appears in later shots from longer distances away.

Fans of the day responded favorably to *The Thing from Another World*, making it one of the top 50 box office draws of 1951. The film has retained a certain level of influence over the years, becoming an inspiration to future directors like Carpenter, Tobe Hooper and Ridley Scott.[73] That influence makes it worth watching, but viewers will also appreciate the smart plotting, the fine acting and compelling story that all make *The Thing from Another World* a crucial piece of horror history.

Horror reached its nadir in 1952, without a single horror film of note appearing in theaters. But 1953 would represent a bounce-back, while also featuring a recent innovation to the film industry. During the 1950s, Hollywood introduced several experimental film techniques. One technique in particular fit in well with the genre of horror. The prospect of three-dimensional viewing gave horror filmmakers the opportunity to scare viewers more thoroughly with an eye-popping special effect that underscored the ability to create both surprise and disgust.

Some fans of horror hoped that 3-D would give the genre a boost in the early 1950s. Premiering in New York City on April 9, 1953, *House of Wax* brought Hollywood into the world of 3-D.[74] It is also an entertaining film that provided a forum for the burgeoning talent of Vincent Price. It remains one of the better pure horror films of the 1950s, at a time when many films had shifted completely into the genre of science fiction.

While *House of Wax* did well during its spring release, it is a film that has drawn criticism over time for its overreliance on trickery that was meant to emphasize the three-dimensional effects. It was the first color film to be produced in 3-D by a major studio,[75] a fact not lost on director Andre De Toth. Some of the effects, like the street performer doing tricks with three paddleballs, add nothing to the story, but simply underscore the 3-D capacity of the film. These gimmicks, some of which lasted far too long on screen, made commercial sense at the time, but do nothing to enhance the quality of *House of Wax* all these years later.

Helping to overcome the gimmickry is the performance of Price as Prof. Henry Jarrod, a skilled sculptor who specializes in creating lifelike wax figures. His business partner Matthew Burke implores him to feature a chamber of horrors in their co-owned museum as a way of drawing larger crowds, but Jarrod refuses. In anger, Burke sets fire to the museum in an attempt to destroy all of Jarrod's creations and collect $25,000 in insurance money. Jarrod tries to stop Burke, a fight ensues, and Burke escapes the blaze, leaving his partner to a gruesome fate. Burke believes that Jarrod has died in the fire, only to stunningly discover his return a year and a half later. Shortly thereafter, Jarrod unveils plans for a new museum, but also hides a secret behind his new creations, one that is rather horrific.

While Price had appeared in films for a number of years, *House of Wax* represented his breakout performance in horror, setting the stage for numerous roles in the genre over the next 20 years. At times, Price received criticism for being over the top in his acting style, but that is not the case here; his performance is more understated, and it is effective. He also has to perform some of the time while wearing makeup that makes him look severely burned. (The makeup was so revolting that a cafeteria worker almost fainted when she saw Price during lunch.[76]) The restriction of heavy makeup might have been a problem for a lesser actor, but not for Price, who succeeds in eliciting sympathy for his disfigured plight—at least for a while.

The supporting cast is also quite good. Three well-known actors all make appearances, including a young Charles Bronson (who portrays a deaf-mute), character actor Dabbs Greer (who would later co-star on *Little House on the Prairie*) and Carolyn Jones, the future Morticia Addams of TV fame. Though unrecognizable from her eventual *Addams Family* role, Jones is especially good as Cathy Gray, Burke's love interest. It was a role that she suffered for months in preparation for; already thin, Jones lost yet more weight in her hopes to look more appealing in the film.

Additionally, there were struggles on the set. Bronson was reportedly difficult to work with, especially for actress Phyllis Kirk, who plays one of the subjects of Jarrod's obsession. More significantly, an incident on set nearly turned into tragedy. At one point, three intentionally set fires raged out of control, damaging the roof of the sound stage and slightly burning Price's eyebrows.[77] Fortunately, no major injuries resulted.

Despite the many difficulties, *House of Wax* emerged as a commercial success. It was not a great film because of its predictability and slow pace, but the 3-D effects proved visually intriguing (at least for the time period), and the story of a sinister wax museum became a hit with viewers. The horror imagery created by De Toth, his ability to create suspense, and the restrained, nuanced performance of Mr. Price all make *House of Wax* a worthwhile experience of 1950s vintage.

Another 1953 release did not rely on any new innovations, but instead drew upon a formula that had been initiated in 1948. While not nearly as good as the famed comedy duo's initial encounter with Frankenstein, Dracula and the Wolf Man, *Abbott and Costello Meet Dr. Jekyll and Mr. Hyde* was a decent follow-up that utilized the talents of Boris Karloff and stuntman Eddie Parker. Released on August 1, 1953, this Universal film once again straddles the line between horror and comedy, making the figure of Dr. Hyde grotesque while still retaining the comedic touch of the two legendary funnymen. As with most Universal productions, the sets and the music are both excellent, giving a Victorian feel to the film.

Abbott and Costello play two American police officers, Slim and Tubby, who have been assigned to work out of London as bobbies. The two bumblers lose their jobs and wind up in jail, where they meet local newspaperman Bruce Adams and his new love interest, Vicky, who is both a showgirl and the leader of a local suffragette movement.

Bruce and Vicky (played capably by Craig Stevens and Helen Westcott) are bailed out by the seemingly amiable and respected Dr. Jekyll (Karloff). The doctor is Vicky's guardian, but he secretly loves his much younger ward. And neither Vicky nor Bruce are aware of the experiments that Jekyll has been conducting, principally his transformation into the horrible Mr. Hyde, who then murders the doctor's rivals. Jekyll consumes his chemical formula and becomes Hyde again, with the expressed intent of murdering Vicky's suitor Bruce. Hyde, played by Eddie Parker, breaks into the music hall where Vicky is performing, but his efforts to kill Bruce are interrupted by Slim and Tubby, who endure their first encounter with the monster.

Joined by Bruce, the two failed policeman pursue Hyde along rooftops and then into a wax museum. Tubby traps Hyde in a cage, but by the time Tubby has summoned the police, Hyde has become Jekyll again. Believing that Jekyll could never be capable of such crimes, the police let the admired doctor go, but he convinces Slim and Tubby to accompany him to his palatial home, with the idea of killing them both. From there, more mayhem ensues, before culminating in a wild daytime chase through the streets and parks of London.

Unlike other movie Jekylls, Karloff's is completely mindful of the ramifications of his experiments. There is no doubt as to Jekyll's complicity in the crimes; he can stop when he wants, but he chooses to continue killing. In fact, he prefers it.

In portraying Hyde, director Charles Lamont opted not to use Karloff in that role. Instead, he called upon Parker, a veteran of over 300 stuntman appearances, including work in *Abbott and Costello Meet Frankenstein*.[78] Parker dons the hideous Hyde mask, which looks like a cross between the traditional look of Hyde and that of a werewolf. Parker brings a physicality and athleticism to his movements that an aging Karloff would not have been able to achieve. The split of the two roles works brilliantly, allowing Parker and Karloff to shine as their respective characters.

Karloff is typically excellent in his performance. While his Jekyll is evil, he is also effective at conveying the dignity and status of Dr. Jekyll, at least initially. In the meantime, Abbott and Costello do their usual fine work, reacting to the presence of a monster with their impeccable sense of comedic timing. At times, their comedy goes overboard and ends up as mugging for the camera, but invariably, Karloff and Parker bring the plot back to more conventional horror. Abbott and Costello also perform a great deal of physical comedy, far more than in their Frankenstein film. In the final reel, Costello's character is accidently injected with Jekyll's serum, allowing for an intriguing transformation and a temporary presence as a monster himself.

The film does suffer by comparison to *Abbott and Costello Meet Frankenstein*. Perhaps that's because of the absence of Bela Lugosi, Lon Chaney and Glenn Strange, all of whom were integral to the earlier story. But the work of Karloff and Parker somewhat counteracts their absences, allowing for *Abbott and Costello Meet Dr. Jekyll and Mr. Hyde* to become an integral part of the comedians' series of monster movies. It's a film that's mostly fun, with just enough horror to keep things intriguing.

Despite the box office success of *Abbott and Costello Meet Dr. Jekyll and Mr. Hyde*, Universal seemed to have reached the downhill side of its horror empire by the mid–1950s. All of the studio's full-fledged classics hailed from the '30s and '40s, leaving Universal a mere afterthought in the horror genre. But the studio did have one last classic in the making, a film that would add a memorable monster to the lexicon that already included a vampire, a man-made creature, a mummy, an invisible man and a werewolf.

Premiering in Denver, Colorado, on March 5, 1954, *Creature from the Black Lagoon* holds its own against most of its preceding classics. The film lacks the iconic name presence of a Chaney, Karloff or Lugosi, but that matters little in the grand scheme. Like *House of Wax*, *Creature from the Black Lagoon* dared to venture into the world of 3-D imagery. That decision created a novelty for theater viewers.

Director Jack Arnold lays out the storyline in cogent, easy-to-follow fashion. A group of scientists, looking for the skeletal remains of a species that could provide the link between sea creatures and land animals, embark on an Amazon River expedition. Much to their surprise, the expedition's crew finds the actual prehistoric creature, living in the depths of a body of water called the Black Lagoon. The Creature stalks the crew, killing two of its members. Now committed to a dangerous struggle, the crew eventually captures the Creature and locks him in a cage, but he escapes during the night. Having become smitten with one of the expedition's members, a woman named Kay Lawrence, the Creature abducts her and takes her to his cavern, setting the stage for a final confrontation with the crew members.

As pointed out by longtime film critic Leonard Maltin, Arnold wisely chose not to keep the camera focused on the Creature for anything more than a few seconds at a time. As Maltin once explained to documentarian Cortlandt Hull, Arnold kept the Creature "dark, deep and distant," which adds to the mystery surrounding the monster.[79]

Rather than rely on the heavy makeup application of a Frankenstein or the Wolf Man, the designers created a suit made of sponge rubber and latex, to be worn by stuntmen Ricou Browning and Ben Chapman. Chapman handled the land scenes, while Browning did all of the swimming stuntwork. Rubber suits have not always worked well in film and television, but the outfit worn by the Gill Man (the official name of the Creature), is realistic and effective. In creating the costume, "form equals function," says an admiring David J. Skal. "It was really an amazing achievement."[80]

The identity of the suit's designers remains a source of mystery and controversy. Universal credited Bud Westmore with its invention, but that was largely because he was the head of the studio's makeup and special effects department. There have been claims that artist Milicent Patrick devised the look of the Creature. Browning has cast doubt on these claims. Speaking at the 2019 Monster Bash convention, Browning claimed that he met Patrick only once; she applied some touch-up makeup to the suit prior to a shooting session. He informed her that unless the paint was water-proof, it would soon wash off in the water.[81]

Browning believes that two other men working under Westmore actually designed and created the suit—and that it was not Patrick or Westmore who served as its inventor.[82]

The designers of the outfit found a distinctive appearance for the Gill Man, who is both unusual and frightening, but still believable. The one detriment of the suit was the poor visibility afforded to the eye slots; Browning and Chapman could barely see as they carried out the physical actions of the Creature.[83]

Browning's work was extraordinary. An accomplished swimmer who was all of 24 at the time of filming, Browning had to wear lead weights on his legs; otherwise the foam rubber suit would not sink into the water.[84] The suit absorbed water, making it heavier the longer that he continued to swim. Browning also needed to be able to hold his breath for minutes at a time. He received some assistance through the use of an air hose, since an oxygen tank would have made the Creature suit bulge awkwardly.[85] Browning's Herculean efforts underwater add to the realism of the Gill Man.

As writer and historian Frank Dello Stritto points out, of the nine monsters spawned by Universal that appeared in multiple films, the Gill Man is the only who is produced from nature. All of the others have either man-made or supernatural origins.[86] The Gill Man is also the only one of those characters who essentially wears a mask, rather than relying on makeup or clothing of some kind.[87] And as analyzed by Dello Stritto, the Gill Man appears to be deaf (and as such, has no ears), cannot speak, and is incapable of changing its static facial expression.[88]

All of these characteristic help separate the Gill Man from other Universal monsters, enhancing his unique and enigmatic nature. The surroundings for the Gill Man also support the story in a highly effective way. The outdoor scenery is strikingly beautiful, from the underwater scenes of the Black Lagoon, which were filmed on location in Wakulla Springs, Florida, to the land scenes, which were shot on the Universal back lot.[89] Somehow Arnold replicated the scenery of the Amazon, referred to by Dello Stritto as "one of the scariest places on Earth."[90]

Somewhat lost amidst the visual imagery and the effects are the fine performances of the cast. With likability as well as physical beauty, Julie Adams keenly plays Kay Lawrence, a colleague and girlfriend to Dr. David Reed, the heroic lead character portrayed by Richard Carlson. Richard Denning is excellent as Dr. Mark Williams, the domineering and jealous man who funds the expedition, while Whit Bissell lends good support as another scientist, Edwin Thompson. Although none have the screen presence or name value of a Karloff or Lugosi, their acting is very capable in support of a fast-moving story that is full of action and movement and fright.

Even the ending of the film is good. As we see the Gill Man, wounded by gunshots and sinking to the bottom of the lagoon, we wonder if he remains alive, or if has left us for good. The answer, of course, would be provided in two popular sequels, *Revenge of the Creature* and *The Creature Walks Among Us*.

Creature from the Black Lagoon succeeds because of its original and creative story, excellent special effects and wonderful underwater cinematography. Many consider *Black Lagoon* to be the last of the great Universal horror films. That is certainly a fair assessment. The Gill Man deserves its place, alongside Dracula, Frankenstein, the Mummy and the Wolf Man, as one of the iconic monsters of the black-and-white era of film.

A different kind of monster made its presence known in June 1954—one that was larger than life size. A number of 1950s films that dealt with oversized insects and bugs of various kinds achieved a dubious quality. Put more bluntly, many of these films ranked as no

7. Creature Features, *Fright Night* *and* Block of Shock (1931–1969) 121

Creature from the Black Lagoon (1954): In this 1950s version of Beauty and the Beast, scientist Kay Lawrence (played by Julie Adams) hopes to survive her encounter with the Gill Man (Ben Chapman). At 6'5", Chapman gave the on-land version of the Creature intimidating dimensions (Historical Media).

better than dreadful, due to stiff acting, poor special effects and ludicrous storylines. There were, however, at least a few exceptions to this trend, including a film that became an artistic and box office success. On June 15, *Them!* premiered in St. Louis and showed the rest of the prospective bugmakers how to make one of these films properly. With its solid pacing, good performances from an excellent cast, and decent special effects (especially for the mid–1950s), *Them!* has become a favorite among the films featuring gigantic insects.

The story begins in the New Mexico desert, where atomic testing has produced an unwanted side effect: the growth of giant ants. A series of desert murders leads a policeman, played heroically by James Whitmore, to the discovery that monstrous insects are responsible for the killings. Whitmore enlists help from federal officials, including an imposing, masculine figure played by James Arness, and a father-and-daughter team of scientists. The elderly scientist, played to perfection by Edmund Gwenn, supplies a reasoned, calm approach to the situation, providing a careful plan of attack, including the use of cyanide gas on the ants' subterranean nest. The application of the gas works, but not without an unforeseen development that complicates matters over the second half of the film.

Them! was supposed to be made in color, but the studio ordered a last-minute switch to black-and-white to save money.[91] That decision did not hurt the film. In fact, the starkness of the black-and-white approach only deepens the atmosphere and heightens the creepiness of the settings. The special effects are surprisingly good for 1954, even if budgetary restraints prevented the director from showing any more than three ants in any one shot. (That's because only three of the giant ants had been constructed.[92]) Up close, the ants look somewhat fabricated, but in longer shots, they take on a more legitimate tone. The effects are especially forceful through the use of sound, specifically the disturbing whirring noise made by the ants when they are first seen in the desert and later in the Los Angeles storm drains.

The film also delivers something of a Cold War message, a common refrain in the 1950s atomic era films. At one point, the script directly references the Cold War. The film also suggests a larger question: Could nuclear war play such havoc with nature that nature turns itself against mankind? The answer would seem to be "yes," though the director chooses not to make an overt political statement.

Politics aside, *Them!* ranks as a classic of 1950s horror–science fiction. Popular at the time of its release, it has held up well over the decades, in part because of the high quality of the acting and the sense of reason and logic that preside over a situation that might otherwise seem preposterous. Of all the giant bug films that gained popularity after World War II, *Them!* stands up as the best. It is good, old-fashioned entertainment.

Much like *Them!*, there is no single monster in the 1956 classic *Invasion of the Body Snatchers*, but rather a more far-reaching doomsday scenario that is powerful and devastating. Debuting on February 5, the film became an example of how horror and science fiction can be mixed effectively, and when done so, create a concoction that is a pure classic. That is certainly the case with *Invasion of the Body Snatchers*, which remains one of the more frightening films of the 1950s, a film that also delivers a biting social commentary for the era.

Told in flashback form, *Invasion of the Body Snatchers* lays out the story of Miles Bennell, who is played capably by character actor Kevin McCarthy. Returning to his medical practice in a small town, Dr. Bennell soon discovers that several of his patients are suffering from something called Capgras delusion—the paranoid belief that their relatives and friends are not whom they seem; rather, they are impostors. Initially skeptical about his patients' claims, Bennell soon realizes that they are not delusional, but clearly on to something nefarious. He and several friends discover bodies that are exact replicas of themselves. Given this development, Bennell comes to share the initial opinions of his patients, as he makes the full transformation from skeptic to true believer. The doctor then tries to makes a long distance phone call to summon federal authorities, but he is told by the operator that all of the phone lines are busy.

Invasion of the Body Snatchers has been interpreted in different ways over the years. Some have called it a metaphor for the growing spread of Communism during the 1950s and a concern that it would overtake democratic society in the U.S. Others take the opposite view, as a kind of warning against the spread of the McCarthyism that targeted Communists, and the recklessness with which the movement unfairly accused so many American citizens. McCarthy always refuted the political interpretations of the film, arguing that it was a thriller and nothing more.[93] Director Don Siegel has argued otherwise, saying that the theme of totalitarianism and its inherent evils are an integral part of the movie.[94] For many viewers and critics, there does appear to be a real-world tie-in; it is up to the viewer to take up the argument for either side.

Whichever view is taken, the film has dark overtones. In fact, studio executives were so concerned by the tenor of the film that they pressured director Siegel to add a prologue and epilogue that served as a way of softening the message. Siegel was reluctant, but ultimately complied with the order from above.[95]

Upon its February release, *Invasion of the Body Snatchers* became a commercial hit. Allied Artists employed creative marketing that may have helped insure that success. The studio placed large papier-mâché pods in theater lobbies, along with cardboard cutouts of McCarthy and co-star Dana Wynter, showing them running away from the alien invaders.[96]

All these years later, the film has established an artistic legacy as well. In 1994, the Library of Congress added *Invasion of the Body Snatchers* to the list of films selected for preservation in the National Film Registry. With its cultural significance, its excellent special effects and overriding sense of dread, the film has become a classic of both the horror and sci-fi genres.

Despite *Body Snatchers*' success, horror films in general had hit somewhat of a lull by the mid–1950s. Universal had seen its prime years of horror come and go, while many other studios had shown a preference for creating larger, otherworldly monsters that fit better into the mode of science fiction. The horror genre needed a jumpstart, part of which would come with the introduction of the "Shock Theater" package to the burgeoning world of TV. But the industry also needed new material, in the form of fresh, first-run films in theaters.

England's Hammer Films would provide that necessary infusion. Although Hammer became best known for productions *The Curse of Frankenstein* (1957) and *Horror of Dracula* ('58), these were not the British company's first horror ventures. A few years earlier, Hammer released *The Quatermass Xperiment*, which some have labeled a science fiction thriller, but which has more than a sufficient tinge of horror to qualify for that genre. Hammer's first try at horror, it was good enough, both in terms of critical and financial success, that it set the stage for a continuing series of horror films that would not cease until the mid–1970s.

Released initially in England in 1955, *The Quatermass Xperiment* would not make its way to the U.S. until April 26, 1956. The film stars American actor Brian Donlevy as Bernard Quatermass, a brilliant scientist who has launched a rocket ship, without official permission, into outer space. When the rocket crashes onto an English farm, only one of its three astronauts is on board—and he is both physically ill and unable to communicate coherently, other than to say, "Help me." Quatermass and English police attempt to interview the astronaut, but soon discover that something is seriously wrong and that a monstrous transformation, perhaps related to the presence of an alien life force, is about to take place.

Donlevy plays Quatermass in a unique way: with a bullying manner that makes him seem more like a military leader than professorial. (And in actuality, he is never referred to as "Professor" throughout the film.) Donley's no-nonsense portrayal reflects the style of director Val Guest, who has a straightforward, documentary-type approach. Along the way, Guest creates a sense of paranoia, a feeling that the worst is yet to come.

Hammer marketed the film deftly by spelling the word "Experiment" as "Xperiment." This decision played up the film's X-rating; at the time, the British Board of Censors used the X certificate to indicate that a film might not be appropriate for viewers under the age of 16.[97] By underscoring the X rating, Hammer made the film more appealing for viewers both young and old, all of whom became curious to see the content that had been deemed too frightening and extreme for some.

Ironically, the film may have contributed to the death of a young viewer. In 1956, a young boy named Stewart Cohen died while watching the film during its double feature showing with *The Black Sleep*. The parents of the boy, who sustained a fatally ruptured artery, sued distributor United Artists, but lost the case. *The Guinness Book of World Records* listed the incident as the only known case of someone literally dying from fright while watching a horror movie.[98]

Of course, it's impossible to know with any certainty if the film's material had anything to do with the boy's passing. But for its time, the horror–sci-fi crossover did supply legitimate scares, thanks to its grit and realism. While not as well-known today as many of Hammer's later releases, *The Quatermass Xperiment* paved the way for the company's entry into the world of horror.

While films like *Invasion of the Body Snatchers*, *Them!*, *Creature from the Black Lagoon* and *House of Wax* are well remembered today, another film from the mid–1950s has become somewhat obscure, despite its heavy-hitting cast. When the list of players includes Basil Rathbone, Lon Chaney, Jr., John Carradine and Bela Lugosi, it would seemingly be difficult not to create a substantial horror film. *The Black Sleep*, which does have its flaws, is an above-average film from the 1950s that remains overlooked, perhaps because of a rather flimsy finale.

Released in June 1956, it stars Rathbone as a renowned surgeon, Joel Cadman, whose wife is afflicted with a seemingly untreatable brain tumor that has put her into a coma. Cadman visits Dr. Ramsey, a wrongly convicted and condemned man in prison on the eve of his execution. Cadman gives the man a sleeping powder to help him calm his nerves prior to his scheduled hanging, but the powder is actually an East Indian drug that induces "black sleep," a condition that mimics death. The next day, believing that he has already died in his sleep, the authorities turn his body over to Dr. Cadman, who revives him with an antidote and brings him to a remote abbey to assist with his (Cadman's) medical research. Grateful that Cadman has saved his life, Ramsey willingly goes along with his new career as an assisting surgeon, but eventually becomes aware that Cadman is involved in bizarre and dangerous experiments on living humans, all part of an effort to develop a treatment to revive his wife.

At one point, another Hollywood heavyweight, Peter Lorre, was scheduled to take part in the movie, but his salary demands proved to be too high.[99] The other actors make up for his absence, particularly Rathbone, who is excellent in the lead role as Dr. Cadman, a seemingly good and just man before he reveals his dark underside. Chaney provides the right characterization for the mentally challenged man named Mungo, but his character's inability to speak limits the actor's usual impact. Carradine is over the top in his performance as a wild-eyed lunatic kept captive by Cadman, but his character appears only in the final act of the film.

Similarly, Lugosi is severely underutilized. He plays a mute butler, and thus has no lines to speak. Lugosi reportedly asked director Reginald LeBorg to give him some dialogue, which he did, but those added scenes never made the final cut.[100] Sadly, this turned out to be Lugosi's last completed and legitimate film appearance (not counting the stock footage of him in *Plan 9 from Outer Space*). The screen legend evokes sympathy with his climactic performance as the butler, but it's unfortunate that we hear no spoken words from this master of horror.

Aside from the small role given Lugosi, *The Black Sleep* has other shortcomings. It is too talky for some, lacking the pacing of some other horror films of the era. It also shows signs of its rushed filming; it was shot over the span of two weeks and carried a budget of only $229,000.[101]

With little doubt, LeBorg accomplished a great deal during a frenetic shooting schedule. Creating terrific sets and creepy imagery, employing wonderful cinematography and good makeup, and allowing some of his brand-name actors to roam free, he succeeded in building a horror romp of decent proportions. Unfortunately, LeBorg's work in putting together an impressive first half of the film is betrayed by the ending, which is rushed and comes across almost comically, a particularly bad fit for a movie that is meant to be taken seriously. With a better conclusion, and with better use of legends like Lugosi, Chaney and Carradine, *The Black Sleep* could have been a classic of the 1950s. Instead, it settles for a status as an intriguing curiosity.

Horror would take a step up the following year. Having warmed up with its earlier *Quatermass Xperiment*, Hammer Films truly turned to full-blown horror with its release of *The Curse of Frankenstein*, which entered American theaters in 1957. *The Curse of Frankenstein* would have an even larger impact than *Quatermass*, to the extent that some film historians credit it as a major factor in reviving the horror industry in the late 1950s.

The Curse of Frankenstein represented Hammer Films' desire to take the black-and-white classics from Universal and offer its own interpretations of the monsters and their stories. Although Hammer would not reach a formal contractual agreement with Universal until 1958,[102] the British company began its reinterpreted series with its version of the Frankenstein Monster in 1957. Over a span of nearly 20 years, Hammer would borrow the themes of the Universal classics, film them in color, and apply a variety of twists and turns to the plots. The end result would be a series of well-done, stylized films that came out during the 1950s, '60s and '70s.

Premiering on June 25, 1957, *The Curse of Frankenstein* made history for Hammer, not only kick-starting the classic monster series but also providing a setting for the first actual meeting of Peter Cushing and Christopher Lee. Although the two actors had worked on two previous films (both of the non-horror variety), they did not actually meet until filming *The Curse of Frankenstein*. They developed a fast friendship, making jokes about their roles and the quality of the script.

Despite the in-house mocking, *Curse* stands as both an artistic and financial success. Directed by the highly capable Terence Fisher, it's an excellent and creative reimagining of its Universal counterpart and remains one of Hammer's best. Hammer's decision to film in Technicolor made this the first Frankenstein movie to be seen in something other than black-and-white.

Found guilty of murder, Baron Victor Frankenstein (Cushing) sits on Death Row recalling the events that brought him here. In flashbacks, we see the baron and scientist Paul Krempe beginning work on several experiments, including the resuscitation of a dead dog. This leads the baron to consider creating a human form out of existing body parts. Krempe agrees to proceed with the experiment, but he withdraws because of the methods by which the baron acquires human corpses. When the baron decides to equip his subject with the brain of an aging professor, whom he targets for murder, Krempe tries to end the experiment. In the ensuing scuffle, the brain intended for Frankenstein's man-made man is damaged.

With the brain's normal activities compromised, the Creature (Lee) is violent, prompting the baron to imprison him. But the Creature escapes and murders a blind man. Pursued by the baron and Krempe, the Creature is shot and buried, but the baron brings him back to life, leading to more mayhem and his own professional and personal downfall.

While Fisher did excellent work in directing *The Curse of Frankenstein*, he was ably assisted by Lee and Cushing. Lee would become best known for his many portrayals of Dracula, but in this film, he plays Frankenstein's Monster for the only time in his long association with Hammer. Due to rights restrictions involving the look of the original Universal version of Frankenstein, Lee looks completely different from the Karloff-Chaney-Lugosi-Strange interpretations of the 1930s and '40s.[103] Gone is the flat-headed look; instead, we see a normally shaped head, but a face that is badly scarred and pockmarked. Since it was created without molds, the makeup application had to be done from scratch each day of filming.[104] The makeup effects work nicely, making Lee a striking figure and an imposing monster.

Much like Karloff in 1931's *Frankenstein*, Lee's Monster does not speak. Lee complained on set to Cushing about being given no lines, but as a relatively unproven actor, he had no power to ask for changes. The role also forced Lee to become physically grotesque, but he didn't care about such inconveniences because of the desperate status of his young career. "I went along and actually convinced them that I would make a suitable creature," Lee told *Hammer's House of Horror* Magazine in 1976. "It didn't worry me that they might make me totally unrecognizable, because I wasn't getting anywhere looking like myself."[105]

In taking the role, Lee significantly advanced his career. Even without the benefit of speech, he used his towering physical presence and his expressiveness to augment his hideous appearance and round out the character of the Creature. While Lee is very good, Cushing emerges as the star of the film. At the beginning, we see him imprisoned, for reasons unknown. His explanation of his fate to a priest, performed in flashbacks, serves as the driving plot of the movie. Cushing carries much of the dialogue throughout, and succeeds in portraying both the good and the evil of the baron, a man driven to the idea of creating another living being out of the body parts of others. At first, we are sympathetic to his genius and thirst for scientific knowledge, but those qualities eventually give way to a dangerous obsession.

The Curse of Frankenstein not only provides quality entertainment, but it stands as one of the most important horror films of any generation. At a time when interest in horror films was beginning to wane, *The Curse of Frankenstein* helped revive passion in the genre.

Another significant film with the word "Curse" in its title made its way into American theaters on March 30, 1958. *Curse of the Demon* is a gem with a creepy, atmospheric tone and well-developed characters. A product of Columbia Pictures, *Curse of the Demon* (also known as *Night of the Demon*) was adapted from M.R. James' short story "Casting the Runes."[106]

Prof. Harrington has been investigating his rival Julian Karswell for his alleged involvement in a satanic cult. In retaliation, Karswell places a curse on Harrington. The professor pleads with Karswell to remove the curse; Karswell promises to do so, but that evening Harrington's car crashes and he is attacked by a giant demon.

Veteran actor Dana Andrews enters the fray as John Holden, an American doctor in London to attend a parapsychology conference. Holden learns of the possible connection between the professor's death and Karsten's cult, but he is skeptical of all talk of supernatural circumstances. Holden meets the professor's niece Joanna, who shows him a diary confirming the fears that her uncle had of Karswell. Over time, Holden's skepticism gives way to a desire to help Joanna and expose Karswell, but Holden finds himself on the wrong end of a deadly curse, one that he desperately tries to shed.

Director Jacques Tourneur succeeded in creating an intriguing and visually striking film while providing excellent guidance for his actors. In fact, he so impressed Andrews that the veteran actor asked him to direct his next film, *The Fearmakers*.[107]

The dialogue and the visual imagery of *Curse of the Demon* are top notch, well above most films of the era. The shots of Stonehenge, the British countryside and the Karswell mansion all add to the atmosphere, making this a truly Gothic experience.

Under Tourneur's direction, the actors deliver good performances. Andrews is solid as the hard-edged and stubbornly skeptical professor, while Irish actor Niall MacGinnis is brilliant as the diabolical Karswell. MacGinnis gives Karswell an exceedingly polite and refined exterior, which only masks his truly sinister intentions. Another key performer is Welsh actress Peggy Cummins, who plays Joanna with genuine likeability while providing moral support to the protagonist.

Tourneur had no intention of showing us the demon referenced in the title, but was forced to do so by the studio, which wanted a more sensational approach to the picture.[108] The decision to reveal the demon could have been disappointing, but the end result was more than respectable. There is a bit of a hokey quality to the demon, particularly by today's standards, but the special effects used in creating the monster are surprisingly good for the time period. Ultimately, the reveal of the demon does not detract from the quality of the film.

All things considered, Tourneur handles the theme of the occult deftly and smartly, while avoiding the camp and silliness of some other films that also tried to tackle the subject matter in the late '50s and early '60s. In the era before satanic themes became exceedingly popular, *Curse of the Demon* represents an excellent foray into the world of devil worshippers, one that keeps us riveted throughout, as we wonder who will win this battle between good and the Devil.

One of the more underrated horror films of the late 1950s is *The Return of Dracula*, an atmospheric movie that would soon become overshadowed by Hammer's *Horror of Dracula*. Featuring a wonderful musical score and an excellent performance by Francis Lederer as the vampire, *The Return of Dracula* has become a cult favorite of fans who prefer black-and-white horror from the 1950s.

Making its debut in American theaters in April 1958, the film reintroduces the famed vampire, who murders a train passenger as he begins his immigrant journey from Transylvania to California. The count takes the identity of his victim Bellac Gordal, an immigrant artist hoping for a better life while residing with relatives in the United States. His stateside family has never seen Bellac, either in person or in photographs, so when Dracula arrives at the Mayberry home in a small California town, Cora and her daughter Rachel assume that he is exactly who he purports to be. Unwittingly, the friendly Mayberrys invite the count into their home, where his strange behavior triggers a few initial alarms before unleashing tragedy.

While Lederer never gained the acclaim of a Lugosi or a Lee, he is excellent in his understated but devilish portrayal of Dracula. Sleek and suave in appearance, Lederer is reminiscent of Lugosi, but his accent is less obtrusive while his portrayal, in some ways, is even more sinister than his more famous predecessor. Surprisingly, Lederer claimed that he despised the film and that he had been tricked into doing the role by his agent.[109] Yet none of his complaints or objections come across during his on-screen performance. He is fully engrossing as the count, charming and charismatic in his disguising himself as Cousin Bellac, before revealing his more ominous and vampiric side. Much like Lugosi in the original *Dracula*, Lederer does not possess fangs and manages to execute his evil deeds without onscreen bloodshed, but his manner is so unsettling that he still creates a sense of fear in each scene in which he appears.

The rest of the cast takes a back seat to Lederer's performance, but Norma Eberhardt is appealing as the young and innocent Rachel, who seems to regard Bellac as something of a father figure. John Wengraf is also effective as a visiting police investigator who comes to realize that Bellac is not who he claims to be.

With its black and white imagery, fine music and careful direction from Paul Landres, *The Return of Dracula* succeeds as a highly atmospheric film that transplants a Gothic story into a modern-day setting. Its simple plot and lack of brand-name actors make it less than a classic, but it is good for what it tries to be: an amusing and frightening film, ideal for late-night viewing.

After its initial success with *Curse of Frankenstein*, and with its deal with Universal signed, Hammer Films realized that it had something good—and profitable—in remaking the monster classics of the 1930s and '40s. So in 1958, Hammer unleashed *Horror of Dracula*, a film that would obscure Lederer and *The Return of Dracula*. Chronologically, *Horror of Dracula* became the fifth of the long series of horror films produced by Hammer Films. But by the consensus of many fans and reviewers, it deserves to be ranked right at the top of the Hammer list for its overall acting, script, plot and cinematography.

Making its U.S. premiere in Milwaukee, Wisconsin, on May 8, 1958, *Horror of Dracula* initially follows the plight of Jonathan Harker, a man who travels to a strange castle in Germany to become the librarian for Count Dracula. There Harker meets the count, along with a young woman claiming to be imprisoned there. It is soon revealed that Harker is actually a vampire hunter, a friend of Dr. Abraham Van Helsing. Van Helsing eventually makes his way to the castle, where he learns the fate of his young friend and associate.

The film takes a number of liberties with Bram Stoker's classic novel—in fact, it bears little resemblance to the book—but does so in ways that enhance the film. *Horror of Dracula* also represents the second unveiling of the dynamic and timeless tandem of Peter Cushing (as Van Helsing) and Christopher Lee (as Dracula), who are billed first and second, respectively. Yet, Cushing does not make his first appearance until 25 minutes into the film.[110] Once Cushing enters, his acting talents become evident, as he establishes himself as the kind of sympathetic and forceful hero that any great horror film needs.

Lee has fewer than 20 lines of dialogue in the entire film—and all are delivered directly to Harker, played by Shakespearean actor John Van Eyssen.[111] The count only hisses and growls at the other characters in the film, but the lack of dialogue does nothing to diminish Lee's screen presence, which is menacing and daunting. But at the same time, the tall and handsome Lee brings a certain level of charm to the role, making him a formidable match for Cushing's Van Helsing. "As soon as Christopher Lee appeared on screen, he was cheered [in theaters]," says historian David J. Skal. "People wanted him to defeat the other forces around him."[112]

For its time, *Horror of Dracula* was considered gory, certainly more so than the counterpart films from Universal. One of the most lasting images involves the character of Lucy, who has a stake driven through her heart. Blood spurts out profusely, and in full color, in a way that would never have been done with any of the Universal classics.

7. Creature Features, Fright Night *and* Block of Shock (1931–1969)   129

Horror of Dracula (1958): In a promotional photograph for Hammer's signature film, Christopher Lee's Dracula moves in on victim Melissa Stribling. At the time of the movie's release, Lee was still relatively unknown, but his memorable portrayal of Dracula, along with his many reprisals of the role, made him a household name.

That graphic scene is one of many iconic moments in a film rich in brilliant images. Another memorable scene involves Harker, who discovers two coffins in the cellar, one of which contains the young woman vampire imprisoned by Dracula. After destroying the female vampire, Harker approaches the other coffin, anticipating the moment that he will drive a strike through Dracula's heart. To his great surprise (and chagrin), the count is gone, filling Harker with a sense of impending doom.

At the end of the film, there is a beautifully filmed maneuver by Cushing's Van Helsing. The vampire hunter forms a makeshift cross with two candlesticks and then pulls down a curtain to allow light to penetrate the room where he battles his nemesis.

The body count of *Horror of Dracula* is merely five. But that shouldn't deceive viewers into thinking that this is anything but a well-done horror film of late 1950s vintage. The photography, the storyline and the skilled direction of Terence Fisher make this a must-see for fans of the era, while setting a template for Hammer's many vampire follow-ups.

More Hammer horror followed during the busy summer of 1958. On June 1, *The Revenge of Frankenstein* made its way into American theaters, as part of a double feature with *Curse of the Demon*. All these years later, *The Revenge of Frankenstein* holds up fairly well, even without the formidable presence of Christopher Lee as the Monster.

The other Hammer lead, Peter Cushing, does return in the title role. Sentenced to death for his crimes in the first film, Baron Frankenstein is about to be executed by guillotine. With the help of his hunchbacked assistant Karl, he arranges for an innocent priest to take his place under the blade. Now the baron flees to Germany, where he renames himself Victor Stein and becomes a successful physician. Apparently having learned nothing from his mistakes in *Curse of Frankenstein*, he resumes his deadly experiments, including the transplanting of Karl's brain into a new body. Such experiments will only lead to a new set of terrors, this time plaguing the German countryside.

In making the sequel, director Terence Fisher re-used many of the sets that had been created for the recently completed *Horror of Dracula*, simply applying some new paint colors and accessories for the Frankenstein sequel.[113] Astute Hammer fans will recognize the re-appropriated sets, but they are still effective in creating the kinds of backdrops that Fisher wanted.

Fisher also presented material that pushed the envelope for its time period. In one scene, Fisher has the baron drop the Monster's brain into a vat of liquid, imagery that created a stir with some of the censors. Given Fisher's willingness to descend into the dark side, the film made an impression on critics of the day. After its release, a writer for the *Daily Telegraph* newspaper suggested that a new movie rating be created for *The Revenge of Frankenstein*: "For Sadists Only."[114]

Fisher did not spare the horror, nor did he shy away from using the talents of Cushing to their fullest. The director relied heavily on Cushing, giving him freedom to develop his character even more substantially than in the original. Cushing plays the baron with a combination of callousness and humor, a blend that creates suspense with the viewers who wonder just what he might do next.

Michael Gwynn plays the newly created monster that employs Karl's brain. This monster is not as physically grotesque as the Lee version; it looks more human and natural. Gwynn also plays the role of the creature far differently than Lee. While Lee emphasized the Creature's monstrous, murderous nature, Gwynn takes a more subtle approach. His monster is more sensitive and somewhat misunderstood, though still dangerous. In some ways, Gwynn's performance outstrips that of Lee, as he gives us a more nuanced monster, and not just a one-dimensional single-minded killer.

While many sequels fail, *The Revenge of Frankenstein* did not. The performances of Gwynn and Cushing, along with the atmospheric sets and the use of intense color and fog, help make it one of the better sequels in Hammer history.

Hammer helped make the summer of '58 a memorable one for fans of horror, but it was not the only company to have an impact. 20th Century–Fox entered the fray on July 16,

7. Creature Features, Fright Night *and* Block of Shock (1931–1969)

1958, with the release of *The Fly*. Though it's not anywhere as gory or as repulsive as David Cronenberg's 1986 remake, the original was still shocking for its day. Blending science fiction with pure horror, the 1958 original left more than a few viewers with nightmares, as they re-lived in their minds a man's horrific transformation into an insect.

The Fly depicts the misfortune of scientist Andre Delambre, who experiments with the transportation of objects from one point to another through the breakdown of their atomic structures. While the process works with inanimate objects, Delambre finds less success with living creatures, such as his family's pet cat. Once he fine-tunes the process, Delambre decides to transport himself—with unforeseen and disastrous results.

Vincent Price is one of the stars of the film, but he does not play the lead role of the ill-fated scientist. Rather, the lead role went to David Hedison, who plays the scientist with naïve enthusiasm in his early scenes before extracting sympathy as the man-turned-man-fly. For much of the film, Hedison appears wearing a cloth on his head, to prevent his wife from seeing the horror beneath.

Third-billed Price takes on the role of the scientist's brother. Unlike most of his screen performances, Price plays the good guy throughout: sympathetic, caring and completely moral. It's an uncharacteristic portrayal that Price takes on, but he shows his acting range by handling the character capably.

In comparison to the Cronenberg remake, the original *Fly* has lost some of its impact and terror over time because of its relative lack of realism and the absence of bloodshed. Limited in its ability to create special effects, the film never shows us the actual teleportation scene involving Delambre and the fly. But director Kurt Neumann compensates by unveiling a dramatic "reveal" for Hedison's character and later giving us a close-up of a fly with a human head, pinned to a spider web, which can be heard crying out, "Help me, help me!" (The special effect here is primitive, but effective.) At the time the film was released, such a scene was truly terrifying; it rattled viewers, particularly younger ones who shrieked and squirmed in their theater seats. Neumann was innovative, too, in the way that he gave us a camera shot that provided us with the vantage point of the monstrous fly.

Neumann himself would become the focal point of tragedy. A German-born director of considerable ability, Neumann died only a month after the movie premiered. Only 50 years of age, he never lived to see the financial success of the film, which became the biggest moneymaker of his all-too-short life. *The Fly* also became his best-known film. Due to his premature death, Neumann has become a forgotten figure in movie lore, but was regarded as such a talent that he was once considered to direct *Bride of Frankenstein*, only to lose out to James Whale.

Like many films of the 1950s, *The Fly* hasn't held up completely over the years, mostly due to its lack of grit and gore, and the primitive special effects of the era. Over the first half of the film, the story is too subdued and slow, lacking the frenzy that one might prefer in a horror film. But for many adults who watched it as children, the film still offers its share of moments that make them cringe and shudder. All these decades later, *The Fly* still manages to wreak some havoc with the minds of a generation that lived it first hand.

Another memorable film that would be remade in the 1980s came out in 1958. The original version of *The Blob*, which entered theaters on September 10, has become the subject of repeated punch lines because of its hokey special effects and a scattered performance from its young star, Steve McQueen. Yet, it's also something of an iconic film that delivers the chills, particularly to those viewing it for the first time. While not an example of great filmmaking, it did exceptionally well at the box office and remains a second-tier classic that is both entertaining and worth further exploration.

Set in a small town with law-abiding citizens and mischievous but harmless teenagers, *The Blob* tells the story of a mysterious alien creature, which looks like a formless, amoeba-like mass of jelly. The mass begins its attack on the community by attaching itself it to the hand of an old man and then slowly making its way up his arm.

Shortly thereafter, as a local doctor prepares to amputate the man's arm, the formless mass consumes the man and then attacks the doctor. Teenager Steve Andrews (played by McQueen) witnesses the attack and attempts to tell the authorities, but they refuse to believe him. By the time the adults realize that his report of a blob is true, it is too late. The alien force, impervious to weapons and growing larger and redder with each consumed victim, invades a movie theater and a diner and kills dozens of citizens. With the town on the verge of doom, Steve makes an important observation that may provide a solution.

The Blob centers on the young McQueen, an unknown at the time who was billed as Steven McQueen. This was not McQueen's first film, but it still marked an appearance from an early stage in his career; his performance reflects that of an actor trying to find his way. His portrayal of the town hero, a teenager with a sense of responsibility, is very uneven. In fairness to McQueen, he was 28 at the time of the filming, making it difficult for him to successfully create the illusion that he was actually a teenager.

McQueen earned only $2500 for his efforts, but could have made much more. The production company offered him a smaller up-front sum, along with a ten percent share of the profits. Believing the movie would not do particularly well, and also needing money immediately, McQueen turned down that offer and took the $2500.[115] That turned out to be a bad choice; *The Blob* grossed $4 million, which would have given the young actor a much larger payday.

Beyond McQueen, the rest of the cast does competent work, but lacks a big-name presence. The film makes up for that shortcoming in two other areas. Director Irvin S. Yeaworth, Jr. presents likable and relatable characters who represent some of the best of small town American ideals in the 1950s. Showing creativity, Yeaworth also unveils a different kind of monster, one that runs in stark contrast to Dracula, Frankenstein and the other definable creatures of Universal lore. This is a monster that is lacking in form or even a face; in fact, other than its color, it has no discernible features. Furthermore, the Blob seemingly cannot be destroyed, which only adds to the level of terror.

To create the effect of the Blob, special effects director Bart Sloane used a modified weather balloon in the early scenes. Later, as the mass grew larger, Sloane concocted a mix of red dye and silicone gel. As each victim fell prey to the creature, more dye was added to the mix,[116] in order to deepen the color of the red and create the impression that the Blob was actually consuming the blood of its victims. In retrospect, many of these special effects look clunky and contrived, but were well accepted by theatergoers at the time.

For all of its flaws, *The Blob* remains a beloved film, particularly to those fans old enough to have seen it during its theatrical release. It has also sustained a strong legacy; the town of Phoenixville, Pennsylvania, one of the filming locations, holds an annual celebration known as Blobfest. *The Blob* will never be considered a horror masterpiece, but it does offer an appealing mix of American nostalgia and 1950s-era monsters, making it an essential part of hosted horror lore.

Thanks to *The Blob*, *The Fly* and the Hammer releases, 1958 emerged as one of the stronger years in horror film history. The year 1959 would not be able to match the impact of the '58 films, but would achieve notoriety in terms of sheer volume. In particular, four films stood out.

Premiering on January 14 in San Francisco, *House on Haunted Hill* enhanced the reputation of its quirky director, William Castle. Unlike some of its 1958 predecessors, the film is not a dense piece of horror filmmaking. It is light and fun, a film not to be taken too seriously, but one that delivers some old-fashioned enjoyment in a classic horror setting.

House on Haunted Hill has a simple and familiar premise: Five visitors are challenged by eccentric millionaire Frederick Loren (played beautifully by Vincent Price), who invites them to spend the night in a rented house that is reputed to be haunted. Loren will lock the doors at midnight; anyone who can endure the night and survive until morning is guaranteed a $10,000 payday. Loren is obviously a strange character, now married to Annabelle, his fourth wife (played by Carol Ohmart), whom he believes once tried to poison him. In spite of the tensions between the two, she agrees to spend the night along with the five guests, all of whom are strangers to one another.

The night in the rented house will be eventful. It will include unexpected screams, ghostly sounds, floating skeletons and a vat of deadly acid. The possibility of death is very much in the air.

Directed by the always creative Castle, the film provides the classic atmosphere of a traditional haunted house. An innovative sort, Castle introduced a "Scare Trick" at the beginning of the film. While the screen is engulfed in darkness, a series of horrific sound effects can be heard. When amplified in the setting of a theater, the effect produced the intended result of momentary terror. Unfortunately, that effect has become somewhat lost as viewers watch a smaller screen with more muted volume in the comfort of their living rooms.

The Scare Trick, and the rest of the film, worked well in theaters. *House on Haunted Hill* did so well at the box office that it motivated Alfred Hitchcock to delve into the world of horror developed on a modest budget. About a year later, Hitchcock released *Psycho*, which remains his signature film piece.

While *House on Haunted Hill* became a moneymaker, it has received its share of criticism for being corny and clichéd, with some over-the-top performances, and for its non-supernatural denouement. The criticism has merit, though the film's defenders say that the corniness plays into its tongue-in-cheek nature.

With his tendency toward campiness, Price was the perfect choice to play the offbeat and mischievous millionaire. He is very good as always, and so is the diminutive Elisha Cook, Jr., who plays Watson Pritchard, the nervous, paranoid, doomsaying owner of the house. The most sympathetic character is test pilot Lance Schroeder, portrayed by Richard Long. A handsome and charismatic actor who was in his early thirties at the time of filming, Long went on to TV success, starring in the popular *77 Sunset Strip* and *The Big Valley*. But he was also wracked with heart disease and died only a decade and a half after *House on Haunted Hill*, at the age of 47.

When judged against the standard of pure horror, *House on Haunted Hill* does not rank particularly well. It is lacking in legitimate scares, particularly to the modern-day viewer. It is the kind of film that is targeted more to fans who are satisfied with mere elements of horror, along with plenty of camp, rollicking fun, and some very good special effects (particularly for the era). Along those lines, *House on Haunted Hill* provides very satisfactory and solid fare, making it worthy of a late-night viewing.

Thanks to the financial success of *House on Haunted Hill*, Castle was able to debut another film later in 1959. On July 29, *The Tingler* premiered in American theaters. Like *House on Haunted Hill*, it stars Vincent Price, who plays Warren Chapin, a pathologist with a history of performing autopsies on executed prisoners. His work leads him to an unusual conclusion: that within each human body, a parasitic creature is attached to the spine; and it grows in size when someone becomes fearful. This creature becomes known as the Tingler.

Chapin eventually meets Oliver and Martha Higgins, who own and operate a silent movie theater. Since Martha is both deaf and mute and is therefore unable to scream during moments of fear, Chapin realizes that the Tingler will grow in size in her.

The Tingler became somewhat controversial because of the inclusion of LSD in the storyline; it's believed to be the first film to show a character in the midst of an LSD trip. While that controversy would quickly die down, Castle tried to make a more lasting impression with one of his patented tricks, an effect called Percepto. At a cost of about $250,000, Castle arranged for some of the larger theaters showing *The Tingler* to install a vibrating device on the bottoms of some theater chairs.[117] At certain moments in the film, the devices were activated as a way of creating a buzzing or "tingling" effect. In a supplementary stunt, Castle also hired people to serve as "screamers" or "fainters" in selected theaters. Typically, the fainter would pretend to lose consciousness, and then be carried out of the theater on a hospital gurney.

Such stunts sometimes distracted from the film itself, which played to mixed reviews upon its 1959 release. *The Tingler* has drawn criticism for being campy—a frequent criticism of Castle films—but the movie is well-paced, decently acted, and full of creepiness and creativity. While hardly a classic, it is a fun film—and a necessary staple of the late-night horror experience.

A later 1959 release falls outside of the ranks of conventional horror, but for a different reason. Debuting on October 21, *A Bucket of Blood* is as much comedy as it is horror. It centers on beatnik culture, and features no major stars. But it is one of the better offerings of the late 1950s, a film that balances the line between horrific acts of murder and an offbeat sense of humor.

Veteran character actor Dick Miller, more recognizable for his distinctive face than his name, fills the lead role as Walter Paisley, a struggling and talentless artist who works as a busboy in a coffee shop frequented by the beatnik crowd. One night Walter goes home and attempts to create a clay sculpture of the café's attractive hostess, Carla. In the midst of his sculpting, he becomes distracted by the neighbor's noisy cat, which he accidentally kills with a knife. Walter decides to cover the deceased cat in clay, thus creating a sculpture, which he attempts to pass off as one of his creations. The sculptured cat is so lifelike that it draws praise from most everyone, including Carla and several beatnik customers, leading to additional work for Walter. But with such little talent for real sculpting, how can he follow up his original masterpiece? Let the horror begin.

With relatively little-known actors and a minuscule budget, *A Bucket of Blood* could have been doomed to fail, but it became an appropriate recipe for the talents of director Roger Corman. In the years before Corman achieved notoriety with his series of Edgar Allan Poe adaptations, the young director made *A Bucket of Blood* work with a good script, inexpensive but realistic sets, an ability to coax good performances from his key players, and a determination to work fast and hard. Given only $50,000 to work with, Corman reportedly shot the film in five days.[118] Even for Corman, it was an incredible pace in which to produce a movie.

For Miller, this was one of only three starring roles in his long career. When Miller saw the film, he criticized the low budget for undermining an excellent script and quality performances from the cast.[119] While there is some truth to the criticism, the film succeeds in spite of its shortcomings. There is little visual evidence that the production was rushed; instead,

7. Creature Features, Fright Night *and* Block of Shock (1931–1969)

the film gives off a vibe of high energy and intense spirit. The film also became an important part of Miller's own legacy: Miller played four more characters named Walter Paisley in future films, including *The Howling* and *Twilight Zone: The Movie*.

A Bucket of Blood succeeds on two levels. First, it provides good old-fashioned entertainment that would be suitable for hosted horror spectacles on a Friday or Saturday night. Second, it effectively satirizes the world of art and the so-called importance of fame. There is fun madness and a message here, making it one of Corman's more effective films and perhaps foreshadowing his eventual success with Poe-related horror in the 1960s.

Before the 1950s closed, Hammer Films gave us one more taste of its brand of horror, but this time without vampires or laboratory monsters. Hammer ventured into the realm of mummies with *The Mummy*, released on December 16, 1959. Although Hammer had reached a formalized agreement with Universal allowing the English company to create remakes of the American studio's classic horror releases, Hammer's version of *The Mummy* is not based directly on Universal's original 1932 classic. Instead, it borrows more directly from two other lesser known Universal releases: *The Mummy's Hand* and *The Mummy's Tomb*. A third Universal film, *The Mummy's Ghost*, became the inspiration for the climactic scene of the Hammer chiller.[120]

As part of the agreement with Universal, Hammer also became free to use the names of the same characters from the Universal series. For *The Mummy*, Hammer called its main character Kharis, the name that Universal introduced 27 years earlier.[121]

Set in Egypt in 1895, Hammer's *Mummy* features three British archaeologists searching for the tomb of Ananka, a high priestess from ancient times. They are told by a learned Egyptian not to disturb the tomb, or else they will unleash a fatal curse. Ignoring the warning, they invade the tomb, putting the curse in motion. One archaeologist, Stephen Banning, is immediately put into a catatonic state. The curse will follow the men to England and create a dire set of circumstances for all involved.

Three years after their return to England, Stephen emerges from catatonia and tells his son John that in the tomb, when he read from the Scroll of Life, he unwittingly returned the spark of life to Kharis, guardian of Ananka. John does not believe his father, but the elder Banning warns his son that Kharis will stalk and murder all those who dared to desecrate the tomb.

For *The Mummy*, Hammer brought back the bankable duo who helped make *Curse of Frankenstein* and *Horror of Dracula* financial and artistic hits: Peter Cushing and Christopher Lee. Not surprisingly, Cushing takes on the role of the heroic lead, John Banning. The Mummy, played by Lee, becomes John's nemesis, leading to a series of skirmishes.

Cushing is surprisingly good in performing the physical aspects of his role, particularly in the scene in which he spears the Mummy. Lee's level of physicality resulted in some personal cost. During one scene, he crashed through a door that had accidentally been locked by one of the film's grips. Lee somehow managed to penetrate the door, but dislocated his shoulder in the process.[122] In another scene, Lee had to make his way through a studio-manufactured swamp. Underneath the water were various pipes and fittings; as Lee waded through, he repeatedly bumped his knees and shins into the pipes, resulting in severe bruises and scrapes.[123] Ever the professional, he used the injuries to his advantage, adding a limp to the Mummy's style of walking.

In some ways, *The Mummy* established the template for Hammer productions that we would see throughout the 1960s and into the early 1970s. The cinematography features bright hues and colored filters and clever back lighting, elements that help create a moody atmosphere so typical of Hammer's later productions.

The Mummy did not escape the censorship of the era. Director Terence Fisher filmed a scene that graphically showed Kharis' tongue being removed, but was forced to tone down the sequence when the censors balked. Another scene involving a shotgun also had to be cut significantly to comply with the standards of the day.[124]

In truth, *The Mummy* did not need the more explicit levels of violence. With its good story, fine acting and atmosphere, it stands well on its own. In fact, it represents one of Hammer's better undertakings, a well-executed and beautifully filmed production delving into the realm of ancient Egyptian lore, hidden tombs, and mummified creatures.

The Mummy closed out the decade of horror in the 1950s. It was a decade that began with an emphasis on science fiction, including alien life forces and oversized creatures, before again reveling in themes of pure horror. It would give way to a new decade that would prove unprecedented, especially in terms of an incredible volume of films, hallmarked by a smattering of masterpieces.

While it can be argued that the 1930s represented the glory days of classic horror, the 1960s might be defined as the decade where *bloody* horror, in full Technicolor, reached new and unprecedented heights. Not only did the number of horror films increase, but so did the intensity, as directors became more willing (and able) to showcase the gorier aspects of the genre. Even American directors became more aggressive, increasingly defying the restrictions placed upon Hollywood by the Code.

One of the first films to defy convention, and challenge the restrictions of the censors, was Alfred Hitchcock's *Psycho*. For the first time in his long and prestigious career, Hitchcock devised a film that could be categorized as pure horror. In the past, he had directed thrillers and murder mysteries, but he also saw the success of films like *House on Haunted Hill* and *The Blob*, noticing that they could be made cheaply and still turn a sizable profit. Hence, *Psycho* was born.

The roots of *Psycho* were modest. Hitchcock anonymously purchased the rights to Robert Bloch's short novel of the same name, paying only $9000.[125] He then bought up every copy that he could find, part of an effort to keep the film's stunning conclusion a secret.[126] Hitchcock reached an agreement with Paramount, which gave him a small sum of money to work with; the studio did not like the novel and felt the film would likely flop. Paramount was so confident about the film's failure that it agreed to give Hitchcock 60 percent ownership in the film and its profits. It would turn out to be the deal of a lifetime for Mr. Hitchcock.[127]

Making its premiere in New York City on June 16, 1960, *Psycho* begins by presenting us with the plight of Marion Crane, a Arizona office worker who has stolen $40,000 from her employer and is now on the run. During her getaway, she stops at the Bates Motel. Marion is played by Janet Leigh, who appears to be the star of the film, only to be taken away from us in midstream. Few directors would have taken such an artistic chance as Hitchcock did in eliminating the protagonist so quickly, but the character of motel keeper Norman Bates, played brilliantly by Anthony Perkins, essentially takes Crane's place as the central figure. Bates alternates between likability and curious strangeness; he is a nervous young man who is both pathetic and charming. He also hides a secret, one that will not be revealed until the film's final reel.

The acting of Leigh and Perkins lifts the quality of *Psycho*, but the performances of supporting actors Vera Miles, Martin Balsam and John Gavin are also very good. At the time of the film's release, only Leigh was considered an A-list film star, but all of the actors, particularly Perkins, rise to the levels of the material. The film reveals Perkins as a newfound star, even if it did create a scenario in which he would be typecast as oddball characters who didn't quite fit into the mainstream of American society.

Psycho reaches its peak of frenzy with the famed shower scene, in which Leigh's Marion is attacked by an unknown assailant whom we believe to be Bates' mother. Chapters of books have been written about this iconic scene of confrontation, in which the shower curtain is suddenly whipped aside, revealing to us the silhouette of a female figure holding a knife over her head. In the coming moments, we never see the knife actually penetrate the skin of Marion. Instead, Hitchcock gives us bold suggestion, accompanied by the most appropriate musical score, creating a scene of shock, a degree of violence that is subtle but personal, and a feeling of absolute terror. As the blood (which actually consisted of Hershey's syrup) flows into the shower drain, we see what is left of Marion's limp body, which clutches at the shower curtain, pulling it down from its rings.

After the murder takes place, Bates is visited by a private investigator who is looking for the missing Marion in the hope that he can retrieve the stolen money. The p.i. reports back to Marion's sister and boyfriend, who will also make memorable visits to the Bates property, which leads to more conflict with the unbalanced Norman Bates.

Spurred by the shower scene, which some have called the most famous scene in horror film history, and Perkins' performance, *Psycho* became a box office hit. Paramount had anticipated a money-losing proposition, but Hitchcock enjoyed the last laugh—and a rich payday. According to historian David J. Skal:

Psycho (1960): The silhouette of Norman Bates (Anthony Perkins) forms an ominous presence next to the Bates house, one of the most recognizable sites in Hollywood history. Located on the Universal lot, the house became one of the highlights of the Universal Tram Tour in 1964. The house has been used in numerous films since being built in 1959.

Psycho was for many years the most profitable black-and-white picture ever produced. Another example where the cost-to-profit ratios are just off the charts. It's something typical of making horror films and low-budget thrillers.

I saw *Psycho* in its re-release, in 1962 or '63, in the theater. It was right around the time that *The Birds* was released. Both films fascinated me. There was a big campaign, "*Psycho* Is Back! See it from the beginning. No one will be admitted into the theater after *Psycho* begins." ...The film had quite a reputation.[128]

Much of that reputation was attributable to the genius of Hitchcock. With only a small budget at his disposal, he opted to film *Psycho* in black and white, a brilliant decision that only enhanced the darkness of the story. He also felt that the absence of color would reduce the level of gore, a concern that he faced with the censors looming over his every decision. In retrospect, the reasons don't matter; it is hard to imagine the film in color and having the same effect. *Psycho* turned out to be Hitchcock's final film in black and white.

Psycho's success became a tribute to Hitchcock's creativity, particularly his ability to tell a story that didn't fit the normal pattern. His editing was also extraordinary, taking what initially was a creation that fell flat, but ended up being a riveting piece of theater. From the cinematography to the casting, Hitchcock hit all the right notes and molded a horror classic.

Hitchcock also exhibited genius when it came to promotion. Each theater that showed *Psycho* during its initial run featured a large cardboard cutout of Hitchcock, who could be seen pointing to his wristwatch. Next to the image of Hitchcock was a message, from the director himself:

The manager of this theatre has been instructed at the risk of his life, not to admit to the theatre any persons after the picture starts. Any spurious attempts to enter by side doors, fire escapes or ventilating shafts will be met by force.
The entire objective of this extraordinary policy, of course, is to help you enjoy *Psycho* more. [Signed] Alfred Hitchcock.[129]

Today's moviegoers might consider such promotion hokey and campy, but it enhanced the experience of 1960s viewers as they watched *Psycho* in theaters. All these years later, fans still feel the power of the film.

By today's standards, *Psycho* is a relatively tame example of horror. There is no gore, just a little blood, and a projection of violence that is far more suggested than it is graphic. "With Hitchcock, less is more," says current-day horror director Harrison Smith. "He didn't have to give you all of the blood and gore. He didn't have to give you all of the nudity. He *implied* things."[130] Even with his subtler touch, Hitchcock defied some of the standards of the Code, particularly through the creatively filmed shower scene and the strange relationship between Norman and his mother. For so many reasons, *Psycho* stands as one of the giants of the genre. It is a classic film that creates tension and suspense throughout while presenting us twists that perhaps only Hitchcock could have filmed so creatively.

As Skal explains, *Psycho*'s success can be found in its ability to blend elements from the old-time horror classics with a more modern sense of violent terror. "*Psycho* is a lot like classic horror," Skal says. "We think of it as a very modern film; obviously it put slasher films into motion and is one of the most imitated movies of all time. ... But it's a haunted house story, [too]. It's a story about the dead possessing the living. The mother's ghost coming out and controlling the son in a way. It's got many, many classic Gothic touches, even though it introduces new trappings."[131]

Filled with tension, suspense, surprises, thrills and subtle terror, Hitchcock's *Psycho* still stands as one of the finest examples of horror on film.

7. Creature Features, Fright Night *and* Block of Shock (1931–1969)

While Hitchcock was an established director testing new waters, a young director was growing into prominence in the early 1960s. Coming off his success with 1959's *A Bucket of Blood*, Roger Corman began a foray into the world of Edgar Allan Poe. From 1960 to 1964, Corman directed eight films adapted from the works of the horror master. The first, *House of Usher,* turned out to be one of the best and also one of the most commercially successful.

Initially premiering in Palm Springs, California, on June 18, 1960, *House of Usher* introduces us to Philip Winthrop (Mark Damon), a man who has traveled a long distance before arriving at the crumbling Usher mansion, where he hopes to find his lost love Madeline (Myrna Fahey). But Madeline and her brother Roderick (Vincent Price) are afflicted with a strange malady: The family is plagued by a curse that will drive all of the Ushers into madness, while also laying waste to the mansion and the adjacent countryside. Upset by Roderick's words and manner, Philip becomes determined to take Madeline away from the deteriorating house.

With his hair dyed white, Price takes on a strikingly different appearance than usual, but the white-haired look is appropriate and fitting for the role. While Price sometimes strayed into campiness and an over-the-top approach in his films, he is more restrained here as the tragic Roderick. Along with *Witchfinder General* and *The Abominable Dr. Phibes*, this is one of Price's top performances and best overall films.

House of Usher represented a major triumph for American International Pictures. Prior to the release of the film, AIP had specialized in low-budget black-and-white films that were usually parts of double features. *House of Usher* was given a larger budget, while filmed in full color and in CinemaScope.[132] Given roughly two weeks to complete the picture, Corman gave it a lavish appearance, heavy on atmosphere and colorful imagery.

Corman also took advantage of an unusual opportunity. Learning that a large barn in Orange County, California, was about to be demolished, he got permission to burn it at night. He filmed the entire conflagration, which became a key part of *House of Usher's* climax.[133] In fact, Corman liked the imagery so much that he would use the footage of the burning structure in subsequent Poe productions. Corman thought that viewers wouldn't recognize the footage, but they did; the scene involving the fire has become iconic to Corman fans.

Audiences responded favorably to the climax—and the rest of the film. *House of Usher* did so well at the box office that it became AIP's largest grossing film, at least until it was succeeded by *Pit and the Pendulum* one year later.

Not only did *House of Usher* essentially remake the company, but it also catapulted Corman's career. He became known as one of horror's most creative directors, an artist who could take a small budget and a limited schedule and turn it into a surprising success. *House of Usher* serves as an ideal example of the Corman way.

September 1960 also produced another notable horror film, an unusual but solid picture from Hammer Films. On September 5, *The Brides of Dracula* made its American debut. It was a sequel to Hammer's 1958 classic *Horror of Dracula*, but it is a curious sequel at that. The character Dracula doesn't appear in the film; in fact, he is mentioned on only two occasions. In spite of his absence, *The Brides of Dracula* plays quite well.

With Dracula (and Christopher Lee) literally out of the picture, the focus switches to female vampires. The story introduces us to a young teacher, Marianne Daniel, who is making her way to Transylvania to begin working at her new job. She agrees to spend a night at the castle of Baroness Meinster, where she helps a young man escape from the shackles his mother put on him. Marianne has unwittingly unleashed a terror that will plague the students at her new school.

Two years after the success of *Horror of Dracula*, Hammer wanted Lee to reprise his role as the fiendish vampire, but he turned down the offer, fearful that he would become typecast.[134] (By the mid–60s, that fear would wear off somewhat, as Lee agreed to play Dracula for a second time in *Dracula—Prince of Darkness*.) Not wanting to cast a lesser actor in the role, Hammer decided to declare Dracula dead, instead shifting the emphasis to a group of female vampires, billed as "the Brides." This could have been a recipe for disaster, but talented director Terence Fisher makes it work, mostly through excellent storytelling and bright visual imagery that create the proper atmosphere. Fisher also made a series of changes to the script just before filming, making the plot stronger and tighter.

With Lee not present to wreak havoc on his victims, the film's star power is supplied by Peter Cushing, back as Van Helsing. He plays the role in his usually sturdy, heroic way and shows unusual physicality for a man of relatively meek stature. Cushing was one of only two actors to return from *Horror of Dracula*; the other was Miles Malleson, who plays a different supporting character in *Brides*, the skeptical Dr. Tobin.

Another key player is handsome British actor David Peel, who portrays Baron Meinster, the young man freed by the unsuspecting Marianne. Proving himself a formidable actor and equal to Cushing's performance, Peel plays the deceptive and arrogant baron in an unusual but highly effective manner. Peel also became involved in one of the film's intriguing footnotes. At the time of the film's release, he was listed at five foot ten, two inches shorter than Cushing. But Peel wanted his character to be the same height as Van Helsing, so he wore two-inch lifts in his shoes.[135]

The Brides of Dracula needed no artificial lifting. The film stands up well, though it does leave one major plot hole that has never been satisfactorily answered. The early moments of the film introduce a foreboding man in a dark suit who hitches a ride into town and then makes a memorable appearance at a pub, his presence frightening the commoners. He then disappears from the balance of the film, and his character's significance is never explained. Is he a vampire, or somehow related to the Meinster family? We are never told. This plot hole leaves us curious.

The Brides of Dracula gives us some of the most famous scenes in Hammer's long line of horror. One memorable scene involves a buried coffin which is repeatedly tapped by a servant in an effort to wake "the dead"; another involves Van Helsing's struggle to deal with a devastating bite wound by applying a red hot iron to it. The film's finale, the famed windmill scene, is especially memorable.

When *The Brides of Dracula* hit theaters, skeptical fans must have questioned how the film could pass muster without the presence of Lee. A *Horror of Dracula* sequel without Dracula? *The Brides of Dracula* manages just fine, the challenge met skillfully by Fisher, Cushing and the rest of the capable cast.

The next film of note, an Italian production, debuted in 1960, but did not make its way into American theaters until February 15, 1961. Director Mario Bava's *Black Sunday* stands as a testament to the power of scenery and mood. Highly atmospheric, it opens with a shocking and gruesome death scene, setting the stage for the revenge motive in the film.

One of the pioneering films to deal in-depth with the subject matter of witchcraft, *Black Sunday* tells the story of a beautiful witch, Asa Vajda, and her lover, both burned at the stake because of their involvement in sorcery. Asa's death sentence is pronounced by her brother, prompting her to vow revenge against him as she utters her final words.

7. Creature Features, Fright Night *and* Block of Shock (1931–1969)   141

Two centuries later, a doctor and his assistant stumble upon her crypt. The doctor cuts his hand on some glass, with some of his blood dripping onto Asa's corpse, reviving her. Asa and her lover eventually reunite at the castle of Prince Vajda, which has long been rumored to be haunted. It is there that Asa will torment her descendants through witchcraft and other nefarious means.

The opening scene, which shows a spiked mask being pounded onto Asa's face, is a very powerful indication of the horrors to come. The imagery of such a scene is why *Black Sunday* works. It also succeeds because of its wonderful sets and its stark black-and-white photography. The latter was critical to *Black Sunday*'s success, according to horror actress-historian-writer Genoveva Rossi: "In a black-and-white film, lighting is so important, because it really affects the quality of the film so much. Bava was meticulous about getting the lighting just right."[136]

The lighting adds to the creepiness of the film. Then there is the talent of scream queen Barbara Steele, who plays both Asa Vajda and her innocent descendant Katia. An inexperienced actress at the time, Steele frequently clashed with Bava, and had difficulty communicating because of her unfamiliarity with the Italian language. Yet Steele does convincing work in the dual roles of witch and innocent descendant. Steele succeeds in making both characters, who are complete opposites, believable and substantial.

Black Sunday lacked a large budget, but Bava's use of scenery and his deft handling of basic special effects belie the relative absence of funds. The dialogue and the general level of acting are mediocre, but Bava overcomes those problems by skillfully using photography and laying down a Gothic foundation that is evident from start to finish. Bava's work represents some of the best low-budget horror filmmaking of the 1960s.

Debuting in American theaters on June 7, 1961, *The Curse of the Werewolf* represents the only Hammer film that dealt with the subject of lycanthropy, or in layman's terms, werewolves and wolf men. The film stars Oliver Reed in the title role, a growling, snarling but reluctant wolf man who would have made Lon Chaney, Jr., proud.

The film is set in Spain and begins by telling the story of a beggar who dares venture into the castle of the evil marquis, where he is horribly mocked and then imprisoned. A young mute girl tends to him, but as she grows into adulthood she runs afoul of the marquis and is thrown into the prison cell with the beggar. Now old and haggard and out of his mind, the beggar rapes her, producing a child who becomes a werewolf.

Right after giving birth, the young woman dies, leaving the boy, Leon, to be adopted by a kind nobleman and his housekeeper. As the story progresses, we see Leon as an adult, portrayed by Reed. While working in a wine cellar, Leon falls in love with the owner's daughter, leading to conflict, particularly when his werewolf tendencies return.

Hammer executive Michael Carreras wanted a Spanish setting because of his desire to see a film done against the backdrop of the Spanish Inquisition. But the Catholic League of Decency threatened Hammer with a ban on the film, forcing Carreras to ditch the initial plot and settle for something completely different.[137]

Rather than rely on action, terror and violence, director Terence Fisher advances the film through atmospheric sets, a distinct mood and an excellent musical score. Reed's character does not appear until roughly midway through the film, but once he surfaces, Fisher gives him ample room to flesh out the dual roles of the werewolf and Leon. Typically excellent in his portrayal, a young Reed gives Leon depth and complexity, with his performance intricate enough that he makes us feel sympathy for the character. As with Lon Chaney years earlier, Reed plays a hesitant and tormented monster, one who tries to fight back against his werewolf tendencies, but his willpower loses out to the power of lycanthropy.

Reed's detailed werewolf makeup was applied by Roy Ashton, the British equivalent to Universal makeup man Jack Pierce. (Ashton also created ghastly makeup for both the marquis and the beggar, making them both detestable in appearance.) In borrowing from Pierce's template, but also enlivening it to take advantage of a color film presentation, Ashton does great work in coming up with his own unique look for the werewolf, one that still has ferocious qualities reminiscent of Chaney's iconic character.[138]

For the most part, Hammer centered its films on Dracula, Frankenstein, the Mummy, and satanic or demonic figures, while staying away from creepy human characters, invisible men and lagoon-dwelling creatures. *The Curse of the Werewolf* represents a departure from Hammer's traditional themes, but it is nonetheless a solid treatment of the subject matter of werewolves. The film does move slowly in the middle stages, but then picks up steam over the final 30 minutes, leaving the viewer with a strong if abrupt conclusion. The film did well enough with critics to force the inevitable question as to why the company did not follow up with additional werewolf movies. Still, Hammer left us with a respectable piece of werewolf film history.

The summer of 1961 continued with another strong showing, this one with a familiar set of horror genre actors. Mixing in a classic horror story, the presence of genre icons Vincent Price and Barbara Steele, and the creative direction of Roger Corman, *Pit and the Pendulum* exhibits the formula of a fine feature film.

Adapted from the famed short story by Edgar Allan Poe, *Pit and the Pendulum* debuted on August 23, 1961. The film tells the tale of a man, Francis Barnard, who travels to Spain to visit the husband of her sister, who has recently died. Her husband Nicholas (Price) tells Francis that she died of a blood disorder. But Francis suspects another cause of death. He will eventually discover that the stated cause of death is not true, but something far more sinister.

Price plays against his usual villainous type for much of the film, portraying the tormented widower. But not all is as it seems with Price's character. In the meantime, the horror legend hams up the effort with his usual flair, delighting his fans who have come to expect nothing else. Genoveva Rossi, a devoted fan of Price, considers this her favorite film on the legend's prolific resumé—and Corman's best, too. "I always go to *Pit and the Pendulum*, because I just feel that's Roger Corman's strongest film," says Rossi. "It's just very artfully done."[139]

Steele handles her modest role quite well, but after the filming, Corman chose to dub all of her lines with those of another actress. Still, she makes her presence felt, even if it's mostly with physical mannerisms. According to Rossi:

> I also enjoy Steele in this film. She's one of the top-billed actors, but doesn't pop up until near the end. She shows her presence, and shows that a small part can have a huge impact on the film. Because you wait for her to appear, and then when she does, she really commands the film. It's a very powerful presence that she has, even though they probably shot her scenes in like a day or so.[140]

Corman practiced his usual magic in completing the film for a paltry $300,000. In creating the second of his Poe adaptations, right after the successful *House of Usher*, he faced a brutal work schedule: only 15 days of filming. Somehow he made it work, thanks to excellent planning prior to production, coupled with beautiful photography and inexpensive effects. For example, the pendulum that Corman's staff devised was made of wood and featured a rubber

7. Creature Features, Fright Night *and* Block of Shock (1931–1969)

Pit and the Pendulum (1961): Nicholas Medina (Vincent Price) puts a stranglehold on his wife Elizabeth (Barbara Steele). According to Steele, the scene was done in one take and literally left a mark: "He really went at me and I had the bruises on my throat to prove it." She added that Price felt bad and expressed concern about hurting her: "[He was] a perfect gentleman" (Historical Media).

blade, but looks authentic on film. Corman also had to convince one of the film's stars, veteran actor John Kerr, that the pendulum was safe. Kerr didn't believe him initially, but changed his mind when he saw how willing Corman was to stand in for him as the crew set up the scene.[141]

If there's a drawback to *Pit and the Pendulum*, it's the film's relatively slow first half, but the pace eventually picks up. The storyline culminates in a terrific sequence of activity over the final 15 minutes. If the viewer has patience, the whirlwind climax is worth the wait.

Pit and the Pendulum represents Corman at his best. His outdoor photography of the shoreline and the castle in the opening sequence is phenomenal, and well supported by a haunting musical accompaniment that plunges the viewer fully into the story. Corman's ability to build tension, his willingness to allow Price to run the gamut of emotions and behaviors, and a beautiful climactic plot twist add up to an entertaining AIP film. It was also a profitable one, outdoing *House of Usher* and becoming the biggest moneymaker among all the Poe films put out by AIP.

Thanks to *Pit and the Pendulum*, Corman was fast making a name for himself in the horror industry. Already well established in that genre was William Castle, whose latest venture premiered in New York City on October 8, 1961. Of all the films that Castle directed in the '50s and '60s, *Mr. Sardonicus* may be the best. Yes, it is silly at times, with a plot that borders on the frenzied, but the makeup and effects are well done and there is enough creepiness as to make this a favorite with genre fans.

Based on a story by Ray Russell, the film centers on the plight and terror of Baron Sardonicus. When a prominent English physician, Sir Robert, visits Sardonicus' castle, he sees the cruel treatment that the baron's henchman, Krull, inflicts on another castle servant. Sir Robert meets Sardonicus, who proceeds to tell him his unusual life story. At one time Sardonicus was a simple farmer named Marek, but he was then convinced by his wife to defile his father's grave in an effort to retrieve the winning lottery ticket in his pocket. In so doing, Sardonicus invoked a curse, his face frozen into a horrible visage, which is revealed dramatically in classic Castle fashion. His wife is so terrified by his horrific look that she commits suicide. Eventually diagnosed with a disease called risus sardonicus, Marek changes his name to Sardonicus and seeks help from Sir Robert. The attempt only worsens the situation for Sardonicus.

There are no big names among the cast, but that doesn't prevent *Mr. Sardonicus* from taking its place among the more entertaining films of the era. Guy Rolfe, who would become known for his role in the *Puppet Master* series of the 1980s and '90s, portrays the cruel and sadistic Sardonicus with relish. His servant Krull is played with equal heartlessness by Oscar Homolka, a capable actor from Hungary. With surprisingly good performances across the board, *Mr. Sardonicus* does not fall victim to the absence of a major player.

The makeup used to create the unusual look to Mr. Sardonicus is so realistic as to be truly horrifying. The effects are also quite good, highlighted by the scene in which Sir Robert first arrives at Castle Sardonicus. When we see the lit windows of the castle from afar, Sardonicus' dwelling takes on the look of a skull. Castle also provides us with other good examples of Gothic atmosphere.

As with all of Castle's horror films, *Mr. Sardonicus* features its share of campy elements. Most prominent is the inclusion of a Punishment Poll: Castle appears on-screen deep into the picture and asks the audience members to determine Sardonicus' fate. The viewers, who were supplied with small glow-in-the-dark cards featuring an illuminated thumb, could register their votes by turning the thumbs upward or downward.[142] This maneuver, in which the audience was made to feel as if it was actively participating, seemed interactive, even though the director had already determined the conclusion to the film. Castle filmed only one ending, thereby rendering the audience poll to the status of entertaining window dressing.

Some of Castle's other films came to rely on such gimmickry, which helped in publicity and promotion while making the theater-going experience more dynamic. In actuality, *Mr. Sardonicus* didn't need such a stunt. The film—atmospheric, eerie and fun—stands on its own legitimate merits.

7. Creature Features, Fright Night *and* Block of Shock (1931–1969)   145

As horror progressed in the 1960s, the subject matter of some films became more controversial, delving into areas that were previously considered verboten. One of the first examples was a film that had its U.S. premiere in San Antonio, Texas, on November 7, 1961: *Peeping Tom*. The product of British director Michael Powell, the film tells the story of Mark Lewis, a young photographer who tries his hand at filmmaking—and also supplies a pornography store with alluring images of young beauties. Lonely and repressed, mostly due to a difficult upbringing, Mark becomes obsessed with the notion of fear; he begins photographing young women whom he has physically attacked. Quickly moving on to murder, he hopes to photograph their expressions as they approach death—and at the very moment they pass on.

Mark eventually comes to know Helen, a kind young neighbor. When Helen catches Mark secretly filming her 21st birthday party, she shows sympathy rather than anger and befriends him. Helen goes to dinner with Mark and the two become closer, at least until she watches in horror one of Mark's "snuff" films.

Peeping Tom was first released in England in 1960. As famed critic Roger Ebert wrote, it "broke the rules and crossed the line. It was so loathed on its first release that it was pulled from theaters, and effectively ended the career of one of Britain's greatest directors."[143] Indeed, British film critics railed against its content, including the nudity and violence, but more particularly the way that Powell portrayed the lead character of Mark so sympathetically. Powell chose Austrian actor Karl Boehm, whose blond hair and handsome features make him look like the antithesis of a serial killer. When not killing women, Boehm seems meek and timid, with a certain level of charm. The criticism and censorship of the film would essentially ruin Powell, who had been making films since the 1930s. Powell continued to make movies, but none would have much impact.

The perception of *Peeping Tom* has changed over time; some now regard it as a masterpiece. It is also believed to be the first slasher movie, predating the 1974 film *Black Christmas*. Given its early 1960s release, the movie quickly became known as the British version of *Psycho*. But while audiences and critics accepted *Psycho* from the beginning, the initial reaction to *Peeping Tom* brought anger and rejection.

A half-century later, *Peeping Tom* seems little different from the slasher movies that came about in subsequent decades. But it was the first of its kind, one delivered in full and bright Technicolor, to an audience that was not yet ready to see murder put on display so explicitly.

Based on pure numbers, 1962 was a relatively lean year in the history of horror filmmaking. Roughly 15 films, a tiny number, could be categorized as horror releases. While quantity may have been lacking, the quality ranked as above average. Five films, all very different, had an impact on moviegoers.

Burn, Witch, Burn, which debuted on April 25, made an impact as one of the period's more effective witchcraft stories. It overachieved, despite the lack a name-brand director and cast, overcoming a plot that is a little bit on the scattered side while operating on a particularly low budget. In England where it was shot, it was released under the title *Night of the Eagle*, but the title was changed for U.S. release to emphasize the theme of the occult and create a feeling of sensationalism. In retrospect, the film did not need the catchier title. The original title was more apt in referencing the plot, which does involve the presence of the eagle; no witches are actually burned in the course of the film.

The distinctive-looking Peter Wyngarde stars as college professor Norman Taylor, who realizes that his wife Tansy (played by actress-singer Janet Blair) has been practicing a form of witchcraft called "conjure magic." When he confronts her about this, she tries to rationalize her behavior by explaining that her witchcraft has helped him advance his career. Angry with Tansy, Norman demands that she cease all of her witch-related activity and burn all of her witchcraft trappings.

Misfortune then starts to plague Norman. One of his female students accuses him of rape, leading to her boyfriend making a violent threat against Norman. In another incident, a criminal attempts to enter the Taylor home. When Tansy nearly drowns, Norman finally agrees to allow her to use witchcraft so that she can save herself—and provide him with help against the unknown dark forces that seem to be trying to ruin his life.

Wyngarde was the third choice for the lead role. Peter Cushing turned down the part so that he could make another movie.[144] The filmmakers then turned to Peter Finch, but he flat-out rejected their offer. Wyngarde was procured at the last minute.[145] Unsubstantiated rumors have maintained that director Sidney Hayers did not want Wyngarde, who was rumored to be gay, because he felt that the actor would be too effeminate in playing the male lead. Even if true, that belief turned out to be incorrect. An excellent actor with a smooth voice, Wyngarde proved himself more than capable, delivering a believable and nuanced performance as the tormented professor.

The work of director Hayers also proves that a headlining star is not essential to effective horror. Hayes overcomes the lack of star power by effectively using a quality screenplay – a product of collaboration between noted writers Richard Matheson and Charles Beaumont, with an assist from a third writer, George Baxt. Their screenplay, combined with Hayers' skilled use of stark black-and-white photography and reliance on some particularly good, low-budget special effects, help lift the picture, making *Burn, Witch, Burn* an important part of 1960s witchcraft lore.

The film has never been regarded as a classic, but it did receive favorable reviews at the time of its release and has maintained a good reputation in the decades since. Hayers' ability to sustain the suspense, which seems to build with each scene, keeps viewers engaged and connected. (So does the performance of Wyngarde, along with the effort of co-star Blair.) The suspenseful storyline leads to a heart-pumping climax, one that gives a fine film like *Burn, Witch, Burn* a fitting conclusion.

Another effective horror film from 1962 was Roger Corman's *Tales of Terror*, a production that represented a union (of sorts) of three horror legends. It premiered in New York City on July 4 while reintroducing theatergoers to the craftsmanship of Edgar Allan Poe. An anthology film, *Tales of Terror* presented three of the macabre master's short stories on screen: "Morella," "The Black Cat" and "The Facts in the Case of M. Valdemar." As with most Corman productions, it was produced on a shoestring budget and completed within the span of a few weeks. In putting together the film, Corman relied on an old trick of reusing sets from earlier movies. In this case, he filmed the conclusion to "Morella," the weakest of the three segments, on the *House of Usher* set.[146]

Like many of Corman's successful productions, *Tales of Terror* belies its budgetary limitations because of good source material, fine storytelling and an excellent cast. The film is perhaps best noted for bringing together three giants of the horror industry: Vincent Price, Peter Lorre and Basil Rathbone. Unfortunately, none of the three stories features the trio of legends simultaneously. Price appears in all three segments, but Lorre is only in "The Black Cat," and Rathbone appears in "The Facts in the Case of M. Valdemar."

The relative brevity of each of the segments has drawn some criticism. Corman generally seemed to work better with a full-length script rather than the anthology format, but

Lorre's presence helps elevate the film from merely satisfactory to something worthwhile. Appearing in the middle segment, which is the best of the three, he brings macabre humor to his role as an irresponsible drunk. The scene in which he and Price, who is over the top as a wine connoisseur, go head to head in a drinking contest is especially funny. Rathbone is also quite good in the third story, bringing a nice level of creepiness to the proceedings, which are already quite morose thanks to Price.

Tales of Terror lacks the gravitas and impact of some of the best anthology films, like *Black Sabbath*, *The House That Dripped Blood* and *Tales from the Crypt*, but its blended balance of horror and comedy has appeal for those who appreciate the genre with a touch of laughter.

One year after dipping into the business of werewolves, Hammer decided to take its turn at another favorite subject, this one a film that saw its origins in the silent era. *The Phantom of the Opera* has been adapted over and over, in movie theaters, on stage, and on television, making it an important part of horror film history. While the 1925 version with the legendary Lon Chaney predates our designated era of hosted horror, the Hammer adaptation falls right into the middle of the timeline. It is not as powerful as Chaney's classic film, but it is still very effective, a solid production that features top-notch directing and acting, along with elaborate sets.

Debuting in the U.S. on August 15, 1962, Hammer's *Phantom* stars prolific actor Herbert Lom as Prof. Petrie, a struggling composer. As revealed in flashbacks, Petrie's compilations, encompassing ten years of his life's work, were stolen by the corrupt and cruel Lord Ambrose d'Arcy (Michael Gough). When Petrie realizes that d'Arcy has put his own name on the professor's work, he breaks into the printing office containing the stolen sheet music and begins to destroy it. As he burns the sheet music page by page, the fire rages out of control, leading to Petrie's severe disfigurement from fire and acid.

Petrie plunges into the local river but is rescued by a deformed man who becomes his assistant. Now masked as the Phantom, Petrie returns years later to terrorize the London Opera House that is featuring a performance based on his stolen music. Rather than commit acts of revenge himself, the Phantom employs his assistant, who is unable to speak but is more than willing to carry out acts of violence.

In casting the film, Hammer gave strong consideration to Christopher Lee but ultimately chose Lom,[147] a highly capable actor who would become better known for his recurring role as Peter Sellers' boss in the *Pink Panther* films. As the Phantom, Lom proves effective, though his screen time is limited. He is no Lon Chaney, but he still plays the part with a capable combination of pathos and anger. In the meantime, Gough is wonderful as the arrogant and lecherous d'Arcy, playing the role deliciously and exceeding the evil of the murderous but sympathetic Phantom.

The rest of the cast is capable, headlined by young actress Heather Sears; she plays the innocent Christine, who becomes the object of The Phantom's obsession. Edward de Souza is very good as Hunter, a likable character who is the perfect hero vying against the horrific d'Arcy.

Directed by Terence Fisher, *The Phantom of the Opera* features plush sets and a Gothic feel that is emblematic of Hammer's best. The Phantom's subterranean lair is particularly well done, complete with a flowing aqueduct that provides access to the outside world. Fisher also manages to create a new interpretation of Gaston Leroux's original novel, making the Phantom more tragic and less villainous. Fisher does well in delivering a creative new spin on an old story.

Somewhat surprisingly, *The Phantom of the Opera* did not do well in theaters, perhaps because it played more like a drama and lacked the typical level of terror found in Hammer films. In fact, *Phantom* proved such a financial flop that Hammer refused to give Fisher another film until 1964.[148] Yet, box office failure does not always accurately reflect a film's quality. That is certainly the case with Fisher's effort. It is a very good film, ranking only behind the classic Chaney version among the many adaptations of *The Phantom of the Opera*.

Released in the United Kingdom in 1960, *The City of the Dead* arrive stateside two years later, on September 12, 1962. By then, this highly effective picture had been renamed *Horror Hotel*. The black-and-white film turned out to be worth the wait, and the title change proved worthwhile, too. *Horror Hotel* presents the viewers with a solid story about witchcraft and Satanism, while also displaying the talents of Christopher Lee in a role of something other than a vampire or man-made monster.

Horror Hotel was the first film produced by a new company, Vulcan Films, which would later become Amicus Productions.[149] Amicus produced *Dr. Terror's House of Horrors*, *The Skull*, *The Beast Must Die et al.*, proving to be a formidable rival to Hammer Films in the '60s and '70s.

Horror Hotel features Venetia Stevenson as Nan Barlow, a college coed who decides to use a winter break as an opportunity to travel and learn more about the subject of witchcraft. Upon the recommendation of her college professor (Lee), she travels to the small village of Whitewood, where she soon begins to notice strange occurrences, including a trap door in her hotel room floor. When Nan disappears, her brother and boyfriend travel to Whitewood in hopes of finding some answers.

The plot of the film bears some resemblance to the far more famous *Psycho*, particularly the way that the protagonist is dispatched in surprisingly fast fashion. As with the Hitchcock film, it's a controversial technique, but it works well here. Stevenson performs capably while she is on screen, but is obviously overshadowed by the presence of veteran actors Lee and Patricia Jessel, an actress with an unusual physical appearance. Lee is cold and unfeeling as duplicitous college professor Alan Driscoll, while Jessel, with her hawk-like facial features, plays her role as the manager of the local Raven's Inn to perfection. Jessel would become a tragic figure in horror history, dying from a heart attack in 1968 at the age of 47.

Led by first-time director John Moxey, *Horror Hotel* succeeds in creating the consummate eerie atmosphere for a 1960s horror film. In underscoring the creepy tension, Moxey skillfully uses raw black-and-white film footage, employs an everpresent, low-lying fog in the secluded village of Whitewood, and beautifully contrasts moody music against moments of stark silence. The end result is the perfect atmosphere for a film about witchcraft, satanic gatherings and a conspiracy of evil against the village's few innocent citizens.

If there is a criticism to this underrated gem, it's the relatively small amount of screen time given to Lee. As is typically the case with him, he is very good while on camera, but he disappears for a long stretch. He also says little during the movie's climactic scene; in this case, silence is not ideal.

Outside of the underuse of Lee, *Horror Hotel* rates as a very entertaining offering from the early '60s. For those who enjoy atmosphere, tension, suspense and a creative ending in which a large shadow cast by a cross proves pivotal, *Horror Hotel* strikes all of the proper chords.

In stark contrast to *Tales of Terror* and *Horror Hotel*, *Carnival of Souls* lacks brand-name actors and received only lukewarm response upon its American premiere in Lawrence, Kansas, on September 26, 1962. None of that should matter. The film has become increasingly appreciated over time, and deservedly so, for its spooky black-and-white imagery and its well-crafted ghost story centered on an abandoned carnival.

The film stars Candace Hilligoss as Mary Henry, a young woman who has remarkably survived a drag racing car accident in rural Kansas that resulted in the drowning of two of her friends. Regaining consciousness with no real understanding of how she was able to survive, Mary will recover from the accident, move to Salt Lake City and take employment as a church organist. Encountering visions of a strange man and an abandoned carnival pavilion located on the shore of the Great Salt Lake, she decides to visit the pavilion. But she is prevented from entering by a minister, who warns her that it would constitute trespassing for her to step onto the grounds. After returning to her rooming house, she sees the strange man from her earlier vision and begins to endure stretches of time where she cannot be heard or seen by other people.

Carnival of Souls was Hilligoss' feature film debut. She would rack up only six film and television credits over a brief career, but does very credible work as the main character of *Carnival of Souls*. She forges a likable and vulnerable character, multi-dimensional and appealing. The rest of the cast is not quite as good, but is certainly acceptable.

In making mostly short educational and documentary films over a career that would end in the early 1980s, director Herk Harvey compiled an obscure resumé that mirrored that of Hilligoss. In fact, he never again made a feature film. But like his lead actress, he rises above the expected level. Despite working with a shoestring budget and a crew that consisted of only five people, he creates a wonderfully atmospheric film full of creepy images and settings.

Harvey's choice of an abandoned amusement park for the site of the defunct carnival was pure genius; the grounds add authenticity and a sense of isolation, creating an excellent backdrop for the hauntings experienced by the solitary Mary. The use of black-and-white, while likely a financial decision, also works perfectly in underscoring the stark and desolate images of the carnival grounds.

Carnival of Souls certainly has its flaws. The editing is choppy and the sound is so poor at times as to make it difficult to hear some of the dialogue. The film's slow start also hurts; it takes a while for the story to gain momentum and take hold. These criticisms have merit and prevent the film from achieving a higher level of acclaim, but ultimately they do not ruin the film. A good ghost story, the surprisingly effective acting, and the persistently eerie atmosphere lift *Carnival of Souls* into the realm of cult favorites from the 1960s.

Despite the lack of depth in the genre, 1962 turned out to be a respectable year for horror. The year of 1963 would become a landmark year for the genre, beginning with a January release and continuing into the fall.

In January, American International Pictures released a new adaptation of *The Raven*, a film idea (and name) that had first been introduced in silent days. Debuting on January 25, the 1963 version of *The Raven* is not an example of classic horror and bears no resemblance to its predecessors. It is a blend of genres: primarily a comedy that mixes in elements of fantasy and horror. Yet it is a film that makes for essential viewing, in large part because of the presence of three screen legends: Karloff, Peter Lorre and Vincent Price. They all play vital roles in creating a memorable experience that is far more humorous than it is frightening.

Purportedly based on the famed poem by Edgar Allan Poe, *The Raven* has little to do with its alleged source. Price stars as Dr. Erasmus Craven, a former sorcerer who has been mourning his wife's death for more than two years. Erasmus is visited by a raven who was once a man. With the help of Erasmus, the raven regains his previous form as Dr. Adolphus

Bedlo, a magician. Bedlo tells Erasmus that his transformation into a raven was caused by the evil Dr. Scarabus (Karloff). He also explains that he saw the ghost of Erasmus' long-lost wife at Dr. Scarabus' castle. Linked by hatred of their oppressor, Craven and Bedlo decide to band together, travel to the castle accompanied by Bedlo's son (Jack Nicholson) and Erasmus' daughter, and seek revenge on the horrid Dr. Scarabus. The situation leads to a memorable climax: an intense duel of magic featuring the heavyweight talents of Price and Karloff.

Rather than give us serious horror, *The Raven* offers a lighter touch. "*The Raven* was really fun," says film historian and actress Genoveva Rossi. "You had Boris Karloff in that, and even Jack Nicholson pops out. You can see that Jack Nicholson was maybe a little green as an actor at that point; he hadn't really come into his own yet, but he was just kind of learning. But it was cool to see him in that movie with all of those great guys."[150]

This marked the first of two collaborations between Nicholson and Karloff; the two would remain together for *The Terror*, which director Roger Corman began filming right after *The Raven*. As if Nicholson and the trio of horror legends are not sufficient in *The Raven*, Hazel Court turns in a memorable performance as Lenore, Erasmus' wife.

Corman gave his cast plenty of latitude in formulating *The Raven*. Lorre and Nicholson ad-libbed many of their lines, especially the punch lines, which did not bother Price, but affected the aging Karloff, who was used to working directly from a written script.[151] Lorre and Nicholson also intensified the anger between the two characters. Those feelings of hostility were not in the original Richard Matheson screenplay, but were improvised by the actors. Corman felt that the byplay worked and he allowed it to continue throughout the film.[152]

Corman wrapped up filming within 15 days,[153] typifying his whirlwind ability to produce a film. With the help of art director Daniel Haller, Corman used elaborate sets in creating a Gothic atmosphere, which is most evident in the cavernous and intricate castle of Dr. Scarabus. But rather than play the film as straight horror, Corman chose a comedic approach. Many of the lines are delivered in tongue-in-cheek fashion in what is essentially a parody of old horror films. For some, the humor might be dated, but for others, it's a fond recollection of a simpler time.

While some critics have wondered how *The Raven* might have fared as serious horror, it nonetheless works in its comedic form. The intermingling of three horror icons, along with the eye-catching sets and costumes, makes for an entertaining and fun-filled romp, if not a film that actually frightens.

After his unexpected success with *Psycho* in 1960, some critics wondered how Alfred Hitchcock could possibly match the impact with his next film. Would he return to thrillers, or would he attempt another horror-themed production? Opting for the latter, Hitchcock created another masterpiece, *The Birds*, which premiered in New York City on March 28, 1963, before receiving a nationwide release one day later.

Although derided by a few current-day film critics, *The Birds* remains a significant piece of horror history. Yes, some of the 1963 effects are dated and the script leaves too many questions unanswered, at least in some fans' opinions. But *The Birds* still delivers, mostly because of its balanced combination of terror and subtly supernatural overtones, its overriding sense of mystery, and its wonderful cinematography, all accomplished without a musical score.

Rod Taylor leads a wonderful cast that also featured Tippi Hedren (who was making her first full appearance in a theatrical film), Suzanne Pleshette and the accomplished Jessica Tandy. While Taylor's heroic character Mitch Brenner is likable and charming, Hedren's Melanie Daniels is strange and out of place (at least during the first half of the film). After

7. Creature Features, Fright Night *and* Block of Shock (1931–1969) 151

Mitch meets socialite Melanie in a San Francisco pet store, an awkward conversation ensues, resulting in his decision not to buy a pair of lovebirds as a birthday present for his young sister. Now interested in Mitch, Melanie decides to buy the love birds for him. She pursues him to Bodega Bay, a remote suburb where Mitch is spending the weekend with his sister and mother. The contrast between socialite Daniels and downhome Bodega Bay enhances the tension over the first hour of the film.

Just as Daniels starts to win favor with Mitch's family and some of the locals, including a schoolteacher (and Mitch's former girlfriend, played by Pleshette), the story takes a major turn. Shortly after Daniels' arrival, a couple of bird attacks took place in Bodega Bay. Those attacks begin to multiply and grow in size, with a variety of birds (including crows, ravens and seagulls) targeting the citizens of Bodega Bay. The attacks create some of the most iconic scenes in Hollywood history. One of the most memorable scenes takes place at the service station, where a sudden assault by an army of birds leads to a gasoline spill and a dropped match. Perhaps the most lasting sequence is the view of the children running from the Bodega Bay schoolhouse, a real-life location that had been rumored to be haunted for decades, even before filming took place. And, of course, there is the dramatic climax with the characters' departure from the Brenner family house—and the presence of what appear to be thousands of birds, patiently waiting to execute their next attack.

It's hard to imagine what Hedren, particularly as a young and inexperienced actress, went through in enduring the production of *The Birds*. She had to fend off the obsessive sexual advances of director Hitchcock,[154] while also enduring several harrowing scenes in which she was pecked and pawed by actual birds that were literally being thrown at her. The scene on the second floor of the Brenner house, in which Hedren is brutally attacked by a large number of birds, was particularly excruciating. (Hedren had been promised that all of the birds in the film would be mechanical ones, but they didn't work to Hitchcock's liking, necessitating the inclusion of live ones.) Through it all, through this "mental prison"[155] that Hitchcock imposed, Hedren manages a very capable performance.

As much hell as Hitchcock put Hedren through, the success of *The Birds* is yet another tribute to his vast filmmaking skills. "I love [*The Birds*]," says historian David J. Skal. He continues:

> It's a film I return to again and again. I watch it again every few years. It's completely fascinating, even if you don't know about the weird backstory on the film, everything that Tippi Hedren had to endure making it. It's a unique movie. It is a completely controlled exercise. Hitchcock was a control freak. That film is a really good example of him not just controlling the script and the image on screen, but all the people involved in the film, especially the leading lady.[156]

The Birds also represented a creative departure for the Master of Suspense. Most of Hitchcock's films, while wonderful samples of horror or thrillers, do not involve the supernatural. *Psycho* did not. *Rear Window* did not. *Frenzy* did not. But there is clearly an otherworldly element to *The Birds*.

Hitchcock did not initiate the content for *The Birds*; he drew his material from Daphne Du Maurier's wonderful short story of the same name. (Du Maurier's ending is more abrupt and even more nebulous than the film, but it is otherwise a classic piece of horror fiction.) Hitchcock's willingness to rely on material with supernatural overtones created questions in the minds of mainstream moviegoers. Could birds really band together, in a way that smacks of some supernatural force governing them, and start attacking people? Most natural historians would dismiss such a scenario. It's certainly unlikely, but the film makes you wonder about that horrific possibility.

The Birds (1963): In a classic scene, Melanie Daniels (Tippi Hedren) and two children flee the Bodega Bay schoolhouse, hoping to outrun the attack of a swarm of violent birds. Throughout filming, Hedren endured a hellish experience, not only fending off birds that were being thrown at her, but also the advances of director Alfred Hitchcock.

"I don't think *The Birds* would have been made without all of the science fiction revenge-of-nature films of the 1950s," Skal maintains. "They really kind of paved the way for an audience to accept something like this. The attack of the giant grasshoppers, and preying mantises, the giant spiders and flies, and the whole menagerie created a kind of fertile ground for Hitchcock to concoct *The Birds*."[157]

The ending of *The Birds* has caused some controversy, particularly for those who desire a clear resolution to their horror. Yet the lack of a definitive answer might be one of the film's strengths. "It ends on such a note of ambiguity," says Skal. "It doesn't close the circle. All you can do is go back and watch it again, and decide what to make of it."[158]

Ultimately, *The Birds* seems believable. Therein lies the real terror. That, along with the creative cinematography, the strong performances, and the good writing, maintain *The Birds* as must-see viewing for fans of horror. While it might not match *Psycho* on a list of all-time greats, *The Birds* remains a cinematic classic. It is one of Hitchcock's best.

A lesser known film also delivered a dose of quality horror in 1963. Premiering in Cincinnati on August 28, *The Haunted Palace* is one of those underrated gems that has become somewhat forgotten over time, perhaps because it is overshadowed by so many other great films from the 1960s. Yet it is one of the more entertaining horror films of the era, a fine pairing of two film legends, and yet another example of Roger Corman's "make the most out of a little" filmmaking ability.

The film gives us our only opportunity to see two iconic genre figures, Vincent Price and Lon Chaney, Jr., working together. This makes *The Haunted Palace* a must-see event for any aficionado of horror. Price takes top billing in a dual role. The film is set in the small New England village of Arkham and in the opening scene, Price is seen as Joseph Curwen, a warlock about to be burned at the stake. Before he dies, he places a curse on the Arkham residents who have sentenced him to death. Several generations later, the warlock's great grandson, Charles Dexter Ward, once again played by Price, returns to the family palace in Arkham, which he has inherited. The spirit of Curwen attempts to take over his body, creating a Jekyll-and-Hyde kind of struggle. Price is simply outstanding in his portrayals of descendant Ward, a kind and moral man, and Curwen, whose evil streak is evident in the shabby treatment of his wife and his vows of revenge against Arkham, a town that has been plagued by a variety of birth defects resulting from the warlock's curse.

Chaney is also good as Curwen's manservant. Originally, Corman had chosen Boris Karloff to play the role, but the actor became ill after filming *Black Sabbath*.[159] So Corman turned to a capable replacement in Chaney as the servant, who is loyal to Curwen but also tries to question him as to when his acts of revenge will be sufficient.

Chaney and Price work well together, even though it was apparent that the elder of the two actors was struggling. "He was very ill at the time," Price said of Chaney. "I had admired him enormously and wanted to meet him. He was not really very happy.... I spent a lot of time with him, trying to talk with him and make him cheer up, but I couldn't do it."[160]

Beyond Price and Chaney, the supporting cast is also quite good. The cast included Debra Paget (who would surprisingly retire from Hollywood only a few years later) and acting veteran Frank Maxwell, who is excellent as the wise and level-headed Dr. Willet.

The Haunted Palace was part of a long line of films that Corman directed for American International Pictures. Like the other Corman-AIP ventures, the film was billed as an adaptation of an Edgar Allan Poe story, but that was an outright deception engineered by the company in the belief that the Poe connection would help sell tickets.[161] In reality, *The Haunted Palace* was actually taken from an H.P. Lovecraft novella, *The Case of Charles Dexter Ward*. Corman desired a break from the Poe adaptations and chose Lovecraft, but AIP did not feel that Lovecraft was as bankable an author as Poe. AIP allowed the Lovecraft story to be used, but insisted on calling the film *The Haunted Palace* to perpetuate the myth that the story was drawn from a Poe work.[162]

Even without much money to work with, Corman employed attractive set designs, some of which he borrowed from *The Raven*.[163] With its sprawling castle, secret passageways and ground level fog, the film's atmosphere complements the story beautifully. Corman also makes good use of an excellent Charles Beaumont script. *The Haunted Palace* is one of the best of the Price-Corman collaborations, with the added bonus of Chaney thrown into the mix.

The film year of 1963 would grow in significance thanks to an important release in the fall. Just a few months after the spring debut of *The Birds*, *The Haunting* entered theaters. In contrast to *The Birds*, its impact would not be felt immediately.

The Haunting provides a perfect example of a film that has gained stature over time. When it was first shown in limited release on August 21, it did acceptably, but not spectacularly, at the box office. It was considered a good film, but also drew criticism because of the plot, which was difficult to follow, and at times became almost indecipherable. Decades later, *The Haunting* has achieved the status of a supernatural classic, part of any essential library of 1960s horror.

The film tells the story of Hill House, an old mansion being investigated because of its sordid history of mayhem, violence and death. Dr. John Markway, played by the capable English actor Richard Johnson, leads an investigation of Hill House in an effort to prove the existence of ghosts. As part of his investigation, he recruits three others—a clairvoyant, a psychic and a skeptic. In due time, a presence manifests itself within the house, creating dangers for its four inhabitants.

The Haunting represents good, old-fashioned, homespun horror. Director Robert Wise relies on wonderful cinematography and the use of unusual camera angles to create a character out of Hill House itself. He also skillfully uses black-and-white, instead of color, as a way of creating an atmospheric and moody film full of disturbing undertones. The special effects are limited but effective, especially the use of a large door that appears to be pulsating.

Wise first became interested in the project after reading a favorable review of the novel *The Haunting of Hill House*. He contacted author Shirley Jackson to secure the movie rights. The film's screenwriter, Nelson Gidding, also consulted Jackson to go over ideas for the film version.[164] With Jackson's cooperation, *The Haunting* soon resulted as a generally faithful adaptation to the book.

Always known as being calm and reasoned, Wise established good relationships with all of his stars. His even-keel temperament helped the film succeed in the face of some of its difficult inner workings. Russ Tamblyn, who played the skeptical Luke Sanderson, initially balked at the role, at least until MGM made threats of legal ramifications. Tamblyn relented.[165] He did not regret it, later recalling *The Haunting* as one of his favorite movies.

The two female leads hardly spoke on set. Claire Bloom, playing the clairvoyant, tried to strike up conversations with Julie Harris, only to have her co-star rebuff those efforts. Bloom did not understand what had caused an apparent rift with Harris. After the filming, Harris approached Bloom, presenting her with a gift and explaining that she had remained aloof in order to remain in character, as someone who was an outsider to the rest of the inhabitants of the house.[166] Perhaps the strategy worked, given how good Harris is in portraying an emotionally unstable character who is laughing playfully at one moment and screaming in anger at the next.

The relationship between the characters established by Bloom and Harris also created controversy at the time. Bloom's character Theodora seems to be a lesbian, and one who has feelings for Harris' Eleanor, bringing a taboo subject to the table of mainstream theater. Rather than present such a relationship blatantly, Wise does so subtly, so that the film passed muster with the censors.

Appreciation for the film has grown over time. As we see repeatedly in good films from this era, a combination of atmosphere, mood, special effects and suspense win out over other areas of inadequacy. That winning combination lifts *The Haunting* to cult status among horror fans.

On January 19, 1964, *Strait-Jacket* kickstarted a new year in horror. Not meant to be taken too seriously, *Strait-Jacket* is so campy that it is occasionally funny, yet it still retains enough of a hardened edge to maintain its status as a legitimate film from the horror genre.

Directed by the prolific William Castle, *Strait-Jacket* provided Joan Crawford with another vehicle during a 1960s comeback that had been triggered by the surprising success of *What Ever Happened to Baby Jane?* Crawford plays Lucy Harbin, a deranged woman who has been held in an asylum for the last 20 years, ever since killing her cheating husband and his mistress with an axe. Now deemed worthy of release, Harbin is taken in by her brother and his wife, who reside on a farm. There Lucy tries to reconnect with her daughter Carol,

7. Creature Features, Fright Night *and* Block of Shock (1931–1969)   155

who had the misfortune of witnessing the murders at a very young age, but seems mostly unaffected by her mother's crimes. As Lucy attempts to reestablish their relationship, and adjust to public life in general, a new series of axe murders ensues. Is she responsible for the new crimes?

Crawford is borderline brilliant in her role, which is accentuated by a rather outlandish wig and outfit. Under the original plan, Joan Blondell was scheduled to portray Lucy, but had to withdraw at the last moment due to an accident.[167] Castle turned to Crawford, with whom he was quite familiar, claiming to have watched *What Ever Happened to Baby Jane?* nearly 20 times. Crawford agreed to do *Strait-Jacket*, but insisted on a complete re-write of the script so that it would meet her specifications.[168] To her credit, Crawford justified the re-writing with a dynamic, full-force acting effort.

Crawford's co-star, Diane Baker, joined the production at an even later date. Replacing the first two actresses who had been chosen to play the daughter, one of whom could not wear a rubber mask because it was too claustrophobic, Baker agreed to the role only one day before shooting began.[169] Crawford and Baker performed well together, so much so that they reunited for another production just a few months later.

The film also has a notable supporting cast, including longtime character actors George Kennedy and Leif Erickson. A young Lee Majors played an uncredited role: In a flashback scene, he plays the tragic Mr. Harbin, Lucy's husband and first victim. It was Majors' big screen debut.

While Castle at times could be so campy in his direction as to eradicate true feelings of horror, he does well in guiding *Strait-Jacket*. He certainly had good material to work with; the film was scripted by acclaimed writer Robert Bloch.[170] Featuring Crawford's high-end performance, plenty of swinging axes and lopped heads, and gruesome sound effects, *Strait-Jacket* is one of Castle's better films, full of fun and thrills and screams. It might not be sophisticated horror, but it is *entertaining* horror, more than worthy of a look on a Friday or Saturday night.

Premiering on May 6, *The Last Man on Earth* delivered an apocalyptic view of the future, a society devastated by a plague that has left the world crawling with zombie-like creatures that are actually vampires. Seemingly only one human remains—a man played by Vincent Price.

Price portrays Robert Morgan, a brilliant man of science who, as seen in flashbacks, was unable to discover a cure for the widespread disease that took his wife and daughter, along with the rest of society. Somehow immune from the plague, he is left alone to fight off the vampires that are the by-products of the worldwide disease. Price's character tackles the task reluctantly; he would much rather save lives than kill the vampire-like creatures, whom he burns in an enormous pit. At the end of each day of vampire-hunting, Morgan retreats to his shuttered house, protected from the creatures that only come out at night.

While initially believing that he is the last remaining survivor, Morgan will eventually discover the presence of a strange woman, Ruth, who has been sent to spy on him. Ruth explains that she is part of a small group of survivors who are infected with the disease but have managed to find a vaccine that temporarily keeps the effects of vampirism from taking hold. The group will eventually turn on Morgan, but Ruth now feels loyal to him. Morgan will then attempt to come up with a permanent cure to treat her infection.

In some ways, Price was an odd choice to play the role, given the physical demands required of his character. Although always erudite and distinguished, Price was never particularly athletic or physical in his film roles. Richard Matheson, who wrote the screenplay based on his own novel, felt that Price was miscast.[171] The role of Dr. Morgan was especially grueling; in one scene, Price insisted on lifting actual bodies, and not dummies, into the back of his car, as a way of enhancing the realism.[172] Despite the physical awkwardness, Price succeeds in portraying a character who is weighed down by the dire, depressing circumstances that he faces.

Filmed in stark black and white, *The Last Man on Earth* presents a dismal and dark view of a world that has collapsed into ruin. But there is hope presented during the second half of the film, which allows Price greater range of expression. The vampires are also intriguing in their presentation. Like most vampires, they only come out at night, but they speak few words and stagger around the fallen city in a fashion more reminiscent of zombies. It's believed that these strange vampires influenced George Romero's depiction of his trademark zombies in *Night of the Living Dead*,[173] which came out four years later.

For the most part, *The Last Man on Earth* is an accurate adaptation of Matheson's novel, which he wrote in 1957. The Matheson novel has subsequently been adapted to film by others, starting with Charlton Heston's *The Omega Man*. *The Last Man on Earth*, with its bleak atmosphere and sympathetic performance from Price, is the better of the two.

Initially released in Italy in August 1963, Mario Bava's *Black Sabbath* did not make its way to American theaters until May 6, 1964, but the content made it worth the wait. A terrific example of 1960s horror cinema, *Black Sabbath* ranks as one of the best horror anthologies of the hosted horror era.

Black Sabbath features three short stories, each introduced by the legendary Boris Karloff. He reportedly had great fun creating the introductions, which he delivered with a mix of comedy and creepiness. The first segment, which is simply outstanding, follows a young nurse who tends to a dying old woman before becoming plagued by a seemingly reanimated corpse. The imagery of the corpse, especially as it moves across the room, is striking.

The second segment features a modern-day prostitute being harassed by a series of telephone calls. The unknown caller is somehow able to see every move she makes, giving us a most unusual kind of stalker. This is very creepy material, particularly for those who live alone.

The third and final segment, "The Wurdulak," stars Karloff as a family patriarch who has become a vampire. The segment is a bit long, but still effective, and it marked the only time that he portrayed a vampire. Horror fans have become so used to seeing Bela Lugosi and Christopher Lee in this role that it's intriguing to see Karloff, in the latter stages of his career, finally taking on such a portrayal. In so doing, Karloff gives us a different look from his roles as Frankenstein's Monster, the Mummy, the body-snatching John Gray and the bevy of mad doctors from his lengthy film catalogue.

The name of the film, *Black Sabbath*, is also noteworthy. It supposedly influenced Ozzy Osbourne's famed heavy metal band to take the name, though that story has been disputed by some. According to the legend, the band's members were playing a small club in Birmingham, England, when they noticed the long line at the movie theater across the street. Somewhat jealous that the lines for *Black Sabbath* were longer than their own, the band reportedly decided to take the name of the competing horror film.[174]

Whatever the true story, director Bava does great work in his use of the camera and in laying out very colorful and decorative sets. His use of color is especially brilliant, in contrast to the way that he used black and white so skillfully in *Black Sunday*. The end result is a highly atmospheric film that has plenty of chills and twists. This is a horror classic emblematic of the early 1960s at its finest.

7. Creature Features, Fright Night *and* Block of Shock (1931–1969) 157

As the 1960s progressed, Vincent Price became a growing presence on the big screen. In 1964, he appeared in a number of films, including AIP's *The Masque of the Red Death*, which premiered in Los Angeles on June 24. The film offers an intriguing storyline that is executed artistically, despite budgetary constraints. While some have criticized it for a lack of a pure fear factor, it's an example of more subtle horror that is achieved through the development of characters and the creation of powerful visual imagery.

Price stars as the evil and greedy Prince Prospero, who lives in a castle on a hill above the poor European village of Catania, which is being ravaged by a plague, the so-called "Red Death." Prospero, who lords over the village with an iron fist, reacts to the news of the Red Death's arrival by burning all of the homes in Catania. Even those who seek haven in Prospero's castle are subject to his whims—including his tendency to mock and belittle his subjects, all for his personal entertainment.

Throughout the film, Prospero expresses his contempt for Christianity, instead praising Satan and making it clear that he is a devout worshiper of the Devil. As usual, Price does his best to make one of his villainous character despicable in every way.

Starring alongside Price are two beautiful actresses, Hazel Court and Jane Asher, who provide a pleasing contrast to the pure evil of Price's character. And then there is Patrick Magee, a hard-drinking character actor whose face just embodied the word "sinister"; he gives one of his typically devious performances. The four principal actors all perform well for director Roger Corman, who once again borrowed from the writing of Edgar Allan Poe. Of all the Corman-Poe productions, *The Masque of the Red Death* is one of the best. Doing justice to a good Charles Beaumont script, Corman coaxes a particularly good performance out of Price, fleshing out Prospero's standing as a follower of Satan.

In addition to skillfully guiding his veteran cast, Corman creates a powerful visual tapestry. He made the film in England, taking advantage of the location by using some sets from *Becket*, another film from 1964. *The Masque of the Red Death*'s climactic scene, a lavish masquerade party at Prospero's castle, is particularly striking, but Corman was disappointed by the final scene, pointing out how a frantic filming schedule forced him to shoot the entire sequence in one day. Corman believed that he could have done better with additional time,[175] and perhaps there is something to that sentiment, but the scene remains highly effective, creating a memorable twist ending for this mini-classic.

Following the masquerade scene, the conclusion to the film is a bit bizarre—highly metaphorical—but it doesn't detract much from this Corman effort. If anything, it makes the viewer consider the story on a grander scale, within a wider context.

Corman was the master of making films on dirt-cheap budgets. As a cost-cutting maneuver, Corman decided to move filming of *The Masque of the Red Death* to England, where he was able to receive a government subsidy to help pay for the production. This marked Corman's first film venture to England.[176] While he has drawn criticism for some of his low-budget productions, *The Masque of the Red Death* is one of his best, an example of how a fine film can be made with minimal outlay of money, thanks to a good story, solid acting and judicious choices by a veteran director.

In September 1964, one of the last respectable films made by Lon Chaney debuted in American theaters. *Witchcraft* stars Chaney as Morgan Whitlock, patriarch of a family with a history of performing acts of witchcraft.

The film centers on a continuing rivalry between the Whitlocks and another family, the Laniers. Three hundred years earlier, the Laniers had buried one of the Whitlocks alive on the charge of witchcraft. Now back in the present day, on the eve of a marriage between a Whitlock and a Lanier, the Laniers hire a construction crew that unwittingly bulldozes the Whitlock Cemetery as part of a land development deal. In doing so without the knowledge of the Laniers, the crew disturbs several graves, including that of Vanessa Whitlock, the witch who was buried alive centuries earlier. Now freed from her grave, and with the assistance of Morgan Whitlock (played by Chaney), Vanessa embarks on a vengeful reign of terror against the Laniers.

Though made on a low budget, the film is heavy on atmosphere and creepiness, which is only enhanced by the cost-saving decision to film it in black and white. The acting is also solid, from the little-known supporting players to an aging Chaney. By now, his physical appearance had changed drastically, his body bloated by years of alcohol abuse and a poor diet. But his acting remains impactful in *Witchcraft*, adding to the melodrama of the story.

Upon its release, *Witchcraft* was double-billed with *The Horror of It All*, a fairly awful horror-comedy starring Pat Boone, of all people. Those who attended the double feature received a prize: a witch deflector, i.e., a green badge that could keep witches at bay! As theatrical posters for *Witchcraft* proclaimed, "Only the witch deflector can save you from the eerie web of the unknown."[177] Indeed.

Despite such creative promotional efforts, *Witchcraft* did not do much business, but has since developed a small cult following. It is certainly entertaining, and features value for its spine-chilling atmosphere. The movie also stands as one of the last favorable testaments to the abilities of Lon Chaney.

With the American release of *The Gorgon* on February 17, 1965, the folks at Hammer ventured into the area of Greek mythology. Despite the film's campiness and cheesy special effects, Hammer succeeded in this effort, thanks to the direction of Terence Fisher and the acting skills of Christopher Lee, Peter Cushing and Barbara Shelley.

The film is set in the early 20th century in Europe: Sacha Cass ventures into the woods, sees an ominous pair of eyes, and literally turns into stone. Soon after, other villagers begin turning to stone for reasons that remain mysterious. Despite early efforts to dismiss the occurrences, the learned and heroic Prof. Karl Meister (Lee) believes that a Gorgon, a supposedly mythical creature made famous by the Greek character of Medusa, is responsible for the tragic incidents. Meister is right; the Gorgon is emerging from her castle at midnight and exposing her face to innocent bystanders, thus turning them into pillars of stone.

The Gorgon, who is named Megaera, is played by middle-aged actress Prudence Hyman. In a critical scene, Lee's character takes a swipe at her with his sword. Forgetting to duck, Hyman was nearly struck and fatally injured, but the film's assistant director pushed her out of the way at the last second.[178] Given the nearly catastrophic level of the incident, Fisher decided to re-shoot the scene the safe way—using a dummy—and thereby avoided any chance of injury.[179]

Near-tragedy aside, Hyman performed well in the role of the Gorgon, even though the special effects lagged well behind in effectiveness. Hyman was fitted with a wig filled with fake snakes. The effects created by the snakes are relatively poor, something noticed by some of the cast members. Lee, who appears almost exclusively during the final act of the film, was particularly critical of the effects.[180] The producers apparently opted for cheap effects as a cost-cutting maneuver.

That decision proved to be short-sighted. With better effects, *The Gorgon* would rank as a true Hammer classic. The quality of the acting is quite good, from the gruffness of Lee's character to the ruthlessness of Cushing's Dr. Namaroff, a medical man who is skeptical of the Gorgon's existence and mistreats his assistant Carla (played nicely by Shelley). In many

7. Creature Features, Fright Night *and* Block of Shock (1931–1969)

other ways—its main plot, the various subplots, the atmosphere, and an ending with a major twist—the film also rates highly. As long as the viewer is willing to tolerate the substandard effects with a grain of salt, the experience of *The Gorgon* is certainly worthwhile.

Another creepy film from 1965 signaled the beginning of a run of anthology films coming from a previously little-known company. Released on February 28, *Dr. Terror's House of Horrors* was something of a groundbreaker: the first in a series of nicely filmed anthologies created by Amicus Productions, which would later create such cult classics as *The House That Dripped Blood* and *Tales from the Crypt*. *Dr. Terror's House of Horror* deserves to share company with those two films in terms of quality, even if it introduces a bit more comedy, which plays against the feelings of suspense and dread that creep up throughout the picture.

If you can work the words "terror" *and* "horrors" into a title, you've accomplished something grand in setting the proper mood for your film. But *Dr. Terror's House of Horrors* is more than just a catchy title; it is one of the better anthologies of the 1960s and '70s, and an excellent showcase for the talents of Peter Cushing, Christopher Lee and a young Donald Sutherland.

Directed ably by Freddie Francis, the beautifully photographed film has an intriguing premise. Five strangers board a train, where they share a small compartment and are joined by a mysterious fortune teller, played by a bearded and mustachioed Cushing. The fortune teller, identified as Dr. Schreck (an apparent homage to actor Max Schreck, the star of *Nosferatu*), accidentally unveils a pack of Tarot cards, which draws attention. Referring to the cards as his "house of horrors," Dr. Schreck proceeds to conduct readings for each of the strangers, laying out their futures through the telling of five different stories, which involve a werewolf, a creeping vine, a voodoo ritual, a vampire and other far-out themes.

In the best of the five, "Disembodied Hand," Lee and another accomplished British actor, Michael Gough, are pitted directly against each other. Lee plays somewhat against type; rather than portray a clear-cut and unquestionable villain, he takes on the role of an arrogant and overbearing art critic who becomes the victim of a vengeful painter (played by Gough). Exacting revenge for a negative review of his painting, Gough pulls a practical joke on Lee, embarrassing him in public. In a fit of rage, Lee counters the action with a far more horrible act, setting the stage for later scenes in which a crawling hand pursues him. Lee is excellent in his portrayal, proving once again his ability to handle much more than standard vampire and monster roles.

Francis' film has drawn some criticism for its slow pacing and for the relative brevity of each of the segments, but it is still fun, atmospheric, creepy and suspenseful, and features a nice twist at the very end. With solid direction and excellent performances by a top-notch cast, *Dr. Terror's House of Horrors* stands as a prime example of high-quality horror anthology.

Amicus Productions had additional success in the summer of '65, this time with a more traditional single-narrative film. With the August 25th release of *The Skull*, Amicus hoped to pose a direct challenge to the dominance of Hammer Films. Ironically, it features the two reliable Hammer stalwarts, Peter Cushing in the starring role and Christopher Lee as a so-called "guest star."

Cushing plays Christopher Maitland, a collector of occult artifacts who is tempted to purchase a skull from a dealer of bizarre objects (played by the underrated Patrick Wymark). The skull happens to be the remains of the Marquis de Sade, the French nobleman who was imprisoned for committing a series of sex crimes and an array of sadistic endeavors. Maitland is warned by his friend and fellow collector, Sir Matthew Phillips (Lee), not to take acquire the skull because of its ability to possess its owner. Maitland ignores the advice and steals the skull, leading to a transformation of his character and personality.

The cast of *The Skull* carries with it an aura of tragedy. Wymark, a supremely talented actor, succumbed to a heart attack only five years later, while still in the prime of his acting career. Jill Bennett, who portrays Maitland's wife, became a victim of spousal abuse and commited suicide by drug overdose at the age of 58. Another supporting player, Nigel Green, cast as a police inspector, died seven years after filming, the result of an accidental overdose of barbiturates. Green, also seemingly in the prime of his career, was only 47.

While few have suggested a curse associated with *The Skull*, as has been said of *Rosemary's Baby* and *The Exorcist*, the release of the film did come with some controversy. The surviving heirs of the Marquis de Sade filed a lawsuit to prevent the filmmakers from using his name in any of the movie's advertising materials. The court action forced promoters to remove original posters and lobby cards, eliminating all reference to the Marquis.[181] In France, the film was originally slated to be released under the title of *Les Forfaits du Marquis de Sade* ("The Infamies of Marquis de Sade"), but that name had to be changed to a French phrase that translates into "The Evil Skull."[182]

Controversies and tragedies aside, *The Skull* has plenty of merit. Directed stylishly by the underrated Freddie Francis, it achieves a good degree of atmospheric tension and features excellent cinematography, including a creative use of light that is cast on the skull. The special effects are good, showing the skull as it floats throughout the Maitland house. There is also an intriguing sequence (which may or may not have been a dream) where Maitland is hauled by police to a strange courtroom and forced to engage in three rounds of Russian roulette.

Based upon on a tale by Robert Bloch, the film was given a half-baked screenplay by a lesser author that amounted to an outline. Francis then developed and rewrote the script so that it could become a workable basis for the film. Perhaps because of the script's initial inadequacies, Francis relied on a minimum of dialogue over the final act of the film; the last 25 minutes of screen time contain practically no spoken words. Francis is also innovative in his approach. At times, he gives us the vantage point of the skull, as if the skull is a living character itself.

Cushing is very good in the lead role, given freedom to run wild with the character's developing insanity and murderous tendencies, especially toward the climax. Lee does well in a non-typical role; rather than a villain, he portrays an innocent and well-reasoned character. But his screen time is far less than what his fans would typically want to see.

Budgetary constraints limited Francis, as did censors, who forced the director to remove some of the eroticism and gore.[183] A greater role for Lee might also have been helpful. In spite of those shortcomings, *The Skull* succeeds as a worthy venture into the occult, with a creative story, fine acting and a willingness by the director to engage in some daring experimentation.

Another intriguing film, one featuring the talents of the venerable Boris Karloff, made its way into theaters on October 27. As one of the later films in Karloff's lengthy and prolific career, AIP's *Die, Monster, Die!* is certainly a worthy stop on the horror trail. Admittedly not a great film, largely due to its plodding pace, it finds strength in the performance of both its star and his much younger co-star, Nick Adams.

Loosely based on a H.P. Lovecraft novel, *Die, Monster, Die!* (aka *Monster of Terror*) centers on American Stephen Reinhart (played with delightful arrogance and swagger by Adams), who visits the British hometown of his fiancée Susan Witley. Reinhart discovers that the Witley name carries bad connotations; no one in the village will even give him directions to their mansion, much less provide him with a ride to the grounds. When he finally does make it to the area near the residence, he sees how barren the surrounding landscape is, and notices a large crater. Despite **No Trespassing** signs aplenty, Reinhart slips onto the property and enters the house, where he gets a chilly greeting from Susan's father, played by Karloff. Karloff's character, a strange man bound to a wheelchair, is harboring some sort of secret in his greenhouse laboratory.

Adams plays the role of protagonist well, combining forcefulness and determination with charm and a sense of morality. A tragic figure among actors, the talented Adams died only three years later, at the age of 36, the result of an overdose of prescription medication. Given his charisma and screen presence, Adams might have enjoyed a long tenure in Hollywood, though his career had already taken a downturn by the mid–1960s. Some of Adams' friends have maintained that he was murdered, due to his plans to write a book revealing the sexual secrets of some of Hollywood's major stars, but this allegation has not been proven.

Die, Monster, Die! marked the directorial debut of Daniel Haller, a disciple of Roger Corman who would later direct 1970's *The Dunwich Horror*. Haller spins the story ever so slowly, which sometimes makes it difficult for the viewer to stay interested. Haller's production also struggles in the area of special effects; the creatures unveiled in the greenhouse look more like puppets than monsters.

In fairness, the rookie director had little budget to work with, but Haller did exceptionally well in devising some wonderful sets portraying an old mansion, where he creates a feeling of Gothic atmosphere and a sense of claustrophobia. Much like Corman, Haller showed the ability to make a film that is striking and eye-catching even with a decided lack of money. He did wisely in seemingly allowing his star to roam free—always a good idea given the talents of Karloff. Haller also creates a level of mystery: Is Karloff's character motivated by madness, or he is involved in some sort of satanic cult, or he is simply an innocent victim of circumstance? The answer does not come until the final act.

All things considered, *Die, Monster, Die!* is an above-average film from the 1960s. It was also one of the last substantial film roles for Karloff, who was nearing the end of his life and whose movements were restricted by declining health. Even in a wheelchair, the venerable and still capable Karloff is compelling in carrying *Die, Monster, Die!* to its conclusion.

The year of 1966 would turn out to be a relatively sparse year for horror productions in general, but a strong year for movies made by Hammer. The year produced an overdue sequel in Hammer's series of Dracula films. A prior effort (*The Brides of Dracula*) had come without benefit of the presence of Christopher Lee, but Hammer made sure to include Lee in its third vampire film, *Dracula—Prince of Darkness*, which debuted in America on January 12. Hammer offered many interpretations of Dracula over the years, but few matched the artistic success of this sequel. The combination of atmosphere, suspense and terror makes it one of Hammer's best, a worthy follow-up to *Horror of Dracula*.

Although *Prince of Darkness* came third in Hammer's series, it picks up directly from the original film. After a replay of *Horror of Dracula*'s dramatic closing scene, *Prince of Darkness* opens with two couples making a trek through Eastern Europe. Despite warnings, they venture into the village of Karlsbad, where they become stranded and must seek refuge in a mysterious castle. That's where they encounter a caretaker named Klove, played with extreme creepiness by Philip Latham. Klove, a faithful servant to Dracula, invites the four visitors to stay in the castle as guests of his deceased master.

When we last saw Dracula in the original Hammer film, he appeared to have been destroyed, so *Prince of Darkness* gives us a creative and powerful resurrection scene. It begins with a shot of Dracula's ashes within a coffin. In sinister and maniacal fashion, Klove holds the body of one of his victims over the coffin, allowing the blood to drip slowly onto the ashes. Using a series of dissolves that last a full minute,[184] director Terence Fisher creates a gradual reanimation of Dracula, from ashes to the formation of a skeleton to the growth of skin. The resurrection of the vampire, accompanied by lightning and loud crashes of thunder, is a disturbing scene, but one that represents some of the best special effects work ever achieved in a Hammer Film.

The reintroduction of Dracula also brings back the great Christopher Lee. According to David J. Skal, Lee took on the role somewhat reluctantly. "Christopher Lee after a while resented playing Dracula so many times," says Skal. "Aside from the first film, he didn't think much, or put too much into his characterizations. He was showing up and doing it. He felt that he was *shamed* into doing it. He was guilt-tripped into doing it; Hammer Films told him if he refused, so many people would be out of work."[185]

Lee's performance is somewhat odd. He utters not a single word throughout the film, but conveys his ominous presence through his stare, his facial expressions and his towering build. Lee claimed that he was originally given a number of lines, but did not like them, opting instead to apply the silent treatment. While that claim has been disputed by screenwriter Jimmy Sangster, who claimed to have written no lines for Lee,[186] the strategy (whether it was the original or the revised plan) worked well, thanks to Lee's physical presence.

Lee's usual foil, Peter Cushing, could not make the film because of his wife's ongoing medical problems, but Andrew Keir performs creditably as Father Sandor, a kind of Van Helsing substitute. Another strong character is played by Barbara Shelley, a seasoned horror film veteran. She capably delivers all of her lines, although her screams were dubbed by Suzan Farmer, a young British performer.[187]

Prince of Darkness succeeds on many levels, from the acting to the atmosphere to the special effects, but the filming almost came at a tragic cost. During a climactic scene in which Dracula can be seen struggling in a pool of water, stunt double Eddie Powell became trapped under the water. He came close to drowning, but was rescued at a critical moment.

A fine film, *Prince of Darkness* was released as part of a double bill with *The Plague of the Zombies*. Theaters distributed plastic vampire fangs and zombie eyeglasses to moviegoers, a campy promotional effort reminiscent of William Castle's methods.[188] But there is little campy about *Prince of Darkness*. Other than an abrupt ending, it is a very good film, representing Hammer near its best.

Also premiering on January 12, *The Plague of the Zombies* is nearly as well-crafted as *Prince of Darkness*, even if it lacks the presence of the usual Hammer screen legends. It is a movie full of chilling moments, including one that proved influential on later films like *Night of the Living Dead*.

Set in 1860, *Plague* is set in a Cornish village ravaged by a mysterious plague which has killed a number of young workers. A physician, Peter Tompson, asks a professor from a distant village, Sir James Forbes, to help him. Forbes and his daughter travel to the village and, along with Tompson, they discover a number of empty coffins. They soon notice a number of zombie-like figures walking near an abandoned tin mine, located on the estate of Squire Clive Hamilton. After some additional investigation, Forbes concludes that the squire practices black magic and voodoo rituals, which seem to be at the root of the bizarre phenomena plaguing the villagers.

Some of the visual imagery contained in the film is striking, including a celebrated dream sequence and the nighttime unveiling of a zombie on a hillside. In some cases, the film was a bit too graphic; a scene involving the decapitation of a zombie was severely censored.[189]

Filmed beautifully in color, and buttressed by effective makeup used to create the zombies, *The Plague of the Zombies* is a well-acted film, with good contributions from Andre Morell, Diane Clare and Brook Williams. It is heavy on atmosphere, creepiness and general frights. It's not as iconic as *Night of the Living Dead*, but offers an interesting alternative view of what a village might look like if faced with a zombie apocalypse. Outside of a somewhat disappointing conclusion, it's a creative and influential venture by Hammer into the world of the undead.

Like *The Plague of the Zombies*, *The Reptile* is another one of the fascinating and off-the-beaten-track films produced by Hammer. Rather than rely on the traditional monsters like Dracula, Frankenstein and The Wolf Man, the movie introduces a new creation, a female monster with a mix of human and snakelike features.

Making its debut on April 6, 1966, *The Reptile* lacks the big-name presence of a Lee or a Cushing, but the film suffers only slightly for it. A cast of lesser-known but highly capable actors, including Ray Barrett, Jennifer Daniel and Michael Ripper, carry the story forward. When the brother of Harry Spalding (Barrett) dies mysteriously, he and his wife Valerie (Daniel) inherit his cottage in a countryside village. The couple finds the villagers unwelcoming, to the point that a local doctor recommends that they leave town. The Spaldings insists on staying.

Some of the locals are dying from what is being called the Black Death. The coroner determines the cause of death as a series of unrelated heart attacks, but that explanation is treated with skepticism by the couple, and they decide to start their own investigation. They invite an eccentric local, Mad Peter, to their house in a quest for answers, but Peter dies later that night, adding to the mystery.

When Mad Peter's body is illegally exhumed, a strange wound, like a snake bite, is found on his neck. Harry and a friend (Michael Ripper) dig up Harry's brother's body, which has a similar wound. Not long after, Harry is bitten by a strange reptilian creature, which appears to be the source of the recent neck wounds—and the accompanying deaths.

One of the strengths of *The Reptile* is the creature itself—a product of legendary makeup man Roy Ashton. Using a mold taken from actual snakeskin,[190] Ashton created a monster that is both memorable and realistic in appearance. Director John Gilling adds to the successful debut of the monster by waiting until the final third of the film to reveal it. The buildup of suspense and anticipation turns out to be more than worthwhile; there is no feeling of disappointment when the reptile monster, played by Jacqueline Pearce, appears for the first time. The look of the Reptile would become iconic, in part because of the film, but also because of the frequency with which the creature appeared within the pages of the magazine *Famous Monsters of Filmland*.

Pearce hated wearing the Reptile makeup. Already plagued by claustrophobia, she felt restricted and enclosed by Ashton's makeup.[191] Those fears did nothing to detract from her fine performance as the half snake, half woman, but she vowed never again to fill a monstrous role that required such heavy makeup.

In many ways, *The Reptile* is an overachieving film. Filmed back to back with *Plague of the Zombies*, *The Reptile* featured many of the same sets as the other Hammer production.[192] Fortunately, the sets were sufficiently moody and atmospheric, and serve *The Reptile* well. The production also faced its share of obstacles, including budget restrictions and frequent script rewrites, but the cast and crew managed to overcome the difficulties and deliver a well above-average horror film.

While *The Reptile* is not quite the classic that some of Hammer's Dracula and Frankenstein adaptations turned out to be, it is one of the company's hidden gems. With its mix of horror and suspense, and its ability to sustain mystery until the final act, it deserves its status as one of Hammer's cult favorites—and a must-see film from the 1960s horror culture.

Ranking lower on the Hammer list is another 1966 release, which would not arrive in the U.S until February 1967. Based on its plotline and casting, *The Witches* is not typical of Hammer horror, but it is entertaining and more than worthy of discussion as an example of a growing interest in witchcraft during the tumultuous 1960s.

The Witches follows the fortunes of traumatized schoolteacher Gwen Mayfield (Joan Fontaine). Gwen has a life-changing encounter with the occult, resulting in a nervous breakdown. Once recovered, she starts a new life as a teacher at a religious school in a remote English village. Shortly after arriving, she begins to realize that the head of the school is not a minister, and that the school has no affiliation with any established church. Then she notices signs of witchcraft, including a headless doll with pins sticking out of it.

Fontaine lends some big-name credibility to the film, which represented her last appearance in a theatrical release. After a nine-year hiatus, she returned to acting with a succession of TV roles, but would never again enter the genre of horror, instead opting for avenues like *The Love Boat* and *Hotel*.

Fontaine is quite good in *The Witches*; so is veteran British actor Alec McCowen (also known for his role in the underrated Alfred Hitchcock horror thriller *Frenzy*), who portrays the purported minister. As well as Fontaine and McCowen perform, both are upstaged by veteran actress Kay Walsh, who plays McCowen's sister and ends up stealing much of the other actors' thunder.

The presence of Fontaine, Walsh and McCowen helps compensate for some of the film's weaknesses, principally an exceedingly slow pace. The ending has drawn criticism for being too frenetic and even silly, climaxed by a long Satanic ceremony that is more comedic than frightening. What does *The Witches* do well? It is well-acted throughout and very atmospheric, the latter characteristic aided by an excellent musical score.

The Witches represents a departure for Hammer. Rather than deal with its traditional subjects of Dracula and Frankenstein, the company decided to tackle the relatively untouched areas of witchcraft and satanic worship. *The Witches* is not nearly as good as another film on the subject, *The Devil Rides Out*, but it is emblematic of a willingness to address a relatively new area of horror. *The Witches* bravely takes on a controversial topic that would gain prominence over the next decade.

In contrast to much of the '60s, 1967 turned out to be a lean year for horror films, salvaged only by *The Witches*, the long-delayed *Spider Baby* and *The Sorcerers*. The latter, which debuted in Florence, South Carolina, on October 25, blended horror and science fiction concepts while starring an 80-year-old Boris Karloff, who maintained the ability to deliver the goods even as he neared the end of his life.

Karloff takes center stage as Prof. Marcus Monserrat, an acclaimed but past-his-prime hypnotist who has devised a machine that allows him to control the minds of others. The professor and his wife (the titular "sorcerers") test the machine on a young man, who essentially becomes their guinea pig. Monserrat's wife becomes hungry with the thrill of mind control, taking the experiment to such a dangerous level that it makes the professor wonder if he should rein her in and end the project before it causes more damage.

Karloff and his co-stars, Catherine Lacey and a young Ian Ogilvy, are all tremendously effective. In some ways, Lacey is the most prominent performer, as she maintains a crazed facial expression throughout the mind-control sessions and manages to come off as more sinister than Karloff, whose character retains more of a pathetic quality. The handsome Ogilvy plays his part with youthful arrogance while also gaining some of our sympathy as a helpless victim of human experimentation.

The film was directed by Michael Reeves, who died two years later from a drug overdose. Although *The Sorcerers* is not nearly as good as his final film *Witchfinder General*, it represents quite an achievement for Reeves. With virtually no budget to work with, he had to rely on creating good characters and dialogue over special effects. He succeeds, creating an atmospheric film that showcases the contemporary culture and scenery of 1960s England, a powerful backdrop against which the aging Monserrats, who live in a dreary and cramped apartment, must work in an effort to stay relevant.

The one drawback to *The Sorcerers* is the editing, which is sometimes so sloppy as to damage the flow of the story. Reeves also attempted some creative camerawork, particularly in the nightclub scenes, but with mixed success. The camerawork in the dramatic car chase at the end of the film is far better, a fitting conclusion to a story that is both horrific and tragic. Even without much in the way of effects and a budget, *The Sorcerers* remains a power-packed film with the ability to shock the viewer.

After making its belated premiere on December 24, 1967, in Corpus Christi, Texas, *Spider Baby* fell into oblivion. It was an obscure film that made its way into drive-in theaters and then quickly made its way out, soon to be forgotten. But the movie has since become a cult classic, fully restored to its original black-and-white brilliance. Part of its newfound status and appeal comes from its intersection of horror icons from two different generations: a latter-day Lon Chaney, Jr., and a young, up-and-coming Sid Haig.

Spider Baby stars Chaney, in what was essentially his last good film, as a chauffeur and caretaker of a large, dilapidated mansion who has taken charge of three children after the death of their father. The children, two girls and a boy, are the products of an inbred family and the victims of a strange inherited disease that causes them to regress mentally. (The film's name comes from the youngest child, a girl who has a bizarre obsession with spiders and their habits.) Chaney has his hands full trying to keep the children out of trouble while also keeping the local authorities at bay. More difficulties come Chaney's way when some distant relatives, along with their intrusive lawyer, visit the strange family and announce their intention to repossess the mansion.

The product of first-time director Jack Hill, *Spider Baby* has its flaws, some of which were caused by Hill's inexperience and some of which stemmed from the low budget. Though intended as a horror-comedy, there are times when the film becomes too humorous, perhaps awkwardly and unintentionally so. For example, the parodied portrayal of the unscrupulous lawyer Schlocker, as played by Karl Schanzer, seems out of place and over the top.

But the good moments outweigh the bad ones. Hill succeeds in creating some memorable scenes, particularly a midnight chase in the woods involving the two deranged girls, and he shows a willingness to tackle taboo subjects like cannibalism and necrophilia, all the while presenting a set of oddball characters. The acting is generally good, particularly from Chaney. He gives us a sympathetic portrayal, a man caught between his desire to hide the indiscretions of the children and his feelings of love for them, amidst the hope that they can be rehabilitated and saved.

Haig is also good handling the physical role of the eldest child, who has so regressed mentally that he is unable to speak. Haig was a young actor at the time, intimidated by a famous horror figure like Chaney.[193] At first reluctant to speak to Chaney, he finally was forced to do so, in order to relay a message from the director. Haig says he addressed his co-star as "Mr. Chaney," but the screen legend quickly shot down such formality. "It's Lon," Chaney told Haig. From that moment on, Haig says he felt much more at ease on set.[194]

Both the production of the film and its eventual release into theaters came under great difficulty. The film was shot in mid-summer, on a minuscule $60,000 budget, with most of the filming taking place on a small sound stage with no air conditioning.[195] The intense heat, which reached over 100 degrees on some days, exhausted all of the performers, particularly the aging and overweight Chaney. As recalled by Haig, the hottest days of the two-week production really took their toll on Chaney. Haig says that Chaney became so soaked with perspiration that movie assistants had to dip towels into a bucket of ice water and wipe down the screen legend, providing him some relief.[196]

The 12-day shoot took place in August 1964, three and a half years before the movie enjoyed its theatrical release. The delay was caused when the film's backers, two real estate developers, went into bankruptcy. Because of their poor financial standing, the film could not be released for a few years, until lawyers worked out a resolution early in 1968.[197]

To add to the jumble of difficulties, the original print of *Spider Baby* was lost. Only video copies existed, and all were grainy and difficult to watch. Then in 2012, the Academy of Motion Picture Arts and Sciences succeeded in restoring and preserving the film, by using the original camera negative. With a remastered sound track, *Spider Baby* has returned to its original glory.[198]

Perhaps all of these obstacles have made *Spider Baby* a must-see for horror fans. There is no doubt that Hill's film is a weird one, full of strange characters that seem like they belong on a deserted island, not in the rural South. With the weirdness comes an enticing series of horror elements, along with an important late-career performance from a screen legend.

While 1966 and '67 represented the low point of horror in the decade, 1968 brought the genre to its peak. No fewer than five noteworthy films were released that year, with two achieving iconic status. By coincidence, that was the same year that the Hays Code was formally abolished, though the enforcement of the Code had grown so lax in the 1950s and 1960s as to make it inconsequential. With the Code eliminated, the Motion Picture Association of America adopted its new film rating system in 1968.[199]

The onslaught of 1968 horror began on May 15 with the Los Angeles premiere of *Witchfinder General*, another film made under the direction of Michael Reeves. It was produced on a low budget and has generated controversy because of its overly sadistic nature and questionable adherence to historical fact, but *Witchfinder General* overcomes all of those drawbacks in creating an entertaining and fast-moving film based on British witchcraft in the 1640s. In some ways, it is as much of a violent action film as it is a product of the horror genre.

The film is also known by the title *Conqueror Worm*. The alternate title, which was used for its American release, comes from an Edgar Allan Poe poem. The movie has nothing to do with Poe's work; the film was simply renamed as a way to capitalize on the brand name value of Poe.

By either name, the movie certainly enhanced the career of Vincent Price, who gives one of his most convincing portrayals. He stars as Matthew Hopkins, a real-life character in the age of Oliver Cromwell; Hopkins traveled the English countryside in pursuit of witches.

(From 1644 to 1647, he reportedly killed 230 or more people whom he charged with the crime of witchcraft.[200]) It's debatable how much of the film is accurate in its depiction of Hopkins, who died in 1647, possibly from tuberculosis.[201] Hopkins' date of birth is not known, but most historians speculate that he was roughly 30 at the time of death, making him much younger than the middle-aged Price.

As portrayed in the film by Price, Hopkins attempts to coerce confessions from so-called witches, most of whom are innocent figures, not for the good of England but to earn money and sexual favors. Hoping to secure confessions at all costs, Hopkins employs torture and violence, which is shown explicitly throughout. His methods include pricking his victims' skin with sharp knives and later submerging them in rivers and lakes as part of a "swimming" test. At first successful in his nefarious efforts, he runs into trouble when he targets a priest, infuriating a British soldier who was about to wed the holy man's niece.

The role almost eluded Price. Director Reeves preferred Donald Pleasence, the acclaimed British actor. Reeves was overruled by American International Pictures, which insisted that the role go to Price, an American and a staple of AIP horror.[202] The company turned out to be right in its insistence; Price is borderline brilliant as Hopkins, showing him as both charming and sadistic, charismatic and ruthless. Rather than rely on the campiness of some of his other AIP roles, Price gives Hopkins a more subtle and serious treatment.

As exceptional as Price is, he regretted his participation in *Witchfinder General*. "He didn't really like to do exploitative horror films," says actress and historian Genoveva Rossi. "He was very much a family man, with children. Other than *Witchfinder General*, which he regretted doing—it's a beautiful film, but he regretted doing it because of how exploitative it was as a horror film—he liked to make films that a child or a young adult could also see, and it wouldn't be too objectionable."[203] *Witchfinder General* was not that kind of film, particularly at that time.

Adding to Price's regret was the direction of Reeves, who made life difficult for his star. Price said that Reeves hated him and that the director made it clear that Price had not been his first choice.[204] In spite of the treatment he received from Reeves, Price delivered a terrific performance. In fact, Price felt that his portrayal of Hopkins turned out to be the finest of his long career in horror.[205]

Price is ably supported by Ian Ogilvy, cast as the heroic and handsome Richard Marshall, the man determined to bring Hopkins to justice. Another horror veteran of the era, Rupert Davies, does well in portraying the aging priest who becomes the subject of torture at the hands of Hopkins and his ruthless assistant John Stearne, another real-life character. Stearne is played forcefully by British actor Robert Russell.

The film turned out to be the swan song of director Reeves. He was only 25, a brilliant director who seemed on the brink of a long career. But Reeves was troubled by depression and insomnia. Only a year after the film's release, Reeves took an overdose of barbiturates, combined with alcohol. The overdose was ruled accidental, not a suicide.[206]

Witchfinder General was Reeves' third and final full-length feature film. It may have been his best. But it is a tough film to watch, especially for fans of the 1960s era who expect a more subtle approach to the genre. "*Witchfinder General* is hardcore violence," says Rossi. "It's a really beautiful film, but it's a little over the top [in terms of violence]."[207] Still, Reeves' daring willingness to showcase the torturous ways of Hopkins, along with a standout effort by Price, make it required viewing for horror fanciers.

Along with movies about witchcraft and witch-hunting, films about Satanism and devil worship became the other horror fad of choice in the 1960s and early '70s. This may have stemmed in part from the lack of enforcement of the Hays Code, which was essentially ignored in its later years before being abolished altogether in 1968. Of all the films to deal with Satanism, none captured the subject matter more skillfully than *Rosemary's Baby*, which premiered in New York City on June 12, 1968, and emerged as a masterpiece for any era.

Adapted very faithfully from the Ira Levin novel, *Rosemary's Baby* starts slowly, creating a web of paranoia around the central figure of Rosemary Woodhouse. She is married to Guy, a struggling actor. The couple moves into a stately apartment at the Brantford, a high-end Gothic apartment building in New York City. On the night that a female resident commits suicide by leaping from the building's seventh floor, Rosemary and Guy meet their next-door neighbors, the Castevets, who had taken in the young woman as part of an effort to curb her drug habit. An elderly and seemingly kind couple, the Castevets quickly take a special interest in their young counterparts. Soon after their meeting with the Castevets, Guy's stagnant film career takes several upturns, while young Rosemary becomes pregnant for the first time.

On the night that Rosemary conceives, she is plagued by a strange dream—or is it a true-life vision? During the sequence, she exclaims, "This is no dream! This is really happening." As the story of the Woodhouses progresses, doubts about Rosemary's pregnancy and Guy's career are placed in the minds of the viewers. Rosemary loses weight and becomes shockingly pale, while one of Guy's rival actors is struck with sudden blindness. Are we to believe that Rosemary is falling prey to the stress of being pregnant, or is she is in legitimate fear for her life, and the life of her unborn child? Is her husband sympathetic to her, or tangled in some kind of conspiracy that casts her as an unwitting victim while his career suddenly advances by leaps and bounds? The answers are not revealed until the final dramatic scene, but only after a series of unexpected and tragic twists of the plot.

The lead character of Rosemary is played beautifully, with innocence and vulnerability, by Mia Farrow. John Cassavetes is nuanced as her ambitious and devious husband, while aging actors Sidney Blackmer and Ruth Gordon play their roles perfectly as the friendly but peculiar Castevets. Adding to the mix are smaller but vital roles handled by Maurice Evans (who plays Rosemary's concerned friend Hutch), Ralph Bellamy (as the seemingly wise Dr. Sapirstein) and a young Charles Grodin (as Dr. Hill, Rosemary's obstetrician).

The first American film directed by Roman Polanski, *Rosemary's Baby* is shot in an unusual way: long, continuous takes with little to no editing involved. One of the most memorable scenes shot in this style occurs in a New York City phone booth, as Rosemary nervously places a call to Dr. Hill and then impatiently awaits his response. Highlighted by Farrow's monologue and the movements of an older man as he waits to use the phone booth, the brilliantly acted scene lasts more than four minutes. Punctuated by these uninterrupted sequences, Polanski's style powerfully adds to the realism of the movie, which was filmed on the streets of New York City and inside the famed Dakota Apartments.

Like some horror classics, *Rosemary's Baby* has produced its fair share of urban legend. For years, rumors have circulated that Church of Satan founder Anton LaVey served as a technical advisor, but that is not true. Nor does LaVey appear in the film, negating another unsubstantiated rumor.[208] One other legend does remain in dispute. Some observers claim that Sharon Tate, the striking wife of the director, has a cameo at the party thrown by Rosemary for her close circle of younger friends. There is photographic evidence that Tate was present for at least part of the filming,[209] but she is not listed in the credits, nor is there firm evidence of her appearance in the background of the party scene. Tate died only a year after the film's release, the victim of one of Charles Manson's orchestrated murders.

7. Creature Features, Fright Night *and* Block of Shock (1931–1969) 169

Rosemary's Baby (1968): The Woodhouses (Mia Farrow and John Cassavetes) and their landlord (Elisha Cook, Jr., on left) observe in horror the aftermath of the suicide of the Castevets' female ward, Terry. Though it is never clearly spelled out in the film, the Castevets will soon try to "replace" the tragic young woman with Rosemary, in a way that she never could have foreseen.

There are those who have contended that *Rosemary's Baby* was a cursed film, and not only because of the horrific death of Tate. Shortly after production ended, composer Krzysztof Komeda endured a fall, went into a coma, seemingly recovered, and then died. He was only 37. Noted horror director William Castle, who produced the film and also makes a brief non-speaking appearance, came down with a severe case of gallstones and had to be hospitalized. Castle himself believed that a curse was in place. "The story of *Rosemary's Baby* was happening in real life," Castle later said. "Witches, all of them, were casting their spell, and I was becoming one of the principal players."[210]

While the matter of a curse has long been debated, there is little doubt that *Rosemary's Baby* had a powerful impact as a film. A certified classic, it is frightening at times, chilling at others, and disturbing throughout. From the direction to the acting to the realism in portraying urban life in the mid–1960s, it succeeds on every level. With little doubt, it remains one of the greatest horror films ever made.

For those who like anthologies, July 19, 1968, brought the New York City premiere of *Torture Garden*. Developed by Amicus Productions, it presents four short stories, but all are tied to a common thread: a fairground haunted house attraction run by a carnival barker named Dr. Diabolo.

Played skillfully by Burgess Meredith, Dr. Diabolo tells five customers that they can enjoy a particularly frightening experience—but only for an additional fee. The attraction will tell people their fortunes while revealing hidden secrets about each of them. The five patrons all decide to pay for the bonus experience, but their fortunes all end badly. A number of name-brand actors make appearances in the vignettes, including Jack Palance and Peter Cushing.

Like a lot of offerings within the genre of horror, the movie title is misleading. There is no garden, and there is no torture, even though there is plenty of horror. Meredith is particularly good as the sinister carnival barker. Palance is also effective as a fanatical collector of Edgar Allan Poe's works. Palance and Cushing, who plays a rival collector, are both featured in the final vignette, the best of the four stories. The ending of the film will then provide a few major surprises.

Written by Robert Bloch of *Psycho* fame, *Torture Garden* is an entertaining if flawed example of the horror anthologies that Amicus specialized in during the 1960s and '70s. The vignettes are uneven—the first and fourth are good, while the middle two are bland—and the sets are cheap-looking. But there is enough here, especially given the efforts of Meredith, Cushing and Palance, to make *Torture Garden* a worthwhile venture.

One of the better and lesser appreciated offerings of the 1960s made its American debut in August 1968. Hammer's *The Devil Rides Out* provided a twist in casting. Rather than portray the villain, as he usually did in Hammer productions, Christopher Lee is cast in the role of the protagonist. He is likable and sympathetic as the Duc de Richleau, who notices Satanic activity brewing around one of his friends and does his best to eradicate it.

Lee often referred to *The Devil Rides Out* as his favorite Hammer film.[211] Not only did it give him a chance to play against type, but it also entertains with a fast-moving plot, a sense of adventure, and a palpable feeling of good doing its best to battle the most evil of forces. Supplemented by excellent cinematography and a terrific musical score, *The Devil Rides Out* represents an effective departure from the Frankenstein and Dracula themes so often explored by Hammer. Director Terence Fisher deftly handles the topic of devil worship, in a way that is far more entertaining than many other offerings from the era.

While Lee carries the film as the heroic Duc, character actor Charles Gray proves nearly his match as the evil Moncata, leader of the satanic cult. Gray is calculating and deceptive as Moncata, who calls upon two evil forces, the Angel of Death and the Goat of Mendes, both of whom supply memorable horror imagery.

As good as *The Devil Rides Out* proves to be, it would not have happened without a hard push from Lee. He pressured Hammer to do at least one film based on a novel by writer Dennis Wheatley.[212] The initial proposal for the film occurred in 1963, but production did not begin until four years later, with the film finally released into theaters in 1968. The delay had to do with censors worried that a film centered on Satanism might be dangerous and inappropriate.[213] Those fears turned out to be unfounded.

The title of the film has created some confusion over the years. When it was released in the United States, the producers changed the title to *The Devil's Bride*, thinking that the original title sounded too much like a Western.[214] The film is now almost universally known by its original name, which might not be the best title at evoking the proper theme and imagery.

There are two weakness to the film. One involves the special effects, which are simply not believable, either by today's or 1960s standards. And then there is the ending, which has proved confusing to some viewers. Some readers of the book have contended that Wheatley wrote a clearer ending for his novel; that is the one area where the movie adaptation suffers.

But the ending does not ruin the film. Though it has its flaws, *The Devil Rides Out* remains an essential part of the Hammer library.

One other selection from 1968 made its mark quite distinctly from the rest. Quietly entering theaters on October 1 in Pittsburgh (near the location of much of the filming), *Night of the Living Dead* remains one of the most frightening horror movies of all time. Made on a shoestring budget, filmed in black and white, and completely lacking in name actors, this gem started the entire zombie craze, though the word "zombie" is never used during the film. Instead, the characters refer to the living dead as "ghouls" or as "those things."

The plotline is one that has become familiar in modern-day horror. *Night of the Living Dead* opens memorably in a remote cemetery, where a brother and a sister are making a late-afternoon visit to the grave of their father. During the visit, the brother, Johnny (Russell Streiner), playfully taunts his sister when he sees a strange man in the distance. "They're coming to get you, Barbra," says Johnny hauntingly, not realizing that the man is actually a walking corpse. After Johnny is killed by the creature, a frantic Barbra flees the cemetery and, in a nearby house, runs into a man named Ben, who offers to help. But they, and a few additional survivors, are trapped there by a swarm of walking corpses. We later learn that a strange microbe has turned the dead into walking zombies who need to consume the flesh of the living.

While the premise might be basic and familiar, *Night of the Living Dead* also provides an allegory for real-world events affecting America in 1968. As college professor Zachary Sanzone points out, the film has become an effective teaching tool in illustrating the horrors of war:

> It was good to use when I taught *The Things They Carried*, a book about the Vietnam War. I was at a military school in the South when I taught the book, and many of the veterans that I worked with weren't crazy about most Vietnam War movies. So I used *Night of the Living Dead* to talk about how people in 1968 saw the film as a metaphor for the Vietnam War. The senseless carnage, the inability of people to comprehend what was happening, the social divides among those in the house, and the time period itself makes it a good film to use to illustrate themes in the book.[215]

The two most sympathetic characters in the film are portrayed by Duane Jones (Ben) and Judith O'Dea (Barbra). In making *Night of the Living Dead*, Jones became the first African-American to be cast in a lead role of a mainstream horror film. He is excellent, displaying the kind of charisma and leadership that typify a leading man. Playing Ben with a sense of smarts and calmness, he gives the small group of humans their only hope of surviving the growing zombie plague.

A highly intelligent and skilled actor who struggled to find meaningful roles throughout the 1970s and '80s, Jones appeared in only nine features, most of them B-horror movies. He spent most of his time teaching theater, a calling that he enjoyed even more than acting and one in which he excelled. He died young (51) from heart failure. O'Dea also performs well. A delightful and humble actress, she makes Barbra a sympathetic character as she struggles to cope with the death of her brother—and the wave of invading zombies.

Thanks to Jones and O'Dea, *Night of the Living Dead* features a much-needed human element to counterbalance the preponderance of walking corpses. Director George Romero also shines, making the most of his limited budget as an independent filmmaker. Romero found local residents in Pittsburgh, where the filming took place, to fill the roles of zombies, and also received assistance from the Pittsburgh police department, which provided him a group of extras and some equipment.[216] With a minimum of makeup and few discernible special effects, these low-budgeteers somehow create a sense of panic and fear throughout the film.

Even with its low budget, and even with the film advancing in age, *Night of the Living Dead* manages to connect with more recent generations. It certainly did with Sanzone's students: "The kids were intrigued by the fact that the film is the grandfather of zombie movies. I also think the kids were surprised by how good of a film it is, too. You'd be surprised how many kids actually like old movies when they get a chance to see them."[217]

Night of the Living Dead, shot on grainy black-and-white film, serves as proof that old low-budget horror can work. Sometimes a meager budget only adds to the grittiness and the terror of what is felt on film. The movie is a classic, one that set the stage for the follow-up *Dawn of the Dead*, and created a platform for the high-budget terror of TV's *The Walking Dead*.

One final warning about the film: Do not watch it alone.

A notable film that debuted in the United Kingdom in 1968 did not appear in American theaters until February 6, 1969. Fourth in Hammer's series of Dracula and vampire films, *Dracula Has Risen from the Grave* picks up where *Dracula—Prince of Darkness* left off. When we last saw Hammer's Dracula, played with the usual flair by Christopher Lee, he appeared to be drowning in ice water. Shortly after the new film begins, we see Dracula rising from the frozen stream, revived by drops of blood that have fallen through cracks in the ice.

A large metal cross has been attached to the front gate of Dracula's castle, preventing him from taking up residence. So he begins to plot revenge against the responsible party, Monsignor Mueller (Rupert Davies). Forcing a priest to reveal the name of the monsignor and provide him with help in enacting his revenge, Dracula targets the monsignor's pale-skinned but beautiful niece Maria (Veronica Carlson).

There is no Peter Cushing to help with the heavy lifting, but Lee, Davies and Carlson carry the day in *Dracula Has Risen from the Grave*, the most profitable horror film ever made by Hammer.[218] Lee reportedly did not like the script, but in his performance he shows no resentment. Instead, Lee puts forth one of his best efforts as the red-eyed fiend. As in other Hammer productions, Lee's Dracula receives relatively little screen time, but he dominates each scene in which he appears, leaving the viewer with vivid images of the unholy antagonist.

Under the original plan, Terence Fisher was scheduled to direct, but an automobile accident forced him to withdraw. Freddie Francis, who was supposed to handle the camerawork for Fisher, stepped in,[219] and did so admirably. He elicits excellent performances from Lee, Davies and Barbara Ewing, playing a barmaid who becomes an early target of Dracula. Any inadequacies within the script are compensated by the actors' efforts and the direction from Francis. All that's missing is Cushing, whom Francis directed on numerous other occasions.

The end result is one of the better films directed by Francis, who also oversaw *Dr. Terror's House of Horrors* in 1965 and *Tales from the Crypt* in 1972. Francis deserves credit for the excellent and colorful sets, the staging of memorable scenes (including an attempted staking of Dracula), creative use of lighting, and an ability to extract the most from his actors. For all of these reasons, *Dracula Has Risen from the Grave* stands as one of Hammer's better vampire films—and a worthy successor to the original *Horror of Dracula*.

Another Lee feature also debuted in theaters in 1969. Premiering in the States on June 11, *The Oblong Box* is not a particularly well-known film, but it is historically significant; it was the first film to co-star Lee and Vincent Price, two giants of the industry who usually worked for rival companies. The film was supposed to be directed by Michael Reeves, but the young filmmaker fell ill during pre-production.[220]

Adapted from the Edgar Allan Poe story of the same name, the film's premise is a good one: Aristocrat Julian Markham (Price) attempts to keep his badly disfigured and mentally ill brother Edward (Australian character actor and horror veteran Alister Williamson) in a tower of his massive mansion. Edward's physical and mental ailments occurred during a trip to Africa, where the two wealthy brothers operate a plantation.

Due to his violent tendencies, Edward is kept in chains. Desperate to secure his release, he makes an arrangement with Trench, his unscrupulous lawyer. With help from a voodoo practitioner, Trench stages the apparent death of Edward, whose body only appears to be lifeless. Julian discovers the body and arranges to have Edward buried, unaware that his death has been faked. In the meantime, Trench makes no effort to rescue Edward from a premature burial.

Lee comes into play as Dr. Neuhartt, who regularly acquires corpses from local grave robbers for use in his questionable medical experiments. Edward's apparently dead body is delivered to Neuhartt, who soon realizes that Edward is alive. Edward blackmails Neuhartt into allowing him to reside in his home. Now donning a crimson hood to cover his disfigurement, Edward seeks revenge against those who betrayed him while trying to determine why he was harmed by voodoo priests during his ill-fated visit to Africa. To add suspense to the film, director Gordon Hessler (Reeves' last-minute replacement) chooses not to show Edward's face until the very end, though the reveal is somewhat disappointing.

While Price's role is fairly prominent, there are long stretches in which he does not appear. Even more puzzling is Lee's role as Dr. Neuhartt, which is so small that it allows him little room to showcase his usual talents as a villain. Lee shares just one brief scene with Price, with little interaction between the two, creating disappointment for those horror fans hoping that the two legends would confront each other within the film.

The film's other drawbacks are its poor special effects and the complexity of the plot, which has numerous elements and side stories, too many of which are left unresolved. Perhaps the confusion could have been avoided if not for the tragic passing of the film's screenwriter Lawrence Huntington, who died 11 days after the start of production.[221]

Still, *The Oblong Box* has some strong points, including a powerful opening scene that shows Edward being tortured during a voodoo ceremony. Hessler, who had previously worked as a producer on *Alfred Hitchcock Presents*, creates a wonderfully Gothic look to the film that reminds us of Hammer Films, even though this is clearly an AIP production. The movie is very stylish thanks to an excellent array of sets that include the tower, a castle and a graveyard. It is also quite graphic, with nudity and public debauchery.

In one memorable scene, which Edward arranges to have the coach of one of his betrayers stopped in the middle of a forest, so that he can confront him. The ending is also well done, throwing an unexpected twist at the viewer, but the film could have been so much more. With a simplified plot and larger roles for the two headliners, it might have become a horror classic of the late 1960s. Horror fans will have to settle for something that is entertaining, but merely acceptable.

A stylish effort from Rod Serling, *Night Gallery* aired from 1969 to 1973 as a regular NBC series. Serling had achieved fame through *The Twilight Zone*; *Night Gallery* represented his effort at more traditional and Gothic horror. *Night Gallery* actually began with a made-for-television film that doubled as its pilot. Airing on November 8, 1969, it showcased three vignettes within a feature-length format.

All three vignettes proved effective, but the first one stands out. "The Cemetery" stars Roddy McDowall as the insolent nephew of a rich and elderly man, whose demise is expedited by impatient heir Roddy. Inheriting his uncle's mansion, McDowall begins to notice a strange painting that changes every few hours, foreshadowing a series of dire circumstances for the nefarious nephew. Thanks to McDowall's skills in playing the villain, a fine supporting performance by Ossie Davis as a butler, and the meticulous reworking of the painting (shown in at least 15 different forms, creating quite a workload for the artist involved with the show),[222] this vignette reverberates with fear.

While the first story is the best of the three, the second vignette has gained more fame, if only because it represented the directorial debut of young Steven Spielberg. "Eyes" stars Joan Crawford, who lends a heavyweight presence to the story, but initially walked out of the production because of Spielberg's youth and inexperience.[223] Changing her mind and returning to the set, Crawford portrays a wealthy New York City woman who has been plagued by blindness since birth. She pays a doctor to conduct a history-making eye transplant, even though its effectiveness will last for only 12 hours. But even that plan backfires.

Night Gallery's third vignette, "The Escape Route," tells the story of a Nazi war criminal living in poverty in South America. Discovered by a concentration camp survivor and pursued by the police, he seeks refuge in a museum, where he is taken by a painting of a man peacefully rowing a boat in a lake. The Nazi yearns to become the man in the painting, a desire that *Night Gallery* is only too pleased to oblige.

While the ensuing episodes of *Night Gallery* were erratic—some excellent and others subpar, especially as Serling lost creative control—the made-for-TV pilot film stands out as one of the highlights of the franchise. Brilliant and forceful in its delivery, the film is creepy and enthralling, a testament to the genius of Serling, who wrote the screenplays for the second and third vignettes. When it came to writing horror-themed scripts for TV, the brilliant Serling succeeded above most others, creating mystery, suspense and a foreboding sense of terror. All of those elements are present in *Night Gallery*.

NBC's airing of the *Night Gallery* pilot closed out the genre of horror for the 1960s. It was a decade that saw major changes in the presentation of horror, from the now common and widespread use of color film to the more graphic themes being explored within the movies. Those themes would only become more extreme—and more disturbing—in the decade to come.

Chapter Eight

Creature Features, Fright Night and *Block of Shock* (1970–1975)

As the new decade of the 1970s began, horror's momentum continued to steamroll. With the Hays Code completely obsolete and with directors feeling the freedom to explore topics previously considered taboo, horror films became more daring and more risqué. In some cases, the content of the films became questionable to the point of bordering on the offensive, irritating critics and even some horror fans.

One such example entered American theaters on February 11, 1970, when the creatively titled *Frankenstein Must Be Destroyed* made its debut. The film stars Peter Cushing, with Freddie Jones in the role of the Creature.

Frankenstein Must Be Destroyed does not live up to the creativity of its name, but it is a well-made Hammer Horror that has become notable because of the controversy surrounding it. The controversy stems from the inclusion of a particularly brutal rape scene. The decision to include the scene came at the last minute, and at the urging of the head of Hammer, James Carreras, who felt pressure from the film's American distributor.[1] The distributor apparently believed that the film needed to be more violent and more adult-oriented than any of its predecessors.

Very much against the inclusion of the scene, Cushing made his feelings known. The Carreras decision so infuriated Cushing that he even apologized to his co-star, Veronica Carlson, who was also upset about the sequence.[2] Director Terence Fisher was also against the scene, but ultimately followed the Carreras directive, though he cut it short, eliminating some of the graphic violence involved.[3] Many critics agreed with Cushing and Carlson, calling the scene gratuitous to the degree of being pointless. Ultimately, the rape scene does nothing to advance the story or enhance the quality of the film.

Cushing's Baron Frankenstein is particularly loathsome in this film. Callous and ruthless, he seems to have become a complete psychopath, as he blackmails a young couple, Anna and her scientist fiancé Karl, into helping him with his goal: freeing a former partner, now deranged, from an insane asylum so that he can acquire the man's medical secrets. Shortly after the partner is brought to the baron's laboratory, he suffers a heart attack. The baron and Karl then kidnap the asylum administrator, Prof. Richter (Jones), with a plan to transplant the partner's brain into his body. And that will lead to all sorts of trouble for the local citizenry—and for the baron.

Cushing is typically good as the Baron, while Jones gives the Creature a far different look than Lee did in his portrayals. Carlson and Simon Ward also do highly credible jobs as the young couple forced to commit crimes for fear that the baron will expose them as drug traffickers.

The film marked the return of Fisher to Hammer; he had been overlooked by the company for years because of criticisms that his films were too slowly paced and too emotional. Fisher felt that the film as a whole was one of his best works. In interviews, he often referred to *Frankenstein Must Be Destroyed* as one of his personal favorites to create, along with the original *Horror of Dracula*.[4]

Frankenstein Must Be Destroyed is a well above-average film, with good pacing and a fast-moving plot. It creates genuine sympathy for the young couple, as they grapple with the moral dilemma of assisting the mad baron against their better judgment. It also serves as a reminder of the never-ending debate of what should be allowed in a film—and what should not. For those of us who believe that some of today's films go too far, *Frankenstein Must Be Destroyed* reminds us that these kinds of issues have been debated for decades.

Frankenstein films would start to fade out in the 1970s, but the new decade brought a new set of vampires, all ready to join Dracula within American popular culture. One of these was a vampire of Bulgarian roots.

Premiering in Los Angeles on June 10, 1970, *Count Yorga, Vampire* is not an example of great filmmaking, but it is an entertaining film that has become a favorite with some fans. "It's really a terrible film," says historian David J. Skal, "but very watchable."[5] That "watchability" stems from the film's erotic tension, along with lots of violence and blood, making it a hit with horror fans on a broader basis, too.

AIP originally planned *Count Yorga, Vampire* to be X-rated soft porn, but the producers changed course and opted for a straight horror approach.[6] Still, they did maintain a group of female vampires, along with the film's pronounced sexual overtones, giving the entire experience a bit of an adult feel. Clearly, this is not a film for children, but one that should be watched by a crowd of adults 21 and older.

Robert Quarry stars as the title character, a vampire who has traveled from Bulgaria to 1960s Los Angeles. Initially seen as a guest at a small house party, he leads a séance to contact the deceased mother of one of the participants. The count was once involved with the mother, but she died suddenly from a kind of blood anemia. The séance participants include a young unmarried couple, Erica and Paul, who agree to give the Count a ride home. After dropping off Count Yorga, the couple's van becomes stuck in the mud, forcing them to sleep in the van. They are both attacked during the night, but they wake up the next morning with little recall of the attack. When Erica realizes that she has two bite marks on her neck, she consults James Hayes, a blood specialist who will soon begin an investigation into the true identity of Count Yorga. His discoveries lead to several frightening confrontations with Yorga, before ending with a skirmish at the count's mansion.

Handsome and debonair, Quarry is quite convincing in the lead role. (He also sports some lavish clothing, including a shirt with a ridiculously large collar, a gaudy chain and pendant, and a garish red cape.) Quarry's looks made him ideal to play a vampire, making us wonder what he might have done with an opportunity to play a more famous vampire like Dracula. With regard to Count Yorga, he brings some erudite charm to the role, along with an overriding arrogance and a sinister streak that will become all too apparent to his new friends in Los Angeles. Yorga's maniacal laugh, evident in a scene in which he uses his powers to unleash his female coven against his principal accuser, is good enough to send shivers.

It all made for a memorable role, even if it was not one for which Quarry wanted to be remembered. "Quarry had a hard time shaking this character," Skal says, "but people dug it."[7]

8. Creature Features, Fright Night *and* Block of Shock (1970–1975)

Quarry was an interesting character himself. He was highly intelligent, with an IQ of 168, and overcame a bout with cancer in the mid–1960s. A few years after *Count Yorga*, he sparred with Vincent Price on the set of *Dr. Phibes Rises Again*. Price, who had heard talk that AIP planned to replace him with Quarry, did not have much respect for his rival's acting ability.[8]

Another good effort is turned in by underrated American actor Roger Perry, who plays Dr. Hayes. He is particularly engrossing in a scene where his character politely confronts Count Yorga about his knowledge of the supernatural, especially vampires. It's quite obvious that Perry knows Yorga's true identity, but the doctor questions him slyly without making a direct accusation. Given the apparent tension, it's a scene that makes the count uncomfortable, along with the viewers.

Director Bob Kelljan succeeds in making *Count Yorga* very dark and atmospheric, with a well-paced

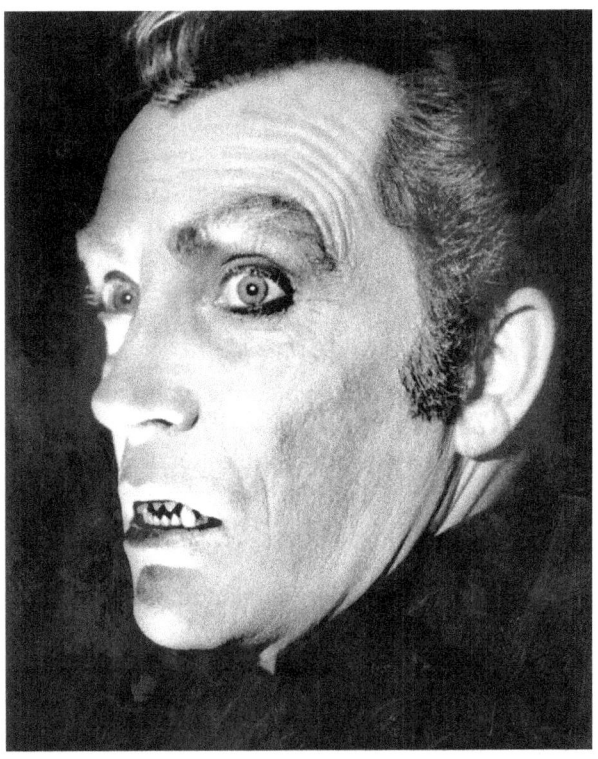

Count Yorga, Vampire (1970): With his handsome, sharp features, and just the right touch of makeup, Robert Quarry cut an ideal look as a good-looking but fearsome vampire. Quarry's acting skill elevated the quality of both of the Yorga films, and they led to several other horror film roles in the early 1970s.

plot that picks up steam after a sluggish beginning. A creative sort who was willing to take chances, Kelljan also includes a fair share of gore, including a scene in which one of the main characters eats a cat. The sequence, which is graphic and stomach-turning, is not for the squeamish. Kelljan would die from cancer at a young age in 1982.

The film also has its share of weaknesses. The special effects are almost nonexistent; when they are used, they look cheesy and cheap. The conclusion also comes a bit too swiftly, with the final encounter between Count Yorga and one of his pursuers lacking in both flair and drama.

In spite of these faults, *Count Yorga, Vampire* represented Kelljan's greatest commercial success. The film did so well that AIP released a sequel one year later, *The Return of Count Yorga*, with Kelljan at the helm. The sequel, while entertaining, would fall short of the original's effectiveness.

Much like Kelljan, *Count Yorga, Vampire* has become an overlooked piece of horror history. While Quarry's rendition of the vampire will never receive the acclaim of the Universal or Hammer counterparts, his vampire is striking and memorable, from his appearance to his evil laugh.

By the start of the 1970s, the most famous vampire in America was not Count Yorga, nor Dracula. No, it was Barnabas Collins, who had succeeded the Lugosi incarnation of

Dracula as the most recognizable revenant in the land. Barnabas was portrayed by Jonathan Frid, who gave Barnabas a complicated and conflicted personality.

Seen in the afternoons on ABC from 1966 to 1971, producer Dan Curtis' *Dark Shadows* was an unusual entity: a daily half-hour soap opera that featured vampires, werewolves, ghosts and even leviathans, along with tormented human characters. Even though the tone and the tenor were completely different from what would come to TV in later years, its supernatural content motivated other daytime serials to incorporate supernatural themes, culminating in the show *Passions* (1999–2007), which explored demons, witchcraft and zombies.[9]

In its day, *Dark Shadows* became so popular that it spawned board games, action figures and two feature films. The first, *House of Dark Shadows*, premiered in New York City on August 24, 1970. It reimagined the early storylines of the TV series and brought them to a forceful conclusion, doing so with a much larger budget, and without the flubbed lines and mechanical gaffes that sometimes made the daily vampire soap opera so unintentionally comical. Given more money and time, the talented Dan Curtis directs early 1970s horror at its finest, including an array of wonderful sets and beautiful cinematography that often characterized his film productions. Free from the censorship restrictions of daytime TV, *House of Dark Shadows* provides large amounts of blood and violence to make matters more interesting for theatergoers.

The key to the success of *House of Dark Shadows* is the presence of Barnabas, accidentally unleashed from the Collins family's mausoleum by Willie Loomis, a bumbling handyman. Barnabas is introduced to the family as a long-lost cousin and offers to host a masquerade ball, where he attacks and kills one of the family members. He also meets local Maggie Evans, the girlfriend of a man named Jeff Clark. She closely resembles Barnabas' long-deceased fiancée Josette. Barnabas begins a pursuit of Maggie, while unleashing a spate of terror against the Collins family. All the while, Barnabas receives help from a local doctor, Julia Hoffman, who believes that his vampirism can be cured.

The role of Barnabas is once again played with dignity and gravitas by Frid, a classically trained Canadian actor who became typecast because of his convincing vampire performance. Though not as well-known as Lugosi or Christopher Lee, Frid's portrayal of Barnabas succeeded in making Barnabas a vampire icon, not through sheer terror, but by alternating Barnabas' sympathetic and sinister sides. In the film, Barnabas is less conflicted and more violent, as he treats his manservant Loomis as if he were Dracula's Renfield, while enslaving the character of Carolyn Stoddard.[10] Even with a harsher approach, the portrayal of Barnabas remains credible and effective.

A number of key players from the television show, including Grayson Hall (Dr. Hoffman), Kathryn Leigh Scott (Maggie), John Karlen (Loomis), Louis Edmonds and Thayer David, also reprise their TV roles for the film. They all do well in lending Frid sufficient support as part of a slick, well-presented film.

House of Dark Shadows works on two levels. For those who did not watch the TV show, the movie stands alone on its ability to tell an entertaining and fast-moving vampire story. And for those who did follow the show, *House of Dark Shadows* succeeds in underscoring the best elements of a daily Gothic soap opera that became a cultural phenomenon.

One of the most overlooked horror films in history, the ABC telemovie *Crowhaven Farm* has stood up well over time. This writer vaguely remembers watching this made-for-TV movie as a child—and remembers it being terrifying. Many years later, a second viewing as an adult confirmed its lasting legacy; it continued to score well for its creepiness and its

8. Creature Features, Fright Night *and* Block of Shock (1970–1975) 179

House of Dark Shadows (1970): After saving the gothic soap opera *Dark Shadows* from cancellation, Barnabas Collins became the central figure of the feature film inspired by the show's success. Played so skillfully by Jonathan Frid, the film version of Barnabas embarked on a path of murderous rage before a final violent confrontation (courtesy of Dr. Jeffrey Thompson).

sense of paranoid terror. The movie's ability to sustain interest from a childhood viewpoint to the perspective of an adult makes it something of a classic. *Crowhaven Farm* easily ranks as one of the better horror films of the color television era.

The telefilm, first shown on November 24, is headlined by Hope Lange, an excellent actress perhaps best known for her lead role in the TV series *The Ghost and Mrs. Muir*. Lange portrays Maggie Porter, half of a sympathetic but troubled couple living in the city who have inherited an old country farmhouse called Crowhaven Farm. They hope that the move to a rural environment will help repair their marriage, but instead the aging farmhouse seems to hold sinister secrets of witchcraft and torture. Lange is terrific, creating a level-headed and likable character who is also vulnerable, one who understandably seems concerned by the strange developments surrounding her.

The supporting cast does good work, too. Horror icon John Carradine, nearing the stretch run of his prolific career, makes a brief but effective appearance as a mysterious caretaker of questionable intelligence—and intentions. The baritone-voiced Lloyd Bochner provides Lange with some much-needed moral support as the circumstances around *Crowhaven Farm* begin to deteriorate hopelessly.

A notable effort also comes from character actress Virginia Gregg, a favorite from the *Alfred Hitchcock Presents* series. She is outstanding as Mercy Lewis, a duplicitous woman named for a key character from Arthur Miller's *The Crucible*. And a very young Cindy Eilbacher skillfully plays Lewis' sinister ten-year-old niece, whom the Porters agree to take in because of her family's tragic circumstances.

In addition to good performances throughout, one of the film's strengths is the strong imagery created by director Walter Grauman. Buttressed by simple but good special effects, the film gives us a large dose of compelling horror imagery, from fire to stoning to torture to other indications of witchcraft. It has the feel of a theatrical release and the appearance of a larger box office production.

Some very good horror films fall apart because of anticlimaxes, but that is not the case with *Crowhaven Farm*, where the conclusion is particularly noteworthy. It feature two plot twists that will have viewers looking over their shoulders. In fact, it's tempting to call the ending of *Crowhaven Farm* one of the better sendoffs in modern horror history.

In the early 1970s, made-for-TV horror films like this appeared with regularity, and some of them were quite good, despite limitations in budget and content (due to TV standards of the day). They had little gore and few major special effects, but succeeded in carrying the story with suspense, tension, plot twists and creepy musical scores. None of these films accomplished those missions any more effectively than *Crowhaven Farm*.

If ever a year of films could be tabbed as wholly underrated, 1971 would rank near the top of the list. The year produced a string of worthy horror selections, beginning on February 26, when *Willard* made its limited release debut in Scranton, Pennsylvania. An above-average horror film that succeeds in attaining a high level of creepiness, *Willard* features the excellent character actor Bruce Davison in the starring role of Willard Stiles, an awkward young man tormented at work by colleagues and his boss. With little in the way of amicable human contact, Willard makes friends with two rats, whom he calls Ben and Socrates. A growing legion of rats soon make their way into Willard's home.

Willard decides to use the rats to his advantage, as a means of taking revenge on his human tormentors. At one point, Willard orders the rats to commit an act of violence by yelling, "Tear him up!" The rats seem to understand.

Davison was only 24 at the time of filming, but he looks like a teenager. He is well supported by an excellent and experienced cast. The great Elsa Lanchester plays his mother while Ernest Borgnine portrays the young man's cruel boss. Sondra Locke, who went on to star with Clint Eastwood in a number of films, plays a key role as a potential love interest. Another key supporting player is Michael Dante, a longtime character actor better known for his work in Westerns.

Dante recalls the filming of *Willard*, where the actors had to share time with dozens of rats:

> Filming *Willard* with the rats was not as bad as it looked. The secret was that the trainers were excellent in getting the rats to do what the director wanted them to do. For instance, the trainers put peanut butter just inside Bruce Davison's ear where you couldn't see it. The rat was trained to go to that area, and it looked like the rat was kissing his ear, all the while licking the peanut butter. Their training was done with the Pavlov Theory. When the trainer rang a bell, it was associated with eating food. When the rats heard [the bell] and wouldn't go toward the working area, they wouldn't be given food. So when they skirted outside the area of work, they knew they had to get back to where they belonged, or they wouldn't eat.[11]

Dante says that the rats acted in a way similar to household pets:

> I actually "met" the rats, and they were most affectionate. I had always thought the opposite [before the experience]. They would cuddle together, the way dogs do in a pack, before they were called to work. Believe it or not, I loved these creatures during and after the film. They were amazing![12]

The lack of action and jump scares may frustrate modern-day followers of horror, but those who have patience may find *Willard* an interesting character study of a young misfit.

8. Creature Features, Fright Night *and* Block of Shock (1970–1975)

For a while, *Willard* was a staple of late-night TV, and left enough of a mark that it spawned a sequel called *Ben* and a 2003 remake with Crispin Glover. For some, *Willard* will come across as dated, but for those fans who appreciate horror from the early 1970s, the film retains some of its original appeal.

The prosperity of 1971 continued with the March 31 San Francisco premiere of *The House That Dripped Blood*. Another Amicus anthology, it includes four separate but related vignettes, all compelling and all centered on a spooky house in the English countryside. The film, with wonderful sets and excellent cinematography, lives up to the creativity of its terrific title. It's also well-written courtesy of Robert Bloch, author of the novel *Psycho*. Its wrap-around scenes feature a Scotland Yard man investigating four criminal cases linked to the empty house. Its previous occupants have all vanished; it is up to Detective Inspector Holloway (John Bennett) to determine where they have gone, and what role the house may have played in their disappearances. Holloway is skeptical as a real estate agent expounds on the house's previous residents.

There is little outward violence and no gore in *The House That Dripped Blood*. In fact, we don't see a single drop of blood on camera, contrary to the title.[13] What does take place is intricate storytelling from Bloch, unending suspense from director Peter Duffell, and high-end acting by some of the genre's legendary figures, including Peter Cushing and Christopher Lee.

For those who are fans of movie artwork, *The House That Dripped Blood* features one of the more creative and memorable promotional posters. Cushing, star of the segment "Waxworks," is the man whose head can be seen as it is served up for dinner by a skeletal female figure. Cushing had tried to excuse himself from the film in order to tend to his ailing wife, but the producers insisted that he fulfill the contract.[14] Lee appears in the segment "Sweets to the Sweet." There's also an effective performance by underrated British actor Denholm Elliott in the initial story, about a horror writer haunted by visions of one of his own villainous characters. Ingrid Pitt, a star of Hammer Films who often crossed over to other studios, makes a good showing in a memorable vampire segment called "The Cloak."

While some anthology films spotlight unrelated stories, *The House That Dripped Blood* effectively weaves a connection across its four segments, which are all linked by central characters who have lived in the home. There is no weak sister among the four tales; they are all well told. As horror anthologies go, *The House That Dripped Blood* is one of the most entertaining ever made. This is old-fashioned horror at its finest.

The Mephisto Waltz, which made its New York City debut on April 9, is somewhat of a forgotten film, but it did give Alan Alda a starring role just before his career breakout on *M*A*S*H*. Produced on a low budget and featuring little in the way of special effects, this 1971 release overachieves because of its stylish imagery, haunting mood and solid performances from supporting cast members Jacqueline Bisset, Curd Jurgens and Barbara Parkins.

It might be difficult to believe that a young Alda, who would become such an accomplished film and TV actor, seems slightly overmatched in the lead role. He plays Myles Clarkson, a failed pianist who must resort to working as a music journalist. By a stroke of luck (or is it bad luck?), he has a chance to interview a legendary virtuoso pianist, a role filled wonderfully by Jurgens. The encounter with the dying pianist turns Clarkson into a brilliant pianist himself, though the means of the transformation soon comes into question.

Despite the lack of a substantial budget, director Paul Wendkos does well in mixing an occult theme, essentially a contract with the Devil, into a film of horror and mystery. The cinematography and the musical score are both top-notch. Wendkos also makes good use of an experienced cast, led by Jurgens, a talented German actor. Despite having limited screen time, his performance is powerful and lasting. The sultry Bisset is excellent as Alda's wife, displaying vulnerability through a torturous series of nightmares, which are beautifully filmed and showcase much of the film's horror. And then there is Parkins, who is nearly as stunning as Bisset; she plays Jurgens' incestuous daughter with flair and gusto. Only Alda seems out of place, perhaps more because of miscasting than his actual merits as an actor, which are substantial.

In some ways, *The Mephisto Waltz* is a poor man's version of *Rosemary's Baby*. (At one point, the movie references the 1968 devil-worshipping classic.) Not as well-crafted as *Rosemary's Baby*, the film still delivers a dose of horror through a good story, excellent camerawork and terrific performances. *The Mephisto Waltz* loses some of its power during the final act, but it is still a worthy entry in the genre of occult horror that became so popular in the early 1970s.

Some horror films fail at the box office even though they are well made, present an entertaining story, and do their part in creating suspense, terror and grisly imagery. *The Blood on Satan's Claw* is one of those films. One of the best horror entries of 1971, it didn't make much money for the small company that made it, but did leave a sizable impression on fans who eventually saw it in the comfort of their living rooms. It also lives up the expectations created by a great film title.

A Tigon British production, it debuted in New York City theaters on April 14, 1971. The film is set in 17th century England, where a farmer discovers the buried remains of what he believes to be a demon. Shortly thereafter, the village children begin to act strangely. Their behavior turns violent, as they commit a series of crimes, culminating in rapes and murders. Why? They appear to have fallen under the influence of a young witch, the leader of a coven of devil worshippers.

Patrick Wymark, in what turned out to be his final major film appearance, takes the lead as the Judge, a kind of witchfinder who must find the source of the Satanism that has taken over the children. Wymark died suddenly of a heart attack in October 1970, shortly after production wrapped. A talented and experienced Shakespearean actor who seemingly had a substantial career in front of him, Wymark was still a young man, though different sources provide different dates of birth. Depending on which source you believe, he was either 44 or 50.

Wymark is excellent in his horror swan song, giving the Judge a stern but heroic quality that runs completely opposite to the sinister and corrupt nature of Vincent Price's character in *Witchfinder General*. Another excellent performer is teenager Linda Hayden, who plays the lead witch, Angel Blake. (Clearly, she is not an angel.) Hayden is stunning, provocative and unabashedly evil in the way that she overtakes the minds of the village's innocent children.

The Blood on Satan's Claw begins slowly, with relatively little of consequence happening over the first 20 minutes, but the mild start should not fool audiences. Director Piers Haggard's film is not for the meek; it is full of unpleasant imagery and intensely displayed horror, particularly for the time period. It caused considerable controversy upon release, largely because of three scenes. One shows a completely nude Hayden, who was only 17 at the time of filming,[15] as she attempts to seduce a local priest. A second depicts a rape scene, and a third involves the removal of deformed skin from an alleged witch.

Haggard also stages a daring and dramatic climax, which is portrayed partially through slow motion effect, something that was rarely used at the time. It is quite effective, though some have criticized the ending for being too rushed.

8. Creature Features, Fright Night *and* Block of Shock (1970–1975)

If the film has a significant flaw, it is a storyline that is somewhat disjointed, as the emphasis shifts awkwardly from a young man's fiancée, who has suddenly become bewitched, to the more central story that involves Angel Blake and her pursuers. That is one of the few flaws of the film, which otherwise ranks as a triumph. *The Blood on Satan's Claw* is as chilling, creepy and intense as its title suggests.

The Blood on Satan's Claw is good, but *The Abominable Dr. Phibes* is better—one of the most underappreciated films of its era. Debuting in the U.S. on May 18, it stars Vincent Price, looking particularly pallid as the disfigured doctor of the title. He delivers one of his finest and most sinister performances as Dr. Phibes, a brilliant doctor who seeks revenge against the surgeons he considers responsible for his wife's death. We never know whether Phibes is justified in placing the blame on the doctors, since the exact circumstances of her death are never quite revealed. And perhaps that's why we don't know whether to consider him sympathetically, or regard him as no more than a vengeful and soulless devil.

Aside from Price's standout effort, this film succeeds because of the creativity of Phibes' gruesome murders, which are based on the Ten Plagues of Egypt. For Phibes, it is not enough to exact revenge; it must be done as part of his formula, which includes bats, rats and grasshoppers. One of the most memorable (and strangest) of the murders involves the liquefying of Brussels sprouts, of all things!

While Price is clearly the star, he does not voice his first words until more than 30 minutes into the film. And even then, his voice was dubbed after the filming. That's because his makeup included the application of collodion, a skin-like substance that immobilized his facial muscles and prevented him from moving his mouth.[16] The relative lack of speaking only makes Dr. Phibes more villainous. We wait for him to speak, and when he does, we hear the struggle in his voice. His words come painfully and carefully, particularly when he addresses his dead wife, who is seen only through photographs (they depict the beautiful actress Caroline Munro).

For publicity purposes, *The Abominable Dr. Phibes* was advertised as Price's 100th film. That number turned out to be inaccurate,[17] but the mistaken milestone may have helped at the box office. After some initial struggles, *Dr. Phibes* eventually became a hit in American theaters.

Beyond Price, the cast of the movie performed well, but with some difficulty. For some reason, Price's co-star Joseph Cotten felt uncomfortable working on the film. (That may have been because Cotten was a last-minute addition to the cast.) While off camera, Price tried to put Cotten at ease by contorting his face in funny ways.[18] In spite of his feelings of tension, Cotten is quite good in his role as Dr. Vesalius, the lead surgeon on the failed operation involving Phibes' wife. And then there is newcomer Virginia North, who is important to the story even though she has no lines in her role as Phibes' striking and mysterious assistant, Vulnavia. North's beauty and screen presence add nicely to the proceedings.

The film falls into the genre of horror, with elements of the supernatural, but there is also plenty of British humor. The comedy is not supplied by Dr. Phibes, who is played with gravity by Price, but mostly by the police who pursue him. Talented British actor Peter Jeffrey successfully dishes up much of the humor as Inspector Trout, the lead investigator of the Phibes serial killings.

On the poster for the film, Dr. Phibes is credited visually with the following catchphrase: "Love means never having to say you're ugly."[19] This was a parody of a line on the poster for the film *Love Story*, which came out the previous year. But Price's alleged words are no more than a funny tagline; Price never voices those words in the film. The film's promotional staff later dropped the tagline, because it had misled some potential customers into thinking they were about to see a film that was primarily a romance. *Dr. Phibes* is many good things, and a love story is tangentially one of them, but it is first and foremost a film from the genre of horror.

"It's a beautiful film," says actress and historian Genoveva Rossi. "Not only the acting, but in terms of the art direction. The art deco that we have from scene to scene is really beautiful. It's a very artful film on so many levels."[20] Harrison Smith considers the Price classic to be at the top of the list among 1970s horror films. "I love *The Abominable Dr. Phibes*," the director says enthusiastically. "*Dr. Phibes* is a very quirky, interesting horror film. I think it's Vincent Price's best. The sequel was not as good.... But the original, my God, I love that movie."[21]

There's little doubt that *Dr. Phibes* is wonderful entertainment. Thanks to Price and a quality script, fans of the legend will not be disappointed as they watch the ghastly murders and the comic elements unfold within the movie. If it is not Price's best film, it's near the top of his many horror entries.

The subject of possession, an increasingly popular theme in 1970s horror, was broached with the August 3rd release of *Night of Dark Shadows*, the follow-up to *House of Dark Shadows*. A film that has long been maligned, it is actually a decent production and one that could have been categorized as great if only director Dan Curtis had been left alone by MGM.

Even before the interference from MGM, Curtis had to deal with the absence of Jonathan Frid, the star of the TV series and the first *Dark Shadows* movie. Frid declined *Night of Dark Shadows* because he felt the first film was overly violent. "I hated it," Frid told writer Will McKinley in referring to *House of Dark Shadows*. "It was all about screeching cars and blood and gore. It had none of the charm of the TV show."[22] With Frid opting out of the follow-up project, Curtis had to turn away from the idea of another film centered on Barnabas and instead opted for a story about witchcraft. So he decided to fall back on the TV show's other male star, David Selby.

In *Night of Dark Shadows*, Selby plays Quentin Collins, an artist who has just inherited the Collinwood estate. He and his new wife (Kate Jackson in her feature film debut) move into the mansion, where they meet an odd caretaker (Grayson Hall). Quentin is soon haunted by the ghost of a woman named Angelique, who had an affair with Charles Collins, one of Quentin's ancestors. Eventually hanged for witchcraft, Angelique has now returned to Collinwood to seduce Quentin, as she once seduced Charles. The haunting leads to episodes of strange behavior from Quentin, who is in danger of becoming completely possessed.

Night of Dark Shadows is rather slow, particularly over its first half, and then becomes somewhat disjointed and frenzied over the final 20 minutes. The latter problem, which included some unexplained jumps in the story, had to do with the studio's mishandling of the film. The head of MGM, a meddler named James Aubrey, not only forced Curtis to cut roughly 25 percent of his film, but made him do so within a ridiculous 24-hour deadline.[23] The forced cuts resulted in the elimination of several excellent scenes, including a compelling séance, and it left major plot holes, ruining the continuity of the film.[24] Faced with the impossible task of making major changes at the last minute, Curtis settled for a film that was a shell of its original intention.

Some who have seen the excised footage have argued that if Curtis had been allowed to maintain the original content and length of the film, *Night of Dark Shadows* would have become a success, and possibly a classic of the early 1970s.[25] With its wonderful outdoor views and indoor backgrounds, which were filmed at Tarrytown's Lyndhurst Mansion on

8. Creature Features, *Fright Night* and Block of Shock (1970–1975)

Night of Dark Shadows (1971): Although betrayed by the interference of a studio executive, the film produced memorable imagery and scenery. Here the ghost of Angelique (Lara Parker) emerges from fog at the far end of a cemetery; the witch haunts Collinwood in order to reunite with Quentin Collins, the reincarnation of her lover (courtesy of Dr. Jeffrey Thompson).

New York State's Hudson River, *Night of Dark Shadows* delivers beautiful cinematography and atmosphere. Curtis also coaxed excellent performances from Selby and Hall, the latter particularly effective as the creepy housekeeper. Jackson, who would later star in *Satan's School for Girls*, is also credible as Selby's wife. And the capable Lara Parker is very good as Angelique.

In spite of all the edits, the ending is also effective and surprising, foreshadowing a similar ending used by Curtis a few years later in *Burnt Offerings*. *Night of Dark Shadows* is not what it should have been, but its atmosphere, mood and strong acting are all major strengths. Even in its lesser form, the film has more than its share of moments, making it a deserving stopover in the world of hosted horror.

Just three days after the release of *Night of Dark Shadows*, another film involving witchcraft entered New York City theaters for the first time. On August 6, *The Brotherhood of Satan* made its debut, albeit with little fanfare. Despite its low budget and lack of big-name stars, *The Brotherhood of Satan* is one of the more entertaining films from the early 1970s to deal with witchcraft and devil worship. With its gritty, somewhat offbeat treatment of the subject matter, the movie packs a good share of scares and makes for compelling late-night theater.

The 1971 film opens by showing Ben, his girlfriend Nicky and his daughter traveling through the California desert to a family birthday party. They come upon an automobile accident and try to report it to authorities, and soon find themselves trapped in the small town of Hillsboro, where children have been disappearing. With the aid of a local priest, Ben and Nicky discover a cult consisting of senior citizens (that's the unusual part of the plot) who are doing their best to lure younger people into the town. Ben's daughter then goes missing.

The film's release came with a promotional gimmick: Upon purchase of their tickets, patrons were given a packet of seeds emblazoned with the movie's logo. According to the instructions on the package, the so-called Satan's Seeds were meant to "protect from the Black Magic of the Brotherhood of Satan."[26]

But the film is more than just gimmicks and promotions. A talented character actor of the era lifts *The Brotherhood of Satan* to a higher level. Strother Martin, a familiar face to fans of 1970s cinema, tended to steal scenes with his unusual vocal delivery and strong physical presence. *The Brotherhood of Satan* was one of his few starring roles, but his performance offers evidence that he could have handled top billing far more often.

Martin is engrossing in his role as Doc Duncan, the physician who also happens to have nefarious intentions. Giving the role the proper nuance and passion, he plays his character with full-steam intensity. He is ably assisted by his real-life friend, fellow character actor L.Q. Jones, who portrays the sheriff (and produced the movie). Another effective performance is turned in by the handsome and charismatic Charles Bateman, the head of the ill-fated family.

Director Bernard McEveety specialized in directing TV episodes for much of his career, but his venture into feature films makes one wonder why he did not gravitate toward the big screen more often. He creates an appropriately creepy atmosphere, with eerie music and decorative sets. McEveety shows particular skill in the way that he arranges the lighting of the main house where much of the horror takes place.

So often the ending of a horror film leaves us wanting something different, but McEveety delivers a climax that is bizarre, surprising and chilling. By the end, we're left with the feeling that we've watched a quietly effective film, one that remains underrated. *The Brotherhood of Satan* isn't quite regarded as a full-fledged cult classic—but perhaps it should be.

The year 1972 turned out to be nearly as strong a year for horror films as '71. The formidable run of movies began on January 11, when ABC debuted the latest in made-for-TV fare. Produced by Dan Curtis and directed by John Llewellyn Moxey, *The Night Stalker* became a sensation.

Television movies have never received much critical respect, but within the genre of horror, several have stood out as important films. *Crowhaven Farm,* a frightening

8. Creature Features, Fright Night *and* Block of Shock (1970–1975)   187

film full of believable performances and memorable horror imagery, served as a signal that made-for-TV horror could work. Nearly two years later, *The Night Stalker* signaled that television horror could be profitable enough to serve as a pilot for a network series.

The Night Stalker stars Darren McGavin as Carl Kolchak, a sarcastic and abrasive newspaper reporter who has been fired from a number of jobs because of his personality and is now relegated to working for a small Las Vegas paper. Looking to break a major story, he begins to study a series of murders on the Vegas strip: Each victim has been drained of blood. Kolchak believes that supernatural forces are at work: that the murders are being committed by a vampire. Neither his hard-nosed editor, played by veteran actor Simon Oakland, nor the police buy into Kolchak's theory.

Supported by the writing of Richard Matheson, McGavin breaks out of the character actor mold that defined much of his career and shows his aptitude for a starring role. His brilliant portrayal of Kolchak is funny at times, coarse at others, but always strangely charming in the ways that he rebelliously interacts with the police and local authorities.

While McGavin dominates the proceedings, Barry Atwater is eerily repellent as Janos Skorzeny, a bizarre, reclusive man who is a kind of modern-day Dracula. The role was first offered to Robert Quarry, but his contract with American International Pictures prevented him from taking the job.[27] Atwater was the second choice, but he delivers like a first-stringer. In Christopher Lee–like fashion, Atwater speaks no lines, but creates a characterization through his hardened physical features and movements. The juxtaposition of Skorzeny, an Old World vampire in modern-day Las Vegas, creates some of the most memorable horror imagery of the 1970s. Atwater died only six years later from a stroke; he became terminally ill with cancer after suffering a number of physical problems, including cranial deformities, because of his earlier use of steroids.

The Night Stalker set records as the most watched TV movie of all time. Because of the response, there was a second Kolchak movie, *The Night Strangler*, and then a series, *Kolchak: The Night Stalker*, which lasted for one season. The made-for-TV movie also directly influenced the creation of a show that became a sensation in the 1990s, *The X-Files*.[28]

Granted, *The Night Stalker* has not held up well over time, in part because of its inexpensive production values and clumsy use of an obvious stunt double for Atwater. But those are small criticisms. It remains remarkably entertaining, largely because of a good script, McGavin's performance and some wonderful vampire imagery.

The parade of quality horror in 1972 continued on March 8 with the theatrical premiere of *Tales from the Crypt*. An underrated film, it is full of twists that bring varying levels of justice to a highly questionable group of characters.

Based on the controversial but well-illustrated and -written comic book series of the 1950s, the film is lifted by the presence of such big name actors as Peter Cushing, Joan Collins and Ralph Richardson (who plays the Crypt Keeper). Cushing's performance is particularly touching. Cushing had just lost his wife at the time of filming, putting him into a deep depression. The screen legend so wanted to be involved with the film that he accepted a lower salary from the producers. In the film, Cushing faced a challenge that mirrored his real life: portraying Arthur Grimsdyke, the grieving, tormented widower who tries to communicate with his late wife through a Ouija board.

Tales from the Crypt begins with five strangers embarking on a tour of an old catacombs, only to be separated from the rest of the tour group. They are now in the presence of the Crypt Keeper, who proceeds to tell them stories that will foreshadow each of their deaths.

Some anthology films suffer because one or two segments fail to live up to the standards of the others, but that is not the case with *Tales from the Crypt*. All five segments are good, with two of them rising to a higher level. The first segment, featuring Collins as a woman who murders her husband and then is stalked in her own home on Christmas Eve, is particularly good, as is the segment with Cushing's Grimsdyke. After the Crypt Keeper tells his five stories, he then makes a disturbing and twisted revelation to his quintet of strangers. It all adds up to a very atmospheric film.

Tales from the Crypt influenced future productions. Stephen King and George Romero drew from the 1972 film in developing the similarly themed *Creepshow* in 1982.[29] Noted producer Robert Zemeckis, who has called *Tales from the Crypt* his favorite movie to watch on Halloween, used the film (along with the original comic book) as the basis for the HBO series that began in 1989.[30] The series, which spanned 93 episodes, ran for seven seasons on the cable network and became a huge hit with horror fans.

Given its influence and stylishness, the 1972 version of *Tales from the Crypt* is easy to recommend. It is one of the best anthologies of its era.

On March 10, just two days after *Tales from the Crypt* debuted, a fairly ridiculous horror film hopped into theaters across the country. *Frogs* is one of those often-parodied films from the early 1970s that is so bad that it's actually fun to watch. In the film, frogs and other forms of wildlife rebel against humans, attacking them in packs without warning. Of all the films showcased in this book, *Frogs* might be the weakest, but it is entertaining. More importantly, it led to a wave of eco-horror movies, including *Food of the Gods* and *Empire of the Ants*.

The headliner of *Frogs* is Ray Milland, who had reached a rather bizarre phase of his otherwise notable career by 1972. (In his later years, Milland appeared in a number of B-level horror films, mostly because he liked to work in films that showed "originality.") The same year that *Frogs* debuted, Milland starred in the wonderfully awful *The Thing with Two Heads*, which co-starred former NFL star Rosey Grier. Milland's characters in both films could have been cut from the same mold: crusty old men who are mad at the world and heartily despise much of their surroundings.

In *Frogs*, Milland portrays a retired millionaire, Jason Crockett, who is aging and disabled, and forced to spend most of his time in a wheelchair at his island mansion. Patriarch of the Crockett family, he hosts a Fourth of July celebration that coincides with his own birthday party. The celebration will be interrupted by a wildlife photojournalist, who is doing a magazine spread on the effects of pollution. He trespasses onto the Crockett property but is invited to the family mansion. There he learns of Jason's hatred of nature, which manifests itself in his decision to spray pesticides every time an unwanted creature shows up on his property. When the island's animal life begins attacking members of the Crockett family and their friends, it seems that nature is rebelling against Jason and his hatred of wildlife. But the later developments of the film call that into doubt, only leaving us with more unanswered questions.

Another one of the stars of *Frogs* was a young Sam Elliott, appearing in one of his first feature films. Without facial hair, Elliott is virtually unrecognizable as the freelance photographer, but he does lend some credible acting to the farcical proceedings. Another notable and capable player is Joan Van Ark, who portrays Milland's daughter and becomes Elliott's potential love interest.

Curiously, the frogs referenced in the film's title are actually never seen killing *anyone*, though the ending does imply that these malevolent creature *will* band together and do something horrible. Director George McCowan had plenty of frogs to work with—a total of

500 frogs and 100 toads—thought most of them escaped during the filming![31] Perhaps that's why most of the physical terror is supplied by other wildlife creatures, who appear to be rebelling against a society that has taken them for granted.

All in all, this is one of those fun 1970s horror flicks that provides a few moments of distracting entertainment and hilarity—assuming, of course, that you don't take any of it too seriously.

Some horror novels have been adapted and re-adapted, sometimes to the point of overkill. But a new twist on an old theme can enliven a story, and that is exactly what Hammer did with *Dr. Jekyll and Sister Hyde* in April 1972. Set in the Victorian Era, the film re-introduces the familiar character of Dr. Henry Jekyll, but assigns him a different task: Instead of trying to separate the good from the evil within man, he embarks on an experiment meant to extend human life. The doctor acquires fresh corpses from two body snatchers, extracting female hormones from each body under the theory that life can be extended because women live longer than men. Jekyll tries the new serum on himself, but much to his surprise, it transforms himself into a woman—and an evil one at that.

Realizing that he (or she) needs a constant supply of hormones to keep the serum potent, Jekyll-Hyde orders the body snatchers to kill young women on the streets of London. When the murderers are caught, Jekyll takes matters into his own hands. To complicate matters, the two personas of Jekyll and Hyde make efforts to dominate one another, leading to a horrific struggle.

The film stars Ralph Bates as Dr. Jekyll and Martine Beswick as "Mrs. Edwina Hyde." Both are very effective under the direction of Roy Ward Baker. For Beswick, the experience was not easy. Baker, perhaps under pressure from his producers, wanted full frontal nudity for his female lead in at least one scene.[32] Beswick balked at Baker's request, leading to a severe disagreement between the two. Although Beswick referred to their dispute as "a little glitch,"[33] the two did not speak for a full week.[34] They eventually reached a compromise, with Beswick reluctantly agreeing to go topless in a few scenes.

Dr. Jekyll and Sister Hyde was Hammer's third venture into the famed Robert Louis Stevenson novella: They released *The Ugly Duckling* in 1959, followed by *The Two Faces of Dr. Jekyll* in 1960. Of the three, *Dr. Jekyll and Sister Hyde* is the best. It's stylish and atmospheric, well-acted and -directed. It isn't entirely serious—there are moments that will make you laugh—but it's admirable for its daring willingness to alter the original source material of a longtime favorite theme.

A more serious horror film made its American debut on June 21, 1972, giving Alfred Hitchcock one more chance to shine within the genre. *Psycho* and *The Birds* had long ago received their due as veritable horror classics from the mind of Hitchcock, but his 1972 film *Frenzy*, remains an underrated gem that skillfully mixes the genres of thriller with psychological horror, while adding a dose of comedy in a way that doesn't detract from the main storyline. Even the ending is punctuated by a humorous line that provides a fitting cap to the proceedings.

The film co-stars two capable British actors in Jon Finch and Barry Foster. Finch portrays Richard Blaney, a former military pilot who has become an unlikable and unreliable alcoholic. After the death of his ex-wife, he is unfairly implicated in a series of rapes and so-called necktie murders. Foster plays Robert Rusk, a handsome and charming businessman hiding a dark secret, and making Blaney twist in the wind. Little does Blaney know that it is Rusk who is committing the rapes and murders, all the while making it seem that he is trying to help Blaney during his current run of bad luck.

Finch and Foster are excellent in their roles, as they each portray nuanced characters who alternate between being sympathetic and repulsive. Barbara Leigh-Hunt and Anna Massey are also exemplary. Another key contributor is veteran actor Alec McCowen, who plays Chief Inspector Oxford. He emphasizes Oxford's professionalism during the murder investigation, but also displays a wonderful sense of comedy through his interactions with his wife (Vivien Merchant) and his subtle displeasure with her hideous cooking recipes.

By the early 1970s, film standards had changed due to the elimination of the Code and the adoption of a ratings system, allowing Hitchcock to portray more risqué material, including murders that carried sexual overtones. As part of *Frenzy*, he included a lengthy rape scene that was particularly graphic for its time. "I think it was the first time I had seen a sexual psychopath coming to orgasm during a murder," says historian David J. Skal. "I don't think Hollywood had ever seen that. So it was a bit transgressive on that level, even though it wasn't explicit."[35] As such, it was the only Hitchcock film that ever received an R-rating at the time of its theatrical release.

The film's screenplay also makes direct mentions of two real-life serial killer cases in London history: the Jack the Ripper murders of the 1880s and the John Christie killings of the 1940s and '50s.[36] Given the violent and sexual themes at hand, even members of Hitchcock's family found the subject material difficult to handle. Hitchcock's daughter Patricia refused to allow her children to see the movie until many years later.[37]

Hitchcock's willingness to delve into dark, unsettling material is just one of the director's successful ventures with *Frenzy*. Filmed in London, the film displays some natural and gritty scenery contained within the city. It also shows us the ugliness of some of the city's disreputable characters. But Hitchcock's greatest success here is his brilliant and unconventional use of the camera. This is most evident in the scene where the rapist lures his latest victim into his apartment. Rather than show us exactly what transpires, Hitchcock has the camera pan away, moving backwards out of the apartment, then making its way down a staircase and out the door of the building onto the crowded streets of inner-city London. The unusual backwards-moving camera work shows us how even the worst crimes can take place right within our midst, only a few hundred feet from the hustle and bustle of main city streets, without anyone else knowing that evil is transpiring.

Given the effectiveness with which Hitchcock oversees the film, it is puzzling that *Frenzy* has remained such an overlooked film. Perhaps it's because Finch and Foster never became household names. There are no Janet Leighs or Rod Taylors here, no future stars like a young Anthony Perkins. Or maybe it's because the film's villain lacks the twisted appeal of a Norman Bates or the supernatural overtones of the assailants in *The Birds*.

Frenzy does have its flaws. "I'm not as bullish on *Frenzy* as some of [Hitchcock's] other films," says Skal. "I think it was workmanlike, but kind of predictable. It didn't have the surprises and twists that I had come to expect from Hitchcock."[38]

These are certainly legitimate criticisms, but *Frenzy* does remain a worthwhile film. It features an intricate and well-developed story and believable, earthy performances. While it falls short of being a masterpiece in the manner of *Psycho* and *The Birds* or non-horror efforts like *North by Northwest* and *Rear Window*, it takes its place on the second tier of the Hitchcock register. Given the director's long list of quality films, that is a good place to be.

Originally released in Great Britain in 1971, *Twins of Evil* had its American premiere in June 1972. One of Hammer's better offerings, it stars real-life twins Madeleine and Mary Collinson as sisters who have recently been orphaned. They are taken in by their uncle, Gustav Weil, played by the great Peter Cushing. A strict disciplinarian and a relentless witch hunter,

Weil is determined to round up all of the attractive women in the area and have them sentenced for witchcraft.

Not long after the twins arrive at their uncle's, they find themselves being targeted by a local devil worshipper, Count Karnstein, who is a bitter enemy of Weil. A devoted practitioner of the black arts, the count conjures up an evil spirit and becomes a vampire, which adds to the intrigue as he begins pursuit of one of the twin sisters.

Prior to the release of the film, the Collinson twins made news by posing nude for *Playboy*. Hammer took advantage of the *Playboy* connection by signing both to appear in the movie.[39] That made sense financially, but did create a problem. The sisters both had thick Maltese accents, which resulted in Hammer dubbing in the voices of two British actresses.[40]

In contrast to some other films of the time period, the dubbing is done almost flawlessly, to the point where it is hardly noticeable. That is consistent with the entire production of the film, which is smoothly executed and fast-moving. Not surprisingly, Cushing is excellent as the zealous witch hunter, a man with good intentions who goes way too far because of his obsession to target followers of the Devil. At times, Cushing's character seems nearly as sinister as Count Karnstein, who is played with equal skill by Egyptian actor Damien Thomas. With his unusually coiffed hair, arrogant manner and maniacal laugh, the count is a sight to behold and observe.

Twins of Evil has not received its due. With its intriguing mix of vampirism and witchcraft and a well-paced, twisty story, it's a highly entertaining Hammer.

July 1972 brought a sequel to the big screen: While not as good as the original film, *Dr. Phibes Rises Again* is another entertaining romp in the bizarre world of the horrible doctor. The blend of comedy and horror showcases Dr. Phibes at the center of the chaos, making for another spirited tale of supernatural pursuits and murderous endeavors.

This time Phibes is no longer consumed with merely revenge, but instead with retrieving a sacred papyrus map that will help him find the River of Life, which will allow him to bring his late wife back to life. Traveling to Egypt, where most of the film takes place, Phibes finds himself in competition with another man seeking the River of Life, and inflicts some collateral damage along the way.

Vincent Price reprises his role as Dr. Phibes, this time with much more dialogue. Also returning is Peter Jeffrey as Inspector Trout, the half-comical police investigator who must once again hunt down Phibes, even though the monstrous killer appeared to die in a suicide at the end of the original movie. Terry-Thomas also returns in a cameo, but this time as a different character; he was one of the doctors who was targeted by Phibes in the 1971 film.

Virginia North was unable to return to the role of Vulnavia because of her real-life pregnancy, so the non-speaking role was given to Valli Kemp. The great Peter Cushing, who was scheduled to appear in the original but had to bow out for personal reasons, makes a cameo as a captain, a role that he shot in one day.

Perhaps the most interesting of the new cast additions was Robert Quarry, an AIP veteran. Under the original plan, Quarry was supposed to reprise his role as Count Yorga, the Bulgarian vampire, and become Phibes' chief adversary.[41] But the script was changed, with Quarry filling a role as the wonderfully named Darrus Biederbeck, the man with the papyrus map that Phibes seeks. It's worth noting that Quarry was billed second in the credits, right behind Price. The two stars reportedly clashed severely on the set, mostly because Price heard rumors that AIP planned to replace him with Quarry as the lead star for the company. Price and Quarry sniped at each other repeatedly, to the point that Price openly questioned his co-star's skills as an actor.[42]

Whether or not the tension between the two leads affected the final product is debatable. But the film certainly lacks the continuity and flow of the original, in part because of the cutting of some scenes for budget reasons, and also because of the use of two different screenwriters. The two writers did not collaborate on the script, but instead wrote separate drafts that were then cobbled together by a third party.

Due to the lack of continuity, budget cuts and the absence of the creativity of the first film, *Dr. Phibes Rises Again* fails to live up to the standard of its predecessor. But it has worthwhile moments and delivers a nice mix of comedy and horror, capably handled through the words and voice of the masterful Price.

By 1972, American cinema had entered its Blaxploitation era: films starring African-American actors in contemporary urban settings, sometimes set against a backdrop dealing with racial injustice.[43] In some cases, the films drew later criticism for fostering and promoting negative stereotypes. Horror and Blaxploitation came together in *Blacula,* an intriguing film that mixes camp with horror while making something of a social statement. Released on August 25, 1972, it initially played to mixed reviews. Not surprisingly, it continues to have its share of detractors, but it is one of those films that any horror fan should want to see, if only because of its historical significance in becoming the first film to combine the genre with Blaxploitation. And as historian David J. Skal points out, *Blacula* serves as further proof of the unending appeal of the original Dracula. "Dracula adapts endlessly—it's remarkable," says Skal.[44]

In a modern-day retelling of the time-honored theme, *Blacula* features an 18th-century African prince who is betrayed by Dracula. The count refuses Prince Mamuwalde's request to bring an end to the slave trade before attacking him and turning him into a vampire. Dracula locks the prince in a coffin, which survives for more than a century and a half and makes its way into the hands of two antique collectors who are visiting Transylvania. They purchase the coffin and ship it back to Los Angeles. Not knowing what they have, the two men open the coffin in their warehouse, allowing Blacula to escape. He quietly emerges from the coffin, murders the two collectors, and embarks on a wave of destruction and death throughout the city.

One of the film's strengths is the effort of the lead actor, William Marshall, who plays the African prince-turned-vampire. Marshall was no lightweight: A classically trained Shakespearean performer and a veteran of Broadway, he brings both dignity and fierceness to his *Blacula* role. (During production, Marshall convinced the producers to use the African prince backstory and insisted on a serious portrayal of the character.[45])

In some ways, the distinguished actor's portrayal is reminiscent of Bela Lugosi, as he gives the vampire an Old World, gentlemanly appearance. At the same time, he connects with the humorous side of the film, especially in the way that he toys with a medical examiner who asks him about the existence of vampires. "Marshall enjoyed the tongue-in-cheek of *Blacula,*" contends Skal.[46]

Marshall's physical appearance as Mamuwalde, complete with a large black cape, stands in stark contrast to the setting of hip Los Angeles and its colorful clothes, large Afros and jargon-filled conversation. Mamuwalde is at first driven by bloodlust and anger; some film critics have likened his plight to the civil rights movement—and the specific struggles that African-American men faced in early 1970s culture. Thanks to Marshall's range and ample acting abilities, viewers can both sympathize with the vampire and come to detest his violent, hell-bent nature.

Mamuwalde becomes smitten with Tina (Vonetta McGee): She bears a striking

8. Creature Features, Fright Night *and* Block of Shock (1970–1975) 193

resemblance to his wife Luva, who was left to die after Dracula imprisoned him in a coffin. Mamuwalde sees Tina as Luva's reincarnation. Denise Nicholas lends strength as Tina's sister. McGee and Nicholas forged successful careers, both during and after the Blaxploitation movement. A particularly good performance is turned in by accomplished actor Thalmus Rasulala, who plays a medical examiner; he is the first to realize that a vampire is behind the recent spate of killings. (Rasulala died young, the victim of a heart attack at the age of 51.)

While these individual performances are good, the film has taken criticism for being too campy and for sometimes coming across as more comical than horrifying. The dialogue is also lacking, though Marshall's presence helps overcome that shortcoming. The portrayal of the antique collectors as flamboyant gay men is so over the top as to play into stereotypes; it's the kind of portrayal that would not be accepted today.

These are legitimate criticisms, but they do not ruin the film. The strong visual settings, an excellent rhythm-and-blues score and some surprising storyline twists make this a fun venture. Not to be taken too seriously, *Blacula* is an entertaining and worthwhile film, with just enough of a message about racism to make the viewer think.

One other film helped make 1972 a good year for horror. On November 17, *Dracula AD 1972* premiered in American theaters. It has been cited as one of the worst Hammer films. That consensus is unfair and off the mark. This is an entertaining film, far better than some critics have led us to believe.

Peter Cushing and Christopher Lee are good in their usual hero-monster roles, respectively, which is no surprise, but most impressive is the performance of a young Christopher Neame as Johnny Alucard. Neame is outstanding as the outspoken leader of group of twentysomething Londoners; unlike the others, who are simply young and rebellious, he is completely evil and obsessed with Satan. He wants all of his friends to become devil worshippers, including Jessica Van Helsing, the granddaughter of Lorrimer Van Helsing, an authority on the occult.

Neame's Alucard really hits his stride in a memorable scene at a defunct church, where he leads a black mass. The ceremony results in the revival of Dracula. The scene is striking, as is the scene where Cushing's elder Van Helsing confronts Alucard at his hip London pad.

Dracula AD 1972 does a good job of juxtaposing Old World characters played by Cushing and Lee against the modern London scene, with plenty of period scenery and jargon thrown into the mix. This could have been very hokey and campy, but it instead delivers a degree of sophistication; the filming is done skillfully, with good sets, some Gothic imagery in the church and cemetery, and solid performances across the board, including those delivered by lead actresses Stephanie Beacham (as Jessica) and Caroline Munro. This film is much better than its reputation.

On November 21, ABC aired its latest made-for-TV horror film. *Gargoyles* became one of the most popular telefilms of the 1970s, putting it in the same category as *The Night Stalker* and *Crowhaven Farm*.

In *Gargoyles*, anthropologist Dr. Boley reads a letter about a mysterious inhuman skeleton found in the American Southwest. Boley, skeptical of its legitimacy, travels with his daughter to visit the old man in possession of the artifact; he runs a small but strange museum in the desert. During their conversation about the skeleton, they are attacked by a small group of gargoyles, descendants of Satan. The museum owner is killed but the Boleys survive, escaping with the skull. Their removal of the artifact enrages the gargoyles, who attempt to kill the Boleys and then unleash additional attacks against residents of a nearby town.

Gargoyles succeeds in part because of its very good cast. The Boleys are played by Cornel Wilde and Jennifer Salt, while the lead gargoyle is portrayed by another accomplished actor, Bernie Casey. They are joined by a young Scott Glenn, veteran actor Woody Chambliss and *Dark Shadows* veteran Grayson Hall. The actors play their parts well, while enduring the brutal weather conditions. Filming took place on location in New Mexico, with temperatures topping 100 during several days of shooting.

The work of the actors was more than matched by the makeup and effects department, even in the face of severe financial restrictions. Stan Winston's gargoyle makeup was so well done that it won him an Emmy. The makeup and costuming are reminiscent of the historic outfit worn by the Gill Man in *Creature from the Black Lagoon*.

Some of the techniques used in *Gargoyles* make it an unusual movie for its time. Produced on a minuscule budget, it was filmed with only one camera. The movie also employs the technique of slow motion, which would become common in later horror films but was used only sparingly in the genre during the early 1970s.

Gargoyles was well received by TV audiences at the time, and the film's stock with horror diehards has risen over time. Most fans are willing to forgive the script, which is over the top in its presentation of a doomsday scenario. Taken with a grain of salt, and with a sense of humor, *Gargoyles* remains a fun venture into the supernatural world of 1970s television. It is arguably one of the best made-for-TV horror movies of the era.

The year 1973 would produce another strong run of horror films, including two classics. The year started with another movie that was part of the growing made-for-TV trend: a sequel designed to capitalize on the success of 1972's *The Night Stalker*. On January 16, ABC debuted *The Night Strangler* – and it was no weakling among sequels. With Dan Curtis now directing, it was a critical hit, matching *The Night Stalker* for entertainment value and perhaps exceeding the first film in some other ways.

Darren McGavin returns in his iconic role as Carl Kolchak, the somewhat disheveled news reporter. He discovers that recent murders in Seattle, apparent strangulations that result in complete blood loss, are part of a pattern of killings that date back over a century. His research reveals the pattern of serial murders occurring every 21 years, convincing him that something supernatural is at work.

Returning from the first film, Simon Oakland plays Kolchak's editor, an old-school type who has little tolerance for stories of monsters and paranormal beings. There's also a memorable cameo by Al Lewis, known for his portrayal of Grandpa on *The Munsters*. Lewis plays a homeless man living within the Seattle Underground; at first, Kolchak believes him to be a vampire, a fitting development given that Lewis played such a creature on *The Munsters*. Lewis' character is no vampire, but he does make his presence felt in his lone scene. And then there is Richard Anderson: Playing the nefarious Dr. Malcolm and hiding dark secrets, Anderson's character becomes involved in a major twist at the end of the film, one that stuns audiences and results in a memorable showdown in the doctor's dark underground laboratory.

Shot in 12 days in Seattle and Los Angeles,[47] *The Night Strangler* does not come off as a hurried production. It is well-paced and fast-moving, both humorous and suspenseful, and surprising in the way the story develops. The creative and unexpected developments mark an upgrade over *The Night Stalker*, as do the cameo roles for Lewis and two other Hollywood favorites, John Carradine and Margaret Hamilton. Given *The Night Strangler*'s success as a sequel to *The Night Stalker*, it's no wonder that a popular TV series would soon come to fruition.

8. Creature Features, Fright Night *and* Block of Shock (1970–1975) 195

The Night Strangler (1973): Carl Kolchak, the flawed but wise investigative reporter played by Darren McGavin, looks back while a resident of the Seattle Underground (Al Lewis of *The Munsters*) tries to sleep on an old mattress frame. Lewis was one of several brand-name actors who made cameos in the film, along with John Carradine and Margaret Hamilton (courtesy of Dr. Jeffrey Thompson).

While Curtis was continuing to have an impact with his telefilms, the first significant theatrical release of 1973 arrived on February 9 when *The Creeping Flesh* made its American debut in New York City theaters. It is often mistaken for a Hammer film; while it certainly looks like a Hammer, especially with Peter Cushing and Christopher Lee in starring roles, and Hammer favorite Freddie Francis in the director's chair, it is actually a production of a little-known company, Tigon British. *The Creeping Flesh* represents the last of a series of horror movies produced by Tigon from 1967 to 1973.[48]

Cushing stars as a scientist returning to his Victorian London home with a gruesome, massive skeleton that he discovered on a research trip to New Guinea. He believes that the skeleton is that of a primitive man predating Neanderthals. By accident, he discovers that exposing the bones to water results in the growth of flesh and blood. He tries to extract the blood and convert it into a vaccine against extreme mental illness, which allegedly claimed the life of his late wife. Foolishly giving the vaccine to his daughter, whom he fears has inherited the mental illness of her mother, he comes to realize that he has unleashed a strain of pure evil.

Lee plays Cushing's half-brother, the cruel operator of a local asylum who has been conducting dangerous experiments on some of his patients. The brothers are rivals, both searching for a cure to the plague of insanity, but Lee is clearly unscrupulous and conniving, to the point that he is willing and eager to steal his brother's ideas.

The Creeping Flesh was supposed to be directed by Don Sharp, but he withdrew at the last moment. Tigon turned to Francis,[49] who did well with the material, especially on such short notice. It was an ambitious project, especially given the complexity of the script, but Francis makes it work. He lays out an excellent Gothic backdrop for the film. Francis also elicits good performances from all of his main players, including Lorna Heilbron who skillfully plays Cushing's daughter. At first, while being suppressed by her overprotective father, she is innocent and naïve, before the vaccine turns her into a dangerous lunatic.

The film has its weaknesses. The special effects and makeup are disappointing, especially when the transformed skeleton takes on skin and flesh. Then there's the side story of a madman on the loose, distracting viewers from the main story involving the skeleton that is just waiting to be revived. But with patience, the viewer will be rewarded with a worthwhile horror experience from an underrated director and two acting giants.

By the early 1970s, Amicus Productions had nearly perfected the art of the horror anthology. After the company's earlier successes, Amicus once again hit pay dirt with *The Vault of Horror*, which premiered in New York City on March 16, 1973. The lavish production, featuring a host of talented and experienced European actors, lays out a series of five vignettes, all very good and highly compelling.

The movie was named after the EC comic book of 1950s vintage, but none of the film's stories came directly from the comic book; they stem from other comic books produced by EC. But the issue of source material really doesn't matter.[50] All five tales are well told and directed by Roy Ward Baker, providing the viewer with an appropriate level of tension and suspense before dramatic and, in some cases, unforeseen conclusions.

Five men board a British office building's elevator, intending to make their way home for the evening. The elevator instead takes them to the building's basement, a finished meeting room—with no means of escape. The men proceed to tell each other stories about bad dreams and nightmarish visions that they have each been experiencing. Each story ends badly, creating a sense of impending doom, and leading to the film's ghoulish finale.

While there are no Peter Cushings or Christopher Lees to headline the cast, an excellent group of less famous but no less skilled actors fill out the excellent ensemble. The first segment features Daniel Massey (son of Raymond Massey), who decides to murder his sister (Daniel's real-life sister, Anna Massey) for her share of an inheritance. Shortly thereafter, he discovers the presence of vampires in a local restaurant, which features a most gruesome menu. Terry-Thomas headlines the second vignette, about an obsessive-compulsive man who drives his new wife to insanity with his calls for cleanliness. The comedic actor is over the top in his portrayal, but his manic manner works to perfection.

Perhaps the best segment is the third, driven by the underrated German actor Curd Jurgens. He plays a traveling magician in pursuit of a new trick to headline his show. His search leads him to murder, and some rather unexpected consequences. The segment features some of the best special effects trickery seen in films from the early 1970s.

In vignette #4, the weakest of the stories but still above average, a man strikes an odd bargain that involves the staging of his own death, all part of a get-rich-quick scheme. He is eventually double-crossed, leading to a thrilling final sequence in the cemetery in which he has been buried.

The final vignette rises to the standards of the first three. An artist (Tom Baker, the future Doctor Who) learns the art of Haitian voodoo, which allows him to seek revenge against a trio of con men who have wronged him. One of the men is played by Denholm Elliott, who only delivers four lines in total but still manages a worthwhile performance.

8. Creature Features, Fright Night *and* Block of Shock (1970–1975)

By the end of the film, themes of vampirism, spousal abuse, evil magic, grave robbery and voodoo have all been fully explored, making *The Vault of Horror* one of the more enthralling and diverse anthologies ever made. *The Vault of Horror* is must-see theater for aficionados of the era's top tier of British anthology horror.

April 5, 1973, saw another notable film of British origins make its way into American theaters. While it is a lesser film than *The Abominable Dr. Phibes*, a movie to which it is often compared, *Theater of Blood* has achieved similar status as a cult favorite among Vincent Price fans. In fact, Price often referred to *Theater of Blood* as his favorite.[51]

Hamming it up to delightfully comic ends, Price plays Shakespearean actor Edward Lionheart, who becomes so angered by negative reviews of his performances that he decides to take his own life and plunges into the Thames. He survives his suicidal dive, rescued by a group of homeless street dwellers of varying moral credibility. Given a second life, Lionheart opts for an extreme Plan B: violent revenge against the critics who wronged him. In each case, Price dons some kind of elaborate costume or makeup and fools his victims, putting them in situations that ultimately lead to their deaths. The creativity of the killings and the element of revenge are reminiscent of the work of Dr. Phibes.

In perhaps the most memorable scene from the film, Price dons a large Afro wig and pretends to be a hairdresser, while costuming himself like a *Starsky and Hutch* extra. In this scene, Lionheart seeks revenge against a character played by veteran Australian actress Coral Browne, who met Price for the first time on the set of the film. The two fell in love, resulting in Price's divorce from his wife and his eventual marriage to Browne.[52]

Theater of Blood co-stars Diana Rigg, who plays Price's daughter, and also features accomplished British actor Robert Morley, who plays one of Lionheart's more pathetic victims: an obese gourmet who is forced to eat pies consisting of his deceased dogs. Then there is Ian Hendry, an extremely talented British actor who would die young, roughly a decade after *Theater of Blood* debuted. He skillfully portrays Lionheart's arch-nemesis, critic Peregrine Devlin, with a keen intensity and awareness, the latter trait allowing him to realize sooner than the others that the actor is still alive and seeking vengeance against his critics.

In addition to a high-end cast, one of the film's real strengths is the authenticity of the locations and background. Rather than rely on the comforts of a studio set, director Douglas Hickox filmed every scene on location in and around London,[53] even in unattractive locales. That decision gives the film some grit, a nice complement to the dastardly deeds being pulled off by one of Price's classic villains.

Theater of Blood is a horror film, but also a black comedy that provides a good share of laughs. Price delivers an over-the-top performance, but given the comedic overtone to the film, such an acting choice fits *Theater of Blood* perfectly.

The Legend of Hell House, a not-so-ordinary haunted house adventure, made its U.S. debut on June 15, 1973. With its pulsating musical score, elaborate and darkly colored sets, wonderful sound effects and extreme level of creepy tension, it rises above the usual standards of the haunted house genre. Only a contrived and awkward ending detracts from the quality of the film.

The film is based on a novel by the legendary Richard Matheson, who wrote the screenplay for director John Hough. Matheson toned down the script, eliminating much of the graphic violence and sexual content in his original work so as to conform to the standards of the film producers.[54] The end result is a horror film that is light in overt violence, but heavy in its atmosphere and tension.

Led by a British scientist who has been lured by a big payday, four paranormal investigators (including two mediums) enter the dreaded Belasco house. It is haunted by the evil Emeric Belasco, a serial killer with a history of sadism and sexual perversion. (Matheson based the Belasco backstory on the life of infamous occultist Aleister Crowley.)

Previous investigations of the Belasco house have ended in doom, but the current investigators must spend a week under its roof to fulfill their mission: supplying evidence that the house is haunted. Not surprisingly, the residing spirit is so daunting as to put all of their lives in peril.

The performances of the four lead actors are all good, but the enormously talented Roddy McDowall leads the way as physical medium Benjamin Franklin Fischer. McDowall puts forth an evolving performance, at first reserved and quietly sarcastic, but then more vocal and outwardly aggressive. Such an effort should come as no surprise; whenever McDowall performed in horror, from *It!* (1967) to *Fright Night* (1985), he always delivered the goods, and *Legend of Hell House* is no exception.

Pamela Franklin, filling the role of mental medium Florence Tanner, also excels with a combination of vulnerability and strength. (Franklin made only two more horror films before retiring from the business in 1981, at the age of 31.) Clive Revill and Gayle Hunnicutt, both capable actors, are also good in playing the scientist and his wife. In particular, Revill leaves us guessing, wondering whether he is strictly motivated by the monetary reward put forth from a rich benefactor, or has more noble intentions in trying to restore peace and order to the disturbed house.

The *Hell House* soundtrack stands as one of the best in horror history. From the stinging sound effects to the commanding music score, the rich track succeeds in bringing *Hell House* into our living rooms at full throttle.

The film really has only two flaws: a pace that is slow at times, along with a clunky ending that lacks any kind of substantial moral impact. The latter flaw prevents *The Legend of Hell House* from becoming a more significant piece of the horror lexicon.

Movie sequels rarely match the quality of original films, but every once in a great while, they actually exceed their predecessors. Such is the case with *Scream Blacula Scream*, which made its debut on June 27, 1973. While the original *Blacula* was a decent and entertaining film, *Scream Blacula Scream* deserves a much higher ranking. It is far less campy, far sleeker in presentation. Bringing back William Marshall in the title role, the sequel features much-improved production values, better and more elaborate sets, and a stronger supporting cast that is aided by the additions of Pam Grier and Michael Conrad.

The storyline, which is more well-defined than in the original movie, begins with family and friends coming together to pay their respects to a dying voodoo priestess. During the vigil, the priestess' son (played well by actor Richard Lawson) argues that he should replace her as leader of the group, but the group instead chooses her adopted apprentice. Furious, the son decides to seek revenge by using voodoo to revive Prince Mamuwalde, now better known as Blacula. But when Blacula returns to the living world, he has no interest in serving the spoiled son; instead, he becomes the master, making the son one of his vampire legion.

In the new film, Blacula is no longer interested in finding a replacement for his long-lost wife, Luva. Instead, his mission is to find a cure for his vampire curse, so that he can resume life as a human. He turns to Lisa Fortier, the adopted daughter of the deceased priestess. Played by Grier, Lisa reluctantly agrees to help Blacula, even though she is aghast at his violent streak and thirst for blood. In the meantime, Blacula is pursued by two detectives, one played by the accomplished Conrad and the other by likable actor Don Mitchell.

The acting is solid across the board, but Marshall once again carries the film. With his

8. Creature Features, Fright Night *and* Block of Shock (1970–1975) 199

Scream Blacula Scream (1973): Played by William Marshall, the title vampire emerges from his coffin, ready to engage in more violence along with a mission to "cure" his condition. Marshall brought dignity and gravity to both of his Blacula portrayals, but a better screenplay and more elaborate sets helped make the sequel the stronger of the two films (courtesy of Tony Calvert).

deep, melodious voice and fully confident manner, he is even more comfortable in the Blacula role than he was in the first film. This time he brings a greater touch of humanity, given his desire to cease being a vampire and his admission that he has no control over his fits of rage and his urge to draw blood and kill. There is a sympathetic quality to Blacula, in some ways similar to what Jonathan Frid achieved with his characterization of Barnabas Collins in TV's *Dark Shadows*.

Scream Blacula Scream also succeeds because of the direction of Bob Kelljan, who oversaw both of the *Count Yorga* films. With Kelljan and Marshall at the helm, *Scream Blacula Scream* becomes one of the better vampire films of the era, and makes us wonder why a third *Blacula* movie was never made. Remaining underrated to this day, it's a very good film about vampires, their ability to convince others to do their bidding, and their inner torments.

Not all of 1973's horrors were found in theaters. Two films had an impact on TV viewers during the fall. September 19 marked the debut of ABC's *Satan's School for Girls*. While it is by no means a great film, it is another necessary part of 1970s horror culture, and a good representation of both satanic cult films and the proliferation of horror telefilms in the era.

Satan's School for Girls give us another fleeting look at Pamela Franklin and an early glimpse at the talent of a young Kate Jackson. Franklin stars as high schooler Roberta, who learns of the death of her sister at a private girls school located in Salem, Massachusetts.

Unconvinced by the police verdict of suicide, Roberta enrolls at the school under a false name and begins an investigation of her own. Along the way, she meets fellow students played by Jackson and Cheryl Ladd, who was still using her original name of Cheryl Stoppelmoor. The film's producer Aaron Spelling would reunite Jackson and Ladd a few years later on the popular TV show *Charlie's Angels*.

Given the relative youth of Ladd, Jackson and some of the other actresses playing students, the acting in *Satan's School for Girls* is a bit scattered. (Veteran actors Roy Thinnes and Lloyd Bochner help out somewhat as teachers, but neither is given enough screen time to make a big difference.) The special effects are also cheesy, but the story is a good one that features several surprises along the way. The opening of the film is especially strong. In a captivating sequence, we see Roberta's sister being pursued outside the school, yet we never see who or what is giving chase. Quite terrifying, the scene culminates in a shot that shows the sister hanging from a beam in her apartment. The film's ending is also effective, with director David Lowell Rich giving us an unexpected twist of the supernatural.

With a better third act, *Satan's School for Girls* would have been a much stronger film. But it remains one of the most memorable TV movies of its era, thanks to its wonderfully creepy atmosphere (including a cavern-like basement), its ability to create and sustain suspense, and its underlying sense of dread. No one will ever call it a masterpiece, but *Satan's School for Girls* has become a requisite part of the 1970s horror experience.

Another made-for-TV film had an impact that fall. ABC's *Don't Be Afraid of the Dark* was so popular upon its network debut (October 10, 1973) that it developed a loyal following, mandating numerous repeat viewings in syndication in later years.

Kim Darby and Jim Hutton star as the Farnhams, a couple moving into a Victorian mansion that they hope to restore. Sally unwittingly unleashes a horde of small, demon-like creatures that can best be described as goblins. They have been inhabiting the walls of the ancient structure for years, and have now become motivated to make their presence felt—and to make Sally one of them.

Darby and Hutton (who would die six years later from liver cancer) play their roles capably, but Darby is clearly the central figure, with Hutton taking a back seat. Also lending a hand is venerable character actor William Demarest, best known for his turn as Uncle Charlie on the long-running TV show *My Three Sons*. Demarest plays his role as caretaker with his usual degree of growly crustiness, a character trait that he perfected as an actor, while also doing his best to warn Sally and Alex of the house's sinister side.

Director John Newland uses an effective technique in first hinting at the presence of the goblins. Initially, they are only heard (a series of repeated whispers), a device that not only adds to the creepy atmosphere but also creates a degree of suspense.

The physical revelation of the goblins is a mixed bag: good special effects for the time, but somewhat lacking in credibility by modern horror standards. Screenwriter Nigel McKeand later admitted that he had wanted the creatures to be quicker and more demonic, but they ended up being slow and somewhat "lumbering."[55] Viewers need to suspend their disbelief if they are to regard them as truly menacing figures.

Even with such a shortcoming, *Don't Be Afraid of the Dark* is an entertaining film—good enough to have spawned a very competent 2010 remake starring Katie Holmes and Guy Pearce.

Don't Look Now is another must-see film from the era. It premiered in New York City theaters on December 9, 1973, before receiving a more widespread release in January 1974. Featuring two high-end actors in Julie Christie and Donald Sutherland, this psychological

8. Creature Features, Fright Night *and* Block of Shock (1970–1975)   201

horror film is ahead of its time, both in terms of its willingness to deal with difficult subject matter and in its execution of quality special effects.

Don't Look Now examines the plight of a married couple, Laura and John Baxter, whose young daughter has drowned. Still grieving, the two travel to Venice, where they happen to meet a pair of elderly sisters. One of the sisters, a psychic, says that she has seen the spirit of the daughter in her visions. Mr. Baxter is resistant to the idea, while his wife is open to the possibility. But he begins to change his mind when he has visions of his own.

Handled beautifully by director Nicolas Roeg, *Don't Look Now* received a vote of approval from author Daphne du Maurier, whose story was the basis for the film.[56] Of particular note is Roeg's brilliant use of Venice as a haunting backdrop to such a tragic story. But the film's release also produced controversy. The theatrical version featured an explicit and intermittently displayed sex scene involving Sutherland and Christie. For the American release, most of the scene was maintained, but Roeg eliminated nine frames of the scene in order to avoid an X-rating.[57] For many years, there were rumors that the sex scene was not simulated but was actually real, an allegation that Sutherland and Christie have repeatedly denied.[58]

Some critics have called the sex scene too long and perhaps even unnecessary. That criticism aside, *Don't Look Now* succeeds in its ability to create suspense, its presentation of chilling imagery (partly through effective camerawork and partly through special effects), the use of Venice's stunning beauty, and its skillful editing. It is one of Roeg's best and most artistic films, aided nicely by the excellent performances of Sutherland and Christie, two accomplished actors who were near the top of their game in the early 1970s. Sutherland's ability to portray the unending grief that a father faces after the loss of a child is particularly powerful, an example of the kind of everyday horror that can infiltrate the lives of any family.

Yet *Don't Look Now* advances beyond real-life drama and tragedy by giving us the supernatural storyline, initiated by the visions of the psychic sister and continued through the imagery endured by Sutherland. That helps to round out the horror aspect of the film, making it appeal to purists of the genre, but also not interfering with the drama faced by the Baxters.

Don't Look Now lacks an abundance of special effects gimmickry and the typical confrontation of a demon pitted against an innocent child. It is not a fun or a light film. It is serious horror, perhaps not totally appropriate for the hosted horror era, but so well executed that it must be included on any list highlighting the era's best offerings.

The lack of recognition given to *Don't Look Now* is somewhat surprising, but may be attributable to bad timing. It came out at nearly the same time as *The Exorcist*, a film that became a nationwide sensation and garnered massive media attention. Debuting in theaters on December 26, *The Exorcist* emerged as the most powerful horror film of 1973.

Based on the bestselling novel by William Peter Blatty, *The Exorcist* has become one of the most discussed and debated films in horror history. Most critics feel that it is an unquestioned classic, others regard it as slightly overrated, while still others view it as a film that no longer seems as frightening given the extremity of films that have appeared since. But there's little doubt that the 1973 release of *The Exorcist* created a commotion and a swirl of controversy, while leaving us with a film that is still impactful, intrusive and disturbing.

The Exorcist tells the story of a young girl, Regan MacNeil, living with her actress mother Chris in Washington, D.C. While they reside temporarily in an apartment house during a film shoot, the teenager suddenly becomes ill, prompting a battery of hospital tests. Doctors can find nothing physically wrong with her.

Now believing that Regan's problems are psychological, the doctors recommend that Chris consult Catholic Church officials about conducting an exorcism. Chris contacts Father Damien Karras, a Jesuit priest and psychiatrist who had previously been consulted by the police when the MacNeils' babysitter died in a mysterious home accident. Father Karras determines that Regan is indeed possessed. He will now collaborate with Father Merrin, an older priest experienced in such matters, in performing a torturous and pain-inducing exorcism in which they do battle with a demon, Pazuzu.

Appearing in only her third motion picture, Linda Blair drew favorable reviews for her portrayal of young Regan. The voice of the demonic Pazuzu was furnished by veteran character actress Mercedes McCambridge, who was best known for her work in radio. For this unusual voice role, McCambridge was aided by chronic bronchitis, the wrapping of a tight scarf around her neck, and the consumption of 18 raw eggs and a "pulpy" apple.[59] Her raspy, growling voice and accompanying array of screams and groans were spectacular, in some ways more frightening than the physical damage being inflicted upon Regan by the demon.

Those possession scenes, including the 360-degree rotation of Regan's head (done with the use of a mechanical dummy) and the famed "spiderwalk" down the staircase railing, are some of the most iconic in horror history. But the film would not have been nearly as effective without the performances of three adult actors who receive top billing: Ellen Burstyn, Max von Sydow and Lee J. Cobb. All three delivered, Burstyn as the concerned mother, von Sydow as the older Jesuit priest, and Cobb as the veteran police investigator looking into recent deaths that may also be related to demonic possession.

But the best performance of all is turned in by Jason Miller. He is inspiring and powerful as Father Karras, who is convinced that Regan's problems are rooted in demonic possession. The real-life father of actor Jason Patric, Miller plays Father Karras with a brooding intensity that underscores the character of a genuinely good-hearted soul. Miller brilliantly portrays a character who has begun to lose his faith because of his own personal problems, including the death of his mother, but is now forced to resuscitate his spiritual beliefs in an effort to save an innocent child.

The filming, which was overseen by volatile director William Friedkin, was not done without difficulty. At one point, Miller was supposed to be hit in the chest with projectile vomit, but was instead hit in the face. This so upset Miller that he wiped away the vomit in actual disgust, intensifying the scene.[60] (Miller later apologized for losing his cool, but the angry gesture only made the film better.) Von Sydow, made-up to look much older than his actual age of 44, had so much trouble with some of the foul language being uttered by Blair (before the re-dubbing done by McCambridge) that at one point he forgot his lines.[61] And then after the film made its way into theaters, Blair faced death threats from religious zealots who believed that *The Exorcist* glorified Satan. Warner Brothers took the threats seriously, hiring bodyguards to watch over Blair for the next six months.[62]

While the merits of *The Exorcist* will continue to be debated, it deserves its consensus ranking as an all-time classic of the genre. After all, it was the first horror movie to ever be nominated for Best Picture, and with good reason, given the many fine performances and the intensity of the story. Only four subsequent horror films have received such Oscars nominations, and they are all standouts (*Jaws, The Silence of the Lambs, The Sixth Sense* and *Get Out*). That kind of company is an acknowledgment of the film's value, coming from a filmland constituency that is often unfairly dismissive of horror. With its critical acclaim, its dramatic tale of good vs. evil, the fervor of the scenes involving demonic possession, and its powerful special effects, *The Exorcist* is a must-see film for any fan of horror.

8. Creature Features, Fright Night *and* Block of Shock (1970–1975)

There have been many versions of *Dracula* created since Max Schreck's *Nosferatu* and Bela Lugosi's *Dracula*; some have been quite good, others have fallen far short of any classic standards. One film that deserves to be placed in the former category is the 1974 telefilm *Dracula* (also known as *Dan Curtis' Dracula*), directed by Curtis and starring Jack Palance.

It was supposed to air in October 1973, but the breaking news of Spiro Agnew's resignation forced the network to delay it until February 8, 1974. Better late than never, *Dracula* not only played to favorable reviews, but has retained a strong following over the years.

In what is a generally faithful retelling of Bram Stoker's novel, Palance stars as the count. He is seen living in Hungary, where he has summoned Jonathan Harker to complete a real estate transaction in England. Dracula soon moves to Great Britain; the landing of his ship results in one of the most stunning images of the film: a dead man at the helm, completely pale and sporting a horrible expression of anguish on his face. Now loose from his coffin, Dracula establishes his new residence and sets his target on Harker's friend Mina, who soon becomes ill with blood loss. Mina's fiancé Arthur turns to the knowledgeable Van Helsing, played skillfully by veteran British actor Nigel Davenport.

On the surface, Palance might have seemed like an odd choice to play the vampire. He was already 54 and did not possess the stereotypical facial features or the lean body type associated with Dracula. But he was also an actor with a well-earned reputation for playing dastardly types, including a wide range of bandits and thugs, and few characters are any more detestable than the Transylvanian vampire. Palance plays the character with his usual sinister gusto, giving us a unique approach that some might call a blending between Lugosi and Christopher Lee. Palance's Dracula is partly fueled by wanting to rekindle a long-lost love (an admirable quality), but he is also thoroughly evil. Lacking in any social grace or civility, he is motivated mostly by a desire for blood and an obsession with gaining power over as many of his "brides" as he can.

Palance is also surprisingly athletic in his portrayal of Dracula. Even at 6'4" and 200+ pounds, he moves easily in portraying the count. When he discovers that one of his brides has been staked through the heart, he has a physical temper tantrum that is both fluid and believable. In another scene, he does hand-to-hand combat with Van Helsing and handles the scene capably, especially for one in his mid–50s.

Palance showed such aptitude for the role of Dracula that he received several offers to reprise the character in sequels. The actor was not interested. As a method actor, Palance became so engrossed in such an evil character that it disturbed him. Relieved when the filming came to an end, he turned down the subsequent offers, making this his sole appearance as the famed vampire.[63] But his lone turn as Dracula was influential. The comic book *The Tomb of Dracula* based its visual imagery of the vampire on Palance's physical appearance in the movie.[64]

While some critics might deride *Dracula* as merely a "television film," it is yet another example of the fine, underrated work of director Dan Curtis, best known for his creation of *Dark Shadows* and his later direction of *Burnt Offerings*. As with many of his films, Curtis creates a stylish presentation, full of both exquisite outdoor shots and wonderful period interiors. One of Curtis' strengths was his ability to create mood and atmosphere, supplemented by appropriate musical backdrops from his friend Bob Cobert. Curtis does all of that in *Dracula*. The Curtis-Palance collaboration will never be as famous as the works of Lugosi and Lee, but it deserves recognition as one of the better *Dracula* adaptations of the last 50 years.

In 1974, Blaxploitation films continued to register with American audiences, while occasionally delving into the genre of horror. Two years after the premiere of *Blacula* and one year after the release of the sequel, *Scream Blacula Scream*, the February 1974 arrival of *Sugar Hill* brought a story of modern-day zombies to the popular culture. Combining Blaxploitation with campy horror, *Sugar Hill* presents an unusual film formula that is surprisingly entertaining, even if it is a little dated.

The plot is outrageous, but eventful. Sugar Hill is not a place but a character: Diana "Sugar" Hill, whose boyfriend is murdered by local gangsters. Rather than pursue conventional means of revenge, Hill seeks out a voodoo queen (played with gusto by Zara Cully of *The Jeffersons*), who calls on the Lord of the Dead, Baron Samedi, for assistance. In exchange for Hill's soul, the baron unleashes an army of zombies against the gangsters.

Marki Bey, a then-unknown actress who left the industry at the end of the 1970s, receives top billing as Sugar Hill. Bey is very good, making the character determined and unwavering. Her co-star came with a great deal of horror experience. Robert Quarry, the star of the *Count Yorga* movies and a veteran of other AIP productions, plays the leader of the gang that killed Hill's boyfriend. Making his one of his final appearances for AIP, Quarry is particularly oily, playing it to the extreme with a fully unredeemable personality. In some films, that kind of performance might not have worked, but it jells beautifully with the rampant wildness and bizarre nature of *Sugar Hill*.

Director Paul Maslansky took an interesting approach with his depiction of the zombies. Rather than have them appear as decaying human corpses, as George Romero did in *Night of the Living Dead*, Maslansky presents them as physically intact beings with pallid complexions, who behave in a trancelike state. The revenants are the preserved bodies of slaves brought to America from New Guinea. They are more like the "living dead" style of revenant that *White Zombie* unveiled in the 1930s. Going against recent film trends, Maslansky's choice of zombie works well here.

While *Sugar Hill*'s premise is based on revenge and violence, the film has its share of comedic overtones. The gangsters are portrayed not just as evil men, but with a degree of goofiness. The facial expressions of the zombies' victims are often over-the-top and unrestrained, giving the viewer more reason to laugh than to scream.

Given the outrageous fashions, the extreme hairstyles and the slang-heavy 1970s dialogue, *Sugar Hill* is a dated film. But that adds to the underlying humor and the general fun. It's an ideal movie for the Halloween season, or for a random weekend night in need of a look back at the offbeat, one-of-a-kind culture of the early '70s.

In late March, the horror spotlight turned to another one of the many works of Vincent Price. Debuting in Albany, Georgia, on March 28, *Madhouse* begins with a title sequence that pays homage to the late Boris Karloff and Basil Rathbone, two other legends of the industry. Karloff and Rathbone are shown in clips from films in which they starred with Price. It's a nice tribute to both men, each of whom had died in recent years, Karloff in 1969 and Rathbone in 1967.

Though it's far from a Price classic, *Madhouse* is a very decent old-fashioned English-made horror film that tells the story of an aging but successful actor, Paul Toombes, whose signature role is a character known as Dr. Death. On the night of Toombes' engagement to Ellen Mason, adult film producer Oliver Quayle (Robert Quarry) announces at a Hollywood party that Ellen once appeared in one of his pornographic films. Toombes becomes angry, upsetting Ellen, who runs to her room. Toombes follows her there, only to discover that she has been murdered, her head separated from the rest of her body. Toombes, suspected of the crime, has a gap in his memory and becomes so distraught that he is confined to a mental institution.

8. Creature Features, Fright Night *and* Block of Shock (1970–1975)

Several years later, Toombes is released from the institution, still unsure if he was the killer. He is summoned to the London home of his screenwriting friend (Peter Cushing), who is planning a TV show starring Dr. Death. On his way to meet his friend, Toombes meets a beautiful and persistent young actress (Linda Hayden) who steals his watch and begins to stalk him. A series of murders ensues. Is Toombes responsible?

This low-budget film marked Price's final appearance for the AIP, a successful run that began with the release of *House of Usher* in 1960. *Madhouse* is aided by a good supporting cast, including Cushing, Hayden and Quarry. Rather cleverly, *Madhouse* makes references to earlier film appearances by Cushing and Quarry, but in different ways. During a costume party scene, Quarry is dressed as a vampire—exactly the way he was dressed in the *Count Yorga* films. In Cushing's case, we see him outfitted as Dracula, an ironic choice given his frequent casting as Dracula's nemesis, Van Helsing.

Cushing and Quarry have important supporting roles, but Price is the star of the show, as evidenced by the many filmclips from his earlier AIP vehicles that are woven into the plot. As an unexpected bonus, Price does some actual singing toward the end of the film, proving that he could be more than an actor of the horror genre.

Thanks to the presence of Price, Cushing and Quarry, all of whom are typically excellent, *Madhouse* delivers its share of memorably macabre moments. Only some slow pacing and a questionable ending detract from the final product. All in all, fans who like Price and 1970s horror will appreciate *Madhouse* as a worthwhile stop on the horror trail.

The Beast Must Die has been described as a lightweight horror film, but it is notable as one of the first of the genre to feature a black actor as its star. It's a compelling mystery, but lacks the special effects, the pacing and the degree of horror that might have elevated it to more significant status.

Debuting in April 1974, *The Beast Must Die* represented Amicus' lone venture into the world of werewolves. In contrast to Hammer's treatment of werewolves (in the form of Oliver Reed's *The Curse of the Werewolf*), *Beast* takes place in a contemporary setting, with a full-blown early 1970s musical score. Even though *Beast* features the legendary Peter Cushing, African-American actor Calvin Lockhart is the star and deservedly receives top billing. A handsome and underrated actor, he plays Tom Newcliffe, a wealthy businessman and accomplished big game hunter who has summoned five guests to join him and his wife at their remote British estate, ostensibly to participate in a relaxing weekend and perhaps do some hunting. In reality, Newcliffe believes one of his guests to be a werewolf, based on his associates having questionable backgrounds and habits. To add to the intrigue, one of Newcliffe's guests is an admitted cannibal, making him #1 on the list of suspects.

Lockhart was not the original choice of the film's director, who wanted Robert Quarry for the lead. The producers chose Lockhart instead, apparently in an effort to capitalize on the current Blaxploitation trend.[65] Second choice or not, Lockhart delivers wonderfully in the starring role. Visually striking while wearing a variety of mod clothing, including a stunning all-leather suit, Lockhart brings an athletic and commanding presence to the role. He delivers his lines in an affected, almost Shakespearean manner, giving his character a degree of dignity and charm. He is more than worthy as the film's central figure, a difficult achievement given Cushing's presence as one of his guests.

Playing an expert on werewolves, Cushing takes center stage in one scene; it's at dinner, when his character graphically expounds on the science of lycanthropy. It's a memorable scene, and by the time Cushing is done with his grisly discourse, several other guests have lost their appetites for dinner's main course of red meat.

The Beast Must Die includes a gimmick reminiscent of the earlier work of director William Castle. About three-quarters of the way through the movie, a 30-second "werewolf break" interrupts the proceedings to ask the viewers to ponder the evidence and hypothesize as to who the werewolf really is.[66] As the camera shows each suspect in isolated stills, a graphic of a ticking clock appears in the background, until the werewolf break comes to an end.

The werewolf break is fun and well-handled, certainly more successful than the special effect of the werewolf itself (nothing more than a large German shepherd). The limited budget prevented director Paul Annett from devising a more frightening, full-sized werewolf creature. Then there is the problem of the "day-for-night" shots; it is quite obvious that the nighttime scenes were filmed in the daylight hours, another sacrifice that came as part of cutting production costs.[67]

Still, the movie has decent entertainment value, thanks to its ability to create and build suspense, and lay out an imaginative storyline. The last half-hour is full of action, surprise and bloodletting, making this a worthwhile ride into the world of lycanthropy.

The Wicker Man initially entered British theaters in October of 1973, but did not make its American premiere until May 15, 1974, in Atlanta, Georgia. Generally well received at the time of its release, it has only grown in stature over time. It skillfully deals with the theme of the occult and provides one of the most surprising twist endings in horror history.

A British police officer, the pious Sgt. Howie, is dispatched to a remote island to search for a young girl, Rowan Morrison, who has been reported missing. The island dwellers claim that the girl never existed to begin with, but Howie remains undaunted in his efforts to find answers. He soon discovers that the locals are quite open with their sexuality and their attitudes of free love. *And,* even more disturbing to the officer, they are involved in strange rites that involve witchcraft and devil worship. He comes into conflict with Lord Summerisle, who rules over the island with his own set of pagan beliefs.

Christopher Lee, who played Lord Summerisle, so liked the film and the opportunity that it offered him that he reportedly agreed to do it for free.[68] His passion for the role shows, as he plays his character with a combination of charm and secrecy. Edward Woodward, the fine British actor who played the good sergeant, proves to be Lee's equal throughout the film. He is at times a bumbling figure, sometimes holier than thou, but keenly determined to find the girl whom he believes does exist and needs to be saved. And to the end, he remains unwavering in his belief in God.

Another effective character is the librarian played by Ingrid Pitt, "the Queen of Gothic Horror," who became a staple of British genre films in the 1970s. The rest of the cast does not quite meet the standard of Lee, Woodward and Pitt, but it does not have to; the atmospheric setting, a remote and mysterious Scottish island full of offbeat inhabitants and practitioners of pagan rituals, helps establish the underlying tension. All of this creates a continuing sense of uncertainty and dread for Sgt. Howie. At times, we wonder if he has been caught in some web of conspiracy, or is truly losing his ability to grasp reality.

The Wicker Man is one of the decade's cult classics. According to George Grella, a longtime film historian and retired professor from the University of Rochester, "It's a fine movie, with a story steeped in myth and folklore, a most thoughtful and distressing film."[69] He believes the film runs far deeper than its surface material. "The movie suggests connections with ancient myth, with fertility rites, with all sorts of literature."[70]

The Wicker Man has also become the source of some controversy, because of unwanted censorship, mandated not by content but because of restrictions in running time. The film was originally 102 minutes, but EMI Films executive Michael Deeley ordered substantial cuts because he disliked the movie. Fifteen minutes were removed, reducing the length to 87 minutes.[71] Even with the unwanted cuts, Lee still felt the movie reached such a high level that it deserved to be seen. A new cut of the film, released in 2013, runs 99 minutes, including most of the original footage that the director intended to be seen.[72] The three remaining minutes from the original 102 have seemingly been lost forever.

An enthralling film, *The Wicker Man* might be simultaneously categorized as a thriller, a mystery and even as a musical (there are a number of singing interludes). But there is such a sense of foreboding and suspicion that it overrides the other themes and gives the movie an overtone of horror. The film has a startling finish, filled with both terror and singing, which will leave most viewers chilled to the point of paranoia.

Some horror films are destined to be underrated, even if appreciation of them grows with time. *Captain Kronos—Vampire Hunter* is one of those films. Debuting in San Francisco theaters on June 12, 1974, it's one of Hammer Films' more creative and dynamic efforts. When several young girls suddenly advance into old age, and then quickly into death, the wise Dr. Marcus suspects that vampires might be responsible. He implores his old British army friend and career vampire hunter, the dashing Captain Kronos, to hunt down the creatures.

Thanks to Kronos, this is a vampire film that emphasizes swashbuckling action and adventure, particularly in the form of the masterful sword work done by the title character, rather than gore and pure violence. It also has a good sense of humor (wonderfully supplied by Kronos' hunchbacked assistant, played by John Cater), and showcases many beautiful women (including the stunning Caroline Munro). In terms of pure fun and entertainment value, *Captain Kronos* is one of the era's more enjoyable offerings.

Perhaps *Captain Kronos'* reputation has been hurt by its lack of big-name actors; the lead role of the aloof but heroic captain is filled by German actor Horst Janson, who has gone on to a long career in foreign films. With his lean, muscular build, Janson was physically ideal for the role, but he spoke his lines with such a thick German accent that director Brian Clemens decided to dub another actor's voice over Janson's.[73] Outside of Munro, who does well in creating the sympathetic character of Carla, a young maiden rescued by Kronos from a stockade, and Ian Hendry, as murderous villain, the rest of the cast lacks name power, but the acting is surprisingly good.

Completed in 1972, the movie did not come out until two years later. Hammer hoped that it would kickstart a series of Captain Kronos movies (which might have been successful with the right marketing), but the initial release did so poorly that plans for follow-up films were cancelled.[74] That turned out to be a loss for devoted fans of Kronos; they would have loved a revival of the characters played by the handsome Janson, the gorgeous Munro and the wisecracking Cater.

A poor showing in theaters should not dissuade horror film buffs from watching this cult classic, one of the last good Hammers before its demise. *Captain Kronos* is beautifully filmed (much of the story takes place in picturesque outdoor locations), has good practical effects, and offers up a nice twist ending that most viewers will not see coming. It's also creative in its portrayal of a unique strain of vampires, who often attack in the daytime and are not bloodsuckers, but instead seize upon the youth of their victims. This is not your typical horror film of the era: There is plenty of comedy, sex, humor and free-flowing action, but the horror is not lost either. This one is pure fun.

Of all the horror films released in 1974, arguably the best one came out on October 1 in Dallas, Texas. No one could have anticipated that it would become a classic of the genre.

That's because *The Texas Chain Saw Massacre* is like no other film that came before it.

With its rough-around-the-edges, nearly documentary style of presentation, its blunt imagery and a story that is so rooted in the twisted evil of its antagonists, it remains powerful in its ability to create legitimate feelings of terror.

Director Tobe Hooper's classic is influenced by the story of Ed Gein, the real-life killer and grave robber who terrorized rural Wisconsin in the 1950s. But the interpretation is so loose and detached that it cannot be accurately considered an adaptation; the film's on-screen claim that it is "based on a true story" is actually a falsehood, one that was created to make the film more relevant. The false perception that the film's events had recently taken place in rural Texas only added to the feelings of fear expressed by theatergoers.[75]

In truth, *The Texas Chain Saw Massacre* is almost completely fiction—and absolutely horrifying. The story begins with Sally Hardesty and her paraplegic brother Franklin, plus three of their friends, en route to visit their grandfather's grave in an isolated part of rural Texas. They decide to make a stop at the Hardesty homestead, but along the way, the group encounters a strange hitchhiker, a young man with a badly scarred face. He begins acting oddly, taking a photograph of the brother and then demanding to be paid for it. When the friends refuse to give the hitchhiker money, he burns the photograph and then cuts the brother with a razor, before being pushed out of the bus.

The siblings and their friends will soon run into more unforeseen trouble, including a failed attempt at buying gasoline. The group's adventure will culminate at a dilapidated country house where a backwoods family of strange men reside. In one final surprise, the inhabitants of the house are all cannibals. As the film's poster asks, "Who will survive and what will be left of them?"

In many ways, the film's minuscule budget only enhances the feel of terror. Gunnar Hansen, who famously played "Leatherface," the family's primary butcher and dinner server, was given only one shirt to wear throughout the four weeks of production.[76] That created obvious problems for his castmates, but the deteriorating condition of the shirt adds to the grit and realism. In an even more gruesome vein, some of the skeletons seen in the remote house are actual human remains; plastic full-body skeletons would have been much more expensive to procure.[77]

How scary is *The Texas Chain Saw Massacre*? When the film was sneak previewed, some moviegoers walked out because they were so affected by the images that they saw. For those who dared watch it in its entirety, those feelings intensified. The film broke all of the rules. Even the disabled Franklin, forced to use a wheelchair at all times, would not be spared the wrath of the cannibalistic family.

Of all the scenes in the film, the most memorable is the prolonged dinner sequence, in which the decrepit grandfather (John Dugan) is revealed for the first time. Dugan was only in his early thirties when he played the part, but the intense makeup made him look like he was in his eighties and on the verge of death. Dugan's gruesome look, combined with his pathetic attempts at sucking blood from one of the family victims, make him one of the most physically objectionable characters in horror history. The reactions of Marilyn Burns, playing the terrified Sally Hardesty, underscore the monstrous nature of the grotesque grandpa.

In spite of the revolting nature of the material, *The Texas Chain Saw Massacre* is, for the most part, a bloodless film. Most of the violence is suggested or implied. "I was surprised by the lack of gore," says horror director Harrison Smith, remembering his first viewing of the movie. "With a title like that, you'd think this is going to be a really bloody film. It's really not. It's gritty, and it has a very documentary-like feel to it, but it's not a bloodfest. Again, it's like Hitchcock; less is more."[78]

When viewers allow their imagination to carry themselves away, the level of horror is elevated. That feeling, coupled with the brutal and unforgiving manner of Leatherface and his family of freaks, makes *Texas Chain Saw Massacre* as powerful as any horror film from the 1970s.

The last significant horror film of 1974 made its debut on December 20, just days before Christmas, which is only appropriate for a film named *Black Christmas*. It has been described by some critics and fans as the first true slasher film, a precursor to *Halloween* and *Friday the 13th* which followed later in the decade. (In truth, such an honor belongs to an earlier movie, *Peeping Tom*.)

Regardless of which film deserves to be called the first, *Black Christmas* made an impact, particularly on later generations. It stars Olivia Hussey and Margot Kidder as sorority house members plagued by anonymous phone calls in the middle of winter. The concern of the sorority house heightens when another resident, Clare Harrison, goes missing. At first, the police express little concern over the matter, believing that Clare has simply left campus without telling anyone. But their attitude changes when the lifeless body of a 13-year-old girl is found in a nearby park.

Initially, the film's script called for a series of graphic murder scenes, but director Bob Clark made an important adjustment. Opting to reduce the level of violence, he took a more cautious and subtle approach to the death scenes, a choice that proved effective.[79] Clark also made a decision *not* to show the killer; all of the murder scenes are viewed from *his* point of view. Clark presents the only physical evidence of the killer through his voice. Three different actors supplied voices for the killer, but most of what is heard in the final edit was done by a young Nick Mancuso, who was working on only the second film of his career.

All of the key actors perform well in executing Clark's revised script. Kidder is particularly good as the foul-mouthed Barb, who finds ways to offend her sorority sisters and the police—along with the unknown killer—with just about every line she delivers. Playing in her first horror film, the top-billed Hussey beautifully fulfills the lead role of Jess Bradford, who is secretly pregnant. Keir Dullea, best known for his work in *2001: A Space Odyssey*, contributes as Jess' high-strung college boyfriend Peter, even if he was a bit old for the part; at the time of filming, he was 38. And there's also horror favorite John Saxon, who lends a veteran presence to the proceedings as the straight-laced police lieutenant who suspects Peter.

Black Christmas is a classic example of a film that was not fully appreciated in its time, but has gained favor over the decades. Upon its release, it received mostly poor reviews and achieved only slightly above-average box office success. The reception began to change after the film aired on television and became available on video. As fan interest grew, to the point where it achieved legitimate cult status, the critical reception also began to change. Many film historians now consider *Black Christmas*, thanks to its atmospheric presentation and creepy overtones, a borderline classic.

On February 10, 1975, the made-for-TV industry again ventured into horror, this time with a historical bent. ABC's *The Legend of Lizzie Borden* proved shocking on two levels. First, it presented a greater degree of on-screen violence and bloodshed than many of its telefilm predecessors. Second, it made a choice of an unexpected actress to play the role of the murderous Borden: the beloved star of TV's *Bewitched*, Elizabeth Montgomery.

From 1964 to 1972, Montgomery played Samantha Stephens on the popular series. She gave Samantha a wholesome attitude: a good witch who looked and behaved like the girl next door. Montgomery's Samantha wouldn't hurt anyone, not even the meddling witches and warlocks in her family. How in the world could Montgomery portray a controversial real-life figure like Lizzie Borden, who was widely believed to have butchered her parents (but was acquitted at trial)?

To the surprise of many, Montgomery aced the role, giving Borden a dazed but hard-edged personality and a sharp temper that ran consistent with someone capable of murder. The supporting cast of TV veterans also proved capable, including Ed Flanders and Bonnie Bartlett (both of whom went on to find success in the show *St. Elsewhere*), along with Katherine Helmond and Fritz Weaver.

In the film, Borden is seen attacking her stepmother and her father, after having stripped down naked so as to avoid staining her clothes. Careful editing makes it clear that Montgomery is nude, but by suggestion and implication rather than full exposure, so as to meet the TV standards of the day. A different version of the film, screened in European theaters, shows a fully naked Montgomery covered in blood.[80]

The film leaves no doubt as to whether Borden committed the murders. We see Montgomery's Borden using the axe on her parents, with one of the murders shown in slow motion. For the time period, this kind of violence rarely made its way onto TV screens.

Much of the film takes place within the courtroom and through flashbacks, which reveal the domestic abuse that Borden suffered at the hands of her parents, and their subsequent murders. Given the abuse, the swinging of the axe and the blood, there is little doubt that *Lizzie Borden* qualifies as horror, albeit historical horror. It is graphic, detailed and mostly accurate to the story from 19th century Fall River, Massachusetts. It stands as one of the best of the many telefilms of the 1970s.

On March 4, another ABC-TV production arrived in American living rooms, cementing the reputation of prolific director Dan Curtis. *Trilogy of Terror* has fostered a cult following that eventually led to a 1990s remake.

The anthology film features three stand-alone stories, but all are connected through the presence of veteran actress Karen Black. She plays the central figure in each of the stories, rather remarkably portraying a total of four characters by the film's end. In the first segment, she plays a repressed, antisocial English teacher who becomes the target of obsession from an overzealous student. In the second story, Black plays two rival sisters, one of whom is unattractive but smart and sensible, the other beautiful but without morals.

Both vignettes are good, but the last one, "Amelia," has had the most lasting impact. In that segment, Black portrays a woman who is plagued by an overprotective and controlling mother. As the daughter prepares dinner in her apartment, she realizes that an African Zuni doll, just purchased at a local curio shop, has come to life. The doll, equipped with sharp, pointed teeth and a small spear, torments Black, frenetically chasing her around the apartment. Black eventually takes extreme measures to end the doll's sudden reign of terror. A twist ending to the vignette will leave the viewer with an image that is shocking—and difficult to forget.

Black did not make an abundance of great films, horror or otherwise, but in many of her appearances, her performance outshined the quality of the film itself. In the case of *Trilogy of Terror*, she was given good material, which she elevated with a quartet of standout performances. Black had a certain charisma, an offbeat kind of attractiveness, and an ability to play both the "angel" and the villain, sometimes within the same film. All of these talents are evident in *Trilogy of Terror*.

For some reason, Black regretted many of her horror film roles, including *Trilogy of Terror*, and referred to that aspect of her career as "a mistake."[81] She had no reason to be ashamed of her association with entertaining films like *Trilogy of Terror*, or even a superior horror film like the 1976 classic *Burnt Offerings*.

Black was an underrated actress, just as Curtis was an overlooked director and producer. He made the two *Dark Shadows* movies of the early 1970s, the Jack Palance *Dracula*, and the aforementioned *Burnt Offerings*, which stands as his horror masterpiece. Yet he remains underappreciated. Perhaps it's because many of his horror films were made-for-TV productions, which generally don't get the level of respect given to theatrical releases.

Television or big screen, Curtis' movies have a strong appeal and are highly watchable. They are good stories that are filmed well, full of creepy music and imagery, and they succeed in capturing the haunting feel of 1970s horror. *Trilogy of Terror* is no exception to the Curtis rule.

With its debut in early March, *Trilogy of Terror* was one of the last significant horror films to come out in the weeks and months before the release of the industry-changing *Jaws*, which debuted on June 20, 1975. Given such a timeline, *Trilogy of Terror* can be viewed to some extent as the final film of our initial era of hosted horror. It's an unofficial and somewhat arbitrary designation; there is no way to pinpoint any particular film as marking the end of the first great era of hosted horror films, if only because late-night horror continually draws from past films and new releases. But *Trilogy of Terror*'s first TV appearance seems to coincide with a time when late-night creature features were beginning to lose some of their edge and following, only to regain their popularity in the 1980s.

In light of the summer 1975 success of *Jaws*, *Trilogy of Terror* seems like an acceptable finishing point to an era of films that became known for cult followings. With the arrival of *Jaws*, a great film that was also highly profitable, horror changed forever, becoming less cult and more blockbuster. That was not necessarily a bad thing, but perhaps it sealed the fate of hosted horror as something that had become more of a niche interest among old-school fans who preferred the Universal and Hammer classics, along with films from Amicus, American International Pictures and other studios.

In some ways, horror went mainstream, a trend that was first hinted at by the success of *The Exorcist*, and then confirmed by the triumph of *Jaws*. Horror then enjoyed an upsurge in popularity in the late 1970s and into the 1980s. But the genre may have also lost some of its old-school charm and quirkiness. Those qualities were certainly on display in the late '60s and early '70s, making it a rich time in the history of a genre that had changed so much since Lugosi's *Dracula* and Karloff's *Frankenstein* first ventured onto the big screen.

CHAPTER NINE

What Might Happen Next

In an era where Roku, a variety of streaming services and cable TV have all created avenues for films to be seen, the future of horror hosting remains uncertain, but promising. After some sputtering in the 1980s, followed by a major falloff in the sheer volume of hosts in the 1990s, we have seen some signs of optimism in the new century. It seems we may be on the verge of another prosperous era for those who specialize in the art of hosting horror films. Joe Bob Briggs, with his combination of sarcastic humor and vast film knowledge, has made a triumphant return to the industry as a Friday night host on the streaming service Shudder. Svengoolie, a throwback to the cornball hosts of the 1960s, has gained a national following since taking his act to the wonderfully nostalgic channel, Me-TV. And yes, Elvira remains a strong presence, even if 40 years have passed since she made her debut on a local affiliate in Los Angeles.

Other hosts, like the offbeat Mr. Lobo and his *Cinema Insomnia,* and Lamia, Queen of the Dark, the host of *Horror Hotel*, have developed strong niche followings in recent years. Given the power of the Internet, the growing number of streaming outlets and cable TV stations, and the rise of Roku, there are now more opportunities for horror hosts to get a foothold in the industry.

Frankly, there is no better time than the 2020s for horror hosting to undergo a revitalization. The genre of horror has reached new heights in the 21st century, with a preponderance of terrific and creative writing, believable special effects and a level of sophistication not seen in previous decades. A number of recent television shows have elevated the genre. Perhaps it started with *The Walking Dead*, which the skeptics initially felt was unsustainable. How could a weekly show centered on a zombie apocalypse possibly last for more than a few episodes, or perhaps a season at most? Well, it has, thanks to sympathetic and highly developed characters, detailed scripts, unforeseen plot twists and groundbreaking special effects. (The show developed such a following that it spawned a "postgame" talk show, *The Talking Dead*.) In becoming a national sensation, *The Walking Dead* essentially kickstarted a new and glorious era of horror.

Other shows have also developed rabid followings. Netflix's *Stranger Things* has become a pop culture sensation (and also an homage to 1980s culture) that nearly matches the fervor for *The Walking Dead*. On a more restrained level, *Bates Motel* has taken the classic story of Norman Bates, as first written by Robert Bloch, and dared to create Bates' young adult past, in a way that Alfred Hitchcock likely never would have envisioned. On network TV, *Hannibal* has created a pre-history for *The Silence of the Lambs* in a sophisticated and layered manner that only enhances the story of Hannibal Lecter and those who pursue him.

Penny Dreadful has collected the classic monsters—Dracula, Frankenstein and the Wolf Man, among others—and interwoven them in Victorian England against a backdrop of excellent cinematography and top-notch special effects. *The Haunting of Hill House*, another successful Netflix venture, has taken Shirley Jackson's original story and turned it into the modern-day tale of a tormented family and its attempt to overcome its tragic past. And with far less publicity but no less quality, *The Frankenstein Chronicles* reimagined the origins of Mary Shelley's iconic novel by incorporating the author into a more involved and complicated plot.

All of these programs have received critical acclaim, and deservedly so, for advancing the notion that horror can be sustained in a repeated, episodic format. It can be done, and it can be done *well*.

On the larger screen, a number of films have had similar impact. *Get Out*, a film that ties horror to the subject of race relations, received an Academy Award nomination for Best Picture, a rarity for the genre. *The Conjuring* has taken the experiences of real-life paranormal investigators, the Warrens, and embellished their stories to make them more compelling for today's horror fan. *It* has successfully revived Stephen King's classic novel, while *Hereditary* has powerfully tied the horrific tragedies of a family to the world of demons. Even more recently, *Doctor Sleep* has taken the story of *The Shining* and introduced a new set of characters while paying homage to the original film. And the newest incarnation of *The Invisible Man* has taken the original story, skillfully applied a number of creative twists, added top-notch special effects, and seamlessly worked in a theme of modern-day domestic abuse.

All of these films have drawn praise from fans and critics alike. They have succeeded in gaining newfound respect for a genre that has too often been the recipient of thumbed noses from the film society "elites." Horror is no longer the "toy department" of film. It is a genre to be appreciated and reckoned with, even if some critics remain averse to giving it full acknowledgment.

Given the current level of quality within the genre, this seems like the ideal time for horror hosts to make a comeback. For fans, a good horror host can only enhance the home viewing experience. The effective host provides information that makes a good horror movie better. The capable host also provides a distraction, often through comedy, that makes a bad horror film more palatable.

In-person interactions have also become essential. Horror and sci-fi conventions have become enormously popular, both in terms of smaller local shows and larger national get-togethers. Other genres lack this kind of community. Have we ever heard of a romantic comedy convention? Are there ever conventions centered solely on war films? Is there such a thing as a non-fiction convention? I've never heard of any of these. If they do exist, they operate on the smallest of scales and draw little to no media attention.

Horror is different. Fans of the genre will spend hundreds of dollars to attend conventions and conferences. And if that demand exists for fans who will venture out of their houses, it only stands to reason that it will exist for those who prefer to stay home on a Friday and Saturday night, but still want to feel like they are part of something interactive, sometime that is live, something that approaches a reciprocal experience.

As pointed out by Joe Bob Briggs, one of the most popular of the contemporary hosts, horror fans have a basic need to communicate with each other, through the Internet, through chat rooms, and through email. "People want to gather together in groups. And groups that have common interests. And movies are meant to be seen in a group,"[1] Briggs told horror writer Patrick Cavanaugh in a 2019 interview. "Movies are communal. Movies are social."

During each of Briggs' live broadcasts on Shudder, sidekick Diana Prince (known by the pseudonym of Darcy the Mail Girl) receives dozens of tweets, emails and letters, and tries to respond to as many as possible. At times, she will present one of the more interesting messages to Briggs, giving the host a chance to respond on-air in real time. It's the kind of interaction with viewers and fans rarely seen in other genres on TV, where so much is scripted and rehearsed ahead of time.

When given the chance, horror hosts like Briggs have helped make the genre even more substantial as a community endeavor. Perhaps more horror hosts will emerge in this age of social media. They certainly do not need to be the same kinds of hosts that we saw in the late 1950s and the 1960s, with their childlike costumes and corny sight gags. It is a different time now, likely a time for more sophisticated hosts (like Briggs), those who don't need to rely on costumes and prop comedy, but can still deliver the combination of humor and information that so many horror fans seem to want. That would be most appropriate, at a time when the horror genre has never been better.

Chapter Notes

Preface

1. "John Zacherley," *Wikipedia*, accessed June 21, 2020, https://en.wikipedia.org/wiki/Chiller_Theatre_(1961_TV_series).
2. "Creature Features," *Wikipedia*, accessed June 25, 2020, https://en.wikipedia.org/wiki/Creature_Features_(1969_TV_series).
3. *Ibid.*
4. "Fright Night on Channel 9," Amazon.com, accessed June 27, 2020, https://www.amazon.com/Fright-Night-Channel-Saturday-1973–1987/dp/0786466782.

Chapter One

1. David J. Skal, interview with author. Tape recording. Scare-A-Con Convention, Verona, NY, October 7, 2017.
2. Frank Dello Stritto, interview with author. Monster Bash Conference, Mars, PA, June 21, 2019.

Chapter Two

1. Al Feldstein and Jack Davis, "Foul Play," *The Haunt of Fear* no. 19, May/June 1953.
2. *Ibid.*
3. Robert Warshow, "Paul, the Horror Comics, and Dr. Wertham," *Commentary Magazine*, June 1954.
4. Fredric Wertham, as quoted in 1954 Senate Subcommittee Transcripts, *The Comic Books*, accessed January 12, 2020, https://www.thecomicbooks.com/wertham.html.
5. *Ibid.*
6. Bruce Markusen, "Cooperstown Confidential: Baseball Meets Horror," *The Hardball Times*, October 31, 2016. https://tht.fangraphs.com/cooperstown-confidential-baseball-meets-horror/.
7. *Ibid.*
8. *Ibid.*
9. "Screen Gems Isn't Scared," *The Billboard*, October 14, 1957.
10. Lint Hatcher and Rod Bennett, "Inside Darkest Ackerman," *Jim Henry*, accessed January 25, 2020, http://jimhenry.conlang.org/wonder/archive/4e_intvw.htm.
11. "Famous Monsters of Filmland," *Encyclopedia of Science Fiction*, accessed March 15, 2020, http://www.sf-encyclopedia.com/entry/famous_monsters_of_filmland.
12. David J. Skal, interview with author. Tape recording. Scare-A-Con Convention, Verona, NY, October 7, 2017.
13. *Ibid.*
14. *Ibid.*

Chapter Three

1. *Life* Magazine, June 14, 1954, pp. 107–110.
2. Jacob Shelton, "Vampira, The First Horror Host: Her Short, Frustrating Story," *Groovy History*, June 19, 2019, https://groovyhistory.com/vampira-horror-host-elvira-true-story.
3. Mark Voger, *Monster Mash: The Creepy, Kooky Monster Craze in America, 1957–1972* (Raleigh, NC: TwoMorrows Publishing, 2015), p. 20.
4. *Ibid.*
5. David J. Skal, interview by author. Tape recording. Scare-A-Con Convention, Verona, NY, October 7, 2017.
6. Jason Nark, "A Cool Ghoul Looks Back," *Philadelphia Inquirer*, April 24, 2015.
7. Mike Barnes, "John Zacherle, Delightfully Schlocky TV Host of Horror Movies, Dies at 98," *Hollywood Reporter*, October 28, 2016.
8. W. Scott Poole, *Vampire: Dark Goddess of Horror* (New York: Soft Skull Press, 2014), p. 168.

Chapter Four

1. "Dracula (1931)," *Internet Movie Database* (IMDb), accessed October 21, 2016, https://www.imdb.com/title/tt0021814/trivia?ref_=tt_trv_trv.
2. *Ibid.*
3. *Ibid.*
4. David J. Skal, David, interview with author. Tape recording. Scare-A-Con Convention, Verona, NY, October 7, 2017.
5. *Ibid.*
6. *Ibid.*
7. *Ibid.*
8. Richard Bojarski, *The Complete Films of Bela Lugosi* (New York: Carol Publishing, 1992), p. 27.

9. "Dracula (1931)," *Internet Movie Database* (IMDb), accessed October 21, 2016, https://www.imdb.com/title/tt0021814/quotes/?tab=qt&ref_=tt_trv_qu.

10. David J. Skal, interview with author. Tape recording. Scare-A-Con Convention, Verona, NY, October 7, 2017.

11. *Ibid.*

12. "Frankenstein (1931)," *Internet Movie Database* (IMDb), accessed October 24, 2016, https://www.imdb.com/title/tt0021884/trivia?ref_=tt_trv_trv.

13. David J. Skal, interview with author. Tape recording. Scare-A-Con Convention, Verona, NY, October 7, 2017.

14. *Ibid.*

15. Gregory William Mank, *Karloff and Lugosi: The Story of a Haunting Collaboration* (Jefferson, NC: McFarland, 1990), p. 21.

16. "Frankenstein (1931)," *Internet Movie Database* (IMDb), accessed October 24, 2016, https://www.imdb.com/title/tt0021884/trivia?ref_=tt_trv_trv.

17. David J. Skal, interview with author. Tape recording. Scare-A-Con Convention, Verona, NY, October 7, 2017.

18. Michael Mallory, *Universal Studios Monsters: A Legacy of Horror* (New York: Universe Publishing, 2009), p. 176.

19. "Murders in the Rue Morgue," *Internet Movie Database* (IMDb), accessed October 28, 2016, https://www.imdb.com/title/tt0023249/trivia?ref_=tt_trv_trv.

20. Michael Mallory, *Universal Studios Monsters: A Legacy of Horror* (New York: Universe Publishing, 2009), pp. 110–113.

21. "The Mummy (1932)," *Internet Movie Database* (IMDb), accessed October 24, 2016, https://www.imdb.com/title/tt0023245/trivia?ref_=tt_trv_trv.

22. Michael Mallory, *Universal Studios Monsters: A Legacy of Horror* (New York: Universe Publishing, 2009), p. 113.

23. "Secret of the Blue Room (1933)," *Internet Movie Database* (IMDb), accessed January 29, 2020, https://www.imdb.com/title/tt0024538/trivia?ref_=tt_trv_trv.

24. "The Invisible Man (1933)," *Internet Movie Database* (IMDb), accessed September 5, 2019, https://www.imdb.com/title/tt0024184/trivia?ref_=tt_trv_trv.

25. "Motion Picture Production Code," *Internet Movie Database* (IMDb), accessed January 5, 2020, https://en.wikipedia.org/wiki/Motion_Picture_Production_Code.

26. Gregory William Mank, *Karloff and Lugosi: The Story of a Haunting Collaboration* (Jefferson, NC: McFarland, 1990), pp. 65–68.

27. "The Black Cat," *Internet Movie Database* (IMDb), accessed November 14, 2016, https://www.imdb.com/title/tt0024894/trivia?ref_=tt_trv_trv.

28. Gregory William Mank, *Karloff and Lugosi: The Story of a Haunting Collaboration* (Jefferson, NC: McFarland, 1990), p. 81.

29. *Ibid.*

30. "The Mystery of Edwin Drood," *Internet Movie Database* (IMDb), accessed November 14, 2016, https://www.imdb.com/title/tt0026758/trivia?ref_=tt_trv_trv.

31. *Ibid.*

32. "Werewolf of London," *Internet Movie Database* (IMDb), accessed November 14, 2016, https://www.imdb.com/title/tt0027194/trivia?ref_=tt_trv_trv.

33. *Ibid.*

34. *Ibid.*

35. Gregory William Mank, *Karloff and Lugosi: The Story of a Haunting Collaboration* (Jefferson, NC: McFarland, 1990), pp. 101, 115.

36. *Ibid.*, p. 117.

37. *Ibid.*

38. Gregory William Mank, *Karloff and Lugosi: The Story of a Haunting Collaboration* (Jefferson, NC: McFarland, 1990), p. 127.

39. *Ibid.*, p. 135.

40. Michael Mallory, *Universal Studios Monsters: A Legacy of Horror* (New York: Universe Publishing, 2009), p. 54.

41. "Dracula's Daughter," *Internet Movie Database* (IMDb), accessed November 16, 2016, https://www.imdb.com/title/tt0027545/trivia?ref_=tt_trv_trv.

42. Michael Mallory, *Universal Studios Monsters: A Legacy of Horror* (New York: Universe Publishing, 2009), p. 54.

43. *Ibid.*

44. David J. Skal, interview with author. Tape recording. Scare-A-Con Convention, Verona, NY, October 7, 2017.

45. "Son of Frankenstein," *Internet Movie Database* (IMDb), accessed November 18, 2016, https://www.imdb.com/title/tt0031951/trivia?ref_=tt_trv_trv.

46. "The Invisible Man Returns," *Internet Movie Database* (IMDb), accessed November 20, 2016, https://www.imdb.com/title/tt0032635/trivia?ref_=tt_trv_trv.

47. Michael Mallory, *Universal Studios Monsters: A Legacy of Horror* (New York: Universe Publishing, 2009), p. 138.

48. "The Mummy's Hand," *Internet Movie Database* (IMDb), accessed December 2, 2016, https://www.imdb.com/title/tt0032818/trivia?ref_=tt_trv_trv.

49. *Ibid.*

50. "Horror Island," *Internet Movie Database* (IMDb), accessed December 2, 2016, https://www.imdb.com/title/tt0033728/trivia?ref_=tt_trv_trv.

51. Michael Mallory, *Universal Studios Monsters: A Legacy of Horror* (New York: Universe Publishing, 2009), p. 186.

52. "Horror Island," *Internet Movie Database* (IMDb), accessed December 2, 2016, https://www.imdb.com/title/tt0033728/trivia?ref_=tt_trv_trv.

53. Don G. Smith, *Lon Chaney, Jr.: Horror Film Star, 1906–1973* (Jefferson, NC: McFarland, 1996), pp. 32–33.

54. *Ibid.*, p. 33.

55. Michael Mallory, *Universal Studios Monsters: A Legacy of Horror* (New York: Universe Publishing, 2009), p. 95.

56. Michael Brunas, John Brunas, and Tom

Weaver, *Universal Horrors* (Jefferson, NC: McFarland, 1990), p. 246.

57. David J. Skal, interview with author. Tape recording. Scare-A-Con Convention, Verona, NY, October 7, 2017.

58. Don G. Smith, *Lon Chaney, Jr.: Horror Film Star, 1906–1973* (Jefferson, NC: McFarland, 1996), p. 37.

59. David J. Skal, interview with author. Tape recording. Scare-A-Con Convention, Verona, NY, October 7, 2017.

60. "The Wolf Man," *Internet Movie Database*, accessed October 24, 2016, https://www.imdb.com/title/tt0034398/trivia?ref_=tt_trv_trv.

61. "Mystery of Marie Roget," *Internet Movie Database* (IMDb), accessed December 8, 2016, https://www.imdb.com/title/tt0035107/trivia?ref_=tt_trv_trv.

62. Gary Don Rhodes, *Lugosi: His Life in Film, on Stage, and in the Hearts of Horror Lovers* (Jefferson, NC: McFarland, 1997), p. 125.

63. "Night Monster," *Internet Movie Database* (IMDb), accessed December 8, 2016, https://www.imdb.com/title/tt0035124/trivia?ref_=tt_trv_trv.

64. Michael Mallory, *Universal Studios Monsters: A Legacy of Horror* (New York: Universe Publishing, 2009), pp. 97–100.

65. *Ibid.*, p. 97.

66. *Ibid.*

67. *Ibid.*, p. 56.

68. "The Mad Ghoul," *Internet Movie Database* (IMDb), accessed December 8, 2016, https://www.imdb.com/title/tt0036125/trivia?ref_=tt_trv_trv.

69. Don G. Smith, *Lon Chaney, Jr.: Horror Film Star, 1906–1973* (Jefferson, NC: McFarland, 1996).

70. "Calling Dr. Death," *Internet Movie Database* (IMDb), accessed December 8, 2016, https://www.imdb.com/title/tt0035706/trivia?ref_=tt_trv_trv.

71. *Ibid.*

72. "Weird Woman," *Internet Movie Database* (IMDb), accessed December 8, 2016, https://www.imdb.com/title/tt0037453/?ref_=fn_al_tt_2.

73. *Ibid.*

74. "The Mummy's Ghost," *Internet Movie Database* (IMDb), accessed December 8, 2016, https://www.imdb.com/title/tt0037099/trivia?ref_=tt_trv_trv.

75. "The Frozen Ghost," *Internet Movie Database* (IMDb), accessed December 8, 2016, https://www.imdb.com/title/tt0037722/trivia?ref_=tt_trv_trv.

76. Michael Mallory, *Universal Studios Monsters: A Legacy of Horror* (New York: Universe Publishing, 2009), p. 161.

77. "Acromegaly," *The Mayo Clinic*, accessed December 14, 2016, https://www.mayoclinic.org/diseases-conditions/acromegaly/symptoms-causes/syc-20351222.

78. "She-Wolf of London," *Internet Movie Database* (IMDb), accessed December 14, 2016, https://www.imdb.com/title/tt0038934/trivia?ref_=tt_trv_trv.

79. *Ibid.*

Chapter Five

1. "The Bride of Frankenstein," *Internet Movie Database* (IMDb), accessed October 24, 2016, https://www.imdb.com/title/tt0026138/trivia?ref_=tt_trv_trv.

2. *Ibid.*

3. *Ibid.*

4. *Ibid.*

5. Lee Pfeiffer, "Bride of Frankenstein," *Encyclopaedia Britannica*, April 7, 2020, https://www.britannica.com/topic/Bride-of-Frankenstein.

6. David J. Skal, interview with author. Tape recording. Scare-A-Con Convention, Verona, NY, October 7, 2017.

7. Harrison Smith, interview with author. Tape recording. Scare-A Con Convention, Springfield, MA, June 4, 2017.

8. "The Man They Could Not Hang," *Internet Movie Database* (IMDb), accessed December 11, 2016, https://www.imdb.com/title/tt0031614/?ref_=fn_al_tt_1.

9. Michael Mallory, *Universal Studios Monsters: A Legacy of Horror* (New York: Universe Publishing, 2009), p, 185.

10. *Ibid.*

11. "The Man with Nine Lives," *Internet Movie Database* (IMDb), accessed December 11, 2016, https://www.imdb.com/title/tt0032753/?ref_=fn_al_tt_1.

12. Matthew Thrift, "Peter Lorre: 10 Essential Performances," *The Buckminster Fuller Institute*, January 11, 2018, https://www.bfi.org.uk/news-opinion/news-bfi/lists/10-best-peter-lorre-performances.

13. "The Devil Commands," *Internet Movie Database* (IMDb), accessed December 11, 2016, https://www.imdb.com/title/tt0033530/?ref_=fn_al_tt_1.

14. Don G. Smith, *Lon Chaney, Jr.: Horror Film Star, 1906–1973* (Jefferson, NC: McFarland, 1996), p. 44.

15. Philip J. Riley, *The Ghost of Frankenstein* (Absecon, NJ: MagicImage Filmbooks, 1990), pp. 8–9.

16. "The Ghost of Frankenstein," *Internet Movie Database* (IMDb), accessed December 11, 2016, https://www.imdb.com/title/tt0034786/trivia?ref_=tt_trv_trv.

17. Gregory William Mank, *Karloff and Lugosi: The Expanded Story of a Haunting Collaboration* (Jefferson, NC: McFarland, 2009), p. 477.

18. "House of Frankenstein," *Internet Movie Database* (IMDb), accessed December 11, 2016, https://www.imdb.com/title/tt0036931/trivia?ref_=tt_trv_trv.

19. "House of Dracula," *Internet Movie Database* (IMDb), accessed December 11, 2016, https://www.imdb.com/title/tt0037793/trivia?ref_=tt_trv_trv.

20. *Ibid.*

Chapter 6

1. Steve Jajkowski, "Terry Bennett and Joy: A Special Blend of Chicago Television," *Chicago Television*, accessed January 4, 2020, http://chicagotelevision.com/bennett.htm.

2. *Ibid.*

3. *Ibid.*

4. *Ibid.*
5. *Ibid.*
6. "Terrence," *Egor's Chamber*, accessed January 5, 2020, https://egorschamber.com/tvhorrorhosts/hostst.html.
7. *Ibid.*
8. "Nightmare Theater," *Internet Movie Database* (IMDb), accessed January 5, 2020, https://www.imdb.com/title/tt10478658/?ref_=nm_flmg_act_1.
9. Dawn Mitchell, "Selwin Was Indy's First Horror-Movie Host," *Indianapolis Star*, October 25, 2015.
10. *Ibid.*
11. *Ibid.*
12. "Fright Night 1958–1963," *Internet Movie Database* (IMDb), accessed January 5, 2020, https://www.imdb.com/title/tt11006448/trivia.
13. Dawn Mitchell, "Selwin Was Indy's First Horror-Movie Host," *Indianapolis Star*, October 25, 2015.
14. *Ibid.*
15. "Fright Night 1958–1963," *Internet Movie Database* (IMDb), accessed January 5, 2020, https://www.imdb.com/title/tt11006448/trivia.
16. "Sammy Terry," *Wikipedia*, accessed January 5, 2020, https://en.wikipedia.org/wiki/Sammy_Terry.
17. Elena M. Watson, *Television Horror Movie Hosts: 68 Vampires, Mad Scientists and Other Denizens of the Late-Night Airwaves Examined and Interviewed* (Jefferson, NC: McFarland and Company, 2013), p. 56.
18. *Ibid.*
19. "The Wacky World of Dr. Morgus," *Internet Movie Database* (IMDb), accessed January 5, 2020, https://www.imdb.com/title/tt0251470/.
20. Doug Maccash, "Morgus the Magnificent Fans Travel Back in Time with Sid Noel, Crazy Inventor of the Crazy Inventor," *The Times Picayune*, October 14, 2019.
21. Jeff Thompson, "Ken Bramming: Nashville's Transylvanian Horror Host," *Filmfax*, no. 20 (May 1990): pp. 9–11.
22. *Ibid.*
23. *Ibid.*
24. Randy Fox, "NashEvil: From Sir Cecil Creape to Dr. Gangrene, A History of Nashville Hosts," *Nashville Scene*, October 27, 2011, https://www.nashvillescene.com/news/article/13040441/nashevil-from-sir-cecil-creape-to-dr-gangrene-a-history-of-nashville-horror-hosts.
25. *Ibid.*
26. *Ibid.*
27. *Ibid.*
28. *Ibid.*
29. David J. Skal, interview with author. Tape recording. Scare-A-Con Convention, Verona, NY, October 7, 2017.
30. *Ibid.*
31. "Moona Lisa," *Wikipedia*, accessed January 5, 2020, https://en.wikipedia.org/wiki/Moona_Lisa.
32. *Ibid.*
33. *Ibid.*
34. *Ibid.*
35. "Once Upon a Time… in Hollywood… Annotated," *The AV Club*, August 2, 2019, https://film.avclub.com/once-upon-a-time-in-hollywood-annotated-1836793225.
36. "Larry Vincent," *Wikipedia*, accessed January 5, 2020, https://en.wikipedia.org/wiki/Larry_Vincent.
37. "Cassandra Peterson," *Wikipedia*, accessed January 5, 2020, https://en.wikipedia.org/wiki/Cassandra_Peterson.
38. *Ibid.*
39. *Ibid.*
40. "Bob Wilkins," *Wikipedia*, accessed January 7, 2020, https://en.wikipedia.org/wiki/Bob_Wilkins.
41. *Ibid.*
42. *Ibid.*
43. *Ibid.*
44. *Ibid.*
45. Russell Streiner, interview with author. Tape recording. Scare-A-Con Convention, Springfield, MA, June 4, 2017.
46. *Ibid.*
47. *Ibid.*
48. *Ibid.*
49. Jason Togyer, "Happy Halloween," *The Tube City Almanac*, October 31, 2017, http://almanac.tubecityonline.com/almanac/?e=736.
50. *Ibid.*
51. "Sir Graves Ghastly Presents," *Internet Movie Database* (IMDb), accessed January 10, 2020, https://www.imdb.com/title/tt0285404/.
52. "Lawson Deming," *Wikipedia*, accessed January 10, 2020, https://en.wikipedia.org/wiki/Lawson_J._Deming.
53. *Ibid.*
54. "Sir Graves Ghastly Presents," *Internet Movie Database* (IMDb), January 5, 2020, https://www.imdb.com/title/tt0285404/trivia?ref_=tt_trv_trv.
55. "Lawson Deming," *Wikipedia*, accessed January 5, 2020, https://en.wikipedia.org/wiki/Lawson_J._Deming.
56. *Ibid.*
57. Mark Simonson, "Price Was Right for TV Station," *Oneonta Daily Star*, October 27, 2008.
58. Dave Allen, "Halloween Fun with TV Personality Mike Price AKA Baron Daemon," *WSYR*, October 31, 2018, https://wsyr.iheart.com/content/2018-10-31-halloween-fun-with-tv-personality-mike-price-aka-baron-daemon/.
59. *Ibid.*
60. Philip Vanno, "Monster Movie Matinee Documentary Celebrates Show's 50th Anniversary," *Utica Observer Dispatch*, October 27, 2014.
61. Elena M. Watson, *Television Horror Movie Hosts: 68 Vampires, Mad Scientists and Other Denizens of the Late-Night Airwaves Examined and Interviewed* (Jefferson, NC: McFarland, 2013).
62. "Chamber 13—Tales of Horror," *Internet Movie Database* (IMDb), accessed January 5, 2020, https://www.imdb.com/title/tt9426590/.
63. "The Cool Ghoul," *Internet Movie Database* (IMDb), accessed January 10, 2020, https://en.wikipedia.org/wiki/The_Cool_Ghoul.
64. *Ibid.*
65. Deb Kremer, "Remember This: Those Who Recall The Cool Ghoul are Now Hearing Bluhbluh-bluhbluhbluh in Their Heads," *WCPO*, accessed

January 10, 2020, https://www.wcpo.com/news/insider/remember-this-those-who-recall-the-cool-ghoul-are-now-hearing-bluhbluhbluhbluhbluh-in-their-heads.
  66. "The Cool Ghoul," *Wikipedia*, accessed January 10, 2020, https://en.wikipedia.org/wiki/The_Cool_Ghoul.
  67. *Ibid.*
  68. "Dr. Creep," *Wikipedia*, accessed January 10, 2020, https://en.wikipedia.org/wiki/Dr._Creep.
  69. *Ibid.*
  70. *Ibid.*
  71. *Ibid.*
  72. *Ibid.*
  73. Tim Kiska, "The Ghoul, AKA Legendary '70s TV Horror Host Ron Sweed, Has Died," *Detroit Free Press*, April 3, 2019.
  74. *Ibid.*
  75. "Ron Sweed," *Wikipedia*, accessed January 10, 2020, https://en.wikipedia.org/wiki/Ron_Sweed.
  76. *Ibid.*
  77. *Ibid.*
  78. "Creature Feature," *Wikipedia*, accessed January 13, 2020, https://en.wikipedia.org/wiki/Creature_Feature_(1973_TV_series).
  79. *Ibid.*
  80. "Dick Bennick, Who as Dr. Paul Bearer, Was Host of WTOP-TV's Horror Movies," *AP News*, February 10, 1995, https://apnews.com/89b104b56d47a511cf1ceb04c746ec5e.
  81. "Richard Koon," *Internet Movie Database* (IMDb), accessed January 13, 2020, https://www.imdb.com/name/nm8213712/bio?ref_=nm_ov_bio_sm.
  82. John Kelly, "The Horror! Homegrown Count Gore De Vol Is Back for Some Halloween High Jinks," *Washington Post*, October 23, 2018.
  83. *Ibid.*
  84. "Eleanor Herman," *Internet Movie Database* (IMDb), accessed January 13, 2020, https://www.imdb.com/name/nm0379124/bio?ref_=wnm_ov_bio_sm.
  85. "Count Gore De Vol," *Wikipedia*, accessed January 13, 2020, https://en.wikipedia.org/wiki/Count_Gore_de_Vol.
  86. *Ibid.*
  87. "Dr. Shock," *Wikipedia*, accessed January 13, 2020, https://en.wikipedia.org/wiki/Dr._Shock.
  88. "Dr. Shock," *Broadcast Pioneers*, accessed January 13, 2020, http://www.broadcastpioneers.com/bp11/drshock.html.
  89. "Dr. Shock," *Wikipedia*, accessed January 13, 2020, https://en.wikipedia.org/wiki/Dr._Shock.
  90. "Doctor Madblood," *Wikipedia*, accessed January 13, 2020, https://en.wikipedia.org/wiki/Doctor_Madblood.
  91. *Ibid.*
  92. *Ibid.*
  93. *Ibid.*
  94. Elena M. Watson, *Television Horror Movie Hosts: 68 Vampires, Mad Scientists and Other Denizens of the Late-Night Airwaves Examined and Interviewed* (Jefferson, NC: McFarland and Company, 2013), page unknown.
  95. "Doctor Madblood," *Wikipedia*, accessed January 13, 2020, https://en.wikipedia.org/wiki/Doctor_Madblood.
  96. "John Bloom," *Internet Movie Database* (IMDb), accessed February 15, 2020, https://www.imdb.com/name/nm0089185/bio.
  97. "Joe Bob Briggs," *Wikipedia*, accessed February 15, 2020, https://en.wikipedia.org/wiki/Joe_Bob_Briggs.
  98. *Ibid.*
  99. "Jerry G. Bishop," *Wikipedia*, accessed January 16, 2020, https://en.wikipedia.org/wiki/Jerry_G._Bishop.
  100. *Ibid.*
  101. *Ibid.*
  102. "FAQ," *Svengoolie*, accessed January 16, 2020, https://svengoolie.com/faq.
  103. "Svengoolie," *Wikipedia*, accessed January 16, 2020, https://en.wikipedia.org/wiki/Svengoolie.

Chapter Seven

  1. "Dr. Jekyll and Mr. Hyde," *Internet Movie Database* (IMDb), accessed January 20, 2020, https://www.imdb.com/title/tt0022835/trivia?ref_=tt_trv_trv.
  2. *Ibid.*
  3. *Ibid.*
  4. "Paramount Pictures: American Corporation," *Encyclopaedia Britannica*, accessed January 9, 2020, https://www.britannica.com/topic/Paramount-Pictures.
  5. "Freaks," *Internet Movie Database* (IMDb), accessed January 20, 2020, https://www.imdb.com/title/tt0022913/trivia?ref_=tt_trv_trv.
  6. David J. Skal, interview with author. Tape recording. Scare-A-Con Convention, Verona, NY, October 7, 2017.
  7. "Freaks," *Internet Movie Database* (IMDb), accessed January 20, 2020, https://www.imdb.com/title/tt0022913/trivia?ref_=tt_trv_trv.
  8. Gary Don Rhodes, *Lugosi: His Life in Film, on Stage, and in the Hearts of Horror Lovers* (Jefferson, NC: McFarland, 1997), p. 94.
  9. "White Zombie," *Internet Movie Database* (IMDb), accessed January 20, 2020, https://www.imdb.com/title/tt0023694/trivia?ref_=tt_trv_trv.
  10. David Brook, "The Old Dark House: Review," *Blue Print Review*, May 2, 2018, http://blueprintreview.co.uk/2018/05/the-old-dark-house/.
  11. "The Old Dark House," *Internet Movie Database* (IMDb), accessed January 20, 2020, https://www.imdb.com/title/tt0023293/trivia?ref_=tt_trv_trv.
  12. *Ibid.*
  13. Tim Masters, "BBFC Anniversary: How Banned Horror Film Island of Lost Souls Got a PG Rating," *BBC*, March 28, 2012, https://www.bbc.com/news/entertainment-arts-17315918.
  14. "Island of Lost Souls," *Internet Movie Database* (IMDb), accessed January 21, 2020, https://www.imdb.com/title/tt0024188/trivia.
  15. Gary Don Rhodes, *Lugosi: His Life in Film,*

on Stage, and in the Hearts of Horror Lovers (Jefferson, NC: McFarland, 1997), p. 49.

16. "Island of Lost Souls," *Internet Movie Database* (IMDb), accessed January 21, 2020, https://www.imdb.com/title/tt0024188/trivia?ref_=tt_trv_trv.

17. "King Kong (1931)," *Internet Movie Database* (IMDb), accessed January 21, 2020, https://www.imdb.com/title/tt0024216/trivia?ref_=tt_trv_trv.

18. *Ibid.*
19. *Ibid.*
20. *Ibid.*

21. "The Ghoul," *Internet Movie Database* (IMDb), accessed January 25, 2020, https://www.imdb.com/title/tt0024055/trivia?ref_=tt_trv_trv.

22. *Ibid.*
23. *Ibid.*

24. Gary Don Rhodes, *Lugosi: His Life in Film, on Stage, and in the Hearts of Horror Lovers* (Jefferson, NC: McFarland, 1997), p. 105.

25. "Mark of the Vampire," *Internet Movie Database* (IMDb), accessed January 25, 2020, https://www.imdb.com/title/tt0026685/trivia?ref_=tt_trv_trv.

26. "Mad Love," *Internet Movie Database* (IMDb), accessed January 25, 2020, https://www.imdb.com/title/tt0026663/trivia?ref_=tt_trv_trv.

27. *Ibid.*
28. *Ibid.*

29. "The Walking Dead," *Internet Movie Database* (IMDb), accessed January 25, 2020, https://www.imdb.com/title/tt0028478/trivia?ref_=tt_trv_trv.

30. "The Hunchback of Notre Dame (1939)," *Internet Movie Database* (IMDb), accessed January 25, 2020, https://www.imdb.com/title/tt0031455/trivia?ref_=tt_trv_trv.

31. *Ibid.*
32. *Ibid.*
33. *Ibid.*
34. *Ibid.*

35. "The Hunchback of Notre Dame (1939)," *Wikipedia*, accessed January 25, 2020, https://en.wikipedia.org/wiki/The_Hunchback_of_Notre_Dame_(1939_film).

36. "Dr. Cyclops," *Internet Movie Database* (IMDb), accessed January 26, 2020, https://www.imdb.com/title/tt0032412/trivia?ref_=tt_trv_trv.

37. "Val Lewton," *Internet Movie Database* (IMDb), accessed January 26, 2020, https://www.imdb.com/name/nm0507932/?ref_=fn_al_nm_1.

38. "Cat People," *Internet Movie Database* (IMDb), accessed January 26, 2020, https://www.imdb.com/title/tt0034587/trivia?ref_=tt_trv_trv.

39. *Ibid.*

40. "At the Rialto," *New York Times*, April 22, 1943.

41. Gary Don Rhodes, *Lugosi: His Life in Film, on Stage, and in the Hearts of Horror Lovers* (Jefferson, NC: McFarland, 1997), p. 130.

42. "The Return of the Vampire," *Internet Movie Database* (IMDb), accessed January 26, 2020, https://www.imdb.com/title/tt0037219/trivia?ref_=tt_trv_trv.

43. Greg Mank, "Laird Cregar." Presentation. Monster Bash Conference, Mars, PA, June 22, 2019.

44. *Ibid.*

45. *Ibid.*
46. *Ibid.*

47. "The Uninvited," *Internet Movie Database* (IMDb), accessed February 3, 2020, https://www.imdb.com/title/tt0037415/trivia?ref_=tt_trv_trv.

48. *Ibid.*

49. Greg Mank, "Laird Cregar." Presentation. Monster Bash Conference, Mars, PA, June 22, 2019.

50. *Ibid.*
51. *Ibid.*
52. *Ibid.*

53. Gregory William Mank, *Karloff and Lugosi: The Story of a Haunting Collaboration* (Jefferson, NC: McFarland, 1990), pp. 257–258.

54. David J. Skal, interview with author. Tape recording. Scare-A-Con Convention, Verona, NY, October 7, 2017.

55. Louis Berg, "Farewell to Monsters," *Los Angeles Times*, May 12, 1946.

56. Gregory William Mank, *Karloff and Lugosi: The Story of a Haunting Collaboration* (Jefferson, NC: McFarland, 1990), p. 256.

57. *Ibid.*

58. Gregory William Mank, *Karloff and Lugosi: The Story of a Haunting Collaboration* (Jefferson, NC: McFarland, 1990), p. 272.

59. "The Picture of Dorian Gray," *Internet Movie Database* (IMDb), accessed February 3, 2020, https://www.imdb.com/title/tt0037988/trivia?ref_=tt_trv_trv.

60. "Isle of the Dead," *Internet Movie Database* (IMDb), accessed January 29, 2020, https://www.imdb.com/title/tt0037820/trivia?ref_=tt_trv_trvIsle.

61. *Ibid.*
62. *Ibid.*
63. *Ibid.*

64. "Val Lewton," *Internet Movie Database* (IMDb), accessed January 29, 2020, https://en.wikipedia.org/wiki/Val_Lewton.

65. "Dead of Night," *Internet Movie Database* (IMDb), accessed February 3, 2020, https://www.imdb.com/title/tt0037635/trivia?ref_=tt_trv_trv.

66. *Ibid.*
67. *Ibid.*

68. "Abbott and Costello Meet Frankenstein," *Internet Movie Database* (IMDb), accessed September 15, 2018, https://www.imdb.com/title/tt0040068/trivia?ref_=tt_trv_trv.

69. Gary Don Rhodes, *Lugosi: His Life in Film, on Stage, and in the Hearts of Horror Lovers* (Jefferson, NC: McFarland, 1997), p. 138.

70. Steven Thrash, "Retro Recommendations: Abbott and Costello Meet Frankenstein (1948)," *Rue Morgue*, February 15, 2018, https://rue-morgue.com/retro-recommendations-abbott-and-costello-meet-frankenstein-1948/.

71. Richard Bojarski, *The Complete Films of Bela Lugosi* (New York: Carol Publishing, 1992), p. 39.

72. Henry Fuhrmann, "'A Thing' to His Credit," *Los Angeles Times*, May 25, 1997.

73. "The Thing from Another World," *Internet Movie Database* (IMDb), accessed September 15, 2018, https://www.imdb.com/title/tt0044121/trivia?ref_=tt_trv_trv.

74. "House of Wax," *Internet Movie Database* (IMDb), accessed September 15, 2018, https://www.imdb.com/title/tt0045888/trivia?ref_=tt_trv_trv.
75. *Ibid.*
76. Mark Mancini, "13 Thrilling Facts about House of Wax," *Mental Floss*, April 25, 2018, https://www.mentalfloss.com/article/81901/13-thrilling-facts-about-house-wax.
77. *Ibid.*
78. "Abbott and Costello Meet Dr. Jekyll and Mr. Hyde," *Internet Movie Database* (IMDb), accessed September 18, 2018, https://www.imdb.com/title/tt0045469/trivia?ref_=tt_trv_trv.
79. Cortlandt Hull, "Creature from the Black Lagoon." Presentation. Monster Bash Conference, Mars, PA, June 21, 2019.
80. David J. Skal, interview with author. Tape recording. Scare-A-Con Convention, Verona, NY, October 7, 2017.
81. Ricou Browning, "Creature from the Black Lagoon." Presentation. Monster Bash Conference, Mars, PA, June 23, 2019.
82. *Ibid.*
83. *Ibid.*
84. *Ibid.*
85. *Ibid.*
86. Frank Dello Stritto, "Creature from the Black Lagoon." Presentation. Monster Bash Conference, Mars, PA, June 21, 2019.
87. *Ibid.*
88. *Ibid.*
89. Ricou Browning, "Creature from the Black Lagoon." Presentation. Monster Bash Conference, Mars, PA, June 23, 2019.
90. Frank Dello Stritto, "Creature from the Black Lagoon." Presentation. Monster Bash Conference, Mars, PA, June 21, 2019.
91. "Them!" *Internet Movie Database* (IMDb), accessed September 20, 2018, https://www.imdb.com/title/tt0047573/trivia?ref_=tt_trv_trv.
92. *Ibid.*
93. "Invasion of the Body Snatchers (1956)," *Internet Movie Database* (IMDb), accessed September 20, 2018, https://www.imdb.com/title/tt0049366/trivia?ref_=tt_trv_trv.
94. *Ibid.*
95. "Invasion of the Body Snatchers (1956)," *Wikipedia*, accessed September 20, 2018, https://en.wikipedia.org/wiki/Invasion_of_the_Body_Snatchers.
96. *Ibid.*
97. "The Quatermass Experiment," *Internet Movie Database* (IMDb), accessed September 26, 2018, https://www.imdb.com/title/tt0049646/trivia?ref_=tt_trv_trv.
98. *Ibid.*
99. "The Black Sleep," *Internet Movie Database* (IMDb), accessed September 21, 2018, https://www.imdb.com/title/tt0049013/trivia?ref_=tt_trv_trv.
100. Gary Don Rhodes, *Lugosi: His Life in Film, on Stage, and in the Hearts of Horror Lovers* (Jefferson, NC: McFarland, 1997), pp. 143–44.
101. *Ibid.*, p. 143.
102. Wayne Kinsey, *Hammer Films: The Bray Studios Years* (Richmond, VA: Reynolds & Hearn, 2005), p. 86.
103. "Curse of Frankenstein," *Wikipedia*, accessed September 26, 2018, https://en.wikipedia.org/wiki/The_Curse_of_Frankenstein.
104. "Curse of Frankenstein," *Internet Movie Database* (IMDb), accessed September 26, 2018, https://www.imdb.com/title/tt0050280/trivia?ref_=tt_trv_trv.
105. "Christopher Lee: The Man Behind the Monster," *The House of Hammer* volume 1, no. 1, October 1976, p. 26.
106. "Curse of the Demon," *Internet Movie Database* (IMDb), accessed September 26, 2018, https://www.imdb.com/title/tt0050766/trivia?ref_=tt_trv_trv.
107. *Ibid.*
108. *Ibid.*
109. "The Return of Dracula," *Internet Movie Database* (IMDb), accessed October 2, 2018, https://www.imdb.com/title/tt0052131/trivia?ref_=tt_trv_trv.
110. "Horror of Dracula," *Internet Movie Database* (IMDb), accessed September 26, 2018, https://www.imdb.com/title/tt0051554/trivia?ref_=tt_trv_trv.
111. *Ibid.*
112. David J. Skal, interview with author. Tape recording. Scare-A-Con Convention, Verona, NY, October 7, 2017.
113. "Revenge of Frankenstein," *Internet Movie Database* (IMDb), accessed September 26, 2018, https://www.imdb.com/title/tt0050894/trivia?ref_=tt_trv_trv.
114. James Egan, *1,000 Facts About Horror Movies* (Lulu.com Publisher, 2019), p. 61.
115. Ryan Lambie, "The Strange History of The Blob Movies," *Den of Geek*, January 29, 2015, https://www.denofgeek.com/movies/the-strange-history-of-the-blob-movies/.
116. "The Blob," *Internet Movie Database* (IMDb), accessed January 21, 2018, https://www.imdb.com/title/tt0051418/trivia?ref_=tt_trv_trv.
117. "The Tingler," *Wikipedia*, accessed September 28, 2018, https://en.wikipedia.org/wiki/The_Tingler.
118. "A Bucket of Blood," *Internet Movie Database* (IMDb), accessed January 3, 2020, https://www.imdb.com/title/tt0052655/trivia?ref_=tt_trv_trv.
119. *Ibid.*
120. "The Mummy (1959)," *Internet Movie Database* (IMDb), accessed September 26, 2018, https://www.imdb.com/title/tt0053085/trivia?ref_=tt_trv_trv.
121. *Ibid.*
122. *Ibid.*
123. *Ibid.*
124. *Ibid.*
125. Shannon Hicks, "Alfred Hitchcock Bought the Movie Rights to the Novel Psycho Anonymously from Author Robert Bloch for Just $9,000," *The Newtown Bee*, October 7, 2005.
126. *Ibid.*
127. Jacob Shelton, "The Studio Sabotaged

Psycho and the Fact That It Was Made is Miraculous," *Groovy History*, August 29, 2019, https://groovyhistory.com/psycho-1960-alfed-hitchcock-paramount.

128. David J. Skal, interview with author. Tape recording. Scare-A-Con Convention, Verona, NY, October 7, 2017.

129. "Psycho," *Internet Movie Database* (IMDb), accessed January 4, 2020, https://www.imdb.com/title/tt0054215/trivia?ref_=tt_trv_trv.

130. Harrison Smith, interview with author. Tape recording. Scare-A-Con Convention, Springfield, MA, June 4, 2017.

131. David J. Skal, interview with author. Tape recording. Scare-A-Con Convention, Verona, NY, October 7, 2017.

132. "House of Usher," *Internet Movie Database* (IMDb), accessed January 3, 2020, https://www.imdb.com/title/tt0053925/trivia?ref_=tt_trv_trv.

133. *Ibid.*

134. Terence Towles Canote, "Hammer Films' The Brides of Dracula," *A Shroud of Thoughts*, August 6, 2016, http://mercurie.blogspot.com/2016/08/hammer-films-brides-of-dracula-1960.html.

135. "The Brides of Dracula," *TV Tropes*, accessed January 3, 2020, https://tvtropes.org/pmwiki/pmwiki.php/Trivia/TheBridesOfDracula.

136. Genoveva Rossi, interview with author. Tape recording. Scare-A-Con Convention, Springfield, MA, June 3, 2017.

137. "Curse of the Werewolf," *Internet Movie Database* (IMDb), accessed January 6, 2020, https://www.imdb.com/title/tt0054777/trivia?ref_=tt_trv_trv.

138. *Ibid.*

139. Genoveva Rossi, interview with author. Tape recording. Scare-A-Con Convention, Springfield, MA, June 3, 2017.

140. *Ibid.*

141. "Pit and the Pendulum," *Internet Movie Database* (IMDb), accessed January 6, 2020, https://www.imdb.com/title/tt0055304/trivia?ref_=tt_trv_trv.

142. "Punishment Poll," *Grindhouse Database*, November 21, 2019, https://www.grindhousedatabase.com/index.php/Punishment_Poll.

143. Roger Ebert, "Peeping Tom." *Roger Ebert*, accessed January 20, 2020, https://www.rogerebert.com/reviews/great-movie-peeping-tom-1960.

144. "Night of the Eagle," *Wikipedia*, accessed January 6, 2020, https://en.wikipedia.org/wiki/Night_of_the_Eagle.

145. *Ibid.*

146. "Tales of Terror," *Wikipedia*, accessed January 6, 2020, https://en.wikipedia.org/wiki/Tales_of_Terror.

147. "The Phantom of the Opera (1962)," *Internet Movie Database* (IMDb), accessed March 15, 2020, https://www.imdb.com/title/tt0056347/trivia?ref_=tt_trv_trv.

148. *Ibid.*

149. "The City of the Dead," *Internet Movie Database* (IMDb), accessed January 7, 2020, https://www.imdb.com/title/tt0053719/trivia?ref_=tt_trv_trv.

150. Genoveva Rossi, interview with author. Tape recording. Scare-A-Con Convention, Springfield, MA, June 3, 2017.

151. "The Raven (1963)," *Internet Movie Database* (IMDb), accessed January 7, 2020, https://www.imdb.com/title/tt0057449/trivia?ref_=tt_trv_trv.

152. "The Raven (1963)," *Wikipedia*, accessed January 7, 2020, https://en.wikipedia.org/wiki/The_Raven_(1963_film).

153. "The Raven (1963)," *Internet Movie Database* (IMDb), accessed January 7, 2020, https://www.imdb.com/title/tt0057449/trivia?ref_=tt_trv_trv.

154. Brent Lang, "Tippi Hedren Recounts What Happened When She Turned Down Alfred Hitchcock's Advances," *Variety*, December 13, 2017.

155. John Hiscock, "Tippi Hedren Interview: 'Hitchcock Put Me in a Mental Prison,'" *The Telegraph*, December 24, 2012.

156. David J. Skal, interview with author. Tape recording. Scare-A-Con Convention, Verona, NY, October 7, 2017.

157. *Ibid.*

158. *Ibid.*

159. Mark McGee, *Faster and Furiouser: The Revised and Fattened Fable of American International Pictures* (Jefferson, NC: McFarland, 1996), p. 206.

160. Steve Biodrowski, David Del Valle, and Lawrence French, "Vincent Price: Horror's Crown Prince," *Cinefantastique*, January 1989, p. 59.

161. "The Haunted Palace," *Internet Movie Database* (IMDb), accessed March 15, 2020, https://www.imdb.com/title/tt0057128/trivia?ref_=tt_trv_trv.

162. *Ibid.*

163. *Ibid.*

164. Farran Smith Nehme, "Terror, Suspense, and the Power of Suggestion in The Haunting," *Library of America*, October 19, 2016, https://www.loa.org/news-and-views/1208-terror-suspense-and-the-power-of-suggestion-in-_the-haunting_

165. Susan King, "Robert Wise's The Haunting Marks 50 Years with Russ Tamblyn," *Los Angeles Times*, October 29, 2013.

166. "The Haunting (1963)," *Internet Movie Database* (IMDb), accessed February 5, 2020. https://www.imdb.com/title/tt0057129/trivia?ref_=tt_trv_trv.

167. "Strait-Jacket," *Internet Movie Database* (IMDb), accessed February 5, 2020, https://www.imdb.com/title/tt0058620/trivia?ref_=tt_trv_trv.

168. *Ibid.*

169. *Ibid.*

170. *Ibid.*

171. "The Last Man on Earth," *Internet Movie Database* (IMDb), accessed February 5, 2020, https://www.imdb.com/title/tt0058700/trivia?ref_=tt_trv_trv.

172. *Ibid.*

173. *Ibid.*

174. "Black Sabbath," *Internet Movie Database* (IMDb), accessed February 5, 2020, https://www.imdb.com/title/tt0057603/trivia?ref_=tt_trv_trv.

175. "Masque of the Red Death," *Wikipedia*, accessed February 11, 2020, https://en.wikipedia.org/wiki/The_Masque_of_the_Red_Death_(1964_film).

176. "Masque of the Red Death," *Internet Movie Database* (IMDb), accessed February 11, 2020, https://en.wikipedia.org/wiki/The_Masque_of_the_Red_Death_(1964_film).
177. "Witchcraft," *Internet Movie Database* (IMDb), accessed March 31, 2020, https://www.imdb.com/title/tt0058753/trivia.
178. "The Gorgon," *Internet Movie Database* (IMDb), accessed February 11, 2020, https://www.imdb.com/title/tt0058155/trivia?ref_=tt_trv_trv.
179. *Ibid.*
180. *Ibid.*
181. "The Skull," *Internet Movie Database* (IMDb), accessed February 11, 2020, https://www.imdb.com/title/tt0059727/trivia?ref_=tt_trv_trv.
182. *Ibid.*
183. Jennie Kermode, "The Skull," *Eye for Film*, accessed February 11, 2020, https://www.eyeforfilm.co.uk/review/the-skull-1965-film-review-by-jennie-kermode.
184. "Dracula: Prince of Darkness," *Internet Movie Database* (IMDb), accessed February 11, 2020, https://www.imdb.com/title/tt0059127/trivia?ref_=tt_trv_trv.
185. David J. Skal, interview with author. Tape recording. Scare-A-Con Convention, Verona, NY, October 7, 2017.
186. "Dracula: Prince of Darkness," *Internet Movie Database* (IMDb), accessed February 11, 2020, https://www.imdb.com/title/tt0059127/trivia?ref_=tt_trv_trv.
187. *Ibid.*
188. Movie Posters Heritage Auctions, accessed February 25, 2020, https://movieposters.ha.com/itm/movie-posters/horror/dracula-prince-of-darkness-the-plague-of-the-zombies-combo-20th-century-fox-1966-very-fine-novelty-glasses-145-x-3/a/161940–51154.s.
189. "Plague of the Zombies," *Internet Movie Database* (IMDb), accessed February 25, 2020, https://www.imdb.com/title/tt0060841/trivia?ref_=tt_trv_trv.
190. "The Reptile," *Internet Movie Database* (IMDb), accessed February 25, 2020, https://www.imdb.com/title/tt0060893/trivia?ref_=tt_trv_trv.
191. *Ibid.*
192. *Ibid.*
193. Sid Haig, interview with author. Scare-A-Con Convention, Verona, NY, October 7, 2017.
194. *Ibid.*
195. "Spider Baby," *Internet Movie Database* (IMDb), accessed February 12, 2020, https://www.imdb.com/title/tt0058606/trivia?ref_=tt_trv_trv.
196. Sid Haig, interview with author. Scare-A-Con Convention, Verona, NY, October 7, 2017.
197. "Spider Baby," *Internet Movie Database* (IMDb), accessed February 12, 2020, https://www.imdb.com/title/tt0058606/trivia?ref_=tt_trv_trv.
198. Marjorie Baumgarten, "From the Vaults: Spider Baby," *Austin Chronicle*, July 26, 2013.
199. "Motion Picture Association of America," *Encyclopaedia Britannica*, accessed March 15, 2020, https://www.britannica.com/topic/Motion-Picture-Association-of-America.
200. "Matthew Hopkins," *Encyclopaedia Britannica*, accessed February 13, 2020, https://www.britannica.com/biography/Matthew-Hopkins.
201. *Ibid.*
202. "Witchfinder General," *Internet Movie Database* (IMDb), accessed February 13, 2020, https://www.imdb.com/title/tt0063285/trivia?ref_=tt_trv_trv.
203. Genoveva Rossi, interview with author. Tape recording. Scare-A-Con Convention, Springfield, MA, June 3, 2017.
204. "Witchfinder General," *Internet Movie Database* (IMDb), accessed February 13, 2020, https://www.imdb.com/title/tt0063285/trivia?ref_=tt_trv_trv.
205. *Ibid.*
206. Paul Gallagher, "Witchfinder General: The Life and Death of Michael Reeves," *Dangerous Minds*, December 2, 2010, https://dangerousminds.net/comments/witchfinder_general_michael_reeves.
207. Genoveva Rossi, interview with author. Tape recording. Scare-A-Con Convention, Springfield, MA, June 3, 2017.
208. Rodrigo Perez, "Seven Things You Should Know about Rosemary's Baby," *Indie Wire*, October 31, 2012, https://www.indiewire.com/2012/10/7-things-you-should-know-about-roman-polanskis-rosemarys-baby-104463/.
209. Keith Dow, "Sharon Tate on the Set of Rosemary's Baby, 1967," *Metaflix*, accessed February 15, 2020, https://www.metaflix.com/movie-news/2019/5/22/sharon-tate-on-the-set-of-rosemarys-baby-1967.
210. Matthew Jackson, "13 Devilish Facts about Rosemary's Baby," *Mental Floss*, October 4, 2017, https://www.mentalfloss.com/article/504972/13-devilish-facts-about-rosemary%E2%80%99s-baby.
211. "The Devil Rides Out," *Internet Movie Database* (IMDb), accessed February 15, 2020, https://www.imdb.com/title/tt0062885/trivia?ref_=tt_trv_trv.
212. *Ibid.*
213. "The Devil Rides Out," *Wikipedia*, accessed February 15, 2020, https://en.wikipedia.org/wiki/The_Devil_Rides_Out_(film).
214. "The Devil Rides Out," *Internet Movie Database* (IMDb), accessed February 15, 2020, https://www.imdb.com/title/tt0062885/trivia?ref_=tt_trv_trv.
215. Sanzone, Zachary. Email interview with author. April 20, 2020.
216. "Night of the Living Dead (1968)," *Internet Movie Database* (IMDb), accessed February 20, 2020, https://www.imdb.com/title/tt0063350/trivia?ref_=tt_trv_trv.
217. Zachary Sanzone, email interview with author. April 20, 2020.
218. "Dracula Has Risen from the Grave," *Internet Movie Database* (IMDb), accessed February 15, 2020, https://www.imdb.com/title/tt0062909/trivia?ref_=tt_trv_trv.
219. *Ibid.*
220. "The Oblong Box," *Wikipedia*, accessed February 15, 2020, https://en.wikipedia.org/wiki/The_Oblong_Box_(film).
221. "The Oblong Box," *Internet Movie Database* (IMDb), accessed February 15, 2020, https://www.imdb.com/title/tt0064747/?ref_=fn_al_tt_1.
222. "Night Gallery Pilot," *Internet Movie*

Database (IMDb), accessed February 17, 2020, https://www.imdb.com/title/tt0064725/trivia?ref_=tt_trv_trv.
   223. *Ibid.*

Chapter Eight

   1. "Frankenstein Must Be Destroyed." *Internet Movie Database* (IMDb). Accessed February 26, 2020. https://www.imdb.com/title/tt0065738/trivia?ref_=tt_trv_trv.
   2. Paul Gallagher, "Peter Cushing as 'the Screen's Most Fantastic Fiend' in Frankenstein Must Be Destroyed," *Flashbak*. December 21, 2019. https://flashbak.com/peter-cushing-as-the-screens-most-fantastic-fiend-in-frankenstein-must-be-destroyed-28205/.
   3. Bruce G. Hallenbeck, *The Hammer Frankenstein: British Cult Cinema* (Baltimore: Midnight Marquee Press, 2013), pp. 167–170.
   4. "Frankenstein Must Be Destroyed," *Internet Movie Database* (IMDb), accessed February 26, 2020, https://www.imdb.com/title/tt0065738/trivia?ref_=tt_trv_trv.
   5. David J. Skal, interview with author. Tape recording. Scare-A-Con Convention, Verona, NY, October 7, 2017.
   6. "Count Yorga, Vampire," *Internet Movie Database* (IMDb), accessed October 16, 2016, https://www.imdb.com/title/tt0066952/trivia?ref_=tt_trv_trv.
   7. David J. Skal, interview with author. Tape recording. Scare-A-Con Convention, Verona, NY, October 7, 2017.
   8. "Dr. Phibes Rises Again," *Internet Movie Database* (IMDb), accessed October 16, 2016, https://www.imdb.com/title/tt0068503/trivia?ref_=tt_trv_trv.
   9. Jeff Thompson, *The Television Horrors of Dan Curtis* (Jefferson, NC: McFarland, 2009), p. 68.
   10. *Ibid.*
   11. Michael Dante, email interview with author. June 19, 2019.
   12. *Ibid.*
   13. "The House That Dripped Blood," *Internet Movie Database* (IMDb), accessed October 16, 2016, https://www.imdb.com/title/tt0065854/trivia?ref_=tt_trv_trv.
   14. *Ibid.*
   15. "The Blood on Satan's Claw," *Internet Movie Database* (IMDb), accessed October 16, 2016, https://www.imdb.com/title/tt0066849/trivia?ref_=tt_trv_trv.
   16. "The Abominable Dr. Phibes," *Internet Movie Database* (IMDb), accessed October 18, 2016, https://www.imdb.com/title/tt0066740/trivia?ref_=tt_trv_trv.
   17. Jon Wamsley, "The Abominable Dr. Phibes Still Hits the Right Notes After 45 Years," *Cryptic Rock*, July 13, 2016, https://crypticrock.com/the-abominable-dr-phibes-still-hits-the-right-notes-after-45-years/.
   18. "The Abominable Dr. Phibes," *Internet Movie Database* (IMDb), accessed October 18, 2016, https://www.imdb.com/title/tt0066740/trivia?ref_=tt_trv_trv.
   19. Jon Wamsley, "The Abominable Dr. Phibes Still Hits the Right Notes After 45 Years," *Cryptic Rock*, July 13, 2016, https://crypticrock.com/the-abominable-dr-phibes-still-hits-the-right-notes-after-45-years/.
   20. Genoveva Rossi, interview with author. Tape recording. Scare-A-Con Convention, Springfield, MA, June 3, 2017.
   21. Harrison Smith, interview with author. Tape recording. Scare-A-Con Convention, Springfield, MA, June 4, 2017.
   22. Will McKinley, "Where's Barnabas? The Vampire-Free Night of Dark Shadows," April 4, 2014, https://willmckinley.wordpress.com/2014/04/04/wheres-barnabas-the-vampire-free-night-of-dark-shadows-1971/.
   23. *Ibid.*
   24. *Ibid.*
   25. *Ibid.*
   26. "The Brotherhood of Satan (1971) Unopened Seeds of Satan," *Trash Video*, December 3, 2012, http://trashvideobrisbane.blogspot.com/2012/12/the-brotherhood-of-satan-1971-unopened.html.
   27. "The Night Stalker," *Internet Movie Database* (IMDb), accessed October 18, 2016, https://www.imdb.com/title/tt0067490/trivia?ref_=tt_trv_trv.
   28. Jeff Thompson, *The Television Horrors of Dan Curtis* (Jefferson, NC: McFarland, 2009), p. 120.
   29. "Tales from the Crypt (1972)," *Internet Movie Database* (IMDb), accessed October 18, 2016, https://www.imdb.com/title/tt0069341/trivia?ref_=tt_trv_trv.
   30. *Ibid.*
   31. "Frogs," *Internet Movie Database*. (IMDb), accessed October 25, 2016, https://www.imdb.com/title/tt0068615/trivia?ref_=tt_trv_trv.
   32. Martine Beswick, "Dr. Jekyll and Sister Hyde." Presentation. Monster Bash Conference, Mars, PA, June 21, 2019.
   33. *Ibid.*
   34. *Ibid.*
   35. David J. Skal, interview with author. Tape recording. Scare-A-Con Convention, Verona, NY, October 7, 2017.
   36. "Frenzy," *Wikipedia*, accessed January 18, 2018, https://en.wikipedia.org/wiki/Frenzy.
   37. "Frenzy," *Internet Movie Database* (IMDb), accessed January 18, 2018. https://www.imdb.com/title/tt0068611/trivia?ref_=tt_trv_trv.
   38. David J. Skal, interview with author. Tape recording. Scare-A-Con Convention, Verona, NY, October 7, 2017.
   39. "Twins of Evil," *Internet Movie Database* (IMDb), accessed January 20, 2018, https://www.imdb.com/title/tt0069427/trivia?ref_=tt_trv_trv.
   40. *Ibid.*
   41. "Dr. Phibes Rises Again," *Internet Movie Database* (IMDb), accessed October 16, 2016, https://www.imdb.com/title/tt0068503/trivia?ref_=tt_trv_trv.
   42. *Ibid.*
   43. "Blaxploitation. What It Is... What It Was," *Grindhouse Database*, December 24, 2019, https://www.grindhousedatabase.com/index.php/Blaxploitation:_What_It_Is...What_It_Was.
   44. David J. Skal, interview with author. Tape

recording. Scare-A-Con Convention, Verona, NY, October 7, 2017.

45. "Blacula," *Internet Movie Database* (IMDb), accessed January 21, 2018, https://www.imdb.com/title/tt0068284/trivia?ref_=tt_trv_trv.

46. David J. Skal, interview with author. Tape recording. Scare-A-Con Convention, Verona, NY, October 7, 2017.

47. Jeff Thompson, *The Television Horrors of Dan Curtis* (Jefferson, NC: McFarland, 2009), p. 122.

48. "Tigon British Film Productions," *Wikipedia*, accessed March 21, 2020, https://en.wikipedia.org/wiki/Tigon_British_Film_Productions.

49. "The Creeping Flesh," *Internet Movie Database* (IMDb), accessed March 21, 2020, https://www.imdb.com/title/tt0068424/trivia?ref_=tt_trv_trv.

50. "The Vault of Horror," *Internet Movie Database* (IMDb), accessed March 20, 2020, https://www.imdb.com/title/tt0070868/trivia?ref_=tt_trv_trv.

51. "Theater of Blood," *Internet Movie Database* (IMDb), accessed January 25, 2018, https://www.imdb.com/title/tt0070791/trivia?ref_=tt_trv_trv.

52. *Ibid.*

53. "The Legend of Hell House," *Internet Movie Database* (IMDb), accessed January 21, 2018, http://www.imdb.com/title/tt0070868/trivia?ref_=tt_trv_trv.

54. *Ibid.*

55. "Don't Be Afraid of the Dark," *Internet Movie Database* (IMDb), accessed February 28, 2020, https://www.imdb.com/title/tt0069992/trivia?ref_=tt_trv_trv.

56. "Don't Look Now," *Internet Movie Database* (IMDb), accessed February 29, 2020, https://www.imdb.com/title/tt0069995/trivia?ref_=tt_trv_trv.

57. "Don't Look Now," *Wikipedia*, accessed February 28, 2020, https://en.wikipedia.org/wiki/Don%27t_Look_Now.

58. Tom Beasley, "Don't Look Now: The Truth Behind One of Hollywood's Most Controversial Sex Scenes," *Yahoo Entertainment*, July 5, 2019, https://www.yahoo.com/entertainment/dont-look-now-true-story-controversial-sex-scene-084114449.html.

59. Jonathan Barkan, "Remember Her Name: Mercedes McCambridge was Pazuzu in The Exorcist but Her Name was Cut From The Credits," *Dread Central*, August 30, 2019. https://www.dreadcentral.com/news/299539/remember-her-name-mercedes-mccambridge-was-pazuzu-in-the-exorcist-but-her-name-was-cut-from-the-credits/.

60. Christopher Fiduccia, "30 Crazy Details Behind the Making of The Exorcist," *Screen Rant*, October 21, 2018, https://screenrant.com/the-exorcist-making-of-behind-scenes-hidden-trivia/.

61. *Ibid.*

62. *Ibid.*

63. "Dracula (1974)," *Internet Movie Database* (IMDb), accessed March 22, 2020, https://www.imdb.com/title/tt0070003/trivia?ref_=tt_trv_trv.

64. *Ibid.*

65. "The Beast Must Die," *Internet Movie Database* (IMDb), accessed March 24, 2020, https://www.imdb.com/title/tt0071200/trivia?ref_=tt_trv_trv.

66. Jacob Knight, "The Amicus Vault of Horror: The Beast Must Die!" *Birth, Movies, Death*, December 22, 2017, https://birthmoviesdeath.com/2017/12/22/the-amicus-vault-of-horror-the-beast-must-die-1974.

67. "The Beast Must Die," *Internet Movie Database* (IMDb), accessed March 24, 2020, https://www.imdb.com/title/tt0071200/trivia?ref_=tt_trv_trv.

68. Jane Rose, "15 Fascinating Facts about The Wicker Man," *Mental Floss*, July 22, 2016, https://www.mentalfloss.com/article/83609/15-fascinating-facts-about-wicker-man.

69. George Grella, email interview with author. September 5, 2016.

70. *Ibid.*

71. Jane Rose, "15 Fascinating Facts about The Wicker Man," *Mental Floss*, July 22, 2016, https://www.mentalfloss.com/article/83609/15-fascinating-facts-about-wicker-man.

72. *Ibid.*

73. "Captain Kronos: Vampire Hunter," *Internet Movie Database* (IMDb), accessed March 25, 2020, https://www.imdb.com/title/tt0071276/trivia?ref_=tt_trv_trv.

74. *Ibid.*

75. Jennifer M. Wood, "11 Things You Didn't Know about The Texas Chainsaw Massacre," *Esquire*, October 21, 2014, https://www.esquire.com/entertainment/movies/a23810/texas-chainsaw-things-you-didnt-know/.

76. "The Texas Chain Saw Massacre (1974)," *Internet Movie Database* (IMDb), accessed March 14, 2017, https://www.imdb.com/title/tt0072271/trivia?ref_=tt_trv_trv.

77. Ted Geoghegan, "11 Facts about The Texas Chain Saw Massacre," *Gorgon Video*, August 11, 2014. https://gorgon-video.com/blogs/blog/15741059-11-facts-about-the-texas-chain-saw-massacre.

78. Harrison Smith, interview with author. Tape recording. Scare-A-Con Convention, Springfield, MA, June 4, 2017.

79. "Black Christmas (1974)," *Internet Movie Database* (IMDb), accessed February 21, 2020, https://www.imdb.com/title/tt0071222/trivia?ref_=tt_trv_trv.

80. "The Legend of Lizzie Borden," *Internet Movie Database* (IMDb), April 2, 2020, https://www.imdb.com/title/tt0073273/trivia?ref_=tt_trv_trv.

81. Mike Barnes and Duane Byrge, "Five Easy Pieces Actress Karen Black Dies at 74," *Hollywood Reporter*, August 8, 2013, https://www.hollywoodreporter.com/news/karen-black-five-easy-pieces-nashville-dies-431637.

Chapter Nine

1. Patrick Cavanaugh, "Why Horror Hosts Need to Return from the Dead," *Comic Book*, March 8, 2019, https://comicbook.com/horror/2019/03/06/horror-hosts-elvira-joe-bob-briggs-return/.

Bibliography

"Abbott and Costello Meet Dr. Jekyll and Mr. Hyde." *Internet Movie Database* (IMDb). Web. Accessed September 18, 2018.
"Abbott and Costello Meet Frankenstein." *Internet Movie Database* (IMDb). Web. Accessed September 15, 2018.
"The Abominable Dr. Phibes." *Internet Movie Database* (IMDb). Web. Accessed October 18, 2016.
"Acromegaly." *The Mayo Clinic*. Web. Accessed December 14, 2016.
Allen, Dave. "Halloween Fun with TV Personality Mike Price AKA Baron Daemon." *WSYR*, October 31, 2018. Web. Accessed March 27, 2020.
"At the Rialto." *New York Times*, April 22, 1943.
Barkan, Jonathan. "Remember Her Name: Mercedes McCambridge Was Pazuzu in *The Exorcist* but Her Name Was Cut from the Credits." *Dread Central*, August 30, 2019. Web. Accessed June 15, 2020.
Barnes, Mike. "John Zacherle, Delightfully Schlocky TV Host of Horror Movies, Dies at 98." *Hollywood Reporter*, October 28, 2016.
Barnes, Mike, and Duane Byrge. "*Five Easy Pieces* Actress Karen Black Dies at 74." *Hollywood Reporter*, August 8, 2013.
Baumgarten, Marjorie. "From the Vaults: *Spider Baby*." *Austin Chronicle*, July 26, 2013.
Beasley, Tom. "Don't Look Now: The Truth Behind One of Hollywood's Most Controversial Sex Scenes." *Yahoo Entertainment*, July 5, 2019. Web. Accessed June 29, 2020.
"The Beast Must Die." *Internet Movie Database* (IMDb). Web. Accessed March 24, 2020.
Berg, Louis. "Farewell to Monsters." *Los Angeles Times*, May 12, 1946.
Biodrowski, Steve, David Del Valle, and Lawrence French. "Vincent Price: Horror's Crown Prince." *Cinefantastique*, January 1989.
"The Black Cat." *Internet Movie Database* (IMDb). Web. Accessed November 14, 2016.
"Black Christmas (1974)." *Internet Movie Database* (IMDb). Web. Accessed February 21, 2020.
"Black Sabbath." *Internet Movie Database* (IMDb). Web. Accessed February 5, 2020.
"The Black Sleep." *Internet Movie Database* (IMDb). Web. Accessed September 21, 2018.
"Blacula." *Internet Movie Database* (IMDb). Web. Accessed January 21, 2018.
"Blaxploitation. What It Is… What It Was." *Grindhouse Database*. December 23, 2019. Web. Accessed March 4, 2020.
"The Blob." *Internet Movie Database* (IMDb). Web. Accessed January 21, 2018.
"The Blood on Satan's Claw." *Internet Movie Database* (IMDb). Web. Accessed October 16, 2016.
"Bob Wilkins." *Wikipedia.com*. Accessed January 7, 2020.
Bojarski, Richard. *The Complete Films of Bela Lugosi*. New York: Carol Publishing, 1992.
"The Bride of Frankenstein." *Internet Movie Database* (IMDb). Web. Accessed October 24, 2016.
"The Brides of Dracula." *TV Tropes*. Web. Accessed January 3, 2020.
Brook, David. "*The Old Dark House*: Review." *Blue Print Review*, May 2, 2018. Web. Accessed March 15, 2020.
"The Brotherhood of Satan (1971) Unopened Seeds of Satan." *Trash Video*. December 3, 2012. Web. Accessed June 5, 2020.
Brunas, Michael, John Brunas, and Tom Weaver. *Universal Horrors*. Jefferson, NC: McFarland, 1990.
"A Bucket of Blood." *Internet Movie Database* (IMDb). Web. Accessed January 3, 2020.
"Burn, Witch, Burn." *Internet Movie Database* (IMDb). Web. Accessed January 6, 2020.
"Calling Dr. Death." *Internet Movie Database* (IMDb). Web. Accessed December 8, 2016.
Canote, Terence Towles. "Hammer Films' *The Brides of Dracula*." *A Shroud of Thoughts*. August 6, 2016. Web. Accessed April 28, 2020.
"Captain Kronos: Vampire Hunter." *Internet Movie Database* (IMDb). Web. Accessed March 25, 2020.
"Cassandra Peterson." *Wikipedia*. Web. Accessed January 5, 2020.
"Cat People." *Internet Movie Database* (IMDb). Web. Accessed January 26, 2020.
Cavanaugh, Patrick. "Why Horror Hosts Need to Return from the Dead." *Comic Book*, March 18, 2019. Web. Accessed June 14, 2020.
"Chamber 13–Tales of Horror." *Internet Movie Database* (IMDb). Web. Accessed January 5, 2020.

"Christopher Lee: The Man Behind the Monster." *The House of Hammer* 1, no. 1 (October 1976).
"The City of the Dead." *Internet Movie Database* (IMDb). Web. Accessed January 7, 2020.
"The Cool Ghoul." *Internet Movie Database* (IMDb). Web. Accessed January 10, 2020.
"The Cool Ghoul." *Wikipedia*. Web. Accessed January 10, 2020.
"Count Gore De Vol." *Wikipedia*. Web. Accessed January 13, 2020.
"Count Yorga, Vampire." *Internet Movie Database* (IMDb). Web. Accessed October 16, 2016.
"Creature Feature." *Wikipedia*. Web. Accessed January 13, 2020.
"Creature Features." *Wikipedia*. Web. Accessed June 25, 2020.
"The Creeping Flesh." *Internet Movie Database* (IMDb). Web. Accessed March 21, 2020.
"The Curse of Frankenstein." *Internet Movie Database* (IMDb). Web. Accessed September 26, 2018,
"The Curse of Frankenstein." *Wikipedia*. Web. Accessed September 26, 2018.
"Curse of the Demon." *Internet Movie Database* (IMDb). Web. Accessed September 26, 2018.
"The Curse of the Werewolf." *Internet Movie Database* (IMDb). Web. Accessed January 6, 2020.
"Dead of Night." *Internet Movie Database* (IMDb). Web. Accessed February 3, 2020.
"The Devil Commands." *Internet Movie Database* (IMDb). Web. Accessed December 11, 2016.
"The Devil Rides Out." *Internet Movie Database* (IMDb). Web. Accessed February 15, 2020.
"The Devil Rides Out." *Wikipedia*. Web. Accessed February 15, 2020.
"Dick Bennick, Who as Dr. Paul Bearer, Was Host of WTOP-TV's Horror Movies." *AP News*, February 10, 1995.
"Dr. Creep." *Wikipedia*. Web. Accessed January 10, 2020.
"Dr. Cyclops." *Internet Movie Database* (IMDb). Web. Accessed January 26, 2020.
"Dr. Jekyll and Mr. Hyde." *Internet Movie Database* (IMDb). Web. Accessed January 20, 2020.
"Doctor Madblood." *Wikipedia*. Web. Accessed January 13, 2020.
"Dr. Phibes Rises Again." *Internet Movie Database* (IMDb). Web. Accessed October 16, 2016.
"Dr. Shock." *Broadcast Pioneers*. 2008. Web. Accessed January 13, 2020.
"Dr. Shock." *Wikipedia*. Web. Accessed January 13, 2020.
"Don't Be Afraid of the Dark." *Internet Movie Database* (IMDb). Web. Accessed February 28, 2020.
"Don't Look Now." *Internet Movie Database* (IMDb). Web. Accessed February 29, 2020.
"Don't Look Now." *Wikipedia*. Web. Accessed February 28, 2020.
Dow, Keith. "Sharon Tate on the Set of *Rosemary's Baby*, 1967." *Metaflix*, February 15, 2020. Web. Accessed May 4, 2020.
"Dracula (1931)." *Internet Movie Database* (IMDb). Web. Accessed October 21, 2016.
"Dracula (1974)." *Internet Movie Database* (IMDb). Web. Accessed March 22, 2020.
"Dracula Has Risen from the Grave." *Internet Movie Database* (IMDb). Web. Accessed February 15, 2020.
"Dracula: Prince of Darkness." *Internet Movie Database* (IMDb). Web. Accessed February 11, 2020.
"Dracula's Daughter." *Internet Movie Database* (IMDb). Web. Accessed November 16, 2016.
Ebert, Roger. "Peeping Tom." *Roger Ebert*, May 2, 1999. Web. Accessed January 20, 2020.
Egan, James. *1,000 Facts About Horror Movies*. N.p.: Lulu.com Publisher, 2019.
"Eleanor Herman." *Internet Movie Database* (IMDb). Web. Accessed January 13, 2020.
"Famous Monsters of Filmland." *Encyclopedia of Science Fiction*. Web. Accessed March 15, 2020.
"FAQ." *Svengoolie*. Web. Accessed January 16, 2020.
Fiduccia, Christopher. "30 Crazy Details Behind the Making of *The Exorcist*." *Screen Rant*, October 21, 2018. Web. Accessed July 3, 2020.
"Foul Play." *The Haunt of Fear* no. 19 (May/June 1953).
Fox, Randy. "NashEvil: From Sir Cecil Creape to Dr. Gangrene, A History of Nashville Hosts." *Nashville Scene*, October 27, 2011. Web. Accessed March 5, 2020.
"Frankenstein (1931)." *Internet Movie Database* (IMDb). Web. Accessed October 24, 2016.
"Frankenstein Must Be Destroyed." *Internet Movie Database* (IMDb). Web. Accessed February 26, 2020.
"Freaks." *Internet Movie Database* (IMDb). Web. Accessed January 20, 2020.
"Frenzy." *Internet Movie Database* (IMDb). Web. Accessed January 18, 2018.
"Frenzy." *Wikipedia*. Web. Accessed January 18, 2018.
"Fright Night 1958–1963." *Internet Movie Database* (IMDb). Web. Accessed January 5, 2020.
"Fright Night on Channel 9." *Amazon*. Web. Accessed June 27, 2020.
"Frogs." *Internet Movie Database* (IMDb). Web. Accessed October 25, 2016.
"The Frozen Ghost." *Internet Movie Database* (IMDb). Web. Accessed December 8, 2016.
Fuhrmann, Henry. "'A Thing' to His Credit." *Los Angeles Times*, May 25, 1997.
Gallagher, Paul. "Peter Cushing as 'the Screen's Most Fantastic Fiend' in *Frankenstein Must Be Destroyed*." *Flashbak*, December 21, 2019. Web. Accessed January 3, 2020.
Gallagher, Paul. "Witchfinder General: The Life and Death of Michael Reeves." *Dangerous Minds*, December 2, 2010. Web. Accessed May 30, 2020.
Geoghegan, Ted. "11 Facts about *The Texas Chain Saw Massacre*." *Gorgon Video*, August 11, 2014. Web. Accessed June 13, 2020.
"The Ghost of Frankenstein." *Internet Movie Database* (IMDb). Web. Accessed December 11, 2016.
"The Ghoul." *Internet Movie Database* (IMDb). Web. Accessed January 25, 2020.
"Good Evening, I Am Vampira." *Life* Magazine, June 14, 1954.

"The Gorgon." *Internet Movie Database* (IMDb). Web. Accessed February 11, 2020.
Hallenbeck, Bruce G. *The Hammer Frankenstein: British Cult Cinema*. Baltimore: Midnight Marquee Press, 2013.
Hatcher, Lint, and Rod Bennett. "Inside Darkest Ackerman." *Jim Henry*. Web. Accessed January 25, 2020.
"The Haunted Palace." *Internet Movie Database* (IMDb). Web. Accessed March 15, 2020.
"The Haunting (1963)." *Internet Movie Database* (IMDb). Web. Accessed February 5, 2020.
Hicks, Shannon. "Alfred Hitchcock Bought the Movie Rights to the Novel *Psycho* Anonymously from Author Robert Bloch for Just $9,000." *The Newtown Bee*, October 7, 2005.
Hiscock, John. "'Tippi Hedren Interview: 'Hitchcock Put Me in a Mental Prison.'" *The Telegraph*, December 24, 2012).
"Horror Island." *Internet Movie Database* (IMDb). Web. Accessed December 2, 2016.
"Horror of Dracula." *Internet Movie Database* (IMDb). Web. Accessed September 26, 2018.
"House of Dracula." *Internet Movie Database* (IMDb). Web. Accessed December 11, 2016.
"House of Frankenstein." *Internet Movie Database* (IMDb). Web. Accessed December 11, 2016.
"House of Usher." *Internet Movie Database* (IMDb). Web. Accessed January 3, 2020.
"House of Wax (1953)." *Internet Movie Database* (IMDb). Web. Accessed September 15, 2018.
"The House That Dripped Blood." *Internet Movie Database* (IMDb). Web. Accessed October 16, 2016.
"The Hunchback of Notre Dame (1939)." *Internet Movie Database* (IMDb). Web. Accessed January 25, 2020.
"Invasion of the Body Snatchers (1956)." *Internet Movie Database* (IMDb). September 20, 2018.
"The Invisible Man (1933)." *Internet Movie Database* (IMDb). Web. Accessed September 5, 2019.
"The Invisible Man Returns." *Internet Movie Database* (IMDb). Web. Accessed November 20, 2016.
"Island of Lost Souls." *Internet Movie Database* (IMDb). Web. Accessed January 21, 2020.
"Isle of the Dead." *Internet Movie Database* (IMDb). Web. Accessed January 29, 2020.
Jackson, Matthew. "13 Devilish Facts about *Rosemary's Baby*." *Mental Floss*, October 4, 2017. Web. Accessed May 1, 2020.
Jajkowski, Steve. "Terry Bennett and Joy: A Special Blend of Chicago Television." *Chicago Television*. Web. Accessed January 4, 2020.
"Jerry G. Bishop." *Wikipedia*. Web. Accessed January 16, 2020.
"Joe Bob Briggs." *Wikipedia*. Web. Accessed February 15, 2020.
"John Bloom." *Internet Movie Database* (IMDb). Web. Accessed February 15, 2020.
"John Zacherley." *Wikipedia*. Web. Accessed June 21, 2020.
Kelly, John. "The Horror! Homegrown Count Gore De Vol Is Back for Some Halloween High Jinks." *Washington Post*, October 23, 2018.
King, Susan. "Robert Wise's *The Haunting* Marks 50 Years with Russ Tamblyn." *Los Angeles Times*, October 29, 2013.
"King Kong (1931)." *Internet Movie Database* (IMDb). Web. Accessed January 21, 2020.
Kinsey, Wayne. *Hammer Films: The Bray Studios Years*. Richmond, VA: Reynolds & Hearn, 2005.
Kiska, Tim. "The Ghoul, AKA Legendary '70s TV Horror Host Ron Sweed, Has Died." *Detroit Free Press*, April 3, 2019.
Knight, Jacob. "The Amicus Vault of Horror: The Beast Must Die!" *Birth, Movies, Death*, December 22, 2017. Web. Accessed April 7, 2020.
Kremer, Deb. "Remember This: Those Who Recall The Cool Ghoul Are Now Hearing Bluhbluhbluhbluhbluh in Their Heads." *WCPO*, January 10, 2020. Web. Accessed March 13, 2020.
Lambie, Ryan. "The Strange History of The Blob Movies." *Den of Geek*, January 29, 2015. Web. Accessed April 14, 2020.
Lambie, Ryan. "The Texas Chainsaw Massacre: How Low-Budget Filmmaking Created a Classic." *Den of Geek*, October 1, 2019. Web. Accessed June 13, 2020.
Lang, Brent. "Tippi Hedren Recounts What Happened When She Turned Down Alfred Hitchcock's Advances." *Variety*, December 13, 2017.
"Larry Vincent." *Wikipedia*. Web. Accessed January 5, 2020.
"The Last Man on Earth." *Internet Movie Database* (IMDb). Web. Accessed February 5, 2020.
"Lawson Deming." *Wikipedia*. Web. Accessed January 10, 2020.
"The Legend of Hell House." *Internet Movie Database* (IMDb). Web. Accessed January 21, 2018.
"The Legend of Lizzie Borden." *Internet Movie Database* (IMDb). Web. Accessed April 2, 2020.
Maccash, Doug. "Morgus the Magnificent Fans Travel Back in Time with Sid Noel, Crazy Inventor of the Crazy Inventor." *The Times Picayune*, October 14, 2019.
"The Mad Ghoul." *Internet Movie Database* (IMDb). Web. Accessed December 8, 2016.
"Mad Love." *Internet Movie Database* (IMDb). Web. Accessed January 25, 2020.
Mallory, Michael. *Universal Studios Monsters: A Legacy of Horror*. New York: Universe Publishing, 2009.
"The Man They Could Not Hang." *Internet Movie Database* (IMDb). Web. Accessed December 11, 2016.
"The Man with Nine Lives." *Internet Movie Database* (IMDb). Web. Accessed December 11, 2016.
Mancini, Mark. "13 Thrilling Facts about *House of Wax*." *Mental Floss*, April 25, 2018. Web. Accessed March 29, 2020.
Mank, Gregory William. *Karloff and Lugosi: The Story of a Haunting Collaboration*. Jefferson, NC: McFarland, 1990.

"Mark of the Vampire." *Internet Movie Database* (IMDb). Web. Accessed January 25, 2020.
Markusen, Bruce. "Cooperstown Confidential: Baseball Meets Horror." *The Hardball Times*. Web. Accessed January 30, 2020.
"Masque of the Red Death." *Internet Movie Database* (IMDb). Web. Accessed February 11, 2020.
"Masque of the Red Death." *Wikipedia*. Web. Accessed February 11, 2020.
Masters, Tim. "BBFC Anniversary: How Banned Horror Film *Island of Lost Souls* Got a PG Rating." *BBC*, March 28, 2012. Web. Accessed April 4, 2020.
"Matthew Hopkins." *Encyclopedia Britannica*. Web. Accessed February 13, 2020.
McGee, Mark. *Faster and Furiouser: The Revised and Fattened Fable of American International Pictures*. Jefferson, NC: McFarland, 1996.
McKinley, Will. "Where's Barnabas? The Vampire-Free Night of *Dark Shadows*." April 4, 2014. Web. Accessed May 2, 2029.
"The Mephisto Waltz." *Internet Movie Database* (IMDb). Web. Accessed September 3, 2018.
Mitchell, Dawn. "Selwin Was Indy's First Horror-Movie Host." *Indianapolis Star*, October 25, 2015.
"Moona Lisa." *Wikipedia*. Web. Accessed January 5, 2020.
"Motion Picture Association of America." *Encyclopedia Britannica*. Web. Accessed March 15, 2020.
"Motion Picture Production Code." *Internet Movie Database* (IMDb). Web. Accessed January 5, 2020.
Movie Posters Heritage Auctions. Web. Accessed February 25, 2020.
"The Mummy (1932)." *Internet Movie Database* (IMDb). Web. Accessed October 24, 2016.
"The Mummy (1959)." *Internet Movie Database* (IMDb). Web. Accessed September 26, 2018.
"The Mummy's Ghost." *Internet Movie Database* (IMDb). Web. Accessed December 8, 2016.
"The Mummy's Hand." *Internet Movie Database* (IMDb). Web. Accessed December 2, 2016.
"Murders in the Rue Morgue." *Internet Movie Database* (IMDb). Web. Accessed October 28, 2016.
"The Mystery of Edwin Drood." *Internet Movie Database* (IMDb). Web. Accessed November 14, 2016.
"Mystery of Marie Roget." *Internet Movie Database* (IMDb). Web. Accessed December 8, 2016.
Nark, Jason. "A Cool Ghoul Looks Back." *Philadelphia Inquirer*, April 24, 2015.
Nehme, Farran Smith. "Terror, Suspense, and the Power of Suggestion in *The Haunting*." *Library of America*, October 19, 2016. Web. Accessed May 6, 2020.
"Night Gallery Pilot." *Internet Movie Database* (IMDb). Web. Accessed February 17, 2020.
"Night Monster." *Internet Movie Database* (IMDb). Web. Accessed December 8, 2016.
"Night of the Eagle." *Wikipedia*. Web. Accessed January 6, 2020.
"Night of the Living Dead (1968)." *Internet Movie Database* (IMDb). Web. Accessed February 20, 2020.
"The Night Stalker." *Internet Movie Database* (IMDb). Web. Accessed October 18, 2016.
"Nightmare Theater." *Internet Movie Database* (IMDb). Web. Accessed January 5, 2020.
"The Oblong Box." *Internet Movie Database* (IMDb). Web. Accessed February 15, 2020.
"The Oblong Box." *Wikipedia*. Web. Accessed February 15, 2020.
"The Old Dark House." *Internet Movie Database* (IMDb). Web. Accessed January 20, 2020.
"Once Upon a Time… in Hollywood… Annotated." *The AV Club*, August 2, 2019. Web. Accessed July 3, 2020.
"Paramount Pictures: American Corporation." *Encyclopedia Britannica*. Web. Accessed January 9, 2020.
Perez, Rodrigo. "Seven Things You Should Know about *Rosemary's Baby*." *Indie Wire*, October 31, 2012. Web. Accessed May 7, 2020.
Pfeiffer, Lee. "Bride of Frankenstein." *Encyclopedia Britannica*. Web. Accessed April 7, 2020.
"The Phantom of the Opera (1962)." *Internet Movie Database* (IMDb). Web. Accessed March 15, 2020.
"The Picture of Dorian Gray." *Internet Movie Database* (IMDb). Web. Accessed February 3, 2020.
"Pit and the Pendulum." *Internet Movie Database* (IMDb). Web. Accessed January 6, 2020.
"Plague of the Zombies." *Internet Movie Database* (IMDb). Web. Accessed February 25, 2020.
Poole, W. Scott. *Vampire: Dark Goddess of Horror*. New York: Soft Skull Press, 2014.
"Psycho (1960)." *Internet Movie Database* (IMDb). Web. Accessed January 4, 2020.
"Punishment Poll." *Grindhouse Database*. 21 November 2019. Web. Accessed May 11, 2020.
"The Quatermass Experiment." *Internet Movie Database* (IMDb). Web. Accessed September 26, 2018.
"The Raven (1963)." *Internet Movie Database* (IMDb). Web. Accessed January 7, 2020.
"The Raven (1963)." *Wikipedia*. Web. Accessed January 7, 2020.
"The Reptile." *Internet Movie Database* (IMDb). Web. Accessed February 25, 2020.
"The Return of Dracula." *Internet Movie Database* (IMDb). Web. Accessed October 2, 2018.
"The Return of the Vampire." *Internet Movie Database* (IMDb). Web. Accessed January 26, 2020.
"Revenge of Frankenstein." *Internet Movie Database* (IMDb). Web. Accessed September 26, 2018.
Rhodes, Gary Don Rhodes. *Lugosi: His Life in Film, on Stage, and in the Hearts of Horror Lovers*. Jefferson, NC: McFarland, 1997.
"Richard Koon." *Internet Movie Database* (IMDb). Web. Accessed January 13, 2020.
Riley, Philip J. *The Ghost of Frankenstein*. Absecon, NJ: MagicImage Filmbooks.
"Ron Sweed." *Wikipedia*. Web. Accessed January 10, 2020.
Rose, Jane. "15 Fascinating Facts About the Wicker Man." *Mental Floss*, July 22, 2016. Web. Accessed April 30, 2020.
"Sammy Terry." *Wikipedia*. Web. Accessed January 5, 2020.
"Screen Gems Isn't Scared." *The Billboard*, October 14, 1957.

"Secret of the Blue Room (1933)." *Internet Movie Database* (IMDb). Web. Accessed January 29, 2020.
"She-Wolf of London." *Internet Movie Database* (IMDb). Web. Accessed December 14, 2016.
Shelton, Jacob. "The Studio Sabotaged Psycho and the Fact That It Was Made Is Miraculous." *Groovy History*, August 29, 2019. Web. Accessed May 3, 2020.
Shelton, Jacob. "Vampira, The First Horror Host: Her Short, Frustrating Story." *Groovy History*, June 19, 2019. Web. Accessed April 25, 2020.
Simonson, Mark. "Price Was Right for TV Station." *Oneonta Daily Star*, October 27, 2008.
"Sir Graves Ghastly Presents." *Internet Movie Database* (IMDb). Web. Accessed January 10, 2020.
"The Skull." *Internet Movie Database* (IMDb). Web. Accessed February 11, 2020.
Smith, Don G. *Lon Chaney, Jr.: Horror Film Star, 1906–1973*. Jefferson, NC: McFarland, 1996.
"Son of Frankenstein." *Internet Movie Database* (IMDb). Web. Accessed November 18, 2016.
"Spider Baby." *Internet Movie Database* (IMDb). Web. Accessed February 12, 2020.
"Strait-Jacket." *Internet Movie Database* (IMDb). Web. Accessed February 5, 2020.
"Svengoolie." *Wikipedia*. Web. Accessed January 16, 2020.
"Tales from the Crypt (1972)." *Internet Movie Database* (IMDB). Web Accessed October 18, 2016.
"Tales of Terror." *Wikipedia*. Web. Accessed January 5, 2020.
"Terrence." *Egor's Chamber*. Web. Accessed January 5, 2020.
"The Texas Chain Saw Massacre (1974)." *Internet Movie Database* (IMDb). Web. Accessed March 14, 2017.
"Theater of Blood." *Internet Movie Database* (IMDb). Web. Accessed January 25, 2018.
"Them!" *Internet Movie Database* (IMDb). Web. Accessed September 20, 2018.
"The Thing from Another World." *Internet Movie Database* (IMDb). Web. Accessed September 15, 2018.
Thompson, Jeff. "Ken Bramming: Nashville's Transylvanian Horror Host." *Filmfax* no. 20 (May 1990).
Thompson, Jeff. *The Television Horrors of Dan Curtis*. Jefferson, NC: McFarland, 2009.
Thrash, Steven. "Retro Recommendations: Abbott and Costello Meet Frankenstein (1948)." *Rue Morgue*, February 15, 2018. Web. Accessed March 2, 2020.
Thrift, Matthew. "Peter Lorre: 10 Essential Performances." *The Buckminster Fuller Institute*, January 11, 2018. Web. Accessed January 22, 2020.
"Tigon British Film Productions." *Wikipedia*. Web. Accessed March 21, 2020.
"The Tingler." *Wikipedia*. Web. Accessed September 28, 2018.
Togyer, Jason. "Happy Halloween." *The Tube City Almanac*, October 31, 2017. Web. Accessed February 6, 2020.
"Twins of Evil." *Internet Movie Database* (IMDb). Web. Accessed January 20, 2018.
"The Uninvited." *Internet Movie Database* (IMDb). Web. Accessed February 3, 2020.
"Val Lewton." *Internet Movie Database* (IMDb). Web. Accessed January 26, 2020.
Vanno, Philip. "Monster Movie Matinee Documentary Celebrates Show's 50th Anniversary." *Utica Observer Dispatch*, October 27, 2014.
"The Vault of Horror." *Internet Movie Database* (IMDb). Web. Accessed March 20, 2020.
Voger, Mark. *Monster Mash: The Creepy, Kooky Monster Craze in America, 1957–1972*. Raleigh, NC: TwoMorrows Publishing, 2015.
"The Wacky World of Dr. Morgus." *Internet Movie Database* (IMDb). Web. Accessed January 5, 2020.
"The Walking Dead." *Internet Movie Database (IMDB)*. Web. Accessed January 25, 2020.
Wamsley, Jon. "The Abominable Dr. Phibes Still Hits the Right Notes After 45 Years." *Cryptic Rock*, July 13, 2016. Web. Accessed April 16, 2020.
Warshow, Robert. "Paul, the Horror Comics, and Dr. Wertham." *Commentary Magazine*, June 1954.
Watson, Elena M. *Television Horror Movie Hosts: 68 Vampires, Mad Scientists and Other Denizens of the Late-Night Airwaves Examines and Interviewed*. Jefferson, NC: McFarland, 2013.
"Weird Woman." *Internet Movie Database* (IMDb). Web. Accessed December 8, 2016.
"Werewolf of London." *Internet Movie Database* (IMDb). Web. Accessed November 14, 2016.
Wertham, Fredric. As quoted in 1954 Senate Subcommittee Transcripts, *The Comic Books*. Web. Accessed January 12, 2020.
"White Zombie." *Internet Movie Database* (IMDb). Web. Accessed January 30, 2020.
"Witchcraft." *Internet Movie Database* (IMDb). Web. Accessed March 30, 2020.
"Witchfinder General." *Internet Movie Database* (IMDb). Web. Accessed February 13, 2020.
"The Wolf Man." *Internet Movie Database* (IMDb). Web. Accessed October 24, 2016.
Wollstein, Hans J. "Cy Schindell Biography." *Fandango*. Web. Accessed January 5, 2020.
Wood, Jennifer M. "11 Things You Didn't Know about *The Texas Chainsaw Massacre*." *Esquire*, October 21, 2014. Web. Accessed May 20, 2020.

Index

Numbers in ***bold italics*** indicate pages with illustrations

Abbott, Bud 102–3, 113–14, 118
Abbott and Costello Meet Dr. Jekyll and Mr. Hyde 118–19
Abbott and Costello Meet Frankenstein 38, ***43***, 102, 104, 113, ***114***, 115, ***115***, 118–19; *see also Meet the Ghosts*
ABC Television 178, 186, 193–94, 199, 200, 209, 210
The Abominable Dr. Phibes 139, 183–84, 197
Academy Award(s) 61, 89–90, 102, 107, 110–11
Academy of Motion Picture Arts and Sciences 166
Ackerman, Forrest J 14–15
Acquanetta 52
acromegaly 53
Action in the Afternoon 18
Adams, Julie 120, ***121***
Adams, Nick 160–61
Addams, Charles 16, 18
The Addams Family (comic) 16
The Addams Family (TV series) 116–17
Alda, Alan 181–82
Alfred Hitchcock Presents (TV series) 15, 85, 173, 179
Alfred Hitchcock Presents: Stories That Scared Even Me 2
Alfred Hitchcock's Daring Detectives 2
Alfred Hitchcock's Ghostly Gallery 2, 4
Alfred Hitchcock's Haunted Houseful 1–2, 4
Alfred Hitchcock's Monster Museum 1
Alfred Hitchcock's Sinister Spies 2
Alfred Hitchcock's Spellbinders in Suspense 2
Allan, Michael 113
Allen, Lewis 106
Allied Artists 123
Alucard, Johnny (vampire) 193
Amazon 2
Amazon Prime 7
American Bandstand 18
American International Pictures (AIP) 3, 74, 139, 144, 149, 153, 157, 160, 167, 177, 181, 191, 204, 211
Ames, Ramsay 52
Amicus Productions 148, 159, 169–70, 181, 196, 205, 211
Anderson, Ernie 74–75, 82; *see also* Ghoulardi
Anderson, Richard 194
Andreas (werewolf) 104–5
Andrews, Dana 126–27
Angel of Death 170
Ankers, Evelyn 42–43, 50, 52–53, 65, 103
Annett, Paul 206
The Ape Man 2–3
Armstrong, Robert 95, ***96***
Arness, James 116, 122
Arnold, Edward 30
Arnold, Jack 119–20
Asher, Jane 157

Ashton, Roy 142, 163
Attack of the 50 Foot Woman 3
Atwater, Barry 187
Atwill, Lionel 30, 37, 41–42, 45, 60, 65, 68, 70
Aubert, Lenore 113
Aubrey, James 184

Baclanova, Olga 90
Baker, Diane 155
Baker, Roy Ward 189, 196
Baker, Tom 196
Balkan Wars 111
Balsam, Martin 136
Banbery, Fred 1
Barclay, John 71
The Baron and His Buddies 80
Baron Daemon 80; *see also* Price, Mike
Baron Frankenstein 130, 175
Baron Latos 67–68
Baron Meinster 140
Baron Samedi 204
Baron Sardonicus 144
Baroness Meinster 139
Barrett, Ray 163
Barrymore, Lionel 98–99
Bartlett, Bonnie 210
Barton, Charles 114
Bateman, Charles 186
Bates, Mrs. 137
Bates, Norman 136, ***137***, 138, 190, 212
Bates, Ralph 189
Bates house 137
Bates Motel 136
Bates Motel (TV series) 212
Batman (TV series) 38
Bava, Mario 140–41, 156
Baxt, George 146
Beacham, Stephanie 193
The Beast Must Die 148, 205–6
Beaumont, Charles 146, 153, 157
Becket 157
Bedlam 111–12
Beebe, Ford 45
Before I Hang 13, 62–63
Behind The Mask 13, 56
Belasco House 198
Bellac, Cousin 127–28
Bellamy, Ralph 43, 65, 168
Ben 181
Bennett, Jill 160

234 Index

Bennett, John 181
Bennett, Terry 13, 70; *see also* Marvin (the Nearsighted Madman)
Bennick, Dick 83; *see also* Dr. Paul Bearer
Berg, Louis 108
Beswick, Martine 189
Bewitched 209
Bey, Marki 204
The Big Valley 133
The Birds 138, 150–52, **152**, 153, 189–90
Bishop, Jerry 86; *see also* Svengoolie
Bishop, Julie 32
Bissett, Jacqueline 181–82
Black, Karen 210–11
The Black Cat (1934 film) 11, 32–34
Black Christmas 145, 209
Black Death 163
Black Friday 13, 61
Black Lagoon 119–20
The Black Room 13, 59–60
Black Sabbath 147, 153, 156
The Black Sleep 124–25
Black Sunday 140–41, 156
Blackmer, Sidney 168
Blacula 192–93, 198–99, 204
Blair, Janet 145
Blair, Linda 202
Blatty, William Peter 201
Blaxploitation 192–93, 203–5
The Blob (1958) 131–32, 136
Blobfest 132
Bloch, Robert 155, 160, 170, 212
"Block of Shock" (film package) 69, 88
Blondell, Joan 155
The Blood on Satan's Claw 182–83
Bloom, Claire 154
Bloom, John 85–86; *see also* Briggs, Joe Bob
The Bob Wilkins Super Horror Show 77
Bochner, Lloyd 179, 200
Bodega Bay 151, **152**
The Body Snatcher 103, 106, 108, 109, **109**, 110–11
Boehm, Karl 145
Bondi, Beulah 36
Bonomo, Joe 95
The Boogie Man Will Get You 13
Boone, Pat 158
Borden, Lizzie 210
Borgnine, Ernest 180
Borland, Carroll 98–99
Bozo the Clown 84
Brahm, John 107
Brain Damage 19
Bram Stoker's Dracula 203; *see also Dan Curtis' Dracula*
Bramming, Ken 73; *see also* Dr. Lucifur
The Bride (monster) 56, 58, **59**; *see also* The Monster's Mate
Bride of Frankenstein 5, 13–14, 21, **24**, 33, 37–38, 56–59, **59**, 80, 92, 131
The Brides of Dracula 139–40, 161
Briggs, Joe Bob 85–86, 212–14; *see also* Bloom, John
British Board of Censors 124
British Film Institute 98
Broadway 192
Bronson, Charles 117
The Brotherhood of Satan 186
Brown, Karl 60
Browne, Coral 197
Browning, Ricou 119–20
Browning, Tod 21–22, 24, 90–91, 98–99

Bruce, David 50
The Brute Man 54
A Bucket of Blood 134–35, 139
Burn, Witch, Burn 145–46; *see also Night of the Eagle*
Burns, Marilyn 208
Burnt Offerings 185, 203, 211
Burstyn, Ellen 202

Cabot, Bruce 95, **96**
Calling Dr. Death 12, 51–52
Capgras delusion 122
Captain Kronos—Vampire Hunter 207
Captive Wild Woman 13
Cardille, Bill "Chilly Billy" 78–79
Carfax Abbey 21, **23**, 41
Carlson, Richard 103, 120
Carlson, Veronica 172, 175
Carnival of Souls 148–49
Carpenter, John 116
Carradine, John 52, 56, 67–69, 73, 79, 124–25, 179, 194, **195**
Carreras, James 175
Carreras, Michael 141
Carter, Bob 72; *see also* Sammy Terry
The Case of Charles Dexter Ward (novella by Lovecraft) 153
Casey, Bernie 194
Cassavetes, John 168, **169**
"Casting the Runes" (short story by M.R. James) 126
Castle, William 133–34, 144, 154–55, 162, 169, 206
Castle of Frankenstein 15
Castle Sardonicus 144
The Cat Creeps 12
Cat People 103–4, 115
Cater, John 207
Cathedral of Notre Dame 101
Catholic Church 202
Catholic League of Decency 141
Chambliss, Woody 194
Chaney, Lon, Jr. 12, 33–34, 41–43, **43**, 45–47, **47**, 48–49, **49**, 50–53, 56, 64–65, **66**, 67, **67**, 68–69, 101, **105**, 113–14, 119, 124–26, 141–42, 147, 153, 157–58, 165–66
Chaney, Lon, Sr. 22, 101, 148
Channel 4 (Britain) 98
Chaplin, Charlie 100
Chapman, Ben 119–20, **121**
Charlie's Angels 200
Chiller Cinema 74
Chiller Theater (Indianapolis) 72
Chiller Theater (New York) 2–5, 19–20
Chiller Theater (Pittsburgh) 78–79
Chinatown Squad 11
Christie, John 190
Christie, Julie 200–1
Christmas Eve 188
Church of Satan 168
Cinema Insomnia 212
CinemaScope 139
City of the Dead 148; *see also Horror Hotel*
Clare, Diane 163
Clark, Bob 209
Clark, Dick 18
Clark, Lisa 75–76; *see also* Cosmomina; Moona Lisa
Clark Sports Center 1
Clemens, Brian 207
Clive, Colin 27, 36, 57, **59**, 99–100
Cobb, Lee J. 200
Cobert, Bob 203
Coglin, Russ 70–71; *see also* Terrence

Cohen, Stewart 124
Cold War 122
Collins, Barnabas 177–78, *179*, 199
Collins, Joan 187
Collinson, Madeleine 190–91
Collinson, Mary 190–91
Collinwood *185*
Columbia Pictures 10, 56–57, 59–60, 62–63, 69, 105, 112, 126
Comics Code Authority 10, 15
Comics Magazine Association of America 10
Communism 122–23
The Conjuring 213
The Conqueror Worm 166; see also *Witchfinder General*
Conrad, Michael 198
Conway, Tom 104
Cook, Elisha, Jr. 133, *169*
The Cool Ghoul 81–82; see also Von Hoene, Dick
"The Cool Ghoul" 18; see also Zacherley, John
Cooper, Merian B. 95
Cooper, Violet Kemble 36
Cooperstown Antiquarian Book Fair 1
Corman, Roger 74, 134–35, 139, 142–44, 146, 150, 152–53, 157, 161
Cornell, Lillian 50
Cosmomina 75; see also Clark, Lisa; Moona Lisa
Costello, Lou 102–3, 113–15, *115*, 118–19
Cotten, Joseph 183
Count Alucard 48, *49*
Count Floyd 79
Count Gore 84; see also Dyszel, Dick
Count Karnstein 191
Count Mora 98–99
Count Shockula 83; see also Bennick, Dick
Count Yorga 176–77, 191
Count Yorga, Vampire 176–77, *177*, 199, 204–5
Countess Von Stauffenberger 84
Court, Hazel 150, 157
Crawford, Joan 154–55, 174
Creature Feature (TV show in Nashville) 73
Creature Feature (TV show in St. Petersburg) 83
Creature Feature (TV show in Washington, D.C.) 84
"Creature Features" (film package) 69, 88
Creature Features (generic name for TV show) 5
Creature Features (TV show in New York City) 3, 5
Creature Features (TV show in San Francisco Bay Area) 77
Creature from the Black Lagoon 103, 119–20, *121*, 124, 194
The Creature Walks Among Us 120
The Creeper 53–54
The Creeping Flesh 195–96
Creepshow (1982 film) 188
Cregar, Laird 106–8
Crisp, Donald 107
Cromwell, Oliver 166
Cronenberg, David 131
Crowhaven Farm 178–80, 186–87, 193
Crowley, Aleister 198
The Crucible 179
The Crypt Keeper 187
Cully, Zara 204
Cummins, Peggy 127
Curse of Frankenstein 123, 125–26, 128, 130, 135
Curse of the Demon 104, 126–27, 130; see also *Night of the Demon*
The Curse of the Werewolf 141–42, 205
Curtis, Dan 178, 184–86, 194–95, 203, 210–11
Curtis Helldiver military planes *97*
Curtiz, Michael 100

Cushing, Peter 6, 125–26, 128, 130, 135, 140, 146, 158–60, 162–63, 170, 172, 175, 181, 187–88, 190–91, 193, 195–96, 205
The Cyclops 2
Czech National Archives 98

Daily Telgraph 130
Dakota Apartments 168
Dallas Times-Herald 85
Damon, Mark 139
Dan Curtis' Dracula 203; see also *Bram Stoker's Dracula*
Danger Woman 12
A Dangerous Game 11
Daniel, Jennifer 163
Daniell, Henry 108, 110
Dante, Michael 180
Darby, Kim 200
Darcy the Mail Girl 213; see also Prince, Diana
Daring Detectives 2
Dark Shadows (TV series) 178, *179*, 194, 199, 203
Darnell, Linda 107
Davenport, Nigel 203
David, Thayer 178
Davies, Rupert 167, 172
Davis, Jack 8
Davis, Joan 103
Davis, Ossie 174
Davison, Bruce 180
Dawn of the Dead 92, 172
Dead Man's Eyes 12
Dead of Night 112–13
Deane, Hamilton 21
Death Row 125
Dee, Frances 104
Deeley, Michael 206
Dekker, Albert 102
Dello Stritto, Frank 120
Del Toro, Guillermo 107
Demarest, William 200
Deming, Lawson J. 79–80; see also Sir Graves Ghastly
Denning, Richard 120
de Souza, Edward 147
Destination Unknown 11
De Toth, Andre 117–18
The Devil 181, 191
The Devil Commands 13, 63–64
The Devil Rides Out 164, 170; see also *The Devil's Bride*
The Devil's Bride 170; see also *The Devil Rides Out*
The Devil's Brood 65; see also *House of Frankenstein*
Dickens, Charles 33
Die, Monster, Die! 160–61; see also *Monster of Terror*
Dmytryk, Edward 64
Dr. Creep 82; see also Dr. Death; Hobart, Barry
Dr. Cyclops 102
Dr. Death 82; see also Dr. Creep; Hobart, Barry
Dr. Diabolo 169
Dr. E. Nick Witty 80–81; see also Milair, Alan
Dr. Gangrene 74; see also Underwood, Larry
Dr. Gangrene's Cinetarium 74
Dr. Jekyll and Mr. Hyde 27, 88–90
Dr. Jekyll and Sister Hyde 189
Dr. Lucifur 73–74; see also Bramming, Ken
Doctor Madblood 85 ; see also Harrell, Jerry
Doctor Madblood Presents 85
Doctor Madblood's Movie 85
Dr. Paul Bearer 83; see also Bennick, Dick
Dr. Phibes Rises Again 177, 191–92
Dr. Schreck 159
Dr. Shock 84–85; see also Zawislak, Joseph
Doctor Sleep 213

Dr. Terror's House of Horrors 148, 159, 172
Doctor Who 196
Donlevy, Brian 123
Don't Be Afraid of the Dark 200
Don't Look Now 200–1
Dorian Gray (monster) 110
Douglas, Melvyn 92
Dracula (monster) 10, 16, 21–24, 31, 36 38, 48, 49, *49*, 50, 55, 65, 67–68, 79–80, 98, 104–5, 113, *114*, 115, *115*, 118, 120, 126–29, *129*, 132, 139–40, 142, 161–64, 170, 172, 176–78, 187, 192–93, 203, 205, 212
Dracula (1931 film) 5, 11, 18, 21–22, 23–24, **23–24**, 25, 27–31, 33, 36, 41–42, 55, 71, 80, 88, 90–91, 98, 104–5, 113, 128, 203, 211
Dracula (novel) 8, 21, 128, 203
Dracula AD, 1972 193
Dracula Has Risen from the Grave 172
Dracula—Prince of Darkness 140, 161–62, 172
Dracula's Daughter 11, 36–37, 47–48
"Dracula's Guest" (Bram Stoker's short story) 36
Drake, Frances 36, 99
Dudgeon, Elspeth 93
Dudgeon, John 93
Duffell, Peter 181
Dugan, John 208
Dullea, Keir 209
Du Maurier, Daphne 151, 201
The Dunwich Horror 161
Dyszel, Dick 84; *see also* Count Gore de Vol

Ealing Studios 112
Earles, Harry 90
Eastwood, Clint 180
Ebert, Roger 145
EC Comics 8–9, 196
Edmonds, Louis 178
Eilbacher, Cindy 179
"The Electric Man" (short story) 41
Elliott, Denholm 181, 196
Elliott, Sam 188
Elvira 20, 76–77, 212; *see also* Peterson, Cassandra
Elvira, Mistress of the Dark (film) 77
Elvira's Movie Macabre 76–77
EMI Films 206
Empire of the Ants 188
Empire State Building 96, **97**
Enemy Agent 11
Erickson, Leif 45, 155
Evans, Maurice 168
Everett, Bill 81; *see also* Lape, Willard
Ewing, Barbara 172
The Exorcist 6, 160, 201–2, 211

The Face Behind the Mask 13, 63
Facebook 87
Fahey, Myrna 139
Famous Monsters of Filmland 14–15, 163
Farmer, Suzan 162
Farrow, Mia 168, *169*
The Fearmakers 127
Feldstein, Al 8
female vampire 36
Festival of the New Wine 46
Field Communications 87
Fields, W.C. 22
Finch, Jon 189–90
Finch, Peter 146
Fisher, Terence 125–26, 130, 136, 140–41, 147–48, 158, 162, 170, 172, 175–76

Flaherty, Joe 79
Flanders, Ed 210
Fleming, Eric 74
Florey, Robert 28, 63
The Fly (1958) 131–32
The Fly (1986) 131
The Flying Nun 76
Fontaine, Joan 164
Food of the Gods 188
"For Sadists Only" 130
Foran, Dick 40–41
Ford, Wallace 40, 57
Foster, Barry 189–90
"Foul Play" (comic book story) 8–9
Fox, Sidney 28
Francis, Freddie 159–60, 172, 195–96
Frankenhooker 19
Frankenstein (monster) 4, 10, 14, 25–26, **26**, 27, 29, 31, 37–39, **39**, 45–46, **47–48**, 54–58, **59**, 60, 64–66, **66**, 67, **67**, 68–69, 80, 97, 108, **109**, 113, **114**, 118–20, 125–26, 130, 132, 142, 156, 163–64, 170, 175–76, 212
Frankenstein (1931 film) 5, 11, 14, 18, 21–23, **24**, 25, **26**, 27–28, 31, 36–38, 46, 57–59, 80, 88, 90, 92, 126, 211
Frankenstein (novel) 25, 57, 59, 213
The Frankenstein Chronicles 213
Frankenstein Meets The Wolf Man 3, 11–12, 45–46, **47–48**, 65
Frankenstein Must Be Destroyed 175–76
Franklin, Pamela 198–99
Freaks 90–91, 98–99
Frenzy 151, 164, 189–90
Freund, Karl 24, 29–30, 100
Frid, Jonathan 24, 178, **179**, 184, 199
Friday the 13th 209
Friedkin, William 202
Friedlander, Louis 35; *see also* Landers, Lew
"Fright Night" (film package) 88
Fright Night (generic name for TV show) 88
Fright Night (1985 film) 76, 198
Fright Night (TV show in Indianapolis) 13
Fright Night (TV show in Los Angeles) 76
Fright Night (TV show in New York) 3
Frogs 188–89
The Frozen Ghost 12, 52–53
Frye, Dwight 23, **24**, 60
Fulton, John P. 36, 39, 42

Gabor, Zsa Zsa 74
Gaines, William 9–10
Gallow, Janet Ann 64, **66**
Gangelin, Paul 50
Gargoyles 193–94
Gaumont British Picture Corporation 96
Gavin, John 136
Gein, Ed 208
George, Thomas 73
George Eastman House 92
The George Gobel Show 20
Gertsman, Maury 54
Get Out 202, 213
Get Smart 76
The Ghost and Mrs. Muir (TV series) 179
The Ghost of Frankenstein 13–14, 46, **47**, 56, 64–65, **66**
The Ghoul 74, 82–83; *see also* Sweed, Ron
The Ghoul (book) 83
The Ghoul (film) 96–98
Ghoulardi 74–75, 79, 82; *see also* Anderson, Ernie
Gidding, Nelson 154
Gill Man 119–20, *121*, 194

Gilling, John 163
Glenn, Scott 194
Glover, Crispin 181
Goat of Mendes 170
Gogos, Basil 15
Gordon, Bert I. 74
Gordon, Ruth 168
The Gorgon (film) 158–59
The Gorgon (monster) 13, 158
Gough, Michael 147, 159
Grand Guignol Theater 99
Grauman, Walter 180
Graves, Doug 87
Gray, Charles 170
The Great Impersonation 11
Green, Nigel 160
Green Hell 40
Greer, Dabbs 117
Gregg, Virginia 179
Grella, George 206
Grey, Nan 38
Grier, Pam 198
Grier, Rosey 188
Grinde, Nick 56, 61–63
Grodin, Charles 168
Guest, Val 123
The Guinness Book of World Records 124
Gwenn, Edmund 122
Gwynn, Michael 130
Gwynne, Anne 52

Haggard, Piers 182
Haig, Sid 165–66
Haitian voodoo 196
Hall, Grayson 178, 184–85, 194
Hall, Manly P. 61
Haller, Daniel 150, 161
Halloween 19, 72, 76, 80, 82, 85, 188, 204, 209
Halperin, Edward 91
Halperin, Victor 91
Halperin Brothers 92
Hamilton, Margaret 194, **195**
Hammer Films 3, 5, 25, 123–28, **129**, 130, 132, 135, 139–42, 147–48, 158–59, 161–64, 170, 172–73, 175–77, 181, 189–91, 193, 195, 205, 207, 211
Hammer's House of Horror 126
Hangover Square 106–8
Hannibal 212
Hansen, Gunnar 208
Hardwicke, Cedric 38, 40, 64–65, 97, 101
Harrell, Jerry 85; *see also* Doctor Madblood
Harrington, Curtis 92
Harris, Julie 154
Harvey, Herk 149
Hatfield, Hurd 110–11
Hatton, Rondo 53–54
The Haunt of Fear (comic) 8–10
The Haunted Palace 152–53
The Haunting 153–54
The Haunting of Hill House 154, 213
Hawks, Howard 116
Hayden, Linda 182, 205
Hayers, Sidney 146
Hays Code 32, 37, 89, 94, 97–100, 136, 138. 166, 168, 175, 190; *see also* Motion Picture Production Code
Hedison, David 131
Hedren, Tippi 150–51, **152**
Heilbron, Lorna 196
Helmond, Katherine 210

Hendry, Ian 197, 207
Hereditary 213
Herman, Eleanor 84
Hessler, Gordon 173
Heston, Charlton 156
Hickox, Douglas 197
Hill, Jack 165
Hilligoss, Candace 149
Hitchcock, Alfred 1–2, 4, 6, 45, 133, 136–39, 148, 150–52, **152**, 164, 189–90, 208, 212
Hitchcock, Patricia 190
Hitler, Adolf 46
Hobart, Barry 82; *see also* Dr. Death
Hobart, Rose 111
Hobson, Valerie 33, 57
Hoerner, Charles 111
Hoffman, Dustin 70
Hogan, James 50
Hold That Ghost 102–3
Holden, Gloria 36
Holmes, Katie 200
Holmes, Sherlock 44, 53
Homans, Robert 45
Homolka, Oscar 144
Hooper, Tobe 116, 208
Hopkins, Matthew 166–67
Hopkins, Miriam 89
horror (definition of), 6
Horror Hotel (film) 148; *see also* City of the Dead
Horror Hotel (TV show) 212
Horror Island 11, 41–42
horror noir 50
Horror of Dracula 123, 127–28, **129**, 130, 135, 139–40, 161, 172, 176
The Horror of It All 158
Horror of Party Beach 77
Horror Theater 85
Hotel 164
Hough, John 197
House of Dark Shadows 178, **179**, 184
House of Dracula 13–14, 56, 68–69
House of Frankenstein 13–14, 56, 65–66, **67**, 68, 85; *see also* The Devil's Brood
House of Horrors 12, 53–54
House of Shock 72
House of Usher 139, 142, 144, 146, 205
House of Wax 117–119, 124
House on Haunted Hill 133, 136
The House That Dripped Blood 147, 159, 181
Howard, Shemp 103
The Howling 135
Hudson River 185
Hugo, Victor 101
Hull, Cortlandt 119
Hull, Henry 33–34
The Hunchback of Notre Dame (1923) 10, 22
The Hunchback of Notre Dame (1939) 101–2, 108
Hunnicutt, Gayle 198
Huntington, Lawrence 173
Hussey, Olivia 209
Hussey, Ruth 106–7
Hutton, Jim 200
Hyde, Mr. (monster) 89, 118
Hyde, Mrs. Edwina 189
Hyman, Prudence 158

I Walked with a Zombie 103–4
Imhotep 29, 40
Indianapolis Star 71

238 Index

Inner Sanctum (films) 51–53
"Inner Sanctum" (radio program) 50
Invasion of the Body Snatchers 122–24
The Invisible Man (monster) 31, 38, 119
The Invisible Man (1933) 11, 30–31, 35, 56–57, 92, 95
The Invisible Man (2020 film) 213
The Invisible Man Returns 11, 38, 40
The Invisible Man's Revenge 13
The Invisible Ray 11, 35–36
Irving, George **49**
Island of Lost Souls 94–95
Isle of Doomed Men 13
Isle of the Dead 111
It! 198
It's a Wonderful Life 31

Jack the Ripper 106, 190
Jackson, Kate 184, 199–200
Jackson, Shirley 154, 213
Jacoby, Michael 44
James, M.R. 126
Janson, Horst 207
Jaws 202, 211
Jeepers Creepers (TV show) 3
The Jeffersons 204
Jeffrey, Peter 183, 191
Jessel, Patricia 148
The Jobblewocky Place 70
Joe Bob's Drive-In Theater 85
Johann, Zita 29
Johns, Mervyn 112
Johnson, Richard 154
Jones, Carolyn 117
Jones, Duane 171
Jones, Freddie 175
Jones, L.Q. 186
The Jungle Captive 13, 52
Jurgens, Curd 181–82, 196

KABC (Los Angeles) 16–17
Kaiser Broadcasting 86
Karlen, John 178
Karloff, Boris 6, 12, 14–15, 25–26, **26**, 27, 29–38, **39**, 40, 42–43, 50, 54–56, 58–59, **59**, 60–66, **66–67**, 68–69, 82, 85, 92, **93**, 96–101, 108, 109, *109*, 110–12, 118–20, 126, 149–50, 156, 160–61, 164–65, 204, 211
KCRA (Sacramento) 77
Kefauver, Sen. Estes 9
Keir, Andrew 162
Keith, Ian 22
Kellaway, Cecil 40
Kelljan, Bob 177, 199
Kemp, Valli 191
Kennedy, George 155
Kenton, Earle C. 95
Kerr, John 143
Keyes, Evelyn 62
KFMB (San Diego) 76
KHJ (Los Angeles) 20, 76
Kidder, Margot 209
Killers from Space 2
King, Stephen 188, 213
King Kong (1933 film) 3, 6, 80, 95, 96, **96**, **97**, 102
King of the Dead 30; *see also The Mummy*
Kirk, Phyllis 117
KMOX (St. Louis) 76
Knowles, Patric 44
KOGO (San Diego) 75
Kolchak: The Night Stalker 187

Komeda, Krzysztof 169
Kong (monster) 95, **96-97**
Koon, Richard 83
Kosleck, Martin 53–54
Koz, Richard 86–87; *see also* Son of Svengoolie; Svengoolie
KRON (San Francisco) 70–71
Kruger, Otto 36
KTLA (Los Angeles) 76–77
KTVU (San Francisco) 77
KTXL (Oakland) 77

Lacey, Catherine 165
Ladd, Cheryl 200
Laemmle, Carl, Jr. 33, 37
Lamia, Queen of the Dark 212
Lamont, Charles 118
Lanchester, Elsa 56, 58–59, **59**, 180
Landers, Lew 35, 105; *see also* Friedlander, Louis
Lang, Charles 107
Lange, Hope 179
Lansbury, Angela 110–11
Lape, Willard 81; *see also* Everett, Bill
Lassie 54
The Last Drive-In with Joe Bob Briggs 86
The Last Man on Earth 155–56
Last Warning 11
Laughton, Charles 92–95, 101
La Vey, Anton 168
Lawford, Peter 110
Lawson, Richard 198
"Leatherface" 208–9
LeBorg, Reginald 52, 124–25
Lecter, Hannibal 212
Lederer, Francis 127–28
Lee, Anna 111–12
Lee, Christopher 6, 24, 32, 125–28, **129**, 130, 135, 139–40, 147–48, 156, 158–62, 170, 172, 178, 181, 187, 193, 195–96, 203, 206–7
The Legend of Hell House 197
The Legend of Lizzie Borden 209–10
Leigh, Janet 136–37, 190
Leigh-Hunt, Barbara 190
Leroux, Gaston 147
Lewin, Albert 110
Lewis, Al 194, **195**
Lewis, Mercy 179
Lewton, Val 103–4, 108–11
Library of Congress 123
Life 16
Little House on the Prairie 117
Locke, Sondra 180
Lockhart, Calvin 205
Lockhart, June 54
The Lodger 106–8
Lom, Herbert 147
London After Midnight 98
London Opera House 147
Long, Richard 133
Lord of the Dead 204
Lorre, Peter 37, 56, 63, 69, 99–100, 124, 146–47, 149–50
Los Angeles Times 108
Lost in Space 54
The Lost World 96
The Love Boat 164
Love Story 183
Lovecraft, H.P. 8, 153, 160
Lowery, Robert 52
Lubin, Arthur 61

Lugosi, Bela 6, 12, 22, **23**, 24–25, 28, 30, 32–38, **39**, 42–46, **47–48**, 49–50, 56–57, 61, 64–65, 68, 73, 76, 79–80, 91–92, 94–95, 98–99, 101, 104–6, 108–10, 113, **114**, 115, **115**, 119–20, 124–28, 156, 177–78, 192, 203, 211
Lukas, Paul 30
lycanthropy 33, 141
Lyndhurst Mansion 184

M (film) 99
Macardle, Dorothy 106
MacGinnis, Niall 127
Mad Doctor of Market Street 11
The Mad Ghoul 12, 50
Mad Love 99–100
Mad magazine 8
Mad Theater 85
Madhouse 205
Magee, Patrick 157
The Magnificent Ambersons 103
Majors, Lee 155
Maltin, Leonard 119
Mamoulian, Rouben 89
Mamuwalde 192, 198
Man Made Monster 11, 41–42
The Man They Could Not Hang 13, 60–63
The Man Who Cried Wolf 11
The Man Who Lived Twice 13
The Man with Nine Lives 13, 62
Mandel, Joseph 40; *see also* May, Joe
Mank, Gregory 35, 106–7
Manners, David 23, 32–33
Mannix 76
Manos: The Hands of Fate 6
Manson, Charles 168
March, Fredric 89
Mark of the Vampire 34, 98–99
Marquis de Sade 159–60
Marshall, William 192–93, 198, 199, **199**
Martin, Strother 186
Marvin 13, 70–71; *see also* Bennett, Terry
M*A*S*H 181
Maslansky, Paul 204
The Masque of the Red Death 157
Massey, Anna 196
Massey, Daniel 196
Massey, Raymond 92, 196
Matheson, Richard 146, 150, 155–56, 187, 197–98
Maxwell, Frank 153
May, Joe 39–40; *see also* Mandel, Joseph
McCambridge, Mercedes 202
McCarthy, Kevin 122–23
McCarthyism 123
McCowan, George 188
McCowen, Alec 164, 190
McCown, Russ 73–74; *see also* Sir Cecil Creape
McDougal's House of Horrors 113
McDowall, Roddy 76, 173–74, 198
McEveety, Bernard 186
McGavin, Darren 187, 194, **195**
McGee, Vonetta 192–93
McKeand, Nigel 200
McKinley, Will 184
McQueen, Steve 131–32
Me-TV 7, 86–87
Medusa 158
Meet the Ghosts 113; *see also* Abbott and Costello Meet Frankenstein
The Mephisto Waltz 181–82
Merchant, Vivien 190

Meredith, Burgess 169–70
MGM Studios 90, 99, 154, 184
Milair, Alan 80–81; *see also* Dr. E. Nick Witty
Miles, Vera 136
Milland, Ray 106–7, 188
Miller, Arthur 179
Miller, Dick 134–35
Miller, Jason 202
Mission: Impossible 76
Mr. Lobo 212
Mr. Sardonicus 144
Mr. X 73
Mitchell, Don 198
Monster Bash convention 119
Monster Chiller Horror Theater 79
Monster Mag 15
Monster Movie Matinee 80–81
Monster of Terrror 160; *see also Die, Monster, Die!*
Monster Vision 86
The Monster's Mate 56; *see also* The Bride (monster)
Montgomery, Elizabeth 209–10
Moona Lisa 75–76; *see also* Clark, Lisa; Cosmomina
Moore, Eva 92–93
Morgan, Ralph 44
Morgus (the Magnificent) 13, 72–73, 78–79; *see also* Rideau, Sid Noel
Morgus Presents 73
Morley, Robert 197
Motion Picture Association of America 166
Motion Picture Production Code 32, 89
The Movie Channel 85
Moxey, John 148, 186
The Mummy (monster) 10, 29, 31, 40, 42, 52, 60, 65, 97, 113, 120, 135, 142, 156
The Mummy (1932) 11, 28–31, 33, 40, 52, 56; *see also* King of the Dead
The Mummy (1959) 135–36
The Mummy's Curse 13
The Mummy's Ghost 12, 52, 135
The Mummy's Hand 11, 40, 135
The Mummy's Tomb 12, 52, 135
Munro, Caroline 183, 193, 207
The Munsters 34, 75, 194, **195**
Murders in the Rue Morgue 11, 27–28
"Murders in the Rue Morgue" (short story by Edgar Allan Poe) 44
Murdoch, Rupert 87
My Three Sons 200
Mystery of Edwin Drood 11, 33
Mystery of Marie Roget 11, 44
Mystery of the White Room 11
Mystery Science Theater 3000 6

Naish, J. Carrol 51, 66–67
Napier, Alan 38, 40, 107
Nashville Network 74
National Film Registry 123
NBC Television 174
Neame, Christopher 193
Neill, Roy William 46, 60
Netflix 212–13
Neumann, Kurt 30, 131
New Orleans Public Library 73
The New Shock Theater 82
New York Mets 3
New York Times 32, 104
New York Yankees 3
Newland, John 200
Nicholas, Denise 193

Index

Nicholson, Jack 150
Night Key 11
Night Monster 11, 44–45
Night of Dark Shadows 184, 185, **185**, 186
Night of Terror 13, 56–57
Night of the Demon 126; *see also Curse of the Demon*
Night of the Eagle 145; *see also Burn, Witch, Burn*
Night of the Living Dead 6, 77–78, 84, 92, 156, 162, 171, 204
The Night Stalker 186–87, 193–94
The Night Strangler 187, 194, **195**
Nightmare (film) 11
Nightmare (TV show) 70
Nightmare Theater 72
North, Virginia 183, 191
North by Northwest 190
Nosferatu (film) 105, 203
Nosferatu (monster) 16
Nurmi, Maila 16–17, **17**, 18, 20, 72, 76; *see also* Vampira
Nyby, Christian 116
Nye, Louis 75; *see also* Zombo

Oakland, Simon 187, 194
The Oblong Box 172–73
O'Brien, Willis 95
O'Dea, Judith 171
Ogilvy, Ian 165, 167
O'Hara, Maureen 101
Ohmart, Carol 133
Oland, Warner 34
Old City Ice House 73
The Old Dark House 30, 57, 92, 93, **93**, 94, 107
The Omega Man 156
Osbourne, Ozzy 156
Ouija board 187
Ouspenskaya, Maria 43–44

Paget, Debra 153
Palance, Jack 170, 203, 211
Paramount 27, 88–90, 112, 136–37
Parker, Eddie 46, 118
Parker, Lara 185, **185**
Parkins, Barbara 181–82
Passions (TV series) 178
Patric, Jason 202
Patrick, Butch 34
Patrick, Milicent 119
Pavlov Theory 180
Pearce, Guy 200
Pearce, Jacqueline 163
The Pearl of Death 53–54
Peel, David 140
Peeping Tom 145, 209
Penney, Ralph 64
Penny Dreadful (TV series) 212
Percepto 134
Perkins, Anthony 136–37, **137**, 190
Perkins, Gil 46
Perry, Roger 177
Peterson, Cassandra 20, 76–77; *see also* Elvira
The Phantom (monster) 147
The Phantom of the Opera (1925) 10, 22
Phantom of the Opera (1962) 147–48
"The Phantom of the Opry" 74
The Picture of Dorian Gray 110–11
Pierce, Jack P. 25, 29, 34, 38, **39**, 40, 42–43, **43**, 65, 142
Pillow of Death 12
Pink Panther films 147
Pit and the Pendulum 139, 142–43, **143**, 144

Pitt, Ingrid 181, 206
The Plague of the Zombies 92, 162–63
Plan 9 from Outer Space 2, 20, 125
Playboy 86, 191
Pleasence, Donald 167
Pleshette, Suzanne 150–51
Poe, Edgar Allan 8, 28, 33, 35, 44, 74, 76, 134–35, 139, 142, 144, 146, 149, 153, 157, 166, 170, 172
Polanski, Roman 168
Poltergeist 107
Porter, Don 54
Powell, Michael 145, 162
Price, Mike 80; *see also* Baron Daemon
Price, Vincent 6, 38–40, 73, 117–18, 131, 133, 139, 142, **143**, 144, 146–47, 149–50, 153, 155–157, 166–67, 172–73, 177, 182–84, 191–92, 197, 204–5
Prince, Diana 213; *see also* Darcy the Mail Girl
Psycho 15, 133, 136–37, **137**, 138, 145, 148, 150–152, 170, 181, 189–90
Punishment Poll 144
Puppet Master films 144

Quarry, Robert 176–77, **177**, 187, 191, 204–5
Quasimodo 101
The Quatermass Xperiment 123–25
Queen of Outer Space 74

Radio City Music Hall 96
Rains, Claude 31, 33, 38–39, 42–43, 101
Randolph, Jane 113, **115**
Rasulala, Thalmus 193
Rathbone, Basil 37, 124, 146–47 204
The Raven (1935) 11, 34–35, 41
The Raven (1963) 149–50, 153
Rear Window 151, 190
Redgrave, Michael 112
Reed, Donna 110
Reed, Oliver 141–42, 205
Reeves, Michael 165–67, 172–73
Reicher, Frank 52
Reported Missing 11
The Reptile 163–64
The Return of Count Yorga 177
The Return of Dracula 127–28
The Return of the Vampire 104–5, **105**
The Revenge of Frankenstein 130
Revenge of the Creature 120
Revere, Anne 64, 110
Revill, Clive 198
Richardson, Ralph 97, 187
Riddick Building 72
Rideau, Sid Noel 72–73; *see also* Morgus (the Magnificent)
Ridges, Stanley 61
Rigg, Diana 197
Ripper, Michael 163
River of Life 191
RKO Pictures 3, 96, 101, 103–4, 108, 111–12, 115
Robson, Mark 111–12
Rod Serling's Night Gallery 85, 173–74
Rod Serling's The Twilight Zone 15
Roeg, Nicolas 201
Roku 7, 84, 212
Roland 12, 18, 84
Rolfe, Guy 144
Rolling Stone 86
Romero, George 78, 156, 171, 188, 204
Rondo Awards 54
Rosemary's Baby 6, 160, 168–69, **169**, 182

Rosen, Philip 44
Rossi, Genoveva 141–42, 150, 168, 184
Rowan and Martin's Laugh-In 81
Roxy Theater 96
Russell, Gail 106
Russell, Ray 144
Russell, Robert 168
Russo, John 78

"St. Creaturesburg" 83
St. Elsewhere 210
Salt, Jennifer 194
Sanders, George 107, 110–11
Sangster, Jimmy 162
Sanzone, Zachary 171–72
Satan 193, 202
Satanism 148, 167–68, 170, 182
Satan's School for Girls 185, 199–200
Satan's Seeds 186
Saturday Night Dead 82
Saturday Night Live 77, 82
Saxon, John 209
Sayre, George W. 60
"Scare Trick" 133
Schanzer, Karl 165
Schoedsack, Ernest B. 95, 102
Schreck, Max 159, 203
science fiction (definition of) 6
Scorcese, Martin 107
Scotland Yard 40
Scott, Kathryn Leigh 178
Scott, Ridley 116
Scream Blacula Scream 198, 199, **199**, 204
Scream-In (TV show in Cincinnati) 81–82
Scream-In (TV show in Philadelphia) 85
Screaming Yellow Theater with Host Svengoolie 86
Screaming Yellow Zonkers 86
Screen Gems 5, 10, 12–13, 16, 55–56
Scroll of Life 135
SCTV 79
Sealed Lips 11
Sears, Heather 147
Seattle Underground 194, **195**
Secret of the Blue Room 11, 30–31
Secret of the Chateau 11
Seduction of the Innocent 9
Selby, David 184–85
Sellers, Peter 147
Selwin 13, 71–72, 78; *see also* Sparenberg, Ray
Serling, Rod 173–74
Seven Arts Theater 77
77 Sunset Strip 133
Seymour 76; *see also* Sinister Seymour; Vincent, Larry
Seymour's Monster Rally 76
Sharp, Don 196
Shaw, Janet 45
She-Wolf of London 12, 54–55
Shelley, Barbara 158, 162
Shelley, Mary 25, 57–59, 213
Shepperton Studios 98
"Shock Theater" (film package) 5, 7, 10–15, 16, 18, 21, 24, 27–28, 30, 37, 44–45, 53, 55–56, 69–70, 88, 94–95, 101, 123
Shock Theater (generic name for TV show) 5
Shock Theater (TV show in Dayton) 82
The Shocktale Party 70
Shudder 86, 213
Siegel, Don 123
The Silence of the Lambs 202, 212
Simon, Simone 103–4
Sinister Seymour 76; *see also* Seymour; Vincent, Larry
Siodmak, Curt 42–43, 46, 104
Sir Cecil Creape 73–74; *see also* McCown, Russ
Sir Graves Big Show 79
Sir Graves Ghastly 79–80; *see also* Deming, Lawson J.
The Sixth Sense 202
Skal, David J. 6, 14–15, 18, 22, 24–27, 37, 43, 58–59, 74–75, 90, 108, 119, 128, 137–38, 151–52, 162, 166, 176, 190, 192
Skorzeny, Janos 187
The Skull 148, 159–60
Skull Island 95
Sloane, Bart 132
Smith, Dave 71
Smith, Harrison 59, 138, 184, 208
Son of Dracula 11–12, 47–49, **49**, 50
Son of Frankenstein 11, 37–38, **39**, 64–65
"Son of Shock" (film package) 5, 13–14, 56, 60, 63, 69–70, 88
Son of Svengoolie (character) 86–87; *see also* Koz, Rich
Son of Svengoolie (TV show) 86–87
The Sorcerers 164–65
Spanish Inquisition 141
Sparenberg, Ray 13, 71; *see also* Selwin
Spelling, Aaron 200
Spider Baby 164–66
The Spider Woman Strikes Back 12
"spiderwalk" 202
Spielberg, Steven 174
Spy Ring 11
The Star Trek Dream 77
Starsky and Hutch 197
Stearne, John 167
Steele, Barbara 141–42, **143**
Steele, Lou 3
Stevens, Craig 118
Stevens, Onslow 30, 68
Stevenson, Robert Louis 89–90, 108, 189
Stevenson, Venetia 148
Stoker, Bram 8, 21–22, 36, 128, 203
Stoloff, Ben 57
Stone, Milburn 53
Stoppelmoor, Cheryl 200
Strait-Jacket 154–55
Strange, Glenn 56, 65, **67**, 68–69, 113, **114**, 119
"The Strange Case of Dr. Jekyll and Mr. Hyde" (novella) 89
The Strange Case of Dr. Rx 12
Stranger Things 212
Streiner, Russell 78–79, 171
Stribling, Melissa 129
Stuart, Gloria 30–31, 92, **93**
Studio Wrestling 78
Sugar Hill 92, 204
Sutherland, Donald 159, 200–1
Svengoolie 86–87, 212; *see also* Bishop, Jerry; Koz, Rich
Sweed, Ron 82–83; *see also* The Ghoul
Sweeney Todd 107

Tales from the Crypt (comic book) 8, 10
Tales from the Crypt (film) 97, 147, 159, 172, 187–88
Tales of Horror 81
Tales of Terror 146, 148
The Talking Dead 212
Tamblyn, Russ 154
Tandy, Jessica 150
Tarantula 20
Tarot 159
Tate, Sharon 168

Index

Taylor, Rod 150, 190
Technicolor 102, 125, 136, 145
Ten Plagues of Egypt 183
Terrence 13, 70–71; *see also* Coglin, Russ
The Terror 150
Terry, Sammy 72; *see also* Carter, Bob
Terry-Thomas 191, 196
Tesla, Armand (vampire) 104–5
The Texas Chain Saw Massacre 207–9
Theater of Blood 197
Them! 6, 121–22, 124
Thesiger, Ernest 57–59, **59**, 92–93, 97
The Thing 116
The Thing from Another World 115–16
The Thing with Two Heads 188
The Things They Carried 171
Thinnes, Roy 200
Thomas, Damien 191
3-D 117, 119
Thriller (Boris Karloff TV series) 15, 85
Tigon British 182, 195–96
The Tingler (film) 133–34
The Tingler (monster) 134
Titanic 30
The Tomb of Dracula (comic) 203
Torture Garden 169–70
Tourneur, Jacques 103–4, 127
Tower of London 41
Transylvania 21, **23**, 80, 98, 127, 139, 192, 203
"The Transylvania Twist" 80
Travers, Henry 31
Trilogy of Terror 210–11
Turner Classic Movies 94
Twentieth Century Fox 106–7, 130
The Twilight Zone 15, 173
Twilight Zone: The Movie 135
Twins of Evil 190–91
Twitter 87
The Two Faces of Dr. Jekyll 189
2001: A Space Odyssey 209
Tyler, Tom 40

The Ugly Duckling 189
Ulmer, Edgar J. 32–33
Underwood, Larry 74; *see also* Dr. Gangrene
The Uninvited 106–7
"Universal 77 Horror Hits" (film package) 85
Universal Studios 3, 5–6, 10–12, 21–22, 24, **24**, 25, 27–38, **39**, 40–46, 49–61, 64–65, **66**, 68–69, 80, 88, 90, 92, 94–95, 102, 104–5, 112–115, **115**, 118–20, 123, 125–26, 128, 132, 135, **137**, 142, 170, 177, 211
Universal Tram Tour **137**
University of California 71
University of Rochester 206

Vajda, Asa (witch) 140–41
Vampira 2, 7, 16–17, **17**, 18, 20, 72, 75–76; *see also* Nurmi, Maila
Vampira's Attic 20
Van Ark, Joan 188
Van Eyssen, John 128
Van Sloan, Edward 22, 27, 29, 36, 62
Variety 32
The Vault of Horror (comic) 8, 10
The Vault of Horror (film) 196–97
Victorian Era 107, 110, 118, 189, 195, 212
Vietnam War 171
Vincent, Larry 76; *see also* Seymour; Sinister Seymour
The Voice 13

Von Hoene, Dick 81–82; *see also* The Cool Ghoul
von Sydow, Max 202

WABC (New York) 13, 18–19
The Wacky World of Dr. Morgus 73
Waggner, George 41–42
Walker, Stuart 33–34
The Walking Dead (film) 100–1
The Walking Dead (TV series) 92, 100, 172, 212
Walsh, Kay 165
Ward, Simon 175
Warner Brothers 100, 202
Warren, James 14
The Warrens 213
Warshow, Robert 9
WAVY (Tidewater) 85
WBKB (Chicago) 70
WBNX (Cleveland) 83
WCAU (Philadelphia) 12–13, 18–19
WCIU (Chicago) 87
WDCA (Washington, D.C.) 84
"We Are the Weird" 85
"We Are the World" 85
Weaver, Fritz 210
Weird Woman 12, 51–52
Weisberg, Brenda 50
Welles, Orson 101, 103
Wells, H.G. 94
Wendkos, Paul 181
"werewolf break" 206
Werewolf of London 11, 33–34, 42
Wertham, Fredric 9, 15
Westcott, Helen 118
Westmore, Bud 119–20
Westmore, Wally 89
WFLD (Chicago) 86
Whale, James 25–27, 31, 36, 57–59, 92–94, 131
What Ever Happened to Baby Jane? 154–55
Wheatley, Dennis 170
White, Doc 9
White Zombie 84, 91–92, 204
Whitmore, James 122
WHRO (Tidewater) 85
The Wicker Man 206–7
WIIC (Pittsburgh) 78
Wilde, Cornel 194
Wilde, Oscar 110
Wilkins, Bob 77–78
Willard 180–81
Williams, Brook 163
Williamson, Alister 173
Willis, Matt 105, **105**
Wise, Robert 108–10, 154
WISH (Indianapolis) 71
Witchcraft 157–58
The Witches 164
Witchfinder General 139, 165–67, 182; *see also* The Conqueror Worm
Withers, Googie 112
The Witness Vanishes 11
The Wizard of Oz 90
WJAS Radio (Pittsburgh) 79
WJBK (Detroit) 79
WKBF (Cleveland) 83
WKEF (Dayton) 82
WNEW (New York City) 3
WNYS (Syracuse) 80
The Wolf Man (monster) 42–43, 45–46, 55, 65, 67–68, 113, 118–120, 163, 212

The Wolf Man (1941 film) 11, 21, 33–34, 42, 43, *43*, 44, *47*, 64, *105*
Wonderama 14
Wood, Ed 6, 20
Woodstock 86
Woodward, Edward 206
WOR (New York City) 19
World War, Second 105
WPHL (Philadelphia) 84
WPIX (New York City) 2, 19–20
Wray, Fay 95, *96*
WSIX (Nashville) 73
WSM (Nashville) 73–74
WSTM (Syracuse) 81
WSYR (Syracuse) 80
WTOG (St. Petersburg) 83
WTTV (Indianapolis) 72
WTVZ (Tidewater) 85
The Wurdulak (vampire) 156
WXIX (Cincinnati) 81

Wyatt, Jane 36
Wymark, Patrick 159–60, 182
Wyngarde, Peter 145–46
Wynter, Dana 123

The X-Files 187
X-Rating 124, 201

Yarbrough, Jean 54
Yeaworth, Irvin S. 132

Zacherley (Zacherle), John 2, 7, 12, 18–19, *19*, 20, 70–71, 81, 84
Zacherley at Large 19
Zawislak, Joseph 84–85; *see also* Dr. Shock
Zemeckis, Robert 188
Zombo 75; *see also* Nye, Louis
Zomboo 75
Zucco, George 40, 50

www.ingramcontent.com/pod-product-compliance
Lightning Source LLC
Chambersburg PA
CBHW060340010526
44117CB00017B/2898